An Introductory
Approach to
Operations Research

The Wiley/Hamilton Series in Management and Administration
Elwood S. Buffa, Advisory Editor   University of California, Los Angeles

An Introductory Approach to Operations Research

Robert J. Thierauf

Xavier University

John Wiley & Sons, Inc.
Santa Barbara ☐ New York ☐ Chichester ☐
Brisbane ☐ Toronto
A Wiley/Hamilton Publication

45641

Library of Congress Cataloging in Publication Data

Thierauf, Robert J

  An introductory approach to operations research.

  (A Wiley Hamilton series in management and administration)

  "A Wiley/Hamilton publication."

  Includes bibliographies and index.

  1. Operations research. I. Title.

T57.T48   658.4'034   77-23031

ISBN 0-471-03125-9

Printed in the United States of America

10 9 8 7 6 5 4 3 2 1

Dedicated to the memory of
D. J. O'CONOR, SR.,
a cofounder of the Formica
Corporation

About The Author

Robert J. Thierauf is a Professor of Quantitative Management and Information Systems at Xavier University in Cincinnati. He has also taught at the University of Cincinnati and The Ohio State University. Prior to coming to Xavier University he was staff consultant for several years with Coopers and Lybrand where he specialized in information systems and operations research studies for business and industry. Many of the studies and applications found in his publications are the direct result of consulting activities. His published works include books on operations research, data processing, management information systems, and management principles and practices.

A native of Cincinnati, Professor Thierauf earned his Ph.D. in management from The Ohio State University. He is a Certified Public Accountant and holds membership in several professional societies including The American Institute for Decision Sciences, The Institute of Management Science, The Academy of Management, The Association for Computing Machinery, and The American Institute of Certified Public Accountants. He is the first recipient of the D. J. O'Conor Memorial Professor of Business Administration endowed chair in Xavier's College of Business Administration.

Preface

Although this book owes much of its content to the highly successful *Decision Making Through Operations Research,* 2nd Edition, by Robert J. Thierauf and Robert C. Klekamp (Wiley/Hamilton, 1975), it possesses its own character and has been written to satisfy a particular need of those who teach the introductory course in Operations Research. Chiefly, it presents the basic techniques of operations research (OR) as well as the important requirements for formulating specifical OR models, resulting in a "model formulation" approach to an introductory study of operations research.

The level of presentation is geared toward the undergraduate business student. Within this framework, the book contains features that assist the student in learning about operations research as practiced within a typical business organization. These student oriented learning activities are found in each chapter:
- [ ] study goals for the chapter, accompanied by a chapter outline
- [ ] the requirements for formulating operations research models to solve specific business problems
- [ ] applications of OR models to specific business problem areas
- [ ] summaries of operations research methodology or steps that are involved in a specific OR model
- [ ] questions, model formulation exercises, and mathematical exercises at the end of each chapter, with answers to the latter (Appendix E)

These pedagogical tools also assist the instructor whose time may be somewhat limited, because of large classes.

The structure of the book follows a logical sequence for presenting a comprehensive treatment of standard OR techniques. Part I, focuses on an overview of operations research and model formulation; Part II presents traditional business models; namely, breakeven and inventory, that rely on algebra for their solution. Decision theory, decision models treating a variable demand, and PERT (Program Evaluation and Review Technique) models that utilize probability and statistics are set forth in Part III. In Part IV, the underlying mathematics of matrix algebra is employed for linear programming, transportation methods, dynamic programming, and Markov analysis. Due to the importance of simulation techniques, queuing and simulation models are presented in Part V. Lastly, advanced operations research topics and an overview of the present and future directions of OR make up Part VI. In addition, background on vectors, matrices, and determinants along with a calculus approach to selected inventory and queuing models are found in Appendix B. Thus, the level of mathematics builds from one chapter to another.

The book is designed for a one-quarter or one-semester undergraduate course where calculus may or may not be required. Chapters can be omitted without destroying the unity of the course since each chapter has been written to stand on its own. This allows for a wide variability of emphasis for each major part covered. Also, several of the problems can be solved by the computer, either in a batch-processing mode or a time-sharing mode.

For a project of this magnitude, I am indebted to many individuals who have helped, in particular, Professor Elwood S. Buffa, Advisory Editor of the Wiley/Hamilton Series in Management and Administration. Likewise, I am deeply grateful to Professors Richard Hall, Robert Klekamp, Marcia Ruwe, and Michael Thierauf of Xavier University for their constructive criticism. Also, I would like to thank the many students who participated in this project, in particular, Herbert Banks, John Benny, Donald Blose, B. Bossard, R. J. Gabelman, Steve Jarvis, Malven R. Johnson, Robert C. Monteith, J. N. Platt, and J. Toron.

Robert J. Thierauf
Xavier University
Cincinnati, Ohio

Contents

Part I

Overview of Operations Research

OPERATIONS RESEARCH—
AN INTRODUCTION

Operations Research— An Introduction

I

Introduction Objectives

☐ To survey the history of operations research and its relationship to computers.

☐ To present a method for formulating standard and custom-made OR (operations research) models.

☐ To examine the essential characteristics of operations research as a means of defining it.

☐ To formulate the six steps in the planned approach for undertaking (and resolving) operations research projects.

☐ To set the stage for the rest of the text by surveying the standard "tools of the trade" employed by OR practitioners.

Introduction Outline

In managing the affairs of modern business and government, managers need considerable assistance in coping with the complexity of their jobs. Unaided, the human mind cannot possibly weigh the manifold complexities involved in the development of a missile, the erection of a large office building or the operation of an enterprise producing hundreds of products for diverse customer needs. A multitude of decisions go into scheduling jobs, ordering supplies, managing inventories, negotiating with contractors, hiring labor, pricing goods and planning production facilities. Furthermore, managers are constrained by such uncertainties as the unpredictable tastes of consumers, the speculative nature of economic forecasts and research and development programs. Thus, all too often, they must act largely on hunches and intuition, wondering if the best decision was made.

In recent years, operations researchers have been showing managers how to avoid some of the perplexity that relates to decision making. They have developed various mathematical or operations research (OR) techniques for evaluating possible courses of action. Some of these techniques are best suited to situations in which all the factors are known or predictable, but the complexity is so great that the human mind cannot arrive at a wholly rational decision. Other techniques cope with "risks"— chances that can be accurately measured or calculated from past experience. Still others deal with "uncertainties" (which operations researchers distinguish from risks)—chances that can be estimated only roughly at best, because they depend on future events which cannot be controlled by the manager. Whatever the orientation of these OR techniques, their central focus is to improve the quality of the manager's final decision.

I

Although this book is devoted to the standard "tools of the trade" found in OR projects, this initial part serves as an introduction to operations research. First, the history of operations research and the essential aspects of model building are set forth. Next, the major characteristics of operations research are enumerated, followed by a definition of operations research. Also, the quantitative models to be covered are briefly noted. In essence, the main thrust of this introduction is to assist the reader in relating the essentials of model building to the requirements for formulating specific OR models found in the remainder of the text.

History of Operations Research

It is difficult to mark the official beginning of operations research. Many early pioneers performed work that today would be considered operations research. In England, as early as 1914, F. W. Lanchester published papers on the theoretical relationships between victory and superiority in manpower and firepower. In the United States, during World War I, Thomas Edison was given the task of finding the maneuvers of merchant ships that would be most effective in minimizing shipping losses to enemy submarines. Instead of risking ships in actual war conditions, he made use of a "tactical game board" for a solution. Around the same time (late 1910s), a Danish engineer, A. K. Erlang of the Copenhagen Telephone Company, was performing experiments involving the fluctuation of demand for telephone facilities upon automatic dialing equipment. His work is the foundation for mathematical models used in waiting line theory today.

In the 1930s, Horace C. Levenson applied sophisticated mathematical models to large amounts of data which would otherwise have been totally unmanageable. One of his most interesting and best-known studies involved customers refusing to accept C.O.D. packages from a relatively small order house. The rejection rate was about 30 percent of gross sales. Two categories of merchandise were most frequently rejected: more expensive orders, and merchandise shipped later than five days after the order was placed. On the average, orders older than five days were not profitable. With such data available, it was relatively easy for the mail order firm to compare the cost of rejection with the higher cost of fast shipping and thereby determine the optimum shipping effort.

Military Operations Research   In 1937, British scientists were asked to help the military learn how to use the newly developed radar in locating enemy aircraft. The scientists, working on different aspects of this problem, were brought together in September, 1939 at H.Q. Fighter Command (RAF). This group, considered to be the nucleus of the first operations research group, steadily extended its scope of activities beyond its original problem of radar and its integration with ground observers.

Not long after the formation of this group, the Anti-Aircraft Command Research Group was brought together to study antiaircraft-aiming problems (September, 1940). The distinguished British physicist P.M.S. Blackett headed the group. They were to study the performance of gun control equipment in the field, especially during its actual use by the troops against the enemy. The first two members of the group were physiologists, the next two were mathematical physicists, then an astrophysicist, an Army officer, and a former surveyor. The team was later completed with a third physiologist, a general physicist, and two mathematicians. They became known as "Blackett's Circus"[1] A broad spectrum of disciplines is apparent in this group of 11 scientists. The group expanded and split into an Army and a Navy group, resulting in all of Britain's military forces having an operational research group engaged in military research early in the war (1941). This type of scientific activity came to be known in Britain as "operational research" since the first studies were devoted to the operational use of radar and were carried out by radar research scientists.

In the United States, Sir Robert Watson-Watt recommended that operations research be introduced into the departments of the Secretary of War and the Secretary of the Navy. By April, 1942 the decision to introduce operational research at a high level had been made and implemented. The initial problems included radar and the development of merchant marine convoys designed to minimize losses from enemy submarines. In the U.S. Air Force, it became known as "operational analysis" and in the U.S. Army and Navy as "operations research and operations evaluation."[2] This type of activity also grew in Canada and France during World War II.

Business Operations Research   When World War II terminated, new types of management problems, created by the nationalization of industry and the need to rebuild large segments of the nation's industrial facilities, called for a new approach in Britain. This call was answered by the operational research workers who had moved in to work on government and industrial problems. Management consulting, which never had been popular in Britain, caught on because British managers were willing to try a new approach to raise productivity and profits—operational research.

For some years after the war, most British industries where operational research was carried out had only a few men in the field. However, during the latter half of the 1950s, there was a rapid growth. Existing OR groups expanded to cope with the greatly increased demand from within their own firms. Other firms went quickly into OR activity. British operational research is characterized by a number of large OR

---

[1]J. G. Crowther and R. Whiddington, *Science at War*, London: Her Majesty's Stationery Office, 1947, p. 96.
[2]Sir R. Watson-Watt, *Three Steps to Victory*, London: Odhams Press, 1959, p. 204.

groups. The United Steel Companies group has over 100 people, the National Coal Board about 100. The British Iron and Steel Research Associates, British Petroleum, and Richard Thomas & Baldwin all have more than 50 OR personnel.[3] Many medium-sized firms have several performing OR work. It is difficult to name any single type of industry where OR is not used. In Britain, operational research has gained a strong foothold in business and government for solving difficult and complex problems.

In the United States, "operations research" (first coined in this country by McCloskey and Trefethen in 1940) took on a somewhat different direction. Military research increased at the end of the war, resulting in OR men being retained by the military. In fact, many more were added. Industry and government were subjected to the same stimulation as their counterparts in Britain. Initially, industry and government were somewhat indifferent to operations research. It was not until 1950 that OR began to be taken seriously by American industry.

The United States began to enter a second industrial revolution of automation as electronic computers began to make their appearance in government and industry (the first industrial revolution had replaced men with machines). In the 1950s, the computer demonstrated new capabilities which were staggering to the present crop of managers. OR personnel, who had spent a decade in military operations research, were quick to adopt the computer as an essential tool. As increasingly significant ways of utilizing the computer were developed, the spread of OR accelerated. The advent of the computer along with the development of OR methods, then, brought the industrial executive and OR worker together in an activity that is still growing at a very fast rate.

During this period (1950s), linear programming gave industrial operations research a major boost. This technique, basically the application of linear algebra to resource allocation, had applications in many industries. It gave OR personnel a foot in the door of many industrial firms. Many techniques known only to operations researchers, such as PERT and simulation, are used widely today. Probability and statistics, basic to any work in operations research, introduced the notions of confidence limits and probability of occurrence in place of simple averages. The various techniques associated with OR form the basis for the subject matter of this book.

Even though there was a large movement of OR personnel to industry, operations research was still evident in the military through its contracts. The Department of Defense gradually shifted to the weapons-system, management concept and imposed contractual requirements for defense industries to undertake operations research. Defense research and development money spurred the growth of "think factories" and "advanced study programs," creating an enlarged demand for operations research and systems analysis. Thus operations research became a key tool in battles for budgets and contracts.

[3]R. L. Ackoff and R. Rivett, *A Manager's Guide to Operations Research,* New York: John Wiley & Sons, 1963, p. 8.

[handwritten margin note: Different Society that OR has developed]

The first industrial operations research conference in the United States, held at the Case Institute of Technology in Cleveland (1951), relied on military studies since it was almost impossible to find industrial studies for presentation. Today, most of *Fortune's* 500 largest corporations are benefiting from operations research. Several societies have been formed here and abroad to bring OR professionals together. These include the British Operational Research Society (founded in 1950), the Operations Research Society of America (1952), The Institute of Management Science (1953), and the American Institute of Decision Sciences (1969). Educational institutions in the United States and the United Kingdom have adopted operations research as part of higher learning curriculums. Today, operations research is practiced and taught extensively not only in the United States and United Kingdom, but also in Europe, Australia, India, Japan, and Israel.

Computers and Operations Research

It is appropriate to conclude this historical overview of operations research with a brief discussion of its close relationship to computer methodology. Earlier it was stated that the computer was a primary factor in the growth of operations research. Partly this was because most of the operations research techniques would be completely impractical for any real problem without the modern computer to produce the final results. Most large scale applications of operations research techniques which require only minutes on a computer could take weeks, months, and sometimes years to produce results manually. But even more significantly, computers have ready access to certain kinds of management information without which many OR projects would be meaningless. OR professionals would be hard pressed to enumerate applications not dependent critically on the computer for implementation.

It is certainly unquestioned that the computer is an indispensable tool and integral part of operations research, and that computer methodology and OR methodology are developing in parallel. Today, most OR personnel are knowledgeable about computers right up to the point of writing the desired OR computer program. It seems likely that in the next decade the dividing line between operations research and computer methodology will disappear and leave the two areas combined in the form of a more general and comprehensive management science.

Model Defined

Operations research makes extensive use of mathematical models. Generally, a *model* is defined as *a representation or abstraction of an actual object or situation*. It shows the relationships (direct and indirect) and the interrelationships of action and reaction in terms of cause and effect. Since a model is an abstraction of reality, it may appear to be less complex than reality itself. The model, to be complete, must be representative of those aspects of reality that are being investigated.

7

One of the basic reasons for developing models is to discover which variables are the important or pertinent ones. The discovery of the pertinent variables is closely associated with the investigation of the relationships that exist among the variables. Quantitative techniques such as statistics and simulation are utilized to investigate these relationships. Many models presented throughout this book will depict explicit relationships and interrelationships among the variables and other factors deemed important in solving business problems.

Model Formulation

Use to illustrate sensitivity.

Having defined what a model is, we can now set forth a general OR model which will be representative of a system under study. The OR model takes the following form:

$$P = f (C_1, C_2, \ldots C_n; U_1, U_2, \ldots U_n)$$

where:

P = objective measure of the system's performance or effectiveness (objective function)

$C_1, C_2, \ldots C_n$ = system variables that are subject to control (controllable or decision variables)

$U_1, U_2, \ldots U_n$ = system variables that are not subject to control (uncontrollable or environmental variables)

To illustrate the foregoing generalized OR model, consider the flow of vehicular traffic at a toll bridge during rush hours. P stands for the average delay experienced by motorists at the toll booths during peak periods. The Cs, which are controllable variables, refer to the manned toll booths, that is, C_1 represents the number of these booths, C_2 the number of automatic collection machines, and so forth. On the other hand, the Us are those variables that are not subject to managerial control. U_1 is the average number of cars arriving at the toll booths during the peak hours; U_2 is the mix of cars, trucks, and buses, and the like. Based on these factors, the problem is to minimize the average delay by motorists subject to the availability of booths, capabilities of these booths, personnel on duty, and funds available to service the toll bridge. Thus, a "best" solution is sought within the framework of the problem's parameters. This generalized model (or any other OR model) entails three stages in its formulation which are:

data analysis

model development

model validation

Each of these will be explained in the text that follows.

Data Analysis The first stage (data analysis) is concerned with defining the parameters of the problem—objective(s), variables, constraints, assumptions, events, relationships, and other factors deemed important to the mathematical modeling process. Basically, these data are a synthesis of the essential information in the problem. In the above generalized OR model, the system's *objective*—overall performance, P—is a function of a set of *controllable* or *decision* variables of the system, C_n, and a set of *uncontrollable* or *environmental* variables, U_n.

In an OR study, perhaps the most difficult part is developing an adequate measure of the system's performance, because this measure must reflect the relative importance of the many objectives involved in every management decision. These objectives are of two types:

those which involve retaining things of value (minimize inputs, expenditures, etc.)

those which involve obtaining things of value (maximize outputs, income, etc.)

The "things" may be resources (like time, money, or energy) or states of the system (like market share, public acceptance, or economic activity). Once a model has been set up, a solution is sought which optimizes the measure of performance. To obtain such a solution, one seeks those values of the controllable variables that maximize (or minimize) the performance. In turn, the optimizing values of the controllable variables are then related to the uncontrollable variables.

The restriction on values of the variables in a problem, commonly called *constraints*, may be expressed in a supplementary set of equations and inequalities. In practical business situations, minus values of the controllable variables are not treated; that is, you either produce the item or you do not. Similarly, you either spend the money or you do not. Another example is the amount allocated to departments in terms of a budget which cannot be exceeded. These constraints are expressed as a set of supplementary equations or inequalities where the greater-than, less-than conditions are used. In addition, it may be necessary to set forth certain *assumptions* in the problem, such as a certain rate of inflation.

Model Development In the second stage (model development), the OR model is structured according to the parameters set forth in the data analysis phase. To state it another way, certain questions must be answered about a problem before a mathematical model can be constructed (see Figure I–1). However, once the important parameters have been selected, it may be convenient to combine or divide their elements. For example, receiving costs are combined with raw material purchase and freight costs. When each element has been finalized, the next step is to assign a symbol to each element, with at least one symbol representing the measure of effectiveness (or ineffectiveness). A single equation or a set of equations then can be constructed to express the effectiveness of the process or system. The resulting formula(s) is (are) a symbolic or mathematical model that allows us to evaluate the results by varying certain elements within the constraints of the problem. Likewise, this formula is the basis for validation—the next stage.

1. What is the objective measure of performance or effectiveness? That is, how will we express the solution to the problem? Examples: in dollars saved, units sold, items produced, lowest cost, highest contribution, etc.

2. What are the factors under our control (controllable or decision variables)? That is, what aspects of the problem can we do something about? Examples: selling prices, number of products manufactured, cost aspects, number of salesmen, etc.

3. What are the factors not under our control (uncontrollable and environmental variables)? That is, what aspects of the problem do we have to accept as given? Examples: level of economic activity, prices of competition, demand of customers, location of customers, etc.

4. What is the relationship between these factors (controllable and uncontrollable) and the objective(s)? Likewise, what is the relationship between other factors (constraints, assumptions, etc.) and the objective(s)? That is, can these relationships be expressed in a mathematical form that will constitute a model of the problem?

Figure I–1
Four questions that must be answered about a problem before a mathematical model can be constructed.

One last point should be noted under model development. Whenever possible, information should be obtained about the model's behavior caused by varying its parameters. Such an analysis is especially needed when the parameters cannot be determined accurately; it is commonly referred to as *sensitivity analysis*. Sensitivity analysis can be defined as a method of observing output changes while systematically varying each factor to determine its relative influence on the model's performance. Such analysis facilitates model development and helps determine suitable opportunities for further simplification of the model.

Model Validation   Since most OR models are computer oriented, the third stage (model validation) focuses on the programming and debugging of the model. It is concerned with the soundness of the programmed logic so that the model's structured components can be verified before undertaking experimentation with the model. In cases where OR packages are available from computer manufacturers, testing of these programmed packages are generally not necessary.

Role of Models in OR Projects

In an OR project, the development of the first model is actually only a part of a larger process, as shown in Figure I–2. The evolution of a successful model generally follows this long drawn-out process. The first model (Model 1) is often very wide of the target. In fact, it can be so far off that operations research personnel may feel like giving up the entire project in utter disgust. However, a fresh look by other OR people; further study, analysis, and serious thinking; and introduction of more statistically controlled data can change the evaluation from "no good" to "poor." Model 2, which is a major or a minor revision of Model 1 plus more representative data, gives a major boost to the OR project. Model 3, a revision of Model 2 plus more refinement of the data, may bring about the desired result. This process can certainly be extended beyond Model 3 if needed. In effect, these successive stages allow the OR group to "zero in" on an optimum solution for the project.

Although Figure I–2 gives the impression that there is an end to the sequence in building the final model (Model 3), there is actually no end to the process. Even after a model has years of successful use by a firm, conditions may change, necessitating reworking of the model to maximize revenue and profits and, at the same time, minimize costs. The process starts all over again and a new model must then be developed. Generally, the model will be easier to develop because the OR team has had previous exposure and experience with it. In effect, any OR model should be reviewed periodically to determine if any changes are desirable. An attitude that the ultimate has been obtained can be misleading and a barrier to progress.

Since changing conditions make it necessary to revise the model, we can say that a model is neither true nor false but is relevant or irrelevant to the problem at hand. The model may be correct for one firm yet fail dismally for another. Alternatively, it may have been an effective model based upon existing market conditions, but later may become inefficient under changed conditions. The criterion from the standpoint of the model's effectiveness is: Does it fit the existing conditions of today and the near future? Referring to Figure I–2, Model 3 is effective for the firm while Models 1 and 2 do not fit current demands of the firm.

Advantages of Models

From the preceding discussion, we can conclude that a model which fails to predict what will happen in the real world must give way to a revised model that correctly reflects reality in order to make a proper evaluation. Otherwise, the relative advantages would certainly by overshadowed by its disadvantages. When standard or custom-built OR models are being properly utilized by the firm, their relative advantages are many. An important advantage of model building is that it provides a frame of reference for consideration of the problem, that is, the model indicates

Figure I–2
Role of models in an operations research project.

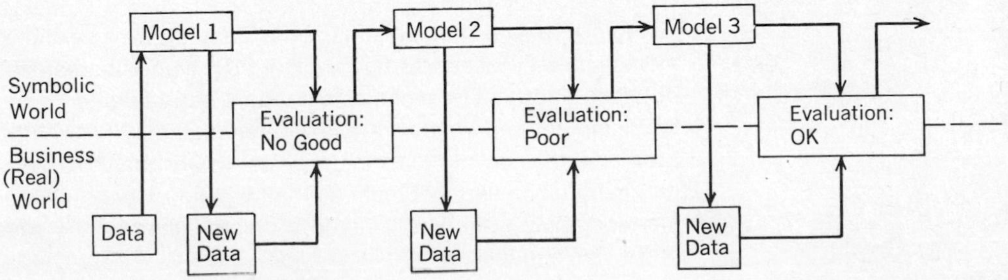

11

gaps which are not apparent immediately. Upon testing the model, the character of the failure might give a clue to the model's deficiencies. Some of the greatest advances in science have resulted from the failure of a particular model.

From a cost standpoint, a complex problem can be expressed in a mathematical model that will allow a firm to change parameters without undertaking actual construction of the project. For example, the use of a model can avoid a placement of plants and warehouses which does not best meet the present and future needs of customers. The time factor is also involved since the results (favorable and unfavorable) can be obtained within a relatively short time as opposed to waiting a much longer time for the completion of the project and actual day-to-day operations. With the constant squeeze on profits, the cost and time savings of operations research models make them worthy of managerial adoption as a decision-making tool.

Once a problem is expressed in mathematical notation and equation form, there is the advantage of the manipulative facility of mathematics. We can insert different values into the mathematical model and study the behavior of the system. If properly undertaken, statements about the sensitivity of the system to a change in any of the variables can be made. Also, the symbolic language offers advantages in communication since it allows a precise statement of the problem as opposed to a long verbal description. The use of mathematical forms makes for better description and comprehension of the facts. It brings to light factors and uncovers relationships that were neglected in verbal description.

Models, which allow one to predict based upon past or present information, can be utilized for training purposes. These allow trainees to see the results of their decisions without having to make the actual decision. By using a model, a wrong decision on their part will not affect the firm's actual position. Models enable the trainees to distinguish between the controllable and noncontrollable variables as well as to determine the relative importance of each variable. Moreover, they allow them to examine cause and effect relationships that may not be readily apparent.

Mathematical models have the ability to expose the abstraction in a problem. In considering a complex world, the individual is made to select those attributes and concepts that are applicable. The mathematical model indicates what data should be collected to deal with the problem quantitatively. It makes it possible to deal with the problem in its entirety and allows a consideration of all the major variables for the problem simultaneously. A computer can be used to manipulate the major variables and factors of a model, which facilitates an understanding of the effect each has on the other.

Stating routine problems mathematically so their solutions can be obtained by mathematical procedures has another advantage. If a satisfactory solution can be obtained through OR methods, managers can relegate these types of problems to the computer and concentrate their efforts on identifying those factors of important problems that do not lend themselves to OR analysis. Many business problems require intuition and judgment for their solution. Hence, OR can release managerial time for solving poorly structured problems, thereby increasing overall efficiency of the firm's resources.

Disadvantages of Models

Mathematical models have their drawbacks, one of which is the usual problem dealing with abstraction. This means that the model may require gross oversimplification and thus may inaccurately reflect the real world. Another problem of abstraction is failing to take into account all the exceptions. This can be an error of omission or commission. Also, it is difficult to define all the elements of a model in mathematical terms and set them down on paper. At the end of the initial process of abstraction, the model is so complex that it becomes very difficult to document the elements properly. This means changes are extremely difficult to make correctly.

There is a danger that operations researchers may become so attached to their models that they will insist it represents the real world when it does not. If the same model were applied to another firm's problem, it might be representative. What was said previously about a model applies here (it is neither true nor false, but relevant to the problem at hand). A model, being the creation of man, is only as good as the originator. If the person who builds the model does not know what he is doing, the output of the resulting model will reflect this fact. The GIGO (Garbage In, Garbage Out) principle of data processing is applicable. This type of situation can be remedied by a competent staff, well trained in the concepts of model building.

Models can sometimes be very expensive to originate compared to the expected return from their use. Not only is there a question of marginal income and marginal cost, but of communications with management personnel who do not understand the models and hence have a difficult time accepting the results. Often it is more efficient to use direct methods than involved mathematical models. Many management people have a tendency to interpret the results too rigidly instead of using them as decision-making tools. The output of the model, tempered with the experience of management and consideration for present and future conditions, is the best way to reap the benefits of operations research.

Major Characteristics of Operations Research

The major characteristics of OR can now be specified. Operations research:

> examines functional relationships from a systems overview.
> utilizes the interdisciplinary approach.
> adopts the planned approach.
> uncovers new problems for study.

Examines Functional Relationships from a Systems Overview The activity of any function or part of a firm has some effect on the activity of every other function or part. In order to evaluate any decision or action in an organization, it is necessary to identify all the important interactions and to determine their impact on the whole organization versus the function originally involved. Initially, the functional relationships in an OR project are deliberately expanded so that all the significantly interacting functions and their related components are contained in a statement of the problem. Thus, a systems overview consists of surveying the entire area under the manager's control instead of one specialized area. This approach provides a basis for initiating inquiries into problems that seem to be affecting performance at a higher or lower level or at the same level.

Many problems that look relatively easy to solve on the surface actually resemble an iceberg. For example, inventory, which may not seem complicated at first inspection, is extraordinarily complex. The manufacturing department is looking for long, uninterrupted runs to reduce set-up costs and clean-up costs. To solve the problem with this viewpoint in mind may not be complex. However, these long runs may result in large inventories of raw materials, work in process, and finished goods in relatively few product lines. This can result in bitter conflicts with the marketing department, not to mention the finance and personnel departments. Hence, inventory, as a manufacturing function, cannot be isolated from other functions. Marketing, wanting to give immediate delivery for a wide variety of products (product lines), desires a diverse and large inventory. Similarly, it would like a flexible manufacturing department that can fill special orders on short notice. Finance wants to keep inventory at a low dollar value in order to optimize capital investments that tie up assets for indeterminate periods. Finally, personnel wants to reduce labor turnover by smoothing out manufacturing runs so as to keep all temporary layoffs to a minimum. The optimum inventory policy then affects the operations of many functional areas.

In view of the preceding difficulties, the OR group should analyze the problem with painstaking care, examining all elements in each department affected. These elements might include: the cost of material procurement; manufacturing, set-up, and clean-up costs; competitive forces and prices; and the costs of holding inventories and stockout costs. When all factors affecting the system are known, a mathematical model can be formulated, as indicated earlier. The solution to this model, having properly related the functions (marketing, manufacturing, finance, and personnel) and their component parts, should result in optimizing profits for the firm as a whole, often referred to as *optimization*.

Suboptimization generally refers to specific profit objectives for the firm's various functions being maximized individually. In the inventory problem, long manufacturing runs may produce the lowest costs for the manufacturing department, but if the merchandise cannot be sold, what good is the merchandise? Thus, the best solution for this inventory problem is one that leads to optimization for the whole firm, but not necessarily to optimization for the various functions (departments) of the firm. It is necessary to modify the action for each level so as to effect balance in the various functions and subfunctions. In addition, suboptimization can be applied to the entire firm rather than its component parts. When this is the case, a suboptimum solution is usually the result of unclear objectives or objectives that conflict with or contradict each other within a firm. Suboptimization similarly results when an optimum solution for the short run is adopted without consideration of the long run. Failure to take into account the intangible and nonquantifiable factors can result in suboptimization. Other cases of suboptimization result from failure to examine all alternatives available or to take into consideration all relevant information.

The opposite of suboptimization is *overoptimization*. This condition results from optimizing to an extreme degree; that is, the costs of applying very exacting OR models are far greater than the expected savings. In the preceding inventory example, an elaborate OR model could be constructed that results in accuracy to several decimal places. Actually, this enlarged approach to optimizing inventory levels is unwarranted since the additional costs of such accuracy far outweigh the potential of the model during its expected life.

Utilizes the Interdisciplinary Approach During the early years of operations research, there was a great shortage of scientists (mathematicians, physicists, chemists, engineers, and statisticians). The military operations research groups had to acquire their personnel not by selection, but by acquisition. Out of this forced approach to operations research came a recognition that the interdisciplinary team was valuable. They found that one can speak of physical problems, chemical problems, biological problems, psychological problems, social problems, and economic problems as though these are categorized in nature. Actually, the various disciplines describe different ways of studying the same problem.

When scientists are confronted with a new problem, they try to abstract the essence of the problem and determine if this same type of problem has been undertaken previously. If they find a similar problem in their own field, they can determine whether or not certain methods used before can be adapted to the problem at hand. In this way, the various members with their respective backgrounds can bring to the problem approaches that otherwise might not be considered. Thus, operations research makes use of this simple principle: people from different disciplines can produce more unique solutions, with a greater probability of success, than could be expected from the same number of people from any one discipline. This principle can be illustrated in the foregoing inventory example.

Mathematicians, looking at an inventory problem, would formulate some type of mathematical relationships between the manufacturing department and final shipment. These relationships might be directly or indirectly tied in with quantity and time factors. Chemical engineers might look at the same problem and formulate it in terms of flow theory since there are methods at their disposal for solutions using this approach. Cost accountants conceive this inventory problem in terms of its component costs (direct material, direct labor, and overhead) and how costs can be controlled and reduced. Several other disciplines could be brought to bear on the problem. Which of the alternative methods from the various disciplines is most beneficial depends upon the existing circumstances. The inventory problem is quite complex when it cuts across the entire firm; thus it is necessary to look at the problem in many different ways in order to determine which one (or which combination) of the various discipline approaches is the best.

One of the main reasons for the existence of operations research groups is that they bring the latest scientific know-how to bear on problems. Just as important is their ability to develop new methods, procedures, and systems which are more ef-

fective in solving problems than any that are presently available. This makes sense since no one person has the time available to acquire all the useful scientific information from all disciplines. The interdisciplinary approach has this added advantage—it recognizes that most business problems have accounting, biological, economic, engineering, mathematical, physical, psychological, sociological, and statistical aspects. It stands to reason that the individual phases of a problem can best be understood and solved by those trained in the appropriate fields.

Adopts the Planned Approach   Operations research, like most other disciplines, makes use of the scientific method, which has been updated to reflect the necessity of solving problems in a business environment. An updated version of this method, called the planned approach, includes mathematical modeling (described earlier), use of the standard techniques of operations research, establishing proper controls, and the utilization of computer capabilities. The planned approach has as its primary goal the development and application of quantitative models to solve specific business problems. Its basic approach consists of the following steps: (1) observation, (2) definition of the real problem, (3) development of alternative solutions (models), (4) selection of optimum solution (model) using experimentation, (5) verification of optimum solution (model) through implementation and (6) establishment of proper controls. It includes model development in conjunction with the current tools of operations research and the utilization of the computer. This will be apparent in the discussion of the planned approach below.

STEP 1. OBSERVATION   The planned approach, as in the scientific method, starts with the observation of the phenomena surrounding the problem, that is, observing the facts, opinions, and symptoms concerning the problem. Observation may be a casual glance or concentrated, detailed, and lengthy, based upon the requirements of the problem under study. Observation is used to identify problems. The capable manager is always alert and sensitive to the presence of problems.

After recognizing the existence of a problem, the manager should call upon the operations research team (located within or outside the firm) to begin work. The operations researchers must be alert during this initial step. They will probably hear such words as "too much," "poor," and "insufficient," which reflect the lack of clarity of established facts as to the nature and extent of the problem. Thus, the operations research group must be observant concerning the conditions surrounding the problem, asking questions of what, where, when, who, and how regarding the firm's resources—management, men, materials, machinery, and money. Basically, understanding the reasons behind the facts comes from asking "why," as illustrated in Figure I–3. Not only does the gathering of facts help to develop a network of knowledge and understanding about the problem, but also assists ultimately in determining the real problem as well as arriving at a sound and worthwhile solution.

STEP 2. DEFINITION OF THE REAL PROBLEM   In the second step, the effective interaction of knowledge (facts) with understanding (reasons behind the facts) leads to the definition of the real problem (Figure I–3) and not just a symptom of it. The

OR team determines those factors affecting the problem, in particular the *objectives, constraints, assumptions,* etc., as set forth earlier. Thus, every effort should be made to quantify those factors affecting the problem. A thorough examination of these factors must be undertaken to insure that the real problem will be solved upon conclusion of the study.

STEP 3. DEVELOPMENT OF ALTERNATIVE SOLUTIONS (MODELS) The next important step in this problem-solving approach is to develop alternative courses of action or tentative solutions to the real problem. To state it another way, several hypotheses are formulated. A *hypothesis* is nothing more than a tentative solution to a problem. Most of the time in an OR study, the alternative courses of action or hypotheses take the form of mathematical models. Mathematical models can be developed by the appropriate tools of the trade or can be custom-built to accommodate the real-world problem. Generally, they are computer oriented for a final solution. (The section on model formulation described the proper approach.)

In this third step of the planned approach, several models may be developed if several approaches initially look promising in terms of a final solution to the problem. As each model is developed, its respective deficiencies become apparent; that is, the model's behavior is inconsistent with that of the modeled problem. Thus certain models which looked promising at the outset may have to be discarded. Instead of a half dozen models, the choice might be narrowed to one, two, or three candidates.

Many times clearly stated objectives are neglected in this step. The OR study tries to take into account as broad a scope of objectives as possible. The problem is to determine which alternative model (course of action) is most effective relative to the set of pertinent objectives. Consequently, in formulating the problem, a measure of effectiveness must be specified in terms of specific objectives. This is helpful in reducing the number of tentative models.

Figure I–3

An *understanding* of the pertinent *knowledge* within the OR project leads to a definition of the *real* problem.

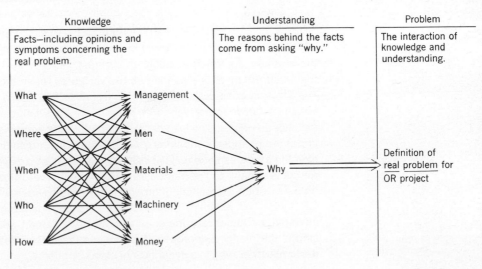

Knowledge	Understanding	Problem
Facts—including opinions and symptoms concerning the real problem.	The reasons behind the facts come from asking "why."	The interaction of knowledge and understanding.

What — Management
Where — Men
When — Materials — Why — Definition of real problem for OR project
Who — Machinery
How — Money

STEP 4. SELECTION OF OPTIMUM SOLUTION (MODEL) USING EXPERIMEN-
TATION   Once the number of alternative models or solutions has been narrowed,
those remaining are evaluated in order to select the optimum one. If the resulting
model fits one of the well-known OR techniques, then a solution may be obtained
by it. On the other hand if the mathematical relationships of the model are too complex for the standard OR techniques, a custom-made model is required. Thus, the
selection of the appropriate model is dependent on the nature and complexity of
the problem under investigation.

STEP 5. VERIFICATION OF OPTIMUM SOLUTION (MODEL) THROUGH IMPLE-
MENTATION   In the next phase of the planned approach, the OR group verifies
experimentally the chosen model. While experimentation is often on a limited basis,
verification involves most or all of the target population (as defined in statistics).
This step is necessary because the reaction of competitors, consumer buying traits,
and comparable factors observed in the limited sample tested experimentally may
not hold true for the target population. In order to verify the optimum model or solution, it must be translated into a set of operating procedures capable of being
understood and applied by the personnel who will be responsible for their use.
Major or minor changes must be specified and implemented. Dual operations,
sometimes called parallel operations, are needed to test the efficiency of the new
method compared to the old method. Initially one phase or section is converted in
order to highlight any shortcomings of the model (solution). This can be a very
trying process since a variable which was initially determined to be insignificant
(was ignored) may be found to be a critical factor (variable). The dynamics of the
business world can cause this to happen overnight. The resistance of operating
personnel to changes can cause additional problems for OR teams.

STEP 6. ESTABLISHMENT OF PROPER CONTROLS   Once the results have been
interpreted and action has been recommended and implemented, the final step of
the planned approach establishes controls. A solution derived from a model remains an optimum one as long as the variables retain their original relationships.
The solution goes out of control when the variables and/or one or more of the relationships between the variables have changed significantly. The significance of
the change depends on the cost of changing the present model versus the deviation
under the changed conditions from the true optimum solution. To establish control
over the model (solution), it is necessary to establish an information system that will
permit feedback to the particular management level(s) responsible and account-
able. Continuous monitoring through feedback provides a means for modifying the
OR model as external/internal conditions and demands change over time. If
changes are necessary, the study should be reviewed, starting again with the first
step of the planned approach. It is obvious that OR projects are continuous since
the firm is operating in a dynamic, not static, economy.

The six steps are seldom, if ever, conducted in a particular order since there is usually a constant interplay between the steps of operations research. For example, an exact and precise formulation of the problem is not completed until the project is about completed. However, these six steps provide a helpful conceptual framework when dealing with a complex problem. The methodology certainly gives direction to one's thinking as some other general method would not. In Figure I–4, the problem-solving steps to be followed by the operations research team are recapped. The first five steps are basically the scientific method with the additions of the sixth step, model development, techniques (tools) of the trade, and computer for a planned approach to OR problems. Also, the feedback loop links the final step back to the beginning one.

Uncovers New Problems for Study A fourth characteristic of operations research, which is often overlooked, is that in the solution of an OR problem new problems are uncovered. All interrelated problems uncovered by the OR approach do not have to be solved at the same time. However, each must be solved with consideration for other problems if maximum benefits are to be obtained. It can be said that operations research is not effectively used if it is restricted to "one-shot" projects. Greatest benefits can be obtained through a continuity of research.

As a member of a consulting firm for many years, I have frequently found that I really have "a tiger by the tail." What originally appears to be a simple and isolated problem frequently turns out to be interconnected with many other operating prob-

Figure I–4

Steps in the planned approach.

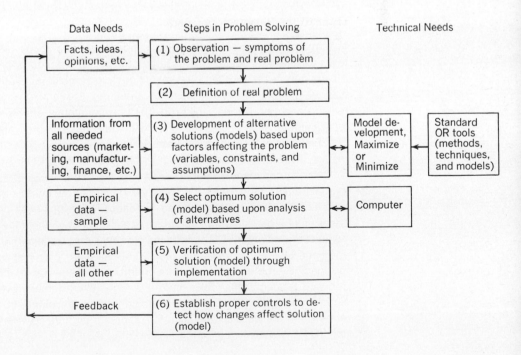

Data Needs	Steps in Problem Solving	Technical Needs
Facts, ideas, opinions, etc.	(1) Observation — symptoms of the problem and real problem	
	(2) Definition of real problem	
Information from all needed sources (marketing, manufacturing, finance, etc.)	(3) Development of alternative solutions (models) based upon factors affecting the problem (variables, constraints, and assumptions)	Model development, Maximize or Minimize / Standard OR tools (methods, techniques, and models)
Empirical data — sample	(4) Select optimum solution (model) based upon analysis of alternatives	Computer
Empirical data — all other	(5) Verification of optimum solution (model) through implementation	
Feedback	(6) Establish proper controls to detect how changes affect solution (model)	

lems. With an initial expansion of the problem, the solutions to the parts should be interrelated to assure best overall performance. This approach avoids the problem of optimization in one area (department or function) at the expense of suboptimization for the entire firm.

For example, consider a warehouse stock control study for a certain paint manufacturer that ended up as an analysis of the paint blending mills. The operations researchers found that warehouse inventory levels were at the mercy of plant production output. This depended on the amount of paint blended in the roller mill each day. An extensive effort was needed to determine why the mill output varied so greatly. When the production problems were identified, several changes in engineering and raw material specifications were made. Thus, the warehouse inventories were brought under control, the physical inventory was reduced, and production costs were lowered.

Based on the interrelationships within a problem, the project may appear to be endless. However, the project can end where the limits of the control exercised by the manager (to whom operations research personnel report) stops. It also can end when more fruitful areas of research compete for the researcher's time or when the added income does not justify added costs. It should be observed that the dynamics of business today necessitate going back and reviewing projects undertaken some time ago, say two to three years. Subsequent findings may require adjusting previous solutions through the use of revised mathematical models, new input data, and similar items. Hence, what is best for the firm today may not be best tomorrow.

Operations Research Defined

In terms of the characteristics discussed above, operations research can be defined as follows: "operations research utilizes the planned approach and an interdisciplinary team in order to represent complex functional relationships as mathematical models for the purpose of providing a quantitative basis for decision making and uncovering new problems for quantitative analysis." In essence, the four characteristics of operations research have been incorporated in the definition. The inclusion of a quantitative basis for decision making was necessary since the results of operations research should be applied to the problem at hand.

One last comment is needed regarding the use of the output from OR methods. In some cases, the answers supplied by mathematical models through a computer system may need to be modified to reflect future business conditions. In other cases, the output is a guide for the manager to follow without the need for changes. Yet in some instances, OR techniques provide a range of feasible solutions for management. Operations research, then, includes more than just developing models for specific problems. Its important contribution is the application of its output for decision making at the lower, middle, and top management levels. The manager's experience, upcoming business conditions, and the output from a mathematical model form the best combination for planning, organizing, directing, and controlling the firm's activities.

Quantitative Models to be Covered

Many OR models have been developed and applied to business problems. They can be grouped into several basic types which will be discussed in the following chapters. No attempt will be made at this point to explain in detail the various methods and models of operations research. Rather, a brief overview is set forth for the following:

breakeven models (chapter 1)

inventory models (chapter 2)

decision theory (chapters 3 and 4)

sequencing models (chapter 5)

allocation models (chapter 6)

assignment models (chapter 7)

dynamic programming models (chapter 8)

competition models (chapter 9)

queuing models (chapter 10)

simulation techniques (chapter 11)

heuristic methods (chapter 12)

behavioral models (chapter 12)

combined OR methods (chapter 12)

Breakeven Models Breakeven models are simplified quantitative devices that permit management to determine its breakeven point, i.e., the point at which total sales equal total costs. These models are also applicable to other areas, such as product planning and decisions to make versus buy.

Inventory Models Inventory models are concerned with two decisions: how much to order at one time and when to order this quantity in order to minimize total cost. Carrying costs, ordering costs of inventory, and shortage costs are determined so that a cost effectiveness relationship (model) can be used by management to select an appropriate balance between costs and shortages. Also, lowest-cost decision rules for inventory management can be obtained by various methods.

Decision Theory The essential characteristic of decision theory is that the consequences of courses of action are generally not known. In these instances, probabilities are associated with the various states of nature. Depending on how much we know about the states of nature in the future, we can make decisions with varying degrees of accuracy. From another view, the future can be predicted even though only a minimum amount of information is available, through Bayesian statistics. In addition to covering these elements of decision theory, Chapters 3 and 4 will treat discrete and continuous probability plus general stochastic models (knowing what will take place, but not with absolute certainty). Thus, it will be shown that decision theory is useful in reducing uncertainty facing the manager.

Sequencing Models   Sequencing models involve determining an optimal sequence for a set of jobs or events or the best sequence for servicing customers in order to minimize total time and costs. Procedures are presented for a network analysis of PERT (Program Evaluation Review Technique)/Time and PERT/Cost. These techniques are currently being applied to research and development, construction, new product planning, and similar areas. Other sequencing problems such as machine scheduling are solved by using simulation and heuristic techniques.

Allocation Models   When there are a number of activities to be performed, alternative ways of doing them, and limited resources or facilities for performing each activity in the most effective way, there is a problem of allocating these scarce resources. The problem is to combine activities and resources in an optimal manner so that overall efficiency is maximized, that is, profit is maximized or cost is minimized. This is known as "mathematical programming." When the objective and the constraints are expressed as linear equations, this is known as "linear programming." If any of the constraints are nonlinear, this is called "nonlinear programming." In addition to linear and nonlinear programming, there are other types of programming—goal, integer, quadratic, convex and stochastic. They differ in the kinds of data they can handle and the kind of assumptions that are made. Some of these latter types are covered in the final chapter.

Assignment Models   The simplest type of allocation model involves the assignment of a number of jobs to the same number of resources (workers). This is called an "assignment problem." This problem type becomes more complex if some of the jobs require more than one resource and if the resources can be used for more than one job. An example of this is the "transportation problem."

Dynamic Programming Models   Dynamic programming, an outgrowth of mathematical programming, is extremely useful for processes that extend over a number of time periods or events. Instead of optimizing each decision as it occurs, dynamic programming takes into account the effects of decisions today on future time periods. Many dynamic programming problems require the use of a computer to manipulate the myriad of data.

Competition Models   The Markov process is a method of predicting competitive changes over time if customer brand loyalties and present market shares are known. If there is high brand loyalty, Markov chains of the first order are used to predict future market behavior. On the other hand, if there is low brand loyalty, Markov chains of a higher order (second, third, etc.) are employed.

Queuing Models   Queuing, sometimes referred to as waiting line theory, is concerned with uniform or random arrivals at a servicing or processing facility of limited capacity. The objective of this model is to allow one to determine the optimum number of personnel or facilities necessary to service arrivals when considering the cost of service and the cost of waiting or congestion.

Simulation Techniques   Simulation, covered briefly in the chapter on queuing theory, makes great use of random numbers which are used to simulate arrivals and service times. Simulation, which lends itself to computer use, generates factors like potential sales or delayed shipments by inspecting random number tables that are integral to the program. The computer output shows the results that could have been obtained if the decision criteria had been used.

Heuristic Methods   Heuristic methods denotes learning or self-adopting systems. The heuristic model uses rules of thumb and educated guesses to explore the most likely paths in coming to a conclusion. This replaces checking all the alternatives (too many for another quantitative approach) to find the best one. This technique appears to be very promising for the future of operations research.

Behavioral Models   Behavioral models represent a new and exciting direction for operations researchers. However, they are relatively unexplored at this time. Initially, it is expected that behavioral phenomena will be incorporated into standard OR methods. Next, problems with strong behavioral aspects, such as marketing problems, will be explored. Considerable behavioral research is necessary before behavioral models become operational.

Combined OR Methods   An important thrust in operations research now and in the future is combining OR methods for some type of master model. Several of the preceding models can be brought together to produce a new group of OR tools for managers. A production control problem, for example, usually includes some combination of inventory allocation and waiting line models. While the usual procedure for solving combined processes consists of solving them one at a time in some logical sequence, operations research must combine the models initially, where there are interrelationships, for an optimum solution.

Even though the foregoing list is incomplete, it does enable managers to perceive what is common to all problems and reminds them that quantitative methods are available for solving problems. The reader should not be too influenced by the name of the model, but rather keep an open mind so as to make analogies to comparable business situations. For example, inventory models are readily applicable to the problems of working capital, personnel, and cash. Waiting line models are readily applicable to inventory. Thus imagination can be an important key to the advancement of OR techniques.

Introduction Summary

Operations research, although originally not so titled, is of somewhat recent origin. Its main roots have arisen for two reasons. The first is the need for scientific study of managerial problems (those involving the interrelationships of functional units of the firm) and the second relates to the opportunity for scientists to attack new problems of the military during World War II. These two motivating forces combined to produce operations research as it is known today. Operations research is defined as "the utilization of a planned approach and an interdisciplinary team in order to represent complex functional relationships as mathematical models for the purpose of providing a quantitative basis for decision making and uncovering new problems for quantitative analysis."

Based on this definition, operations research is an aid or guide to *supplement* business judgment—not supplant it. OR is a managerial tool designed to increase the effectiveness of managerial decisions as an objective supplement to the subjective feelings of managers. In brief, operations research attempts to supply meaningfully analyzed information on those "how," "when," and "what if" questions that were traditionally left to hunch, intuition, judgment, and hopeful guesses. It is an approach to operational analysis which enables managers to improve their decision-making ability.

Questions

1. What contributions has operations research made to business and government in the United States and in Britain?
2. (a) What are the basic steps in constructing a model?
   (b) What is its relationship to the real world?
   (c) How can one decide whether a model should optimize profits, sales, costs, or some other factor?
3. What are the advantages and disadvantages of models?
4. Distinguish among the following: optimization, suboptimization, and overoptimization.
5. What are the essential characteristics of operations research? Explain.
6. What is the planned approach? How does it differ from the scientific method?
7. What areas of operations research have made a significant impact on the firm?
8. Under what conditions would operations research have a difficult time in arriving at an optimum answer? Explain.
9. Why is it important to keep an open mind in utilizing OR techniques?
10. Operations research has been characterized as a "tool designed to increase the effectiveness of managerial decisions as an objective supplement to the subjective feelings of the decision maker." Explain what is meant by this statement.

Bibliography

R. L. Ackoff and M. W. Sasieni, *Fundamentals of Operations Research,* New York: John Wiley & Sons, 1968.

C. W. Churchman, *The Systems Approach,* New York: Dell Publishing Company, 1968.

F. S. Hillier and G. J. Lieberman, *Operations Research,* San Francisco: Holden-Day, 1974.

J. H. Huysmans, *The Implementation of Operations Research,* New York: John Wiley & Sons, 1970.

D. W. Miller and M. K. Starr, *Executive Decisions and Operations Research,* Englewood Cliffs, N.J.: Prentice-Hall, 1969.

C. M. Paik, *Quantitative Methods for Managerial Decisions,* New York: McGraw-Hill Book Company, 1973.

P. Rivett, *Principles of Model Building—The Construction of Models for Decision Analysis,* New York: John Wiley & Sons, 1973.

H. M. Wagner, *Principles of Operations Research, With Applications to Managerial Decisions,* Englewood Cliffs, N.J.: Prentice-Hall, 1975.

Part II

Operations Research Models — Algebra

Chapter 1

Breakeven Analysis

Chapter Objectives

Chapter Outline

Breakeven analysis is a management decision-making tool designed to relate the factors of total sales and total costs at a certain level of volume. Because a firm's profits (or losses) are determined by the relationship between total revenue and total costs at a certain volume, the crucial managerial decisions are those which affect these factors. If drawn as a simple chart based on the assumptions that selling prices do not change and that fixed costs remain constant over the entire range of activity, while other costs vary in direct proportion to volume, breakeven analysis can be no more than an academic tool. However, when derived from an intensive study of price and cost behavior with due consideration for all the factors that influence selling prices and costs, breakeven analysis can be an effective managerial instrument. The approach advocated in the chapter is that breakeven analysis is most useful when it is based upon the "planned performance" method—*one that recognizes the importance of developing costs for current ranges of operating activity.*

For the most part, a manufacturer, a wholesaler, a retailer or a seller of services expects total sales revenue to exceed total costs over time. However, when total sales just equal total costs, the firm has neither made nor lost money. For the year, the firm has just broken even, or operated at the breakeven point. The *breakeven point,* then, is the volume or level of operation at which total sales and total costs are exactly equal. Had the firm operated at a higher level than the breakeven point, the firm would have shown a profit. Conversely, had the firm operated at a level lower than the breakeven point, there would have been a loss for the period.

Requirements for Formulating Breakeven Problems

The requirements for formulating breakeven problems must take into account a thorough analysis of costs and sales. Due to the complexity of developing reliable cost data, this section will focus on the cost component. Traditionally, breakeven analysis is based on the premise that all costs can be segregated into *fixed* and *variable* components. Under this premise, the total cost line is linear in relation to volume, as shown in Figure 1–1. The validity of the breakeven analysis hinges on whether the total cost line is, in fact, linear in relation to volume and whether costs can be separated into fixed (manufacturing, selling, and general and administrative expenses) and variable (direct material, direct labor, manufacturing, and selling expenses) components with an acceptable degree of accuracy. Some costs, such as depreciation, rent, property taxes, and insurance are in no way related to volume and, therefore, have no variable element. Other costs, such as direct material, direct labor, and commissions on sales, have no fixed component and can be controlled as variable costs. Neither of these cost categories presents any problem in cost analysis. However, the problem of separating costs into fixed and variable components is encountered primarily for those costs that contain a

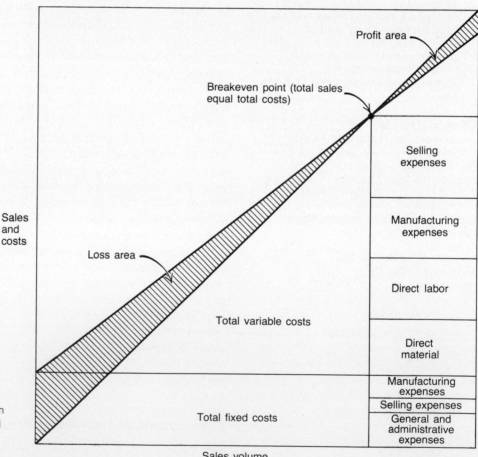

Figure 1–1
Conventional breakeven chart depicting a situation in which total sales equal total costs (fixed and variable).

Applications — Breakeven Analysis

- **Profit planning** — assists management not only in determining its break-even point, but also is an essential part of the annual budgeting process for profit planning.
- **Product planning** — helps the market research group in determining what new products should be added and what old products should be dropped to enhance the firm's profitability.
- **Product pricing** — useful in relating price and volume sensitivity so that the firm can take advantage of the "elasticity of demand" to increase its profits.
- **Selection of advertising media** — useful to marketing management in selecting the best of the various advertising media, e.g., television, radio, magazines, newspapers, etc.
- **Selection of distribution channels** — employed in determining whether the firm should maintain its own distribution network or use others' distribution channels.
- **Make versus buy** — assists management in optimal allocation of capital resources in deciding to make all or part of the components of a product or buy some parts from the outside.
- **Leasing versus owning** — determines for management whether it is best to lease or own machinery and equipment to maximize profits.
- **Equipment selection and replacement** — relates the important cost factors of buying new equipment versus keeping the present machinery so as to minimize overall production costs.

mixture of fixed and variable elements. They are called *semivariable* costs because they do not react to volume changes in the same proportion to the amount of change in volume. Inasmuch as there is no readily ascertainable relationship between cost and volume, their behavior pattern must be determined by analysis.

For purposes of accurate analysis, semivariable costs can be further broken down into three general types. The first type includes those costs which have a fixed element that can be easily identified and segregated, and a variable element that varies in direct proportion with volume. One example of this type of cost is purchased electric power for which there is a fixed charge per period which is constant and an energy charge which varies with consumption. Another example is salesmen's salaries and commissions in which salaries represent the fixed portion and commissions represent the variable portion. This category presents no problem in cost analysis. The total cost line follows a set pattern and passes through all ranges of volume at the same variable rate.

The second type of semivariable costs consists of those charges which cannot be, or for some reason, are not precisely fitted to the level of activity attained; consequently, they increase with volume in a step-like manner. Prime examples are supervisory costs and clerical salaries. Increases in the labor force are made only when volume reaches certain levels, with the result that the cost is held constant over wide ranges of activity, and then suddenly takes a sharp climb upward. This category of semivariable costs presents a special problem because the cost line may move through different ranges of activity at a rate which differs from the overall average.

The third type of semivariable costs includes those expenditures that bear no measurable relationship to activity, and therefore, do not vary in proportion to volume, but vary rather as management thinks they should. Examples are advertising, sales promotion and research and development. The number of employees required to prepare payrolls for computer processing at different volumes is determinable from studies of workload requirements and a cost can be set accordingly; but who is to say with certainty how many dollars must be spent on advertising to achieve a given sales goal? Behavior patterns in this category may be erratic. Influenced by management policy, and therefore highly discretionary, costs in this third category defy logical analysis. They may appear to fluctuate in some definite pattern in relation to volume, but no significant conclusion can be drawn from the relationship, nor is there good reason to presume that the same relationship will hold true in future periods.

Due to the problems encountered with semivariable costs, they are generally segregated into fixed and variable components by using a scattergraph on which a number of cost observations at different levels of activity are plotted, as in Figures 1–2 and 1–3. A trend line is then fitted to the data by inspection or by some statistical method, such as the method of least squares. The intersection of the trend line with the cost axis is the fixed portion, while the variable portion slopes upward from the cost axis for the semivariable cost. Although the task of developing accurate cost factors may be somewhat time consuming for semivariable costs, it is necessary for a proper segregation of fixed and variable components.

Figure 1–2
Segregation of semivariable costs with discernible fixed ($1,000 per month) and variable ($0.05 per unit) components.

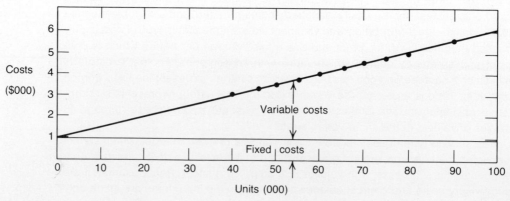

Building the Cost Structure

As a first step in the planned performance method, it is necessary to reclassify fixed costs (determined by the above procedures) into two broad categories:

prior-commitment costs

planned (or managed) costs

Prior-commitment costs are determined by the capacity that has been provided. Examples are straight-line depreciation, taxes, rent, and insurance on plant and equipment. These costs are the result of actions that have been taken in the past and are not presently subject to management control on a short-run basis. Since their amount will remain constant over a whole range of operations, they represent a barrier that management must overcome with volume. Prior-commitment costs present no problem when a cost analysis is undertaken.

Planned costs, on the other hand, are those costs that management deems necessary to accomplish a desired objective. Taken as a whole, planned costs are directly related to the volume of activity planned. By their nature, they can seldom be precisely fitted to the anticipated volume; they must be budgeted in steps. Furthermore, once the planned level of activity has been determined and costs budgeted, the planned costs tend to remain at a constant amount, for short periods at least, even though the level of activity actually attained may differ from the planned level.

Some of the planned costs, such as clerical wages and officer salaries, can be budgeted to fit a specific workload; others, such as advertising and research and development, are discretionary in nature and are based on judgment and opinion rather than analysis. In the final analysis, the budget for planned costs is some amount that appears to be acceptable at the moment. What is acceptable is largely a matter of the expected activity level.

This foregoing reclassification of costs leads to the question of the validity of the cost equation, $C = F + V$ (where C equals total costs, F equals total fixed costs, and

Figure 1–3
Segregation of semivariable costs with discernible fixed ($9,000 per month) and varying levels of variable ($0.46 per unit) components.

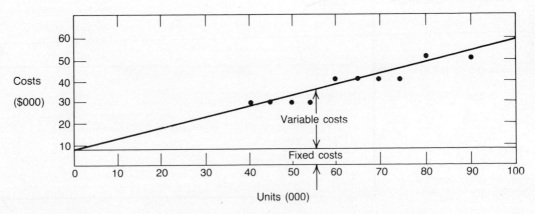

V equals total variable costs), in which F represents total fixed costs that will remain constant at all volumes. The equation should be rewritten to read: $C = (F_c + F_p) + V$, in which F_c represents the prior-commitment costs and F_p represents the planned costs. In this equation, F_c remains constant at all volumes but F_p does not; the latter can be made to fluctuate with volume. Because of their nature, the planned costs do not vary in proportion to volume nor do they remain fixed at all levels of activity. They move in steps, a behavior which cannot be depicted with a straight line through all levels of activity. Consequently, they must be built into the cost structure in blocks at different levels of activity.

To illustrate the use of the planned performance method, prior-commitment costs are developed, followed by an analysis of planned costs at different levels of capacity (see Figure 1–4). To these fixed cost components, the variable costs are added

---

Fixed costs that remain at a constant amount at all levels:

Prior-commitment costs—depreciation, property taxes, insurance, and similar costs $9,000

Fixed costs that are budgeted in steps:

Planned costs:

a. Advertising, sales promotion, research and development, and similar costs

b. Fixed component of purchased power and similar costs

Capacity	
0	$ 6,000
1– 19,999	16,000
20,000– 39,999	21,000
40,000– 59,999	31,000
60,000– 79,999	41,000
80,000–100,000	51,000

Variable cost *per unit:*

Direct material, direct labor, sales commissions, and
similar costs $0.45
Variable component of purchased power and similar costs 0.05
$0.50

Figure 1–4
Fixed and variable cost data using the planned performance method.

to determine the total cost structure. When the data in Figure 1-4 are plotted in Figure 1-5, there are several cost lines, not one. This stair-stepping approach, then, presents a realistic picture of the firm's cost structure in the future.

Building the Sales Structure

Just as a method is needed for building an accurate cost structure, the same can be said for a sales structure. Fundamentally, the sales line follows the pattern set by competition or by the company's pricing policy. If the selling price is determined by competition, the sales line presents no problem. It can be drawn as a straight line sloping through all levels of planned activities for short-time periods. When the company is in a position to control the price, e.g., it is a leader in an industry or it is introducing a new product, the sales line can be drawn as a straight line through all levels of planned activity for short time periods. The price in this case would be set at an amount to achieve a desired profit goal based upon a desired return on investment.

If a company's plan is to reap maximum profits from a new product, it will set the initial price high and will sell as many units as possible at that price, gradually reducing the price as the demand decreases. Even under these conditions, the sales line for a short period will be a straight line through all levels of activity. The slant of the line, however, will change with each decrease in selling price for different periods.

When a company is operating in a highly competitive market, profitable operations can result only through a proper balance between costs and selling prices at different volume levels. Under these conditions, the selling price must be set at an amount to produce a certain profit under alternative combinations of price and volume. One straight sales line can be only tentative. The various alternatives can be determined only by drawing several sales lines at various levels of operations. Once the most profitable level of operations has been determined, the sales line will be a straight line through the level of planned operations. In any event, it should be constructed for the planned operational level, i.e., the period under consideration. Once the sales level has been established, it becomes a gauge with which to measure performance of sales personnel.

Assuming a selling price of $1.20 per unit for the above example, the sales line can be drawn (Figure 1-5). Notice there are three breakeven points and several different profit patterns. Each planned level has its own profit pattern. The term *planned* is used advisedly since the cost structure would be influenced more by planned performance than actual past attainment. The basic profit structure is as follows:

Selling price per unit	$1.20	100.0%
Variable cost per unit	.50	41.7%
Contribution	$ .70	58.3%

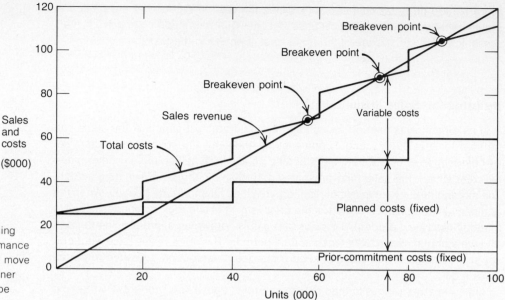

Figure 1–5
Breakeven chart using
the planned performance
method: total costs move
in a step-wise manner
and total sales slope
upward in a linear
fashion.

The profits (losses) at the midpoints of the various levels of operation in Figure 1–5 are tabulated in Table 1–1. The equations used in calculating the breakeven in dollars and units in Table 1–1 will be developed below.

Table 1–1
Net Income (Losses) and
Breakeven in Dollars and
Units Using the Planned
Performance Method

Units Sold	10,000	30,000	50,000	70,000	90,000
Contribution	$ 7,000	$21,000	$35,000	$49,000	$63,000
Fixed Costs:					
Prior-Commitment	$ 9,000	$ 9,000	$ 9,000	$ 9,000	$ 9,000
Planned	16,000	21,000	31,000	41,000	51,000
	$25,000	$30,000	$40,000	$50,000	$60,000
Net Income (Loss)	($18,000)	($9,000)	($5,000)	($1,000)	$ 3,000
Breakeven ($)			$68,570	$85,700	$102,860
Breakeven (units)			57,114	71,429	85,800

Approaches to Conventional Breakeven Analysis

Four conventional approaches to breakeven analysis are presented: standard graphic, inverted graphic, gross graphic, and algebraic. These approaches are based upon linear relationships. More emphasis is placed on the algebraic approach. In addition, two other approaches are presented: multiproduct algebraic and nonlinear algebraic. In all of these approaches, we will assume that all calculations are made within a limited range of capacity. From this view, the stair-stepped effect of planned costs for the planned performance method is eliminated. Also, this approach tends to simplify the presentation of traditional breakeven analysis.

Standard Graphic The standard graphic approach is illustrated in Figure 1–6. (A comparable example using the planned performance method was presented in Figure 1–5.) For this conventional approach, revenue and costs in dollars are plotted on the vertical or *y* axis. Volume or output in units is plotted on the horizontal or *x* axis. The intersection of the total revenue line with the total cost line locates the breakeven point. At this point, total revenue is exactly equal to total variable costs plus total fixed costs. Any vertical distance between the total revenue line and the total cost line to the right of the breakeven point measures profit at that volume. To the left of the breakeven point, any vertical distance between those two lines measures a loss.

Figure 1–6
Breakeven chart with fixed costs at bottom of chart.

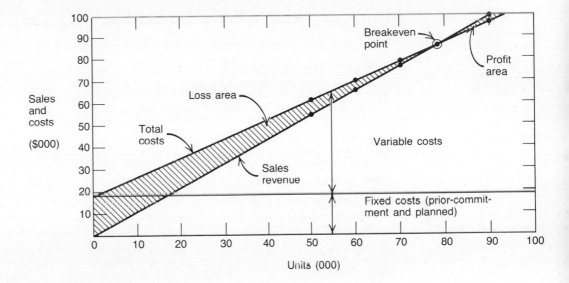

Inverted Graphic The inverted graphic approach, shown in Figure 1–7, differs from the standard graphic breakeven chart in that fixed costs are charted above variable costs—not under. In some types of manufacturing, the variable costs and the selling price of the product are relatively stable. In such cases, a major factor affecting profits is the ability to control overhead, mostly a fixed cost. The effect of greater overhead on breakeven, as well as profit, is more easily seen on this type of chart than the standard graphic.

Gross Graphic It is sometimes possible to construct a breakeven chart even though the variable cost figure per unit is not known. In order to do this, an estimate of fixed costs, total revenue and total cost for some percentage of capacity utilized is needed.

The first step in graphing this approach is locating the fixed costs on the vertical or *y* axis. Secondly, the total revenue figure and total cost figure are spotted on a vertical line that relates to a percentage of capacity on the horizontal or *x* axis. A line is drawn from the origin through the total revenue point and another line is drawn from the fixed cost point through the total cost point. The intersection of these two lines determines the breakeven point on the y axis and percentage of capacity on the x axis. My consulting experience has shown that this method should be used with extreme caution, since estimates can produce an incorrect breakeven point.

Algebraic   The algebraic formulas for breakeven in terms of units, dollars, and capacity are not difficult, but they do need an explanation. In order to simplify the analysis, the following terms are used:

R = total revenue (dollars)

C = total costs (dollars)

V = total variable costs

F = total fixed costs or $F = F_c$ (prior-commitment costs) $+ F_p$ (planned costs)

x = volume or output (units)

v = variable cost per unit (dollars)

p = selling price per unit (dollars)

Total revenue equals the volume in units multiplied by the selling price per unit; thus, $R = xp$. Total cost equals total fixed costs plus total variable costs or $C = F + V$. Likewise, $C = F + xv$ or $C = (F_c + F_p) + xv$. The total revenue equation and the total cost equation, at breakeven, must be equal; thus, $R = C$. Substituting for each of these terms results in the following:

$xp = F + xv$

$xp - xv = F$

$x(p - v) = F$ (Equation 1–1)

$x \text{ (units)} = \dfrac{F}{(p - v)}$ at breakeven

Referring to the earlier illustration for the planned performance method (Table 1–1), the breakeven point in units for a volume range of 60,000 to 79,999 units is 71,429, computed as follows:

$\text{units} = \dfrac{\$50,000}{(\$1.20 - \$0.50)}$

$\text{units} = \dfrac{\$50,000}{\$0.70}$

$\text{units} = 71,429 \text{ at breakeven}$

A graphic verification of this value can be found in Figure 1–5.

   The formula for breakeven in dollars is Equation 1–1 multiplied on both sides by p (selling price). Since $R = xp$, the resulting formula is:

$$R = \frac{F}{(1 - v/p)} \text{ at breakeven} \qquad \text{(Equation 1-2)}$$

Using the same example as above, breakeven in dollars for a volume range of 60,000 to 79,999 units is $85,700.

$$R = \frac{\$50,000}{(1 - \$0.50/\$1.20)}$$

$$R = \frac{\$50,000}{(1 - 41.7\%)}$$

$$R = \frac{\$50,000}{58.3\%}$$

$$R = \$85,700 \text{ at breakeven}$$

This breakeven value can be verified graphically in Figure 1-5. Note that the fixed-cost percentage can be used for the contribution percentage. Why is this so? Since there is no profit or loss at breakeven, the contribution percentage (ratio) and the fixed costs percentage (ratio) must be equal.

The last formula for breakeven in terms of capacity in units is derived as follows:

$$x \text{ (units)} = \frac{\text{total capacity in units} \times \% \text{ capacity}}{100\%}$$

Substituting the above equation in Equation 1-1 for the term x, the following results:

$$\frac{\text{total capacity in units} \times \% \text{ capacity}}{100\%} - \frac{F}{(p - v)} \qquad \text{(Equation 1-3)}$$

$$\% \text{ capacity} = \frac{F}{(\text{total capacity in units}) (p - v)} \times 100\% \text{ at breakeven}$$

Figure 1-7
Breakeven chart with variable costs at bottom of chart.

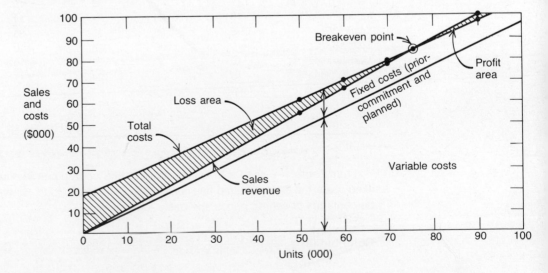

39

The calculation for percentage of capacity in units at breakeven from 60,000 to 79,999 units is 71.4%:

$$\% \text{ capacity} = \frac{\$50,000}{100,000 \ (\$1.20 - \$0.50)} \times 100\%$$

$$\% \text{ capacity} = \frac{\$50,000}{100,000 \ (\$.70)} \times 100\%$$

$$\% \text{ capacity} = \frac{\$50,000}{\$70,000} \times 100\%$$

$$\% \text{ capacity} = .714 \times 100\%$$

$$\% \text{ capacity} = 71.4\% \text{ at breakeven}$$

Multiproduct Algebraic   Up to this point, for the purpose of simplification, the discussion has centered around breakeven as it applies to a business with a single product or to one product of a multiproduct firm. Most manufacturers, wholesalers, and retailers are engaged in selling many products. In this part, breakeven is applied to a multiproduct firm.

Again, using the planned performance method, the data for a multiproduct manufacturer of better lamps, shown in Table 1–2, will illustrate the calculations for breakeven. The sales data comes from the marketing department while the cost figures are obtained from the cost accounting department working in conjunction with the marketing and production departments.

Table 1–2
Breakeven for a
Multiproduct Firm

Lamps— Planned Line	Percentage of Dollar Sales Volume	Selling Price per Unit	Variable Cost per Unit	Contribution to Fixed Costs	Planned Fixed Costs*
Early American	20%	$25	$15	$10	$ 50,000
Colonial	15	25	15	10	40,000
French Provincial	15	40	28	12	42,000
Italian Provincial	10	35	21	14	30,000
Louis XV	5	60	35	25	15,000
Spanish	10	30	20	10	28,000
Mediterranean	10	30	20	10	29,000
Danish Modern	15	35	24	11	41,000
	100%				$275,000
				Prior-Commitment Costs	121,000
				Total Fixed Costs	$396,000

*These costs are based upon anticipated (planned) production volume range for each lamp.

From Table 1–2, the Early American lamp line contributes $10 per unit toward fixed costs, the Colonial lamp line contributes $10, and so forth. Converting these to percentages of selling prices, the basic formula is:

$$\text{Contribution} = \frac{\text{selling price} - \text{variable cost}}{\text{selling price}} \times 100\% \qquad \text{(Equation 1–4)}$$

The per unit contribution for the Early American lamp line is illustrated to be:

$$\frac{\$25 - \$15}{\$25} \times 100\% = \frac{\$10}{\$25} \times 100\% = 40\%$$

The next step is to multiply the contributions by the percentage of sales volume for that particular lamp and then add these figures. The resulting figure is the total contribution per sales dollar for all lamps. As shown in Table 1–3, 36 percent is the total contribution per overall sales dollar at the planned product-sales mix. The breakeven point in dollars (modified Equation 1–2) for this firm is calculated as follows:

$$\text{Breakeven (\$)} = \frac{\text{Fixed costs}}{\text{Contribution percent}} = \frac{\$396,000}{36\%}$$

$$\text{Breakeven (\$)} = \$1,100,000$$

Lamp	Percentage Contribution × per Lamp	Percentage of Dollar = Sales Volume	Total Contribution
Early American	40%	20%	8.0%
Colonial	40	15	6.0
French Provincial	30	15	4.5
Italian Provincial	40	10	4.0
Louis XV	42	5	2.1
Spanish	33	10	3.3
Mediterranean	33	10	3.3
Danish Modern	32	15	4.8
		100%	36.0%

Table 1–3
Contribution of a
Multiproduct Firm

Nonlinear Algebraic This chapter has stressed the proper handling of nonlinear costs. Similarly, in this part, the nonlinear aspects of sales will be treated from a graphic and algebraic standpoint. A different illustration will be used since the selling price changes for different sales volume; that is, total revenue increases at a diminishing rate as output is increased.

Experience has indicated that consumer demand is sensitive to price and that as the firm's price is lowered, an increasing number of units will be sold, as shown in Table 1–4. Variable costs per unit are $0.50 while prior-commitment costs are

Price (p)	Units Sold (x)	Total Revenue (xp)
$3.333	900	$ 3,000
2.000	2,500	5,000
1.000	10,000	10,000
.666	22,500	15,000
.500	40,000	20,000

Table 1–4
Analysis of Nonlinear
Sales Data

$1,000 and planned costs are $3,000 for a production output range of 2,500 to 25,000 units. The revenue (Table 1–4) and cost data are illustrated graphically in Figure 1–8.

The solution for breakeven points is somewhat more complex since the non-linear revenue function is expressed by the equation R = $100 $\sqrt{x}$ where x represents the units of output or sales. Equating $100 $\sqrt{x}$ with the total costs ($4,000 + 0.50x$) for a range of 2,500 to 25,000 units, the resulting equation is:

$100 $\sqrt{x}$ = $4,000 + 0.50x$ (Basic equation for breakeven)

$10,000$x$ = $16,000,000 + $4,000$x$ + 0.25x^2$ (Square both sides to remove square root sign)

0.25x^2$ − $6,000$x$ + $16,000,000 = 0

Since this equation is in the proper format for using the quadratic formula, a represents the coefficient of the x^2 term (.25); b, that of the x term (−6,000); and c, the constant (16,000,000). The calculations for two breakeven points are:

$$X = \frac{-b \pm \sqrt{b^2 - 4\,ac}}{2a}$$

$$X = \frac{+\$6,000 \pm \sqrt{\$36,000,000 - 4\,(\$0.25)\,(\$16,000,000)}}{2\,(\$0.25)}$$

$$X = \frac{+\$6,000 \pm \sqrt{\$20,000,000}}{\$0.50} \qquad \text{(quadratic formula)}$$

$$X = \frac{+\$6,000 \pm \$4,472}{\$0.50}$$

X = 3,056 units and 20,944 units

Figure 1–8 shows that the company will make a profit only when operating in the range above 3,056 units and below 20,944 units.

Breakeven Analysis for Decision Making

Once breakeven data are available, they can be applied to measure the profitability of the entire business or any part of it. After all, management wants to do more than just break even; it wants to maximize profits and its return on total assets. This means that the methods of breakeven analysis are readily applicable to many areas of an organization. In the following illustrations the reader might find it helpful to graph the data as given for a complete understanding of the material. As in the previous approaches to breakeven, the planned performance method is used within a limited range of capacity to simplify the presentation.

Product Planning   Planning for new products lends itself to breakeven analysis. The market research group must make critical decisions about adding or dropping a line or product. Also considered is how packaging will affect the sales volume as well as the fixed and variable costs.

A manufacturer of several product lines is contemplating dropping one item from its product line and replacing it with another. The present volume and cost data shown in Table 1–5 are representative of next year.

The change contemplated consists of dropping product C and replacing it with product E. The manufacturer has compiled in Table 1–6 the anticipated volume and cost data if this change is made. Contribution for the present and proposed product mix is computed as set forth previously and forms the basis for profits before federal income taxes. The calculations are found in Table 1–7.

Figure 1–8
Nonlinear breakeven chart using the planned performance method where the revenue curve is nonlinear.

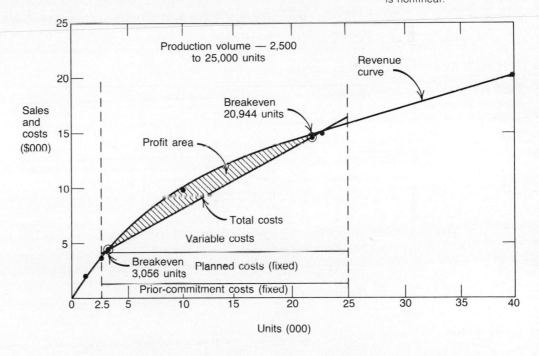

Product Line	Percentage of Sales Volume	Selling Price	Variable Costs per Unit	Contribution
Product A	20%	$ 6	$ 4	$2
Product B	25	10	5	5
Product C	15	12	9	3
Product D	40	18	10	8
	100%			

Total fixed costs per year = $75,000
Sales (this year) = $250,000

Table 1–5
Product Planning—
Present Product Line

Product Line	Percentage of Sales Volume	Selling Price	Variable Costs per Unit	Contribution	Planned Fixed Costs
Product A	20%	$ 6	$ 4	$2	$10,000
Product B	25	10	5	5	10,000
Product E	20	15	9	6	15,000
Product D	35	18	10	8	20,000
	100%				$55,000
Sales (next year) = $280,000				Prior-commitment costs	23,000
				Total fixed costs	$78,000

Table 1-6
Product Planning—
Proposed Product Line

Based upon the data in Table 1-7, the proposed change should be initiated. In the example, if the sales and fixed costs had remained the same, the overall contribution percentage could have been used for reaching a final decision.

Table 1-7
Contribution and Net Income Before Federal Income Taxes—Present and Proposed Lines

Product			Present Line			
A	$\dfrac{\$ 6 - \$ 4}{\$6}$	=	$\dfrac{\$ 2}{\$ 6}$	× 20%	=	.067
B	$\dfrac{\$10 - \$ 5}{\$10}$	=	$\dfrac{\$ 5}{\$10}$	× 25%	=	.125
C	$\dfrac{\$12 - \$ 9}{\$12}$	=	$\dfrac{\$ 3}{\$12}$	× 15%	=	.038
D	$\dfrac{\$18 - \$10}{\$18}$	=	$\dfrac{\$ 8}{\$18}$	× 40%	=	.177
						.407 contribution

$250,000 × .407 = $101,750 contribution
$101,750 − $75,000 = $26,750 net income before federal income taxes

Product			Proposed Line			
A	no change					.067
B	no change					.125
E	$\dfrac{\$15 - \$ 9}{\$15}$	=	$\dfrac{\$ 6}{\$15}$	× 20%	=	.080
D	$\dfrac{\$18 - \$10}{\$18}$	=	$\dfrac{\$ 8}{\$18}$	× 35%	=	.155
						.427 contribution

$280,000 × .427 = $119,560 contribution
$119,560 − $78,000 = $41,560 net income before federal income taxes

Product Pricing Before discussing the application of contribution to pricing, it should be noted that price is a function of volume. If the demand for a product changes with price, it is said to have an *elastic* demand. If it does not change, then demand is *inelastic* and has a low price-volume sensitivity. For example, if the price of table salt sold in supermarkets increases or decreases by 20 percent, the sales volume will remain about the same since people consume about the same amount of salt in their diets. However, suppose the price of color television sets increases or decreases by 15 percent. In this case, a price increase will reduce volume while a price decrease will generate an important increase in volume (assuming all things are equal). The rationale is that color television sets are not as essential to people as is table salt.

Businessmen can take advantage of this important economic principle when the contribution concept is used in pricing. For example, a firm states that its product's competitive price or current market price is $19.95 and its variable costs are $15 per unit. However, it decides that instead of meeting competition, it will price somewhat higher to $23.95 and will accept the resulting drop in volume because of the greater contribution. The calculations are:

	Selling Price $19.95	Selling Price $23.95
Volume of units sold	50,000	30,000 (drop of 40%)
Revenue generated	$997,500	$718,500
Contribution per unit	$4.95	$8.95
Total contribution	$247,500	$268,500

This example shows the effect of knowing the characteristics of prices and volume sensitivity for the firm's products. So often, expansions are undertaken to support volume sales with little consideration given to the contribution-generating capacity of products (i.e., properly pricing to take advantage of the elasticity of demand).

In the above case, the drop in volume created by higher prices could be less or it could be more. All products and markets have widely varying demand elasticities. It is management's job to find the optimum combination between prices and volume for their products in order to achieve the greatest contribution within the limits of the operating and financial constraints of the firm. Often management is confronted with the question of maintaining, lowering, or increasing prices. Obviously, the selection of any one of these alternatives will produce risks. The best course is to test their respective effects in terms of units and breakeven. As indicated in the sample problem per Table 1-8, a price increase produces the lowest breakeven point for arriving at a decision.

	No Price Change	Decrease Price 5%	Increase Price 5%
Selling price per unit	$1.00	$0.95	$1.05
Variable cost per unit	0.70	0.70	0.70
Contribution per unit	$0.30	$0.25	$0.35
Fixed costs—prior-commitment and planned	$50,000	$50,000	$50,000
Breakeven in units	166,667	200,000	142,857

Table 1-8
Breakeven and Pricing

Promotional Mix   Most firms employ a "promotion mix" which fundamentally includes three broad categories: personal selling, advertising, and sales promotion. The addition of more salesmen or advertising has a direct effect on the firm's fixed costs. As an illustration, additional fixed costs that produce a new breakeven point are shown in Table 1–9.

Fixed costs will rise from $80,000 to $94,000, resulting in a new breakeven of 47,000 units. However, if the firm wishes to make a profit (*P*) of $25,000, the firm must sell 59,500 units, computed as follows (let x = unknown unit of sales):

$$P = R - C$$

$$\$25,000 = x(\$4.95) - [\$94,000 + x(\$2.95)]$$

$$\$25,000 = \$4.95x - \$94,000 - \$2.95x$$

$$\$119,000 = \$2.00x$$

$$x = 59,500 \text{ units}$$

The same problem can be solved by the breakeven formula (Equation 1–1), modified for the desired profit as follows:

$$x \text{ (units)} = \frac{F + P}{(p - v)}$$

$$x = \frac{\$94,000 + \$25,000}{(\$4.95 - \$2.95)}$$

$$x = \frac{\$119,000}{\$2.00}$$

$$x = 59,500 \text{ units}$$

Table 1–9
Breakeven and Promotion

Present Situation	
Selling price per unit	$4.95
Variable cost per unit	2.95
Contribution per unit	$2.00
Fixed costs	$80,000
Breakeven in units	40,000

Proposed Addition to Fixed Costs	
Additional advertising	$ 4,000
Additional salesmen	10,000
Increase in fixed costs	$14,000

Selection of Distribution Channels   Every company should select the best distribution channels for its products and services. A manufacturer, for example, must decide whether to have his own salesmen, use sales agents, or employ manufacturer's representatives. In effect, management must decide whether to place a salesman on their payroll to develop new territories or to engage an outside agent.

Another decision is whether to have one distributor or several distributors in a city. Hence, breakeven can be readily applied to a distribution channel problem.

Breakeven data for the present situation and the two alternatives for expanding sales territories of a manufacturing firm are shown in Table 1–10. The result is an estimated $500,000 sales increase. Commissions payable to the manufacturer's representatives are 10 percent of sales and it is estimated that the employment of a salesman will add $15,000 annually to fixed costs. From the analysis, the employment of a company salesman is more profitable.

Suppose there is some question about being able to obtain the additional $500,000 in sales. At what sales point below the $500,000 figure will it be more economical to use the manufacturer's representatives? First, find the incremental profits generated by the additional sales, shown in Table 1–11. Next, determine the difference in the contribution between the two alternatives for the $500,000 sales increment. The manufacturer's representative generates a contribution at the rate of $0.50 for every sales dollar while the salesman generates it at the rate of $0.57 for every sales dollar. The salesman obtains a $0.07 greater contribution. The sales at which both will produce the same profit is the point at which the $0.07 contribution pays for the $15,000 of fixed expenses; thus:

$$\text{Breakeven (dollars)} = \frac{\text{Fixed costs}}{\text{Contr. of salesman} - \text{Contr. of mfgr. rep.}}$$

$$\text{Breakeven} = \frac{\$15,000}{.57 - .50}$$

$$\text{Breakeven} = \frac{\$15,000}{.07}$$

$$\text{Breakeven} = \$214,286$$

It is more economical to use the manufacturer's representative for incremental sales under $214,286.

	Presently	With Mfgrs. Rep.	With Salesmen
Sales	$2,800,000	$3,300,000	$3,300,000
Variable costs	1,400,000	1,650,000	1,600,000
Contribution	$1,400,000	$1,650,000	$1,700,000
Fixed costs	1,000,000	1,000,000	1,015,000
Net income before federal income taxes	$ 400,000	$ 650,000	$ 685,000

Table 1–10
Breakeven and
Distribution Channels

	With Mfgrs. Rep.	With Salesmen
Additional sales	$500,000	$500,000
Additional variable costs	250,000	200,000
Additional fixed costs	—	15,000
Total additional costs	$250,000	$215,000
Incremental profit	$250,000	$285,000
Contribution	50%	57%

Table 1–11
Incremental Profits
Analysis for
Manufacturer's
Representatives
and Salesmen

Make Versus Buy   There are many reasons why a firm does not manufacture all of its component parts. Some of these are: lack of capacity, avoidance of overtime or second-shift operations, desire to use capacity on more profitable work, desire to use vendors' facilities and technical skill, and insufficient volume for full-time employment of a company's labor force. From the viewpoint of maximizing a firm's return on total assets, a motive for buying is to reduce the company's investments in cash, inventory, and fixed assets. Generally speaking, the smaller the operation, the more dependence is placed on outside vendors. As a company grows, the volume may approach the point at which it becomes economically feasible to install fixed assets for making, instead of buying from vendors. The question is, at what volume is the investment justified? This is readily solved by breakeven analysis.

The data, found in the sample problem per Figure 1–9, forms the basis for making a decision to invest or buy. The breakeven for the make decision is 20,000 units versus the present buying from outside vendors of 25,000 units. Since the manufacturer will be needing more than 20,000 units per annum, "to make" is more attractive than "to buy."

Figure 1–9
Make versus buy decision.

Present cost of buying

Annual volume of parts used	25,000 pieces
Purchase cost of parts	$2.00 each
Annual cost of parts used	$50,000

Proposed cost of investing to make

Additional annual fixed costs (planned costs)	$30,000
Variable costs	$0.50 per unit

Breakeven for make decision

$$\text{units} = \frac{F}{(p - v)} \text{ at breakeven}$$

$$\text{units} = \frac{\$30,000}{(\$2.00 - \$0.50)}$$

(Equation 1–1)

$$\text{units} = \frac{\$30,000}{\$1.50}$$

$$\text{units} = 20,000 \text{ at breakeven}$$

Equipment Selection and Replacement   Selection of fixed assets in terms of machinery and equipment can have a lasting effect on a firm's profitability. New technology creates improved machinery and equipment, making older machinery and equipment more expensive to operate and, many times, completely obsolete. Newer equipment saves on labor (a high cost for most manufacturers), permits greater output, raises product quality, or possibly even saves on materials. Based upon these factors, newer equipment can also lower the firm's breakeven point.

Instead of using the term breakeven analysis for equipment selection and replacement, a better name is *indifference analysis*. This can be illustrated by an example. The engineering department has proposed two alternatives to the existing process for making shafts. The present machine (hand operated) is fully depreciated on the books, except for the scrap value which is equal to the cost of removing the hand-operated equipment. Thus, fixed costs are ignored. Its variable costs are $2 per unit. A semiautomatic machine will add $3,000 a year to the fixed costs while variable costs per unit will be $1. The faster method, utilizing the completely automatic machine, will add $9,000 a year to fixed costs and will lower variable costs to $0.50 per unit. The marketing department's long-run forecast indicates that sales will not fall below 14,000 units for the next eight years, the expected life of each new machine.

The first step is to relate mathematically the total costs (TC) of the hand-operated (A), semiautomatic (B), and automatic (C) machines to one another. This can be accomplished by relating A to B, B to C, and A to C, and then solve using simultaneous equations.

$TC_{(A)} = \$0 + \$2N$ (hand-operated machine)

$TC_{(B)} = \$3,000 + \$1N$ (semiautomatic machine)

$0 = -\$3,000 + N$ (subtract equation $TC_{(B)}$ from $TC_{(A)}$)
$N = 3,000$ units

$TC_{(D)} = \$3,000 + \$1N$ (semiautomatic machine)

$TC_{(C)} = \$9,000 + \$0.50\ N$ (automatic machine)

$0 = -\$6,000 + \$0.50N$ (subtract equation $TC_{(C)}$ from $TC_{(B)}$)
$N = 12,000$ units

$TC_{(A)} = \$0 + \$2N$ (hand-operated machine)

$TC_{(C)} = \$9,000 + \$0.50N$ (automatic machine)

$0 = -\$9,000 + \$1.50N$ (subtract equation $TC_{(C)}$ from $TC_{(A)}$)
$N = 6,000$ units

In order to graph the above indifference points, it is necessary to substitute the quantities back into the total cost equations:

$TC_{(A)} = \quad \$0 \quad + \$2\ (3,000) \quad = \quad \$0 \quad + \quad \$6,000 = \quad \$6,000$

$TC_{(B)} = \$3,000 + \$1\ (3,000) \quad = \$3,000 + \quad \$3,000 = \quad \$6,000$

$TC_{(B)} = \$3,000 + \$1\ (12,000) \quad = \$3,000 + \$12,000 = \$15,000$

$TC_{(C)} = \$9,000 + \$0.50\ (12,000) = \$9,000 + \quad \$6,000 = \$15,000$

$TC_{(A)} = \quad \$0 \quad + \$2\ (6,000) \quad = \quad \$0 \quad + \$12,000 = \$12,000$

$TC_{(C)} = \$9,000 + \$0.50\ (6,000) \quad = \$9,000 + \quad \$3,000 = \$12,000$

49

The preceding data are plotted in Figure 1–10. The hand-operated machine is most economical up to a volume of 2,999 units. At a volume of 3,000 units, the firm is indifferent as to the selection of the hand-operated machine or the semiautomatic machine. In the 3,001 to 11,999 range, the semiautomatic machine is most economical. At a volume of 12,000, the firm is indifferent as to the selection of the semiautomatic machine and the automatic machine. At a volume over 12,000 units, the automatic machine is most economical. Since the annual sales will not fall below 14,000 units for the next eight years, the firm should acquire the automatic machine.

Figure 1–10
Equipment indifference analysis for three machines.

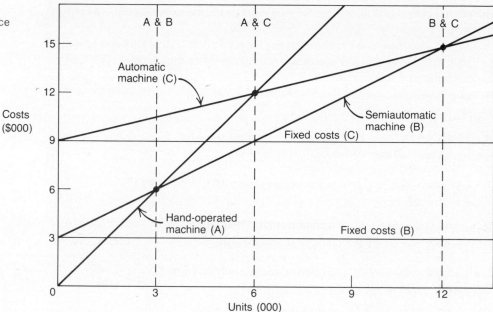

Chapter Summary

Breakeven analysis, a quantitative device that depicts cost-revenue-volume relationships, permits management to look into the future (from one month to one year) in order to estimate the effects of certain decisions on the firm's profits. Since it is basically a profit-planning device for the short run, it should be an integral part of the budgeting process. After all, management's goal is to maximize its profit and return on total assets, rather than just break even.

Within the chapter, costs were not assumed to be either fixed or variable over the entire range of a company's capacity. Such an assumption places very heavy restrictions on the reliability of breakeven analysis. The presentation of breakeven analysis was based upon actual cost behavior and constructed in blocks, with each block representing the cost structure at each level of operations. Linear cost lines were utilized only within limited ranges of activity. Such a structure resulted in costs being segregated into three categories: variable costs, prior-commitment costs, and planned costs. Thus, cost segregation, as an integral part of the planned performance method, is the preferred method for accurate and reliable breakeven studies.

Questions

1. How does the planned performance method of breakeven analysis differ from the conventional method in segregating costs?
2. What is the major advantage of the standard graphic approach to breakeven over the inverted graphic approach and vice versa?
3. What are the cautions of breakeven analysis?

Model Formulation Exercises

1. (a) When building the cost structure in breakeven analysis for a typical manufacturing firm, list five costs each for prior-commitment and planned costs (planned performance method).
   (b) When building the sales structure in breakeven analysis for a typical manufacturing firm, list four factors that affect the slope of the sales curve.

2. As illustrated in Figure 1–5 (based upon the data in Table 1–1) for the planned performance method, what effect does the stair-stepped effect of total costs—in particular, planned costs—have on profits? To state it another way, in formulating such a problem, what cost-volume-profit relationship would typically be found at the various levels of capacity?

3. Inasmuch as most firms are interested not in a breakeven situation, but making a profit, how can the breakeven formula in dollars (Equation 1–2) be reformulated to include a certain level of profits?

4. (a) In the formulation of the breakeven formula in dollars (Equation 1–2) for a single product, the right-hand side is expressed as $\dfrac{F}{(1 - v/p)}$. Show that this expression can be written simply as $\dfrac{F}{C}$ where C equals a certain contribution percent.
   (b) In the formulation of a multiproduct problem, of what value is the breakeven formula in dollars: $R = \dfrac{F}{C}$?

5. Within the nonlinear algebraic approach to breakeven presented in the chapter, prove that the revenue function can be formulated as $R = \$100 \sqrt{x}$, based upon the data set forth in Table 1–4. In the equation, x represents sales in units.

Mathematical Exercises

1. The Ajax Manufacturing Company produces a complete line of card tables. An analysis of its flexible budgets for the coming year reveals the following data:

Variable cost per unit:	
Direct material, direct labor, variable	
manufacturing expenses, sales commissions, and similar costs	$ 6.25
Fixed costs—Total:	
Prior-commitment—depreciation, property	
taxes, insurance, and similar costs	$10,000
Planned—fixed manufacturing expenses, marketing	
expenses, and general and administrative expenses	
Capacity in units	
25,001 to 30,000	$25,000
30,001 to 35,000	30,000
35,001 to 40,000	35,000
40,001 to 45,000	40,000
Capacity (practical): 45,000 card tables	
Average selling price: $7.50 per card table	

(a) Graph the above data.
(b) Compute the breakeven point(s) in units and dollars.
(c) What is the breakeven point(s) in terms of capacity?
(d) What is the fixed cost per card table at 80 percent of capacity?
(e) Determine the number of card tables the company must sell to show a profit of $5,000 in the 35,001 to 40,000 capacity range.

2. The G & R Company is considering an additional marketing program for the year which will add $22,532 to fixed costs. Their product, now selling for $15, has a variable cost of $8 per unit. Its current fixed costs (prior-commitment and planned) are $55,000. What is the new breakeven in units? The company desires to make a profit of $15,000 after consideration for the additional marketing program. How many units must the company now sell?

3. Carriage Trade, Inc., sells many distinctive lines of clothes. From the available records, the following data are applicable to the dress department's present line:

Dress Lines	Average Selling Price per Dress	Average Variable Cost per Dress	Percent of Total Sales Volume
Holiday	$60	$30	40%
Dior	80	30	20
Fath	72	32	25
Prix	64	24	15
Annual fixed costs allocated to dress department: $80,000			

The dress department is considering adding one more line of dresses. The following data has been developed for the coming year:

Dress Lines	Average Selling Price per Dress	Average Variable Cost per Dress	Expected Sales
Henri	$75	$25	$ 35,000
Holiday	60	30	40,000
Dior	80	30	55,000
Fath	72	32	45,000
Prix	64	24	35,000
No change in fixed costs			$210,000

(a) Find the breakeven point in dollars for both situations.
(b) Find the total variable cost at the breakeven point for both situations.
(c) What should the dress department of Carriage Trade, Inc., do?

4. Universal, Inc., has many plants scattered around the country. One of its plants has excess plant capacity available for production of a new product. The market research department has been given the job of developing the new product in conjunction with the engineering and production departments to utilize excess capacity. The cost department was brought in to develop reliable cost data, while the market research group has related expected demand at various selling prices. The following data has been compiled by the various departments:

Proposed Selling Prices	Potential Demand	Total Revenue
$20.000	2,500	$ 50,000
$16.666	3,600	60,000
$14.285	4,900	70,000
$12.500	6,400	80,000
$11.111	8,100	90,000
$10.000	10,000	100,000

Variable cost per unit: $10

Fixed Costs:

Prior-commitment (allocated to new product)	$ 2,000
Planned	8,000
	$10,000

Cost data are based upon production output rates up to 10,000 units.

(a) Graph the above data. Consider the sales demand as a continuous function.

(b) Find the breakeven point(s) in units. Verify by inspecting the graph drawn in (a).

(c) Upon close inspection of the graph in (a), what are the optimum profits that could be expected based upon the project sales and cost data?

(d) What should the selling price be to obtain optimum profits?

5. The Norris Publishing Company is considering various prices for a new book that will be published next month. The marketing manager is considering four prices: $5.95, $6.95, $7.95, and $8.95 per book. Variable costs are $3.25 per book while fixed costs allocated to this book are $7,500. Sales forecasts are: 3,000 at $8.95, 4,000 at $7.95, 4,750 at $6.95, and 5,400 at $5.95. What price should the firm charge to maximize its profits?

6. Concrete Block, Inc., is considering a new plant which will operate at a capacity of 85 percent. Capacity of 100 percent for this plant is 1,500,000 concrete blocks annually. Sales price per block is $1.50. Two types of plants are available, one semiautomatic and the other almost completely automatic. Production costs will be different since the semiautomatic plant has a higher labor cost while the other has a higher fixed cost. Below are the estimated figures:

Cost Factors	Semiautomatic Plant A	Automatic Plant B
Material cost per unit	$0.42	$0.40
Direct labor cost per unit	0.30	0.23
Other variable cost per unit	0.50	0.47
Total annual fixed costs	$200,000	$300,000

(a) Which plant would result in the more profitable factory, assuming all units produced can be sold?

(b) Find the breakeven in terms of capacity utilization.

7. The Gordon Foods Company is a manufacturer of a line of food products, mostly for the consumer market. The firm is thinking of replacing its present food brokers with its own sales staff. The company feels it will be able to cover more sales territory and do a better selling job. Its present financial condition is as follows:

	Current Year, Just Ended
Sales	$20,000,000
Variable costs	11,000,000
Contribution to fixed costs and profits	9,000,000
Fixed costs	7,500,000
Net income before federal income taxes	$ 1,500,000

The company's own sales staff should result in a 10 percent increase in sales. The present cost of food brokers is 5 percent of sales while company salesmen would cost the firm $1,000,000 for commissions and traveling expenses.

The company has another alternative: take on more food brokers in order to enlarge its sales territory. Again, the food broker's fee is 5 percent of sales. Expected gain in sales would be 5 percent.

(a) What should the company do?

(b) At what point are you indifferent as to whether to add more food brokers or use company salesmen?

8. The Argo Machinery Company currently purchases an exhaust muffler for its line of machinery from the outside. Current costs are $10 each versus projected variable costs of $2.50 and total annual fixed costs of $5.000. The company's annual requirements are at least 1,000 per year. No drastic change is expected in this volume for the next few years. What should the company do, continue to buy or make the part? At what percentage of capacity does it pay the company to manufacture its own mufflers?

9. The Arcose Manufacturing Company is currently operating an older press (machine 1) for stamping parts with a variable cost of $10 per unit and a zero book value since it has been completely depreciated. (The cost of removing the older press equals its salvage value.) Being considered in its place are two different presses manufactured by the E. W. Bliss Company. The faster press (machine 2) will increase hourly production, but it will increase fixed costs by $10,000 per year and reduce variable costs by $4 per unit. An even faster press (machine 3) will increase fixed costs by $12,500 per year, but will reduce variable costs by $5 per unit. Long-run forecast for sales indicates that

sales will not fall below 5,100 units per year for the next five years. At what point are you indifferent as to which press to purchase? Should the old press be kept or should one of the two proposed presses be purchased?

10. The Brown Company's engineers recently proposed two alternatives to an existing process for forming the grid of an industrial vacuum tube. Any of the three processes—existing or proposed—would be capable of performing the forming operation at a rate far in excess of requirements. The equipment has an indefinite life, but it is highly specialized and has no salvage value. Given the following:

A. Existing process—foot-operated press
        Original cost $300 (fully depreciated)
        Variable cost per piece $0.25
B. Proposed process—solenoid-operated press
        Original cost $350
        Variable cost per piece $0.15
C. Proposed process—dial-type motor press
        Original cost $1,000
        Variable cost per piece $0.10

(a) Sketch an indifference graph, showing each of these processes.
(b) Give the range of volumes for which you would use each of these processes.

Bibliography

C. T. Horngren, *Accounting for Management Control: An Introduction,* Englewood Cliffs, N.J.: Prentice-Hall, 1970.

C. Kim, *Quantitative Analysis for Managerial Decisions,* Reading, Mass.: Addison-Wesley, 1976.

R. I. Levin and C. A. Kirkpatrick, *Quantitative Approaches to Management,* New York: McGraw-Hill Book Company, 1975.

J. L. Riggs, *Economic Decision Models for Engineers and Managers,* New York: McGraw-Hill Book Company, 1968.

M. K. Starr and I. Stein, *The Practice of Management Science,* Englewood Cliffs, N.J.: Prentice-Hall, 1976.

Chapter 2

Inventory Control Models

Chapter Objectives
- [ ] To develop the basic economic ordering quantity (EOQ) formula as an optimum basis for purchasing.
- [ ] To formulate complementary inventory models to the basic EOQ model for keeping overall costs at a minimum.
- [ ] To determine the reorder point, i.e., the appropriate inventory level, for purchasing on an optimum basis.
- [ ] To show how inventory models used for purchasing on the outside can be used in scheduling production.

Chapter Outline
Requirements for Formulating Inventory Problems
Concept of Average Inventory
Economic Ordering Quantity Approach
EOQ Nomographs
EOQ and the Computer (ABC Method)
Optimum Number of Orders per Year
Optimum Days' Supply per Order
Optimum Amount of Dollars per Order
Quantity Discounts
Reorder Point and Safety (Buffer) Stock
EOQ Applied to Production
Chapter Summary
Questions
Model Formulation Exercises
Mathematical Exercises
Bibliography

The problem of analyzing and establishing appropriate inventory levels is common to almost every organization. Starting about 1915, attention was focused on the development of mathematical approaches designed to aid the decision maker in setting optimum inventory levels. Since that time, increasingly sophisticated analytical tools have been brought to bear on the problems of inventory management. The reason for greater attention to inventory is that this asset, for many firms, is the largest one appearing on the balance sheet. Inventory problems of too great or too small quantities on hand can cause difficulties. If a manufacturer experiences a stockout of a critical inventory item, production can be halted. Moreover, a shopper expects the retailer to carry the item wanted. If an item is not stocked when the customer thinks it should be, the retailer loses a customer not only on that item but on many other items in the future. The conclusion is that effective inventory management can make a significant contribution to a company's profit.

Requirements for Formulating Inventory Problems

The fundamental concerns of management in formulating basic inventory decisions are: the quantity to order at one time and when to order this quantity. In approaching these two decisions, one path is ordering large amounts (to minimize ordering costs), while the other path is ordering small amounts (to minimize inventory carrying costs). Either course pushed too far will have an unfavorable effect on profits. The best course in terms of minimizing costs is a compromise between the two extremes.

Inasmuch as the basic objective of formulating inventory control models is to minimize total annual inventory costs, it is necessary to determine these costs, which can be grouped into three

outage costs — простой в
[áutidʒ] работы

stock-out - a situation in which
a company or shop has no more
of a particular item available

categories. The first two are ordering costs and inventory carrying costs, which are equated to one another in the basic inventory models presented in the chapter. The third, outage costs, is the loss realized by the firm if stockouts of items occur. Sales may be lost if inventories are not adequate to meet consumer demand or production may come to a halt if the critical inventories are insufficient to meet its need. The first two costs are our concern initially because stockouts are assumed not to occur in the basic inventory models. That is, inventory is assumed to be received in a fixed-size order quantity and is then withdrawn (e.g., sold or issued to production) in response to demands that arrive at a constant rate. Under these idealized conditions, the firm experiences no stockouts. Hence, only ordering costs and inventory carrying costs are needed in formulating basic inventory control models.

Applications — Inventory Control Models

поставщик

- **Purchasing from vendors** — uses the basic EOQ model (as is or modified) for specific operating conditions when buying on an optimum basis from vendors.
- **Producing manufactured items** — employs the basic EOQ model (modified) for producing the desired manufactured items at minimum annual inventory costs.
- **Production scheduling** — relates the total cost of production with the desired level of service to customers.
- **Quantity discount determination** — keeps overall inventory costs low with respect to large quantities.
- **Safety stock determination** — determines the optimum level of safety stock by considering the effects of inventory stockouts throughout the year.
- **Reorder point computed** — determines the reorder point before an order is placed for the economic ordering quantity.

Ordering or Acquisition Costs   Costs related to acquisition of purchased items are those of getting an item into the company's inventory. Ordering costs, incurred each time an order is placed, start with the purchase requisition. Other costs include issuing the purchase order, follow-up, receiving the goods, quality control, placing them into inventory, and paying vendors.

Acquisition costs pertaining to company-manufactured items include several of the above-mentioned items, but they also comprise other categories. A sample list of costs for both conditions is found below:

Purchased Items	Manufactured Items
Requisitioning	Requisitioning
Purchase order (includes expediting)	Setup
Trucking	Receiving and inspection
Receiving and inspection	Placing in storage
Placing in storage	Accounting and auditing:
Accounting and auditing:	Inventory
Inventory	Product costs
Disbursements	

Very often, determination of these costs must be made by special study. Because the incremental cost per order is needed, costs estimates for the purchasing, receiving, and accounting departments are determined at different levels of ordering for the year. For example, if 1,000 additional orders are estimated to cost $20,000 for these departments, the incremental cost per order is $20.

Some caution is necessary in assuming that manufacturing costs may be directly replaced by purchasing costs when considering how much to purchase rather than how much to manufacture. First, reordering costs are usually less than setup costs. Second, external considerations surround the purchase decision. Items such as short-term interest rates, price speculation, and labor stability of suppliers make the decision to purchase somewhat less straightforward than the internal considerations involved in deciding to manufacture.

Inventory Carrying or Holding Costs Carrying or holding costs of inventory are those incurred because the firm has decided to maintain inventories. Of course, a firm cannot operate without a certain amount of process and movement inventories. In arriving at these costs, it is best to consider those items that meet the following two tests: out-of-pocket expenditures and forgone opportunities for profit.

An example of applying these tests would be the consideration of warehouse space costs—only to the extent that additional facilities would need to be acquired or that unused space could be rented for profit. Also, these rules would indicate that interest is considered from the standpoint of forgone profit opportunity only when sufficient capital exists in the business and need not be borrowed to finance inventories.

These costs, like ordering costs, are somewhat difficult to determine precisely because the required records do not always exist. The following composite of data, taken from various references, gives representative ranges for these costs:

Item	Approximate Range
Interest (on money invested in inventory)	6–14%
Insurance	1–3
Taxes	1–3
Storage (may include heat, light, or refrigeration)	0–3
Obsolescence and depreciation	4–16

Carrying costs for most manufacturing firms are normally about 20 to 25 percent. Obviously, any extreme situation may fall outside the ranges shown. These costs are stated on an annual basis and are expressed as a percentage of average inventory value. This percentage can be obtained in much the same manner as was used to obtain the incremental cost per order, that is, by estimating total carrying costs at two different inventory levels.

Outage Costs   This category of costs is mentioned primarily because it exists, and not because definitive rules can be set forth for computing outage costs. Outages result in decreased customer service level, less efficient production operations, and high costs resulting from "crash" procurements. Since outages affect the items just named, the unanswered question in most cases is by "how much?" Unless some very direct relationships exist, the cost of an outage is difficult to quantify. The fact that answers to the determination of outage costs are approximate and arbitrary in nature does not necessarily mean that their significance should be ignored. Knowledge of cost alternatives enables the application of enlightened judgment to produce satisfactory answers to the problem of just how great an outage rate is acceptable.

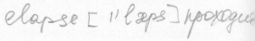

Concept of Average Inventory

Before developing the economic lot size inventory model, certain assumptions must be made regarding the purchase of a single item of inventory. First, usage of the item is at a constant rate and is known to the decision maker in advance. Second, the lead time, which is the elapsed time between the placement of the order and its receipt into inventory, or the time necessary for acquiring an item is constant. Although these assumptions (constant usage and constant lead time) are rarely valid for inventory problems in the business world, they do permit us to develop a simplified model into which more realistic, complicating factors can be introduced.

   If we let Q be the order size under the preceding assumptions, it can be shown in Figure 2–1 that the number of units in inventory is equal to Q when each new order is physically received into inventory and that the inventory is gradually depleted until it reaches zero just at the point when the next order is received. It is observed that the average inventory $(Q/2)$ is equal to one-half the number of units in the lot size. As illustrated in Figure 2–1, the average inventory is affected by the order quantity and the number of orders per year. Furthermore, each new order is received into inventory at exactly the time at which the previous order is depleted, resulting in no stockouts.

Economic Ordering Quantity Approach

Now that the means for determining incremental ordering costs, carrying costs, and average inventory have been set forth, the next step is the development of an inventory model in terms of economic ordering quantity. A key feature of this model, first developed by F. Harris in 1916, is that management is confronted with a set of opposing costs—as the lot size increases, the carrying charges will increase while the ordering costs will decrease. On the other hand, as the lot size decreases, the carrying costs will decrease, but the ordering costs will increase. (In the cases under discussion in this chapter, only minor deviations from these trends are assumed to occur.) *Economic ordering quantity* (EOQ) is that size order which minimizes total annual (or other time period) cost of carrying inventory and cost of ordering. Within the model, conditions of certainty and known annual requirements are assumed.

Tabular Approach One approach for solving the EOQ is by trial and error. The method is as follows: (1) select a number of possible lot sizes to purchase; (2) determine total costs for each lot size chosen; and (3) select the ordering quantity which minimizes total cost. Table 2–1 illustrates this approach.

Figure 2–1
Concept of average inventory (Q/2) and the effect of order quantity (Q) and orders per year on average inventory level.

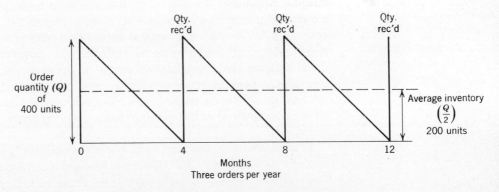

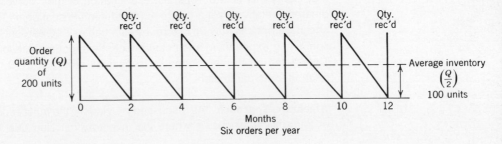

61

In the example, annual requirements equal 8,000 units, ordering cost per order is $12.50, 20 percent per year is the carrying cost of average inventory, and the cost per unit is $1. The table indicates that an order size of 1,000 units will result in the lowest total cost of the seven alternatives evaluated. Note that this minimum total cost occurs when carrying costs are equal to ordering costs. In this example we were fortunate in determining the lowest possible cost. Suppose the computation for eight orders per year had not been made. We could choose only among the six remaining alternatives for the lowest cost solution. This points up a serious limitation of the tabular approach. In many cases, a relatively large number of alternatives must be computed before the best possible least cost combination is determined.

Table 2–1

Tabular Approach to EOQ

Orders Per Year	Lot Size	Average Inventory	Carrying Charges 20% Per Year	Ordering Costs $12.50 Per Order	Total Cost Per Year
1	8,000	4,000	$800.00	$ 12.50	$812.50
2	4,000	2,000	400.00	25.00	425.00
4	2,000	1,000	200.00	50.00	250.00
8	1,000	500	100.00	100.00	200.00
12	667	333	66.00	150.00	216.00
16	500	250	50.00	200.00	250.00
32	250	125	25.00	400.00	425.00

Graphic Approach   The preceding data which can be graphed show the nature of the opposing costs involved in an EOQ problem. Figure 2–2 indicates that the total cost curve is V-shaped. It shows that annual total costs of inventory carrying costs and ordering costs first decrease, then hit a low point where inventory carrying costs equal ordering costs, and finally increase as the economic ordering quantity increases. Our basic objective is to find a numerical value for EOQ that will minimize the total variable costs on the graph. However, without specific costs and values, an accurate plotting of the carrying costs, ordering costs, and total costs is not feasible.

In actual practice, few firms have found it economically sound to calculate the costs for each inventory item. Inventory, however, can be grouped by similarities. The economic ordering quantity logic is then applied to these groups. The reader may decry this lack of rigor but examination of their curves, as in Figure 2–2, indicates a relatively flat area around the minimum cost point. This means that certain cost assumptions may be in error by as much as ±10 percent (based on the author's consulting experience) and not significantly affect the economic ordering quantity. Thus, referring to the concept of sensitivity analysis, EOQ is not too sensitive in relation to its parameters.

Algebraic Approach   As discussed previously, the most economical point in terms of total inventory cost is where the inventory carrying cost equals ordering cost.

This is the basis of the algebraic approach. In order to derive the EOQ model, the following definitions are needed:

Q = economic ordering quantity or optimum number of units per order to minimize total cost for the firm

C = cost of one unit

I = annual inventory carrying costs, expressed as a percentage of the value of average inventory

R = total annual quantity requirements

S = ordering costs per order placed (also can be defined as setup costs per run).

In order to develop annual inventory carrying costs (on the left-hand side of the equation), reference is first made to Figure 2–1 where the average inventory is one-half the order quantity or $Q/2$. If it costs so many dollars per year to carry one item in stock, i.e., C (cost of one unit) times I (annual inventory carrying costs, expressed as a percentage of the value of average inventory), then the annual inventory carrying costs, expressed on an average inventory basis, can be written as $Q/2\ CI$. Thus, total inventory carrying costs are:

$$\frac{Q}{2} \quad \times \quad C \quad \times \quad I \quad = \quad \frac{Q}{2}CI$$

$$\begin{pmatrix} \text{Average} \\ \text{inventory} \\ \text{quantity} \end{pmatrix} \times \begin{pmatrix} \text{Cost of} \\ \text{one} \\ \text{unit} \end{pmatrix} \times \begin{pmatrix} \text{Inventory} \\ \text{carrying cost} \\ \text{percentage} \end{pmatrix} = \begin{pmatrix} \text{Total inventory} \\ \text{carrying} \\ \text{costs} \end{pmatrix}$$

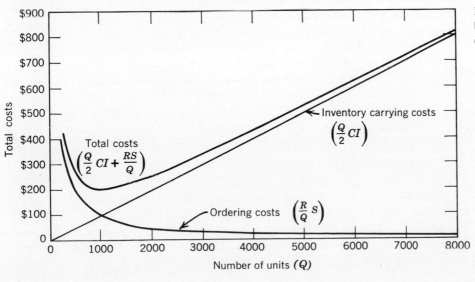

Figure 2–2
Economic ordering quantity graph.

In order to develop the total ordering costs (on the right-hand side of the equation), the expected number of orders per year has been determined to be proportional to the total forecasted annual quantity requirements (R) and to be inversely proportional to the order quantity (Q). The number of orders per year which equals R/Q is then multiplied by the fixed cost of placing each order (S), thereby giving the total ordering costs or $R/Q\ S$. Thus, total annual ordering costs are:

$$\frac{R}{Q} \quad \times \quad S \quad = \quad \frac{R}{Q}S$$

$$\left(\begin{array}{c}\text{Number of orders}\\\text{per year}\end{array}\right) \times \left(\begin{array}{c}\text{Ordering cost}\\\text{per order}\end{array}\right) = \left(\begin{array}{c}\text{Total ordering}\\\text{costs}\end{array}\right)$$

Equating total annual inventory carrying costs to total annual ordering costs results in the following:

$$\frac{Q}{2}CI = \frac{R}{Q}S$$

$$QCI = \frac{2RS}{Q}$$

$$Q^2CI = 2RS \qquad\qquad \text{(Equation 2–1)}$$

$$Q^2 = \frac{2RS}{CI}$$

$$Q = \sqrt{\frac{2RS}{CI}}$$

The EOQ model may be illustrated by taking the same set of data as used previously with the tabular and graphic examples where $C = \$1$, $I = 20$ percent, $R = 8,000$ units, and $S = \$12.50$:

$$Q = \sqrt{\frac{2(8,000)\ (\$12.50)}{\$1\ (20\%)}}$$

$$= \sqrt{\frac{(16,000)\ (12.50)}{0.20}}$$

$$= \sqrt{\frac{200,000}{0.20}}$$

$$= \sqrt{1,000,000}$$

$$= 1,000 \text{ units}$$

Substituting the value for Q in the original terms of the model, total inventory carrying costs $= (Q/2)CI$ or $(1,000/2)(\$1) \times 20\% = \$100$, and total ordering costs $= (R/Q)S$ or $(8,000/1,000)(\$12.50) = \$100$. These costs can be compared with those obtained by the tabular approach. The adding of the two costs equals the lowest minimum cost per year of $200 for the economic ordering quantity. This analysis demonstrates that we have solved for a minimum cost. But how can we be sure? This will be determined by referring to Figure 2–2 or the calculus approach set forth in Appendix B.

EOQ Nomographs

A simplified method to find the economic ordering quantity is the use of EOQ nomographs. As illustrated in Figure 2–3, for a sample EOQ nomograph of $10 ordering costs, the procedure is to place one end of a ruler on the appropriate point of the monthly usage scale (1) and the other end on the unit cost scale (2), then read the EOQ in units on the center scale (3). At times, it may be difficult to read the exact quantity. However, as indicated above, the total cost curve is relatively flat at its lowest cost point, thereby allowing costs to be in error by as much as ± 10 percent before adversely affecting the accuracy of the economic ordering quantity. Thus, an incorrect reading of the appropriate quantity should have little or no effect when buying on an optimum basis.

EOQ and the Computer (ABC Method)

Under the assumptions of the EOQ model (constant usage and constant lead time), the placing of an order for 1,000 units in the above example with a weekly demand of 154 units requires a lead time of one week. Each reorder would be placed one week before the depletion of the existing inventories or when the inventory level has fallen to the level of 154 units. This number represents usage during the delivery period and assumes a condition of certainty relative to delivery predictability.

Since numerical values can be used for acquisition lead time, this method is easily adaptable to a computer program. As the inventory is updated daily or on some other periodic basis, a comparison can be made between the balance on hand and the quantity necessary for the acquisition lead time. In Figure 2–4 this comparison of a greater than condition means nothing is to be done. However, an equal to or less than condition signals for a printout of the economic order quantity. In effect, a purchase order for the number of EOQ units, in this example 1,000 units, can be prepared automatically by a single comparison of the new updated inventory with the acquisition lead time in units. The computer can also be used annually (or on some other time basis) for computing new economic ordering quantities on each inventory item since the current annual usage can be added and stored with a minimum of cost. All the other factors for computing EOQs should not be too difficult to obtain.

Since the EOQ model can be readily programmed, it appears convenient to keep all inventory items on-line within a computer system. However, it may not always be practical for a computer system to handle all of them. Hence it is helpful to divide the many component parts that must be handled by the computer into three categories (A, B, and C), based on annual dollar usage and number of items. The rela-

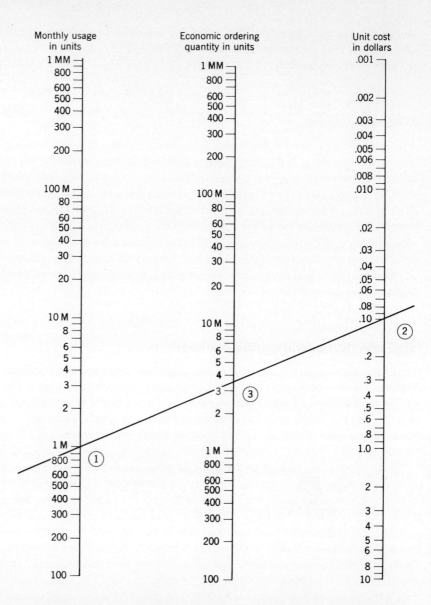

Monthly usage
in units

Economic ordering
quantity in units

Unit cost
in dollars

Figure 2-3
Sample EOQ nomograph
for $10 ordering costs.

tionship of annual dollar usage and number of inventory items for a typical manufacturing firm is shown in Table 2–2. The A items are valuable enough to justify
close control by the computer as well as inventory management. In some companies, A items may not be ordered until the customer's order is actually received.
The particular circumstances would dictate the best approach for the individual
firm. The B and C items, being more numerous and less costly, are also ideal candidates for computer control. When the reorder point has been reached, the EOQ
is automatically placed without further management intervention. However, some
C items might be so insignificant in cost that they may be ordered quarterly or on

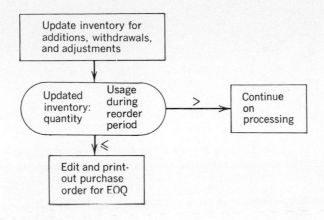

Figure 2–4
Subroutine for computer
inventory program.

some other logical time basis. The cost of ordering nuts, bolts, and like items might exceed their value. Again, the attendant circumstances must be examined.

Optimum Number of Orders Per Year

The equating of inventory carrying costs to ordering costs for the basic EOQ model can likewise be applied to the *optimum number of orders per year*. It should be noted that the answer for the number of orders per year can be converted to ordering every so many days.

For the optimum number of orders per year, the following terms are needed:

N = optimum number of orders per year to minimize total costs for the firm

A = total dollar amount of annual usage

S = ordering costs per order placed (or setup costs per run)

I = annual inventory carrying costs, expressed as a percentage of the value of average inventory

Total inventory carrying costs are derived as follows:

$$\frac{A}{N} \times \frac{1}{2} \times I = \frac{AI}{2N}$$

$$\left(\begin{array}{c} \text{Dollar} \\ \text{amount} \\ \text{per order} \end{array} \right) \times \left(\begin{array}{c} \text{Average inventory} \\ \text{under} \\ \text{constant usage} \end{array} \right) \times \left(\begin{array}{c} \text{Inventory} \\ \text{carrying} \\ \text{cost percentage} \end{array} \right) = \left(\begin{array}{c} \text{Total} \\ \text{inventory} \\ \text{carrying costs} \end{array} \right)$$

Total ordering costs per year = $N \times S = NS$

Again, equating total inventory carrying costs to total ordering costs, the formula (refer to Appendix B for the calculus approach) is:

$$\frac{AI}{2N} = NS$$

$$2N^2S = AI$$

$$N^2 = \frac{AI}{2S}$$

$$N = \sqrt{\frac{AI}{2S}}$$

(Equation 2–2)

By using the data from the prior illustration for the basic EOQ model, N, the optimum number of orders to be placed per year, is calculated as follows:

$$N = \sqrt{\frac{\$8,000 \times 20\%}{2(\$12.50)}} = \sqrt{\frac{\$1,600}{\$25}} = \sqrt{64} = 8 \text{ orders per year or order}$$
every 45.6 days

Table 2–2
Importance of
Inventory Items

Inventory Distribution by Value	A	B	C
Annual dollar usage	65%	20%	15%
Number of inventory items	15%	35%	50%

Another way of solving for N is to divide the total annual quantity requirements (R) by the economic ordering quantity (Q). Thus, a simplified formula for determining the optimum number of annual orders to be placed is:

$$N = \frac{R}{Q}$$

(Equation 2–3)

Applying the data developed above, the calculation for Equation 2–3 is:

$$N = \frac{8,000}{1,000}$$

$N = 8$ orders per year

Optimum Days' Supply Per Order

Having developed the inventory model for the optimum number of orders, we can now develop a formula for the *optimum days' supply per order,* based upon 365 days per year. In the model, the following terms are used:

$D =$ optimum number of days' supply per order in one year

$R =$ total annual quantity requirements

$S =$ ordering costs per order placed (or setup costs per run)

I = annual inventory carrying costs, expressed as a percentage of the value of average inventory

C = cost value of one unit

365 = calendar days per year

Again, total inventory carrying costs per year equal ordering costs per year (refer to Appendix B for the calculus approach):

$$\frac{RC}{365/D} \quad \times \quad \frac{1}{2} \quad \times \quad I \quad = \quad \frac{RCI}{730/D}$$

$$\left(\begin{array}{c}\text{Dollars}\\\text{per order}\end{array}\right) \times \left(\begin{array}{c}\text{Average}\\\text{inventory}\\\text{under constant}\\\text{usage}\end{array}\right) \times \left(\begin{array}{c}\text{Inventory}\\\text{carrying}\\\text{cost}\\\text{percentage}\end{array}\right) = \left(\begin{array}{c}\text{Total}\\\text{inventory}\\\text{carrying}\\\text{costs}\end{array}\right)$$

Total ordering costs per year:

$$\frac{365}{D} \quad \times \quad S \quad = \quad \frac{365S}{D}$$

$$\left(\begin{array}{c}\text{Number of orders}\\\text{per year}\end{array}\right) \times \left(\begin{array}{c}\text{Ordering cost}\\\text{per order}\end{array}\right) = \left(\begin{array}{c}\text{Total}\\\text{ordering}\\\text{costs}\end{array}\right)$$

$$\frac{RCI}{730/D} = \frac{365S}{D}$$

$$\frac{RCID}{730} = \frac{365S}{D} \qquad \text{(Equation 2–4)}$$

$$D^2RCI = 266,450S$$

$$D^2 = \frac{266,450S}{RCI}$$

$$D = \sqrt{\frac{266,450S}{RCI}}$$

Returning to the prior illustration, the number of days' supply per optimum order is 45.6 or 46 days, computed as follows:

$$D = \sqrt{\frac{266,450 \times \$12.50}{8,000 \times \$1 \times 20\%}} = \sqrt{\frac{3,330,625}{1,600}} = \sqrt{2,082} = 45.6 \text{ days or about 46}$$
$$\text{days' supply per optimum order}$$

A simplified formula for determining the number of days' supply per optimum order is dividing 365 days by the optimum number of orders (N). Thus, the equation is:

$$D = \frac{365}{N} \qquad \text{(Equation 2–5)}$$

69

Inserting the N value of 8 in the sample problem, the value for D is:

$$D = \frac{365}{8}$$

$$D = 45.6 \text{ days}$$

Optimum Amount of Dollars Per Order

Now that three optimum inventory formulas have been developed, this section focuses on another one, the *optimum amount of dollars per order*. For this final equation, the terms are as follows:

$O =$ optimum amount of dollars per order

$A =$ total dollar amount of annual usage

$S =$ ordering costs per order placed (or setup costs per run)

$I =$ annual inventory carrying costs, expressed as a percentage of the value of average inventory

Total inventory carrying costs are:

$$\frac{A}{A/O} \quad \times \quad \frac{1}{2} \quad \times \quad I \quad = \quad \frac{OI}{2}$$

$$\left(\begin{array}{c}\text{Dollar amount} \\ \text{per order}\end{array}\right) \times \left(\begin{array}{c}\text{Average} \\ \text{inventory} \\ \text{under constant} \\ \text{usage}\end{array}\right) \times \left(\begin{array}{c}\text{Inventory} \\ \text{carrying} \\ \text{cost} \\ \text{percentage}\end{array}\right) = \left(\begin{array}{c}\text{Total} \\ \text{inventory} \\ \text{carrying} \\ \text{costs}\end{array}\right)$$

Total inventory ordering costs are:

$$\frac{A}{O} \quad \times \quad S \quad = \quad \frac{AS}{O}$$

$$\left(\begin{array}{c}\text{Number of orders} \\ \text{per year}\end{array}\right) \times \left(\begin{array}{c}\text{Ordering costs} \\ \text{per order}\end{array}\right) = \left(\begin{array}{c}\text{Total} \\ \text{ordering} \\ \text{costs}\end{array}\right)$$

As before, total inventory carrying costs per year are equated to total ordering costs per year (refer to Appendix B for the calculus approach):

$$\frac{OI}{2} = \frac{AS}{O}$$

$$O^2 I = 2AS$$

$$O^2 = \frac{2AS}{I} \hspace{4cm} \text{(Equation 2–6)}$$

$$O = \sqrt{\frac{2AS}{I}}$$

To illustrate this formula, the optimum amount of dollars per order, utilizing data from the previous problem, is determined as follows:

$$O = \sqrt{\frac{2 \times \$8,000 \times \$12.50}{20\%}} = \sqrt{\frac{\$200,000}{20\%}} = \sqrt{1,000,000} = \$1,000$$

A simplified way for calculating how many dollars of an inventory item to purchase at one time is to divide the annual usage (A) by the optimum number of orders per year (N). Hence, the formula is:

$$O = \frac{A}{N} \qquad\qquad \text{(Equation 2–7)}$$

Using the data developed above, the calculation for Equation 2–7 is:

$$O = \frac{\$8,000}{8}$$

$$O - \$1,000 \text{ per order}$$

Quantity Discounts

The EOQ model, as set forth at this point, does not take into account the factor of quantity discounts. Buying in large quantities has some favorable and some unfavorable features. The advantages of buying in large quantities are: lower unit cost, lower ordering costs, fewer stockouts, and lower unit transportation cost. On the other hand, quantity buying presents these disadvantages: higher inventory carrying costs, more capital required, greater chance of deterioration and depreciation of inventory, and older stock.

Cost Comparison Approach   Two approaches are presented for evaluating quantity discounts. Again, the demand and acquisition lead time are constant and known in advance by the decision maker. The first one, widely used due to its simplicity, is the *cost comparison approach*. The present total annual inventory costs, using an optimum purchase basis or economic ordering quantity, is compared to the proposed total annual inventory cost conditions which qualify the buyer for the quantity discount. The formula for total annual inventory costs (an extension of the basic EOQ equation) is:

$$T = RC + \frac{Q}{2}CI + \frac{R}{Q}S \qquad\qquad \text{(Equation 2–8)}$$

where T = total annual inventory costs
  R = total annual quantity requirements
  C = cost value of one unit at the appropriate price break level

71

Q = economic ordering quantity or optimum number of units per order to minimize total costs for the firm

I = annual inventory carrying costs, expressed as a percentage of the value of average inventory

S = ordering costs per order placed

To illustrate the cost comparison approach, the Precision Company purchases solenoid valves for use in its line of spot welders. Precision buys at least 400 of these valves annually. With a cost of $50 each, inventory carrying costs are 20 percent of the average inventory value and ordering costs are $20 per order. The firm has received a proposal from the Ross Valve Company which offers Precision a 2 percent discount on purchases of 100 or more valves.

The initial step is to calculate EOQ without taking the 2 percent quantity discount. Using Equation 2–1, the result is 40 units:

$$Q = \sqrt{\frac{2RS}{CI}} = \sqrt{\frac{2(400)(\$20)}{\$50(20\%)}} = \sqrt{\frac{\$16,000}{\$10}} = \sqrt{1,600} = 40 \text{ units per order}$$

The annual total cost of purchasing the Ross valves is 400 units times $50 per unit or $20,000. Inventory carrying costs are 20 percent of the average inventory of $1,000 (40 units × $50 per unit = $2,000 ÷ 2 = $1,000) or $200. Ordering costs are $20 per order times 10 orders for the year or $200. The present cost is given in Table 2–3.

The final step is to compute the total annual costs with the proposed 2 percent discount. The cost of the valves is the annual cost times 98 percent. The method for computing inventory carrying costs and ordering costs are the same as above, except consideration must be given to average inventory at the discounted price. Based upon the data in Table 2–3, the Precision Company should take advantage of the quantity discount offered since total annual costs will be reduced by $230.

Table 2–3
Comparison of Present and Proposed Inventory Costs

Present Annual Inventory Costs	
Cost of valves ($50 × 400)	$20,000
Inventory carrying costs (20% × $\frac{40 \times \$50}{2}$ av. inv.)	200
Ordering cost (10 × $20)	200
Present annual costs of Ross valves	$20,400

Proposed Annual Inventory Costs	
Cost of valves ($50 × 400 × 0.98)	$19,600
Inventory carrying costs (20% × $\frac{100 \times 0.98 \times \$50}{2}$ av. inv.)	490
Ordering cost (4 × $20)	80
Proposed annual costs of Ross valves	$20,170

Another way of approaching this method is to first calculate the savings because of the discount. In the illustration, savings of $1 ($50 × 2%) will be realized on each unit. For 400 units, total savings are $400. Next, the total costs of present inventory carrying and ordering costs are subtracted from the total costs for the proposal. From the above data, $400 ($200 + $200) from $570 ($490 + $80) is $170. Last, a comparison is made between the total discount amount and the additional cost of the proposed costs. If the total discount is greater than the additional proposed costs, the offer should be accepted. If the situation results in a less than condition, the offer should be refused. The total discount of $400 is greater than the additional cost of $170, for a net gain of $230, the same answer as the earlier one.

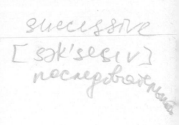

Price Break Approach The previous approach to quantity discount was limited to the case in which only one discount price is offered. Instead, it is possible to determine the economic order quantity with any number of successive discounts taking effect as the purchase quantity increases. These are known as *price breaks*.

To examine this approach, consider the Randall Company, which has been offered a discount schedule for the purchase of a small bracket used in the production of the firm's principal product. The term PB_{n-1} (PB_{n-2}, PB_{n-3}, . . .) in parentheses in the discount schedule below relates to price breaks, starting with the lowest price. The cost of ordering is $25, the annual average inventory carrying cost is 20 percent, and annual usage is 30,000 brackets. These figures plus the varying unit prices are used in calculating EOQ_n (EOQ_{n-1}, EOQ_{n-2}, . . .). The discount schedule offered by a vendor along with corresponding economic order quantities is:

EOQ for Each Price	Price Break Quantity	Unit Price
7,454 (EOQ_n)	9,001 and over (PB_{n-1})	$0.135
6,955 (EOQ_{n-1})	7,001–9,000 (PB_{n-2})	0.155
6,646 (EOQ_{n-2})	5,001–7,000 (PB_{n-3})	0.170
6,284 (EOQ_{n-3})	3,001–5,000 (PB_{n-4})	0.190
5,975 (EOQ_{n-4})	1–3,000 (PB_{n-5})	0.210

Initially a series of comparisons are made between the economic order quantities and the lowest quantity offered for sale at each price break such that the first greater than condition is determined. In Figure 2–5, EOQ_{n-2} is 6,646 brackets and is greater than the 5,001 brackets or PB_{n-3}—the first greater than condition. Next, it is necessary to compute the annual inventory costs (utilizing Equation 2–8) for the selected number of units, as shown in Figure 2–5. Thus, total costs must be computed for the following: 6,646 items (EOQ_{n-2}), 7,001 items (PB_{n-2}), and 9,001 items (PB_{n-1}). The resultant values in Table 2–4 indicate that the economic ordering quantity for lowest cost is 9,001 brackets at $0.135 each.

An alternative price break approach is to calculate the annual inventory costs per Equation 2–8 for all price levels (like those illustrated in Table 2–4 for prices

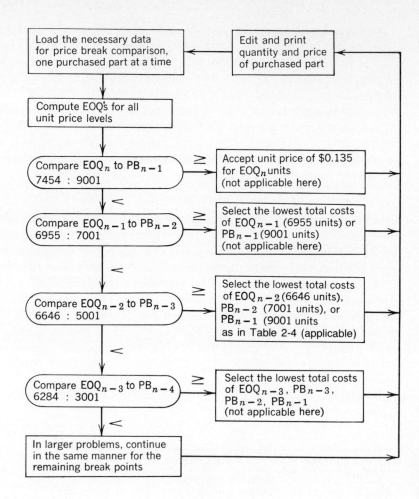

Figure 2–5
Subroutine for computer price break inventory program.

Table 2–4
Computations for Total Costs for Selected Quantities and Prices

Number of Units	Cost of Goods, 30,000 Annual Units × Unit Price	Inventory Carrying Costs, 20 Percent × Average Inventory	$25 Ordering Costs × Average Orders Per Year	Total Costs Per Year
6,646	× ($0.170 each) = $5,100.00 +	× ($564.91) = $112.98 +	× (4.51) = $112.75	= $5,325.73
7,001	× ($0.155 each) = $4,650.00 +	× ($542.58) = $108.52 +	× (4.28) = $107.00	= $4,865.52
9,001	$ ($0.135 each) = $4,050.00 +	× ($607.57) = $121.51 +	× (3.33) = $ 83.25	= $4,254.76

of $0.135, $0.155, and $0.170). That price break level which gives the lowest costs per year is selected.

The foregoing quantity discount approaches—cost comparison and price break—lend themselves to computer systems. The costs of implementing and using quantity-discount computer packages are generally minimal.

Reorder Point and Safety (Buffer) Stock

The obvious problem of the prior inventory models is that certainty does not exist in most inventory situations. Both usage and acquisition lead-time usually fluctuate in a manner not completely predictable. In cases where these two factors are relatively constant and known, the previous inventory models provide a close approximation of reality. Another problem in applying inventory models is that accurate cost information may be difficult to obtain. However, relatively good approximations should be obtainable from a proper study of costs. Close watch should be maintained on all cost factors whose change could affect results greatly.

The assumptions dealing with economic ordering quantities per Figure 2–6 are not applicable to all inventory situations. Demand or usage of inventory items can be greater or less than anticipated due to external and internal factors, such as labor strikes and power failures. Similarly, the acquisition lead time can also vary from favorable to unfavorable due to supplier(s) and/or transportation carrier(s).

If inventory is not available when needed due to any internal or external factor, a stockout occurs. This situation can lead to a noticeable decrease in profits and possibly losses. Figure 2–7 shows the problem of no stock when needed. It should be noted that the inventory level does not return to its original point as in Figure 2–6 since back orders must be filled.

The reorder point is defined as a condition that signals someone, usually a purchasing agent, that a purchase order should be placed to replenish the inventory stock of some item. Thus the two variables (usage and lead time) mentioned previously as a source of potential trouble are an integral part of the reorder point. The computation for the reorder point (R) is the result of multiplying usage (U), expressed in terms of number of units per day, times the lead time in days (L). However, what

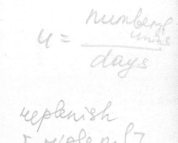

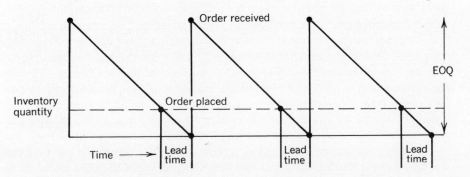

Figure 2–6
Inventory with constant usage and constant lead time.

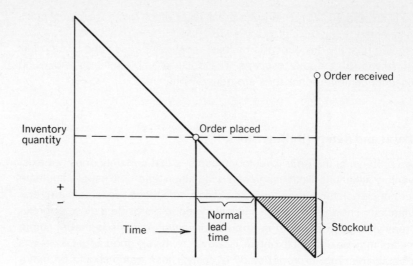

Figure 2–7
Inventory level with no
safety stock, resulting
in stockout.

must a firm do to provide for stockouts? The calculation for the reorder period must
be adjusted to provide for stockouts, resulting in the addition of buffer or safety
stock (B) to the above computation. Thus:

$$R \quad = \quad (U \quad \times \quad L) \quad + \quad B \quad \text{(Equation 2–9)}$$

$$\text{(Reorder point)} = \left[\left(\begin{array}{c} \text{average daily} \\ \text{usage} \end{array} \right) \times \left(\begin{array}{c} \text{lead time} \\ \text{in days} \end{array} \right) \right] + \left(\begin{array}{c} \text{buffer or} \\ \text{safety stock} \end{array} \right)$$

The term *safety stock* refers to extra inventory held as a buffer or protection against
the possibility of a stockout. As was pointed out previously in this chapter, a larger
inventory of safety stock means higher inventory carrying costs. On the other hand,
safety stock will decrease stockout costs. The decision on how much safety stock
to carry in order to provide minimum total costs to the firm is not an easy one. One
of the best approaches is the use of probabilities (to be explained in the next two
chapters).

The first step, utilizing the probability approach, is to analyze past inventory
records in order that a probability percent of usage during the reorder period can
be assigned to the various quantities. For example, the Brown Manufacturing Company has compiled data for a purchased flange (Table 2–5). The company has found
the economic ordering quantity to be 250 units with an average daily usage of 5
units. Lead time for this purchased flange is 21 days. Based upon the data in Table
2–5, the firm could reorder 250 units when the level of its stock falls to 105 units
[5 (average daily usage) × 21 (lead time in days)], but it will be out of stock 8 percent of the time (.06 + .02). What should management do about this condition of
8 percent stockouts? The answer may or may not be a certain level of safety stock.
A procedure for determining safety stock is needed.

Obviously, management desires to pick that level of stock which will yield the
lowest total cost for stockouts and inventory carrying costs of safety stock. Since

notm. garay

Usage During Reorder Period	Number of Times This Quantity Was Used	Usage Probability
90 units	7	7/100 or .07
95 units	10	10/100 or .10
100 units	25	25/100 or .25
105 units	50	50/100 or .50
110 units	6	6/100 or .06
115 units	2	2/100 or .02
	100 times	1.00

Table 2–5
Probabilities of Usage
During Reorder Period

the firm's reorder point is 105 units, the following safety stocks are considered: 5 units for a usage of 110 units and 10 units for a usage of 115 units. Five units of safety stock would cover a usage of 110 units during the reorder period, resulting in the firm being out of stock .02 of the time. Ten units of safety stock would take care of all usage during the reorder period, thereby never having a stockout occur.

The next step is to construct a table reflecting, for each level of safety stock, the total annual stockout costs. In order to do this, the cost of being out of stock for each unit must be calculated. For the example, the cost is $30 per item. Also, consideration must be given to the number of times per year the company reorders since a firm will be in danger of running out of stock that many times during the year. In the example, the EOQ formula indicates that five orders per year is optimum. The costs of being out of stock for each level are shown in Table 2–6.

Table 2–6
Costs of Being
Out of Stock

Stock Safety	Probability of Being Out of Stock	Number Short	Expected Annual Cost (No. Short × Prob. of Being Short × Cost of Being Out Per Unit × No. Orders/Yr.)	Total Annual Stockout Costs
0	.06 when use is 110	5	5 × .06 × $30 × 5 = $45	
	.02 when use is 115	10	10 × .02 × $30 × 5 = 30	$75
5	.02 when use is 115	5	5 × .02 × $30 × 5 =	$15
10	0	0	0	$ 0

The final step after determining the total annual stockout costs is to calculate the annual carrying costs per year. In this example, the cost per year of carrying each flange in inventory is $4. Table 2–7 gives total costs of safety stock. The lowest total cost in this table is $35 for a safety stock of 5 flanges. The present reorder point of 105 units must be increased to provide for the safety stock of 5 units. Thus the reorder point is 110 flanges.

Safety Stock	Cost of Being Out of Stock Per Table 2–6	Annual Carrying Costs (No. Carried × Cost/Year)	Total Costs/Year (Stockout Costs Plus Carrying Costs)
0	$75	0	$75
5	$15	5 × $4 = $20	$35
10	$ 0	10 × $4 = $40	$40

Table 2–7
Costs of Safety Stock

EOQ Applied to Production

Heretofore, all purchased items were treated as being received into inventory at one time. However, when a firm manufactures the items, there is a continuous flow into the inventory as units are completed, illustrated graphically in Figure 2–8. Formulas for determining the optimum run size may be developed in much the same manner as the previous inventory models.

Many companies produce certain items in production lots or batches since sales are not sufficient to warrant a continuous, year-long run. If this is the case, these firms incur setup costs each time a production lot is started. Setup costs are similar to the ordering costs per order. Included in setup costs is the time to set up and tear down the machine for the batch being run, production control cost, and the ordering cost to provide raw materials for the batch order.

Just as inventory carrying costs were determined for our previous economic ordering formula, the same holds true for a production batch order. A firm incurs carrying costs on the finished product from the time it is manufactured until it is sold. The carrying charges will be higher on finished goods than raw materials since the finished goods inventory is a composite of direct material, direct labor, and variable-fixed manufacturing expenses.

Production for Stock   The basic concept for an optimum number of production lots is similar in theory to that used for purchased parts. Three approaches are set forth, the first being a case where finished goods are to be placed in stock and sold at a constant rate until some low level of finished goods inventory is reached. At that point, another production lot is run. The approach for finding the optimum an-

Figure 2–8
Production flow into inventory.

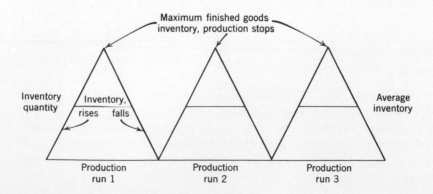

nual batch runs is the same as for the optimum number of orders per year; that is, the symbols of the equation are the same, but the descriptions have been changed. The symbols with the appropriate descriptions are:

N = optimum number of runs per year (was optimum number of orders per year)

A = annual sales of item at factory cost (was total forecasted dollar amount of annual usage)

S = setup cost per production run (was ordering cost)

I = annual inventory carrying cost expressed as a percentage of the value of average inventory—finished goods (same, except for average inventory—raw materials)

For example, the Hobart Manufacturing Company manufactures many parts for its products, many of which are stocked while sales are at a constant rate. Part #624 is an example of the items stocked. The firm sells $10,000 (at factory cost) worth of this part with average carrying costs on finished goods of 25 percent per annum. The setup costs have been determined to be $50 per production run. Using the formula for the optimum number of orders per year (Equation 2–2), the results are:

$$N = \sqrt{\frac{AI}{2S}} = \sqrt{\frac{\$10,000 \times .25}{2 \times \$50}} = \sqrt{\frac{\$2,500}{\$100}} = \sqrt{25} = 5 \text{ runs per annum}$$

It should be noted that we could use other inventory models, developed previously, for the optimum number of units per run and the optimum number of month's sales per run.

Simultaneous Sales and Production for One Item   The second case where the concept of an optimum production lot size can be applied is the simultaneous sales and production of the finished goods. Referring again to Figure 2–8, the inventory of finished goods does not build up immediately to its maximum point as was the case with the optimum order of purchased parts. Rather, it builds up gradually since goods are being produced faster than they are being sold. The mathematical derivation of this formula is given below. First, the terms are defined:

Q = optimum number of units per production run

R = total annual quantity requirements

S = set-up costs per production run

U = usage (or sales rate) in units per day

P = production rate in units per day

C = cost value of each unit

I = annual inventory carrying costs, expressed as a percentage of the value of average finished goods inventory

D = number of days in the production run

The setup costs, referred to previously as ordering costs in the purchase-size model, utilize the same expression $(R/Q)S$. This is the total annual requirement divided by the number of units per run or the number of production runs times the setup costs per run for the total annual setup costs of production.

The inventory carrying costs on finished goods inventory require a more complex mathematical expression. Referring to Figures 2–1 and 2–8, average inventory and, in turn, inventory carrying costs are different when there is a continuous flow of items into the finished goods inventory than when the entire lot is received at once. In the production run model, inventory is at its maximum size at the time each production run is completed (Figure 2–8). The maximum point is equal to the number of days in the run (D) times the daily production rate in units (P) minus the daily usage rate (U), or $D(P - U)$. The average inventory, then, is $D(P - U)/2$. The number of days in the run (D) is equal to the optimum number of units per run (Q) divided by the production rate in units (P), or $D = Q/P$. Substituting this foregoing term for D in the equation $D(P - U)/2$ gives $[(Q/P)(P - U)]/2$. Using the same reasoning as in the economic ordering quantity model, average inventory, or $[(Q/P)(P - U)]/2$, times the cost of one unit (C) times the inventory carrying percent of average finished goods (I) gives the inventory carrying costs of $[(Q/P)(P - U)/2](CI)$.

After determining the proper mathematical expressions for setup costs and inventory carrying costs, it should be apparent from our previous derivation of inventory models that manufacturing costs are at their minimum when these sets of cost are equal. Equating these expressions results in the following:

$$\frac{RS}{Q} = \frac{(Q/P)(P - U)}{2}CI$$

$$\frac{RS}{Q} = \frac{Q}{2}\left(\frac{P - U}{P}\right)CI$$

$$Q^2\left(\frac{P - U}{P}\right)CI = 2RS$$

$$Q^2 = \frac{2RS}{CI(1 - U/P)}$$

$$Q = \sqrt{\frac{2RS}{CI(1 - U/P)}} \qquad \text{(Equation 2–10)}$$

Although the preceding inventory model can be graphed using real-world data to prove that minimum costs have been obtained, an alternative approach utilizes calculus, as set forth in Appendix B.

It should be noted that this model gives a lower total cost for the firm than when the entire purchased quantity is received into inventory at once. The rationale is that the production of a continuous flow into inventory brings about an increase in the optimum lot size and thus fewer runs. Furthermore, a decrease in the size of the average inventory results in smaller finished goods carrying costs. This can best be illustrated by comparing costs for the two models. The original data ($C = \$1$, $I = 20\%$, $R = 8,000$ units, and $S = \$12.50$) must be modified for the two new terms, U and P. Daily production is 44 units per day (p) while the usage rate is 22 units per day, based on 365 days per year (plants operate seven days a week), which approximates a yearly demand of 8,000. The preceding formula gives the following results:

$$Q = \sqrt{\frac{2(8,000)(\$12.50)}{(\$1)(.20)(1 - 22/44)}} = \sqrt{\frac{200,000}{.10}} = \sqrt{2,000,000} = 1,414 \text{ units}$$

The average number of runs that should be scheduled is 8,000 units divided by 1,414 or 5.6, while the comparable number of orders for the purchase order model is 8,000 units divided by 1,000 (EOQ) or 8. The total ordering and carrying costs for the simplified formula are $200, while the comparable costs for the optimum quantity per production run are as follows:

$$TC = \frac{RS}{Q} + \frac{Q}{2}\left(\frac{P - U}{P}\right)CI$$

$$TC = \frac{8,000 \times \$12.50}{1,414} + \frac{1,414}{2}\left(\frac{44 - 22}{44}\right)\$1 \times .20$$

$$TC = \$70.70 + \$70.70 = \$141.40$$

Thus total costs are minimized with the optimum lot size production model.

Simultaneous Sales and Production for Two or More Items Some manufacturing firms have purchased special machinery whose entire production is allocated to two products. Having developed the preceding model for the optimum number of units per production run, we now may modify the formula for this condition. Thus, it is possible to determine the number of units required for each production run in order to minimize costs for the firm.

The basic approach to setting an economical cycle length is the same as in the case of one product, that is, to find the cycle length or number of cycles per month or year which will minimize the total setup (or changeover costs) and inventory costs. The changeover costs increase with more cycles in a given period while inventory costs tend to fall because of more frequent cycles. The resulting formula is very similar to that for a one-product condition.

The starting point for the model is: the number of cycles per year (N) equals annual usage requirements (R) divided by the economic ordering quantity per production run (Q), or $N = R/Q$. Substituting Equation 2–10 for Q, the following model is:

$$N = \frac{R}{\sqrt{\dfrac{2RS}{CI(1 - U/P)}}} = \sqrt{\frac{\dfrac{R^2}{1}}{\dfrac{2RS}{CI(1 - U/P)}}}$$

$$N = \sqrt{\frac{R^2CI(1 - U/P)}{2RS}} = \sqrt{\frac{RCI(1 - U/P)}{2S}}$$

The preceding equation reflects the quantities and costs for only one part produced on the machine. In order to reflect the same for the second part, the model must be modified for this addition:

$$N = \sqrt{\frac{R_1C_1I_1(1 - U_1/P_1) + R_2C_2I_2(1 - U_2/P_2)}{2(S_1 + S_2)}}$$ (Equation 2–11)

Notice the use of the subscript one for the first part and subscript two for the second part.

In order to apply this formula, the following example is used for two pistons, parts K and L, produced on an automatic machine. Data from the production and accounting records are:

	Part K	Part L
Production rate	2,000 parts/day	1,500 parts/day
Usage or sales rate	1,000 parts/day	500 parts/day
Changeover cost	$200 (L to K)	$100 (K to L)
Cost per part	$0.20	$0.40
Inventory carrying costs	25%	25%
Average number of working days per year = 250 days		

Based upon the foregoing data, how many runs per year should the firm consider to minimize costs for each part?

$$N = \sqrt{\frac{(1,000)(250)(\$0.20)(0.25)(1 - 1,000/2,000) + (500)(250)(\$0.40)(0.25)(1 - 500/1,500)}{2(\$200 + \$100)}}$$

$$N = \sqrt{\frac{250,000 \times 0.05(1 - \frac{1}{2}) + 125,000 \times 0.10(1 - \frac{1}{3})}{2(300)}}$$

$$N = \sqrt{\frac{12,500(0.5) + 12,500(0.667)}{600}}$$

$$N = \sqrt{\frac{14,588}{600}} = \sqrt{24.3} = 4.9 \text{ (approx.) number of runs per year for each part}$$

Another question can be raised: What quantities per run should be manufactured for parts K and L during the year? This is easily determined. The ordering quantities per production run for each part equal the annual usage of the particular part divided by the number of production runs annually for each product. In the illustration the required number of units per production run for part K is 250,000 divided by 4.9 or 51,020 parts. For part L, the number of units per run is 25,510 units. If the number of production days for each run is desired, this can be obtained by taking the order quantities and dividing by the daily production rate. The number of continuous production days for K is about 26 days (51,020 divided by 2,000) and approximately 17 days for part L.

The preceding formula (Equation 2–11) is not restricted to two products. It can be expanded to include several products. Written in compact notation, the equation becomes:

$$N = \sqrt{\frac{\Sigma R_j C_j I_j (1 - U_j / P_j)}{2\Sigma S_j}}$$
(Equation 2–12)

where j represents values for each product. Equation 2–12 can be illustrated for several products by using the paper-making industry. It is normally desirable to go from fine to coarser grades on the same paper-making machine. The data for this example is found in Table 2–8. It should be noted that the production rate is based upon 250 working days a year. This yearly basis will be used in computing U_j / P_j below.

Product	Units—Production Rate/Day	Days—Yearly Usage Rate	Units—Yearly Usage	Cost Per Piece	Inventory Carrying Costs	Changeover Costs
1	800	100	80,000	$0.10	20%	$16
2	1,100	100	110,000	0.15	20	22
3	800	50	40,000	0.08	20	36
		250 days				

Table 2–8
Rate of Production, Usage, Cost, Inventory, and Changeover Costs Based on 250 Working Days

The calculations, using Equation 2–12, are shown in Table 2–9. The least cost operation is approximately five runs per year, each run lasting 50 days (250 days divided by five runs) in order to produce one-fifth of the usage or sales requirements.

Product	$R_j C_j I_j$	U_j / P_j	$1 - U_j / P_j$	$\Sigma R_j C_j I_j (1 - U_j / P_j)$	Changeover Costs, ΣS_j
1	80,000 × $0.10 × 20% = $1,600	100/250 = 0.4	1 − 0.4 = 0.6	$ 960	$16
2	110,000 × $0.15 × 20% = $3,300	100/250 = 0.4	1 − 0.4 = 0.6	1,980	22
3	40,000 × $0.08 × 20% = $640	50/250 = 0.2	1 − 0.2 = 0.8	512	36
				$3,452	$74

Table 2–9
Length of Production Cycle per Year for Three Products

$$N = \sqrt{\frac{\$3,452}{2 \times \$74}} = \sqrt{23.3} = 4.8 \text{ (approx.) or about 5 cycles per year}$$

Chapter Summary

The subject matter of this chapter has focused upon the analysis of key decision variables and their interrelationships in formulating inventory control models. Although these models are incorporated as an essential part of a computer system, their fundamental decision criterion is the minimization of total inventory costs. The reason is obvious if one examines the large amount invested in inventories. For more details on advanced inventory models, consult the bibliography of this chapter.

Questions

1. What is the basic function of inventory? What is the basic function of safety stock?
2. How is the EOQ formula derived, using the algebraic method?
3. Discuss the similarities and differences between the EOQ derived for purchasing raw materials and producing finished goods.
4. What is the relationship of inventory models to computers?

Model Formulation Exercises

1. In a reformulation of the basic economic ordering quantity formula (Equation 2–1), simplify the terms C (cost of one unit) and I (inventory carrying cost percentage) as one term and solve for Q.

2. A vendor has informed your company that there will be an order processing charge of $X per order in the future, regardless of the order's size. How should your company reformulate the basic EOQ formula (Equation 2–1) to handle this new variable?

3. In reformulating the basic economic ordering quantity formula (Equation 2–1), indicate how it can be simplified for the following:
   (a) Cost of placing an order is the same for all inventory items.
   (b) Carrying charges are the same for all inventory items.
   (c) Carrying charges and ordering costs are the same for all inventory items.

4. Referring to the inventory formulas (Equations 2–1 and 2–2) derived in the chapter, formulate an equation for each of the following conditions:
   (a) The economic ordering quantity on a quarterly basis.
   (b) The optimum number of orders to place monthly.

5. Referring to the formula for the optimum number of days' supply per optimum order (Equation 2–4) derived in the chapter, reformulate the equation so that 365 days precede the square root sign.

Mathematical Exercises

1. The Erlanger Manufacturing Company has determined through analysis of its accounting and production records that it uses $36,000 per year of a component part purchased at $18 per part. Erlanger's purchasing cost is $40 per

order and its annual inventory carrying charges are $16\frac{2}{3}$ percent of the average inventory

(a) Determine the most economic quantity to order at a time.
(b) Determine the most economic number of times to order per year.
(c) Determine the average days' supply of ordering the most economic quantity.
(d) Determine the optimum amount of dollars per order.

2. The Harmon Manufacturing Company has determined, from an analysis of its accounting and production data for part number 625, that its cost to purchase is $35 per order and $2.20 per part. Its inventory carrying charge is 18 percent of the average inventory. The firm currently purchases $22,000 of this part per year.
   (a) What should the economic ordering quantity be?
   (b) What is the optimum number of days' supply per optimum order?
   (c) What is the optimum number of orders per year to minimize the firm's costs?

3. The Jarmon Shoe Company has found it purchases a large amount of industrial tapes for production of its shoes. Currently, it purchases $40,000 a year of the various sized tapes from the O'Donnell Company. A proposal was made by its supplier, whose offer consists of a $1\frac{1}{4}$ percent discount if Jarmon places an order quarterly. Jarmon has calculated the cost to purchase at $22.50 per order and inventory carrying costs at 22 percent. Should Jarmon accept the discount offer from O'Donnell? If the answer is no, what counteroffer should be made in terms of a discount?

4. The Wilcox Electric Company is considering the feasibility of changing suppliers for coupling hardware. Presently the firm has an optimum purchasing policy with Ace Hardware at a 1 percent discount. Current yearly purchases are $81,000 and the unit cost is $8.10. The administrative charge is $125 per purchase and the carrying charges are 25 percent of the average inventory level. Bids received from other suppliers are: Nutz, Inc., offers a 5 percent discount if ordered twice a year and Grabbers, Inc., offers a 3 percent discount if ordered four times a year. Which of the proposed offers should be accepted or should the present supplier be retained?

5. Arco, Inc., has a monthly usage for part #L25241 of 125 units. Inventory carrying costs are 25 percent of average inventory and ordering costs are $15 per order. Each part costs $2 and its economic ordering quantity is 300 units. The freight on a shipment of 300 units is $95. If 500 units are shipped, the freight is $122. Should a quantity of 500 be purchased in order to effect the savings in freight?

6. The QM Company uses Part No. 1150 at an average rate of 110 units per day, 250 days per year. It buys the part from the Marmo Manufacturing Corporation in Nashville for $75. The firm is contemplating using air freight instead of motor

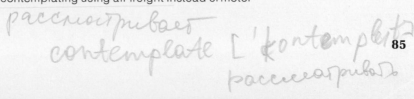

85

freight since it would reduce lead time from 10 days to 4 days. Ordering costs are $40 per order; Part No. 1150 weighs 15 pounds; and inventory carrying costs are 25 percent of product cost. Air freight cost is $388 per ton, and motor freight is $110 per ton. Assume that there is no safety stock in the problem.
(a) What is the economic ordering quantity?
(b) What is the optimum number of orders per year?
(c) Do savings during the first year for reduced inventory investment and carrying costs justify the additional costs for air freight?

7. The Coca-Cola Company buys a large number of pallets every year which it uses in the warehousing of its bottled products. A vendor has offered them the following discount schedule for pallets:

Order Quantity	Price Per Unit
1–500	$10.00
501–1,000	9.50
1,001–1,500	9.15
1,501–over	9.00

The average yearly replacement for the past two years has been 1,650 pallets, which looks realistic for this year. The cost per order is $12.50 and its carrying costs are 18 percent of average inventory. What quantity should be ordered?

8. The Jones Manufacturing Company has been incurring out-of-stock problems lately, which has caused a slowup in the company's shipments. Management has approached you to study the inventory items critical to its manufacturing operations. You have selected at random from this group part #3516, which has a long lead time. Your data, compiled from production records, are:

Usage During Past Reorder Period	Percentage of Times This Quantity Was Used
1,200	0.02
1,225	0.12
1,250	0.13
1,275	0.15
1,300	0.20
1,325	0.25
1,350	0.07
1,375	0.04
1,400	0.02

Other information compiled is:

Normal lead time = 53 days

Average use per day = 25 units

Optimum number of orders per year = 5

Cost to store one unit per year = $4

Cost of being out of stock per unit = $30

What is the reorder point?

9. A municipal water treatment plant purchases 100-pound bags of lime for use in the water treatment process. The number of bags used per day varies with the water consumption and past records have yielded the following data:

Usage During Past Reorder Period	Number of Times This Quantity Was Used
225	9
300	15
375	20
450	3
525	2
600	1

The normal lead time is 15 days and the average usage per day is 25 bags. Inventory cost is $2 per bag per year and being out of stock necessitates buying at the regular price of $5 per bag. The optimum orders per year are 15. As a consulting engineer for the municipality, you are asked to determine the reorder point.

10. Central Electric manufactures a light unit for assembly by another department into a finished plug-in lighting package. Since the machinery making the light unit is much faster than the final assembly, it is used to make other light units. The following information is available for the light unit:

Production rate = 6,500 light units per day

Assembly requirements = 1,000 light units per day

Inventory holding cost per light unit = $0.02 per year

Setup costs = $500

Acquisition lead time = 4 working days

Working year = 250 days

(a) Determine the economic ordering quantity.
(b) Determine the reorder point.

11. The Margo Company manufactures part B-2000 on a special lathe for use in a continuous assembly. The assemblies that use B-2000 are manufactured at a slower rate. This allows time for doing odd jobs on the special lathe when it is not being used for part B-2000. When parts are being run, deliveries are made to the assembly area; otherwise, the assembly department draws parts from inventory. The following information is given for part B-2000:

Production rate = 4,000 pieces per day

Assembly requirements = 1,200 pieces per day

Inventory holding cost per piece = $0.02 per year

Setup cost = $110

Acquisition lead time = 10 working days

Use a 250 working day year.

(a) Calculate the economic ordering quantity.
(b) Determine the reorder point.
(c) Suppose the use rate fluctuates. Would your answer to question (b) be altered? How?

12. The Margo Company has decided to expand its product line. All the odd jobs (as explained in Problem 11) have been taken off the special lathe. Instead, production on this lathe will be alloted to parts B-2000 (see Problem 11 for data) and F-1000 (part for a new product). The estimated figures for F-1000 from the production and accounting departments are:

Production rate = 8,000 pieces per day

Assembly requirements = 5,000 pieces per day

Inventory holding cost per piece = $0.01 per year

Changeover cost from F-1000 to B-2000 = $110

Changeover cost from B-2000 to F-1000 = $90

(a) Calculate the optimum number of cycles per year.
(b) Determine the length of run for each part.

13. The Hudson Chemical Company manufactures dyes for the textile industry. Several of these products are manufactured on the same equipment. As inventory control manager, the production superintendent has requested you to determine how many cycles per year are needed to minimize cost. The accounting department has supplied you with the following data:

Product	Production Rate— Lbs./Day	Daily Usage Rate	Lbs. per Year	Cost per Lb.	Inventory Carrying Cost	Changeover Cost
Yellow	2,000	50	100,000	$1.20	20%	$250
Red	4,000	50	200,000	$1.43	20%	$160
Blue	500	150	75,000	$6.50	20%	$320
		250				

Bibliography

R. G. Brown, *Decision Rules for Inventory Management,* New York: Holt, Rinehart and Winston, 1970.

E. S. Buffa, *Modern Production Management,* New York: John Wiley & Sons, 1977.

E. S. Buffa, *Production Inventory Systems: Planning and Control,* Homewood, Ill.: Richard D. Irwin, 1972.

J. H. Greene, *Production and Inventory Control Handbook,* New York: McGraw-Hill Book Company, 1970.

F. S. Hillier and G. J. Lieberman, *Operations Research,* San Francisco: Holden-Day, 1974.

B. E. Lipman, *How to Control and Reduce Inventory,* Englewood Cliffs, N.J.: Prentice-Hall, 1972.

D. W. Miller and M. K. Starr, *Executive Decisions and Operations Research,* Englewood Cliffs, N.J.: Prentice-Hall, 1969.

Part III

Operations Research Models — Probability and Statistics

Chapter 3

Decision Theory

Decision theory in business today plays an important role in helping managers make decisions. Since we live in a world where the course of future events cannot be predicted with absolute certainty, the best we can do is to reach approximate solutions based upon the likelihood of possible future events. Hence, we assign a certain value or a probability factor to the future events. When one or more individuals are involved in assigning a probability factor to a particular event, we have come to accept this assigned probability as being valid. In a similar manner, probability can be based on historical data, managers' feelings about an event, or some other basis. Thus managers, having some knowledge about the possible outcomes of their many decisions, can reach better decisions in the long run by organizing their information and structuring it within the framework of decision theory.

Requirements for Formulating Decision Theory Problems

Within the framework of decision theory, there are various criteria for solving business problems under conditions of future uncertainty. The requirements for solving for any criterion begin with an objective which is defined and chosen—perhaps from a group of conflicting objectives—by managers working with OR practitioners. Once the objective is established, various possible outcomes are determined and arranged according to some measure of utility, i.e., payoff measure. The problem is, then, analyzed to determine those variables which may affect the outcomes. Those variables which are beyond the control of managers, such as weather conditions and competitor's actions, are termed *states of nature*. Those variables which are within managers' control, such as appropriate actions they can take, including the decision to do nothing, are termed *strategies*. Through analysis, the outcomes which will result from all possible combinations of states of nature and strategies are determined. Finally, the managers' measure of utility or payoff measure for each outcome is associated with each combination of strategy and state of nature. This takes the form of a "payoff matrix." A typical matrix example is shown below:

Payoff Matrix
States of Nature

		Good	Average	Bad
	1st	O_{11}	O_{12}	O_{13}
	2nd	O_{21}	O_{22}	O_{23}
Strategies	3rd	O_{31}	O_{32}	O_{33}
	nth	O_{n1}	O_{n2}	O_{n3}

where O_{nn} equals an outcome for each combination of strategy and state of nature. Thus, the table is a matrix of all the possible outcomes which are presented in a systematic fashion. Within this chapter, various approaches for utilizing this payoff matrix in conjunction with probability factors regarding an uncertain future will be explained.

Applications—Decision Trees

- **Selection of investment alternatives**—evaluates the numerous investment opportunities available for company funds to determine the most profitable one(s).
- **Contract bidding**—reduces a myriad of detail about prices on contract bidding to the more promising ones for evaluation.
- **Evaluation of a business**—provides a means for management to evaluate the most profitable approach for disposing of a business or a subsidiary of a firm.
- **Relates sales to investment decisions**—provides a logical method for relating potential sales demand to investment in machinery and equipment versus working overtime.
- **Reduction of production downtime**—assists in determining whether or not production machinery should be serviced on a periodic basis or as it fails to reduce production downtime and overall production costs.
- **Competitive pricing**—useful in analyzing possible outcomes based upon various selling prices to select the best price to optimize profits.
- **Buying from vendors**—assists a buyer in determining whether to buy from one vendor versus another when considering factors such as price, delivery, and quality of product.

Probability Terms

Before discussing the six basic types of probability under statistical independence and dependence, the probability terms to be used throughout this chapter are explained. An understanding of these terms allows us to pursue a logical framework for decision theory models. The utilization of probability trees is also helpful for an understanding of the subject.

Subjective and Objective Probabilities   Upon examination of a business problem that can be solved at least in part by probability, the question arises: What kind of probabilities should be used? First, probabilities can be subjective or objective. *Subjective* probabilities are educated guesses, whereas *objective* probabilities are based upon historical data and common experience to support the assignment of probabilities. Frequently, historical data are not available, which means the decision maker must rely on an estimation of the various possible outcomes. It should be recognized that one has to guess only in part for subjective probability since much is known from experience and intuition. Of the two approaches, objective probability is preferred to subjective probability. However, there may be a need to reconsider the distribution of probability factors. The past is not a complete predictor of the future. The objective probabilities may have to be tempered based upon the judgment and intuition of the decision maker. Thus in certain cases, subjective and objective probabilities may have to combined. The attendant circumstances must be surveyed to determine what type of probability should be employed within the problem.

An example of subjective probability deals with the purchase of a new seasonal item by a retail store. The outside salesman and the retailer, working together, can determine the optimum quantity to stock. The retailer, knowing the local market in depth, and the outside salesman, having been through this type of experience many times, will generally assign about the same probability of success for the various possible quantities to stock. Based upon agreement on these subjective probabilities, the salesman and retailer could determine the optimum level for this seasonal product. Methods for solving such problems will be found in this chapter and the next.

Considering the toss of a fair coin (with a head on one side and a tail on the other), both heads and tails are equally likely to occur. The probability of .5 that the coin will come up heads on any toss is called objective probability because it is empirically evident. Half the time in an infinite number of tosses the result will be heads, and half the time it will be tails. Translating this objective probability into probability terms, we have a .5 or 50 percent probability that heads will occur on any toss and a .5 or 50 percent probability that tails will occur on any toss. This is written as follows: $P(H) = .5$ and $P(T) = .5$ where their probabilities total 1.0.

Unconditional (Marginal) Probability   The probabilities associated with tossing a coin (or any comparable events) are called *unconditional* or *marginal* probabilities because the outcome of any toss is in no way conditioned or affected by the preceding toss. In effect, each toss of the coin stands on its own. For example, if we toss a fair coin five times and get tails on all five tosses, what is the probability of a head on the next toss? If the coin is not biased, we know that any toss is not conditioned by a prior toss. We can assign a probability of .5 to heads and .5 to tails on the sixth toss or any other toss.

The unconditional or marginal probability of any given outcome for a given action must be between zero and one inclusively. If we assign a probability of zero to an occurrence, we are stating that the occurrence will never take place. On the other hand, if we assign a probability of one to an occurrence, we are expressing with complete certainty that the event will take place. Most business problems have probabilities that range somewhere between zero and one. Any probability between zero and one inclusive is written as $0 \le P \le 1$. This means that the probability of an outcome must be greater than or equal to zero and less than or equal to one.

Mutually Exclusive Events   In the example of the fair coin, there are two possible outcomes, heads and tails. On any one toss, either heads or tails can come up, but not both at the same time. Events are said to be *mutually exclusive* if one and only one outcome can occur at a time. The important point in determining whether events are mutually exclusive is: Can two or more events occur at one time? If the answer to this question is yes, the events are not mutually exclusive.

The probabilities of events that are mutually exclusive can be added. For example, the list of all the possible outcomes for two tosses of a coin is as follows:

Events	Probability
$H_1 H_2$	.25
$H_1 T_2$	.25
$T_1 H_2$	.25
$T_1 T_2$	.25
	1.00

These events add up to 1.0 since there are only four possible outcomes and each event (two tosses of a coin) is equally likely to occur. Mutually exclusive events are those where only one outcome can take place at a time and whose list of all possible outcomes totals 1.0.

Collectively Exhaustive Events   In the fair coin example, there are two possible outcomes—heads and tails. The list of these outcomes is *collectively exhaustive* since the results of any toss must be either heads or tails. To state it another way, a list which contains all of the possible outcomes for a given action is said to be collectively exhaustive. In the case of two tosses in a row, there are four possible outcomes and no others. The list of four outcomes is collectively exhaustive. A list of events, then, may be not only mutually exclusive but also collectively exhaustive.

Statistical Independence

Events in probability theory may be either statistically independent or dependent. If two events are independent, the occurrence of the one event does not affect the probability of the occurrence of the second event. Under statistical independence (as well as statistical dependence), there are three probability types: marginal, joint, and conditional.

Marginal Probabilities   The simplest of all probabilities is *marginal probability* under statistical independence, which is defined as the probability of the occurrence of an event. Each event stands alone and is in no way connected with the preceding or succeeding event(s). This is found, for example, in each toss of a coin no matter how many tosses may precede it and succeed it or what their respective outcomes may be. In effect, each toss of a coin is a statistically independent event and stands on its own.

The formula for marginal probability under statistical independence is

$$P(A) = P(A) \qquad \text{(Equation 3–1)}$$

This is read as: the probability of event A occurring is the probability of event A. In the fair coin example, the probability of getting heads (event A) equals .5 and the probability of tails (event A) equals .5. Using a biased coin, the $P(H) = .9$ and $P(T) = .1$ because the outcome of each toss is completely unrelated to the outcomes of other tosses. It does not matter whether the coin is fair or biased in order to have marginal probability under statistical independence.

Joint Probabilities   When two or more events are independent, the *joint probability* of these events occurring together or in succession is equal to the product of the probabilities of the individual events. Stated mathematically, the equation for joint probability is

$$P(AB) = P(A) \times P(B) \qquad \text{(Equation 3–2)}$$

where

$P(A)$ = probability of event A occurring

$P(B)$ = probability of event B occurring

$P(AB)$ = probability of events A and B occurring together or in succession

Referring again to our fair coin, the probability of heads in two successive tosses is the probability of heads on the first toss (.5) times the probability of heads on the second toss (.5). Using Equation 3–2, the probability of two heads in a row is

$$P(H_1 H_2) = P(H_1) \times P(H_2) \qquad \text{or} \qquad P(HH) = .5 \times .5 = .25$$

Using the same equation, the probability of three heads in three successive tosses is

$$P(H_1H_2H_3) = .5 \times .5 \times .5 = .125$$

From the foregoing illustration, it should be apparent that joint probability deals with "mutually exclusive events" and "collectively exhaustive events." The construction of a *probability tree,* showing all possible outcomes for three tosses of a fair coin, is shown in Figure 3–1. The starting point for the probability tree is the first toss. The first toss is connected to the second toss and the third toss is linked in a similar manner. Notice that the sum of all the possible outcomes for each toss is 1.0, which is a requisite for mutually exclusive and collectively exhaustive events. It should be noted that the same type or probability tree can be constructed for a biased coin. The resulting probability tree would be like the one in Figure 3–1, except that the probability factors and circled figures would be changed.

Figure 3–1
Probability tree for three tosses of a fair coin.

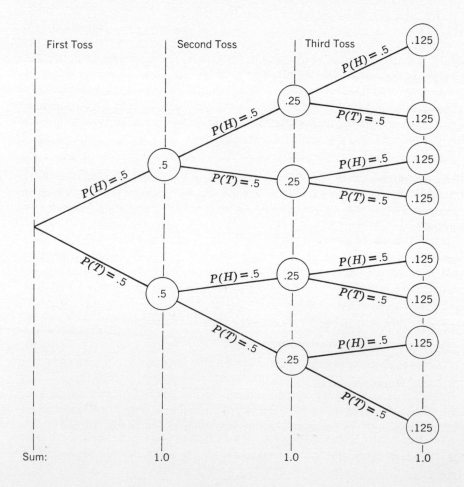

Based upon the outcomes of a probability tree, a tabular list of outcomes can be constructed as shown in Table 3–1. This table shows the results for a fair coin where $P(H) = .5$ and $P(T) = .5$ and a biased coin where $P(H) = .9$ and $P(T) = .1$. The values in Table 3–1 are for three tosses of a coin, which means it is possible to get three heads or three tails in a row initially. However, over a long series of tosses, results will reflect the equal chance or bias condition.

First Toss			Second Toss			Third Toss		
	Probability			Probability			Probability	
Possible Outcomes	Fair Coin	Biased Coin	Possible Outcomes	Fair Coin	Biased Coin	Possible Outcomes	Fair Coin	Biased Coin
H_1	.5	.9	H_1H_2	.25	.81	$H_1H_2H_3$	.125	.729
T_1	.5	.1	H_1T_2	.25	.09	$H_1H_2T_3$	.125	.081
	1.0	1.0	T_1H_2	.25	.09	$H_1T_2H_3$	.125	.081
			T_1T_2	.25	.01	$H_1T_2T_3$	.125	.009
				1.00	1.00	$T_1H_2H_3$	.125	.081
						$T_1H_2T_3$	.125	.009
						$T_1T_2H_3$	.125	.009
						$T_1T_2T_3$	.125	.001
							1.000	1.000

Table 3–1
List of All Possible Outcomes for Three Tosses of a Fair Coin and a Biased Coin

Conditional Probabilities Having considered marginal and joint probabilities, the remaining probability under statistical independence is conditional probability. *Conditional probability* is written $P(A|B)$: the probability of event A, given that event B has occurred. Thus, conditional probability is given as $P(A|B) = P(A)$ where the term to the right of the equal sign is the same as Equation 3–1. Its meaning can be clarified by recalling that independent events are those whose probabilities are in no way affected by the occurrence of any other event—preceding, following, or occurring at the same time.

To illustrate the meaning of conditional probability, a question can be raised: What is the probability that the second toss of a fair coin will be heads, given that heads resulted from the initial toss? This can be written as: $P(H_2|H_1)$. It should be remembered that the result of the initial toss has no effect on the result of the second toss since the events are independent of one another. The probability of heads on the second toss is .5 for this fair coin. Thus we can say that $P(H_2|H_1) = P(H) = .5$.

Statistical Dependence

Statistical dependence is present if the probability of some event is affected by or dependent upon the happening of some other event. Dependence adds a new dimension to probability theory from that set forth in the previous sections. The types of probabilities associated with dependence are the same as for independence.

Marginal Probabilities The *marginal probability* of a statistically dependent event is the same as that for a statistically independent event or $P(A)$ in Equation 3–1. Why is this so? "Marginal" means one and only one probability is considered. Even if two dependent events are involved, marginal probability under statistical dependence applies to only one of them by definition.

In order to illustrate the idea of dependence, in place of the fair coin, three urns containing colored balls will be used. The urns which contain the balls are as follows:

Urn 1	3 red and 6 white
Urn 2	5 blue and 4 green
Urn 3	7 yellow and 2 orange

If a red ball is drawn from urn 1, we draw a ball from urn 2. If a white ball is drawn from urn 1, we draw a ball from urn 3. This arrangement can be diagrammed as follows:

```
                              | 3 Red   |
                              | 6 White |   Urn 1

              If Red ↓                ↓ If White

   Urn 2   | 5 Blue  |        | 7 Yellow  |  Urn 3
           | 4 Green |        | 2 Orange  |
```

It is logical to ask whether the probability of drawing a blue ball is affected by the color of the ball we draw from urn 1. It certainly is, since only urn 2 has blue balls. The only way to draw from urn 2 is to draw initially one of the red balls from urn 1. In effect, the two events—the drawing from urn 1 and the drawing from urn 2—are statistically dependent.

When applying marginal probability under statistical dependence to the above example, the probability of drawing a red ball $P(R)$ from urn 1 is three red balls out of nine balls or a .333 probability. Similarly, the probability of drawing a white ball $P(W)$ from urn 1 is .667 probability. The values for this first draw are shown in Figure 3–2. Thus, Equation 3–1 or $P(A)$ is used.

Conditional Probabilities The conditional probability of a statistically dependent event is different from that of a statistically independent event. The formula for *conditional probability* is:

$$P(A|B) = \frac{P(AB)}{P(B)} \hspace{3cm} \text{(Equation 3–3)}$$

The equation is read: the probability of event A, given event B has occurred, is the probability of events A and B occurring together or in succession divided by the probability of event B.

Conditional probability can be understood by continuing the illustration of the three urns and the colored balls. If someone draws a ball from urn 1 and it is red, what is the probability of drawing a blue ball from urn 2? Stating the problem in terms of probability, what is the conditional probability that the second ball is blue, given that the first ball is red or $P(B|R)$? The question can be expressed in the form of a probability tree, as in Figure 3–2. From the original statement of the data, we know there are three red and six white balls in the first urn and five blue and four green balls in the second urn. The problem, first, is to find the simple probabilities of the red and white balls in the first urn. This can be done by dividing the number of balls in each category by the total number of balls in urn 1. This is done as follows:

$$P(R) = \tfrac{3}{9} = .333$$
$$P(W) = \tfrac{6}{9} = \underline{.667}$$
$$1.000$$

Of the nine balls in urn 1, .333 are red and .667 are white, as shown in Figure 3–2. Similarly, calculating the probability of a blue ball in urn 2, given that the first ball in urn 1 is red, as in Figure 3–2, the total of blue balls (five) is divided by the total of all the balls (nine) in urn 2. The $P(B|R)$ is .556 and $P(G|R)$ is .444. The same type of calculation is made for urn 3 where $P(Y|W)$ is .778 and $P(O|W)$ is .222.

We can assure ourselves that these events are dependent in Figure 3–2 by observing that the color of the ball from urn 1 determines the color of the ball from the other two urns. Since the color of urn 1 directly affects the color for urn 2 or urn 3, these two events are said to be dependent. Before illustrating Equation 3–3 for conditional probability under statistical dependence in our example, we shall first examine joint probability under statistical dependence, which is actually a restatement of Equation 3–3.

Joint Probabilities Having solved for conditional probability under conditions of dependence, or $P(A|B) = P(AB)/P(B)$, we can solve this equation for $P(AB)$. This can be done by cross-multiplication, resulting in the equation for *joint probability* under statistical dependence:

$$P(AB) = P(A|B) \times P(B) \qquad\qquad \text{(Equation 3–4)}$$

The equation reads: the joint probability of events A and B equals the probability of event A, given that event B has occurred, times the probability of event B.

Returning to our example, the question can now be asked, what is the probability of drawing one red ball and one blue ball in a row? This is joint probability under statistical dependence which can be solved by using Equation 3–4 as follows:

$$P(BR) = P(B|R) \times P(R)$$
$$= .556 \times .333$$
$$= .185$$

Referring to the probability tree in Figure 3–2, the joint probabilities at the end of the second draw, after initially drawing from urn 1, are the following:

Event	Marginal P(B)	× Conditional P(A|B)	= Joint P(AB)
BR	$P(R) = .333$	$P(B\|R) = .556$	$P(BR) = .185$
GR	$P(R) = .333$	$P(G\|R) = .444$	$P(GR) = .148$
YW	$P(W) = .667$	$P(Y\|W) = .778$	$P(YW) = .519$
OW	$P(W) = .667$	$P(O\|W) = .222$	$P(OW) = .148$
			1.000

Figure 3–2
Probability tree for first
draw from urn 1 and
second draw from urns
2 and 3.

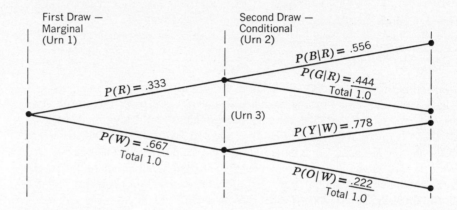

Notice the sum of the joint probabilities is 1.0 since the events are mutually exclusive and collectively exhaustive. The four figures above normally would be shown at the end of the four legs in the probability tree in Figure 3–2 and would be termed joint probability.

Based upon the preceding data, a joint probability table can be constructed as in Table 3–2. The intersections of the rows and columns are joint probabilities. The column to the extreme right gives the marginal probabilities of the outcome for the first draw while the bottom row gives the marginal probabilities of the outcomes of the second draw. Basically, Table 3–2 summarizes the data for our example of the three urns and the colored balls.

Having developed data for marginal, conditional, and joint probabilities under statistical dependence in our illustration, we can return to demonstrating that $P(B|R)$ = .556 and $P(G|R)$ = .444. The lack of values for joint probabilities necessitated this delay. Using Equation 3–3, the calculations are

$$P(B|R) = \frac{P(BR)}{P(R)} = \frac{.185}{.333} = .556$$

$$P(G|R) = \frac{P(GR)}{P(R)} = \frac{.148}{.333} = .444$$

$$1.000$$

Comparable calculations for $P(Y|W)$ and $P(O|W)$ are

$$P(Y|W) = \frac{P(YW)}{P(W)} = \frac{.519}{.667} = .778$$

$$P(O|W) = \frac{P(OW)}{P(W)} = \frac{.148}{.667} = \underline{.222}$$

$$1.000$$

The formulas developed for probability under statistical independence and dependence in the preceding sections are summarized in Table 3–3.

First Draw ↓	Second Draw →	B or Y	G or O	Marginal Probability of Outcome on First Draw
R		P(BR) .185	P(GR) .148	.333
W		P(YW) .519	P(OW) .148	.667
Marginal Probability of Outcome on Second Draw		.704	.296	1.000

Probability Type	Symbol	Formula Under Statistical Independence	Formula Under Statistical Dependence
Marginal	$P(A)$	$P(A)$ (Equation 3–1)	$P(A)$ (Equation 3–1)
Joint	$P(AB)$	$P(A) \times P(B)$ (Equation 3–2)	$P(A|B) \times P(B)$ (Equation 3–4)
Conditional	$P(A|B)$	$P(A)$ (Equation 3–1)	$P(AB)/P(B)$ (Equation 3–3)

Relationship of Statistical Independence and Dependence

Relationships between probability formulas under statistical independence and dependence can be shown within a business environment where the original investment value is altered. For example, consider a firm which has excess cash funds of $50,000 only for investing in two projects during this month and next month. The firm can invest in the first project, which is equally likely to result in a profit of $7,000 or a loss of $3,000 on an investment of $40,000. Assuming that the investment plus the profit or minus the loss is available one month hence, the second project is equally likely to result in a profit of $8,000 or a loss of $3,500 within one month on an investment of $38,500. It is further assumed in the problem that the firm is offered the opportunity of investing in projects of this kind periodically. Also, the return on excess cash funds is to be ignored within the problem.

Using the information set forth above, what should the firm do? Should it invest in the first project only, the second project only, both projects, or do nothing (the return is negative, zero, or below the established rate of return for the firm)? In addition, suppose that the excess cash funds available are $40,000 and not $50,000 as initially; what should the firm do?

To answer the first question above, a logical starting point is determining if sufficient funds will be available to undertake the second project since there are more than ample funds for undertaking the first project. If there is a profit on the first project, the firm should have $57,000 ($50,000 cash funds + $7,000 profit) available for the second project. If there is a loss, $47,000 ($50,000 cash funds − $3,000 loss) will be available to undertake the second project. In both cases, there is sufficient capital to undertake the second investment of $38,500. Thus, we can say that the first and second projects are statistically independent, that is, whether we gain or lose on the first project, there is sufficient capital to undertake the second project.

Based on the original investment, the calculations for *expected payoff* or *expected profits* — profits that can be expected over a series of the same investment opportunities — are set forth in Table 3–4. Although all values are calculated under statistical independence, marginal probability (Equation 3–1) is employed for the first project only and the second project only while joint probability is utilized for the combined projects. It should be noted that the combined projects could have been solved by marginal probability under statistical independence, that is, the first project (expected profit of $2,000) and the second project (expected profit of $2,250) could be summed for the highest expected profit of $4,250.

Table 3–4
Expected Profits Based
On Original Investment
of $50,000

First Project Only (marginal probability under statistical independence)		Combined Projects (joint probability under statistical independence)	
$ 7,000 × .5	= $3,500	$7,000 + $8,000 =	
$-3,000 \times \dfrac{.5}{1.0}$	= −1,500	$15,000 × .25	= $3,750
		$7,000 + (−$3,500) =	
Total expected profits	$2,000	$3,500 × .25	= 875
		−$3,000 + $8,000 =	
Second Project Only (marginal probability under statistical independence)		$5,000 × .25	= 1,250
		−$3,000 + (−$3,500) =	
$ 8,000 × .5	= $4,000	$-6,500 \times \dfrac{.25}{1.00}$	= −1,625
$-3,500 \times \dfrac{.5}{1.0}$	= −1,750	Total expected profits	$4,250
Total expected profits	$2,250		

Having solved the initial investment problem, we can now solve for the condition where only $40,000 of excess cash funds is available initially. This amount is just equal to the first investment requirement. If the firm experiences a gain of $7,000 on the first project, there is sufficient money available for the second project — $47,000 ($40,000 investment + $7,000 profit) is greater than the $38,500 required for the second project. On the other hand, if the firm loses on the first project, there is insufficient capital for the second project—$37,000 ($40,000 investment — $3,000 loss) is less than $38,500. Thus, statistical dependence has been determined within the problem.

Calculated values in the restatement of the problem are given in Table 3–5. The calculations and the type of probability for both projects alone remain the same. However, the value for the combined projects is different as well as the type of probability. As illustrated, the highest expected profit is $3,125 based on joint probability under statistical dependence.

Table 3–5
Expected Profits Based
On Revised Investment
of $40,000

First Project Only (marginal probability under statistical independence)		Combined Projects (joint probability under statistical dependence)	
$7,000 × .5	= $3,500	$7,000 + $8,000 =	
$-3,000 × \dfrac{.5}{1.0}$	= −1,500	$15,000 × .25	= $3,750
		$7,000 + (−$3,500) =	
Total expected profits	$2,000	$3,500 × .25	= 875
Second Project Only (marginal probability under statistical independence)		$-3,000^a × \dfrac{.50}{1.00}$	= −1,500
		Total expected profits	$3,125
$8,000 × .5	= $4,000		
$-3,500 × \dfrac{.5}{1.0}$	= −1,750		
Total expected profits	$2,250		

aUndertaking the second project is impossible.

Revision of Probabilities

Prior estimates of probabilities can be revised as more knowledge is gained about the event(s). These altered probabilities are called *revised probabilities* and can be of great help in decision making under uncertainty. For example, consider a manufacturer who has several semiautomatic machines in his plant which produce very low-cost parts. The firm has found from past experience that if the machine is properly set up, it will produce 90 percent acceptable parts, whereas if it is incorrectly set up, it will produce 30 percent acceptable parts. The firm has also learned from previous experience that 75 percent of the setups have been correctly made. Given the first part is good on the first machine, what is the revised probability that the setup has been correctly made?

The first step in answering the question for this first semiautomatic machine is to prepare a table that contains the given information (Table 3–6). An examination of Table 3–6 reveals that the sum of the probabilities for correct and incorrect setups is 1.0 since two types of setups constitute a mutually exclusive and collectively exhaustive list. However, the sum of figures .9 and .3 does not equal 1.0 since they represent conditional probabilities of getting one good part, given a correct setup or an incorrect setup, respectively. The last column is the joint probability of one good part and a correct setup occurring together, or $.75 \times .9 = .675$. Likewise, the joint probability of one good part and incorrect setup occurring together is .075 or $.25 \times .3$. The total of these joint probabilities, .75, is the marginal probability of getting one good part. To determine the revised probability that the setup has been correctly performed, the formula for conditional probability under statistical dependence is used as follows:

$$P(A|B) = \frac{P(AB)}{P(B)} \qquad \text{(Equation 3–3)}$$

$$P(\text{correct setup}|1 \text{ good part}) = \frac{P(\text{correct setup, 1 good part})}{P(1 \text{ good part})}$$

$$= \frac{.675}{.75} = .9$$

The probability of a correct setup, given one good part, is .9, which is compared to the previous experience of .75. Based upon this comparison, the operator should continue to operate the machine. However, due to the low value of each item, two more parts might then be run. Suppose the next two parts were also found to be good. What is the revised probability that the setup has been correctly made? The calculated values are found in Table 3–7.

Table 3–6
Probability Table Given One Good Part for the Event

Event	$P(B)$ Marginal $P(\text{event})$		$P(A\|B)$ Conditional $P(1 \text{ good part}\|\text{event})$		$P(AB)$ Joint $P(1 \text{ good part, event})$
Correct setup	.75	$\times$	.90	=	.675
Incorrect setup	.25	$\times$	.30	=	.075
	1.00				.750

Table 3–7
Probability Table Given Three Good Parts for the Event

Event	$P(B)$ Marginal $P(\text{event})$	$P(A\|B)$ Conditional $P(3 \text{ good parts}\|\text{event})$	$P(AB)$ Joint $P(3 \text{ good parts, event})$
Correct setup	.75	$.9 \times .9 \times .9 = .729$	.5468
Incorrect setup	.25	$.3 \times .3 \times .3 = .027$	.0068
	1.00		.5536

Now that the necessary probabilities have been computed in Table 3–7, we can again revert to Equation 3–3 for an answer. Thus the calculations are

$$P(\text{correct setup}|3\text{ good parts}) = \frac{P(\text{correct setup, 3 good parts})}{P(3\text{ good parts})}$$

$$= \frac{.5468}{.5536} = .988$$

The revised probability that the machine is correctly set up is 98.8 percent. In effect, we have revised our original probability (.75) of a correct setup to a much higher figure (.988) based upon three good parts produced initially.

Suppose in this problem, instead of getting one good part initially, we got one bad part. What is the probability that the machine is set up correctly? Data in Table 3–6 would have to be revised as shown in Table 3–8. The conditional probabilities for one bad part would be the complement of conditional probabilities for one good part. These are entered in Table 3–8 as well as new figures for the joint probabilities. Using the general formula $P(A|B) = P(AB)/P(B)$, the calculations are

$$P(\text{correct setup}|1\text{ bad part}) = \frac{P(\text{correct setup, 1 bad part})}{P(1\text{ bad part})}$$

$$= \frac{.075}{.250} = .3$$

Event	$P(B)$ Marginal $P(\text{event})$	$P(A|B)$ Conditional $P(1\text{ bad part}|\text{event})$	$P(AB)$ Joint $P(1\text{ bad part, event})$
Correct setup	.75	.1 (1.0 − .9)	.075
Incorrect setup	.25	.7 (1.0 − .3)	.175
	1.00		.250

Table 3–8
Probability Table Given One Bad Part for the Event

The probability that the machine is correctly set up is .3 versus .75. This revised probability indicates that the machine is not correctly set up and adjustment is deemed necessary.

In the illustration, it would have been possible to have combinations of acceptable and unacceptable parts. Suppose the first five parts were found to be: bad, good, bad, good, and good. Based upon these operating conditions, should the operator continue? The data appears in Table 3–9. The revised probability that the machine is correctly set up again utilizes the formula for conditional probability under dependence. The calculations are

$$P(\text{correct setup}|BP,\ GP,\ BP,\ GP,\ GP)$$

$$= \frac{P(\text{correct setup},\ BP,\ GP,\ BP,\ GP,\ GP)}{P(BP,\ GP,\ BP,\ GP,\ GP)}$$

$$= \frac{.0054675}{.0087750}$$

$$= .623 \text{ (do not continue manufacturing, but check machine setup)}$$

The origin of the preceding examples for revised probabilities goes back to Thomas Bayes in the eighteenth century. The basic formula for conditional probability under statistical dependence is attributed to him. Basically, his theorem states how probabilities, or opinions about how likely an event is to occur, ought to be appraised in the light of new information.

Table 3–9
Probability Table Given Three Good and Two Bad Parts for the Event

Event	$P(B)$ Marginal P(event)	$P(A\|B)$ Conditional $P(GP\|$ event)	$P(BP\|$ event)	$P(3GP,2BP\|$event)	$P(AB)$ Joint $P(3GP,2BP,$event)
Correct setup	.75	.9	.1	$.1 \times .9 \times .1 \times .9 \times .9$ $= .00729$	.0054675
Incorrect setup	.25	.3	.7	$.7 \times .3 \times .7 \times .3 \times .3$ $= .01323$	.0033075
	1.00				.0087750

Selection of Best Criterion

With this brief background, we are now in a position to discuss the selection of a best decision criterion that centers on the utilization of probability factors. Depending on how much we know about the states of nature or the business environment, we can refer to decision making under

1. certainty
2. risk
3. uncertainty

Even though the foregoing criteria have important distinctions in their decision-making processes, they all utilize a payoff matrix—outlined briefly in the opening section of the chapter. By way of review, the entry at the intersection of each row and column is the payoff or the measure of the utility of the specific outcome that occurs for a particular strategy and a given state of nature. Since the payoff matrix contains all of the possible outcomes in a business problem and takes into account the probability of them happening, the problem is to determine which strategy is best in light of the existing or possible states of nature. As will be seen below, the determination of the optimum strategy depends upon conditions existing in the business environment.

Decision Criterion under Certainty *Decision making under certainty* occurs when the decision maker knows the state of nature that will occur with complete certainty, that is, a probability of 1.0 can be assigned to a specific state of nature. In a payoff matrix, there is only one column that applies. The strategy (row) which has the largest payoff should be selected since there is no logical reason for doing otherwise. For example, consider the following payoff matrix, which has the profits shown from undertaking a certain project. The decision maker, knowing with certainty that N_2 state of nature (N_2 might be a period of no change in GNP while N_1 is a period of 2–5 percent increase in GNP and N_3 is a period of 2–5 percent decrease in GNP) will occur, will select strategy S_3 since it offers the highest return. The decision criterion for certainty is to select that strategy which has the largest payoff based upon a given state of nature.

		States of Nature		
		N_1	N_2	N_3
	S_1	$22,000	$15,000	$ 8,000
Strategies	S_2	25,000	17,000	10,000
	S_3	28,000	19,000	11,000

In some cases, the payoff matrix cannot be determined since the number of strategies is enormous. This can best be illustrated by an example in a manufacturing plant where there are several machines of differing designs and for different purposes. Each machine requires various amounts of total time for each customer contract. The resulting cost difference makes one machine suited for a particular contract. To set forth all possible rows and columns would not be economically feasible. However, this problem may be solvable by other operations research methods.

Decision Criterion under Risk   *Decision making under risk* refers to the condition in which there are a number of states of nature, and the decision maker knows the probability of occurrence for each of these states of nature. In certain business problems, the probabilities of the respective states of nature are known since they are based upon past experience or objective probabilities. An inventory decision problem for optimum stocking of machinery replacement parts is an example of decision making under risk since historical data on parts replaced can be compiled for a certain period of time. Another example is life insurance where insurance rates are based on life expectancy factors. A common example is a food processor which grows its own crops. Based on the firm's past experience with planting three types of crops in a particular area of the country, the following payoff matrix has resulted over the past years for the three states of nature (N_1 = good weather, N_2 = variable weather, and N_3 = bad weather):

		States of Nature		
		N_1	N_2	N_3
Probability		.25	.50	.25
	S_1	$40,000	$60,000	$10,000
Strategies	S_2	50,000	40,000	15,000
	S_3	60,000	20,000	12,000

This problem leads to the question: What strategy is best? The logical decision maker, as in the case for decision making under certainty, will select that strategy which has the largest payoff. The equations for computing expected payoffs for the strategies (ES) are as follows:

$$ES_1 = P_{11}p_1 + P_{12}p_2 + \cdots + P_{1j}p_j$$
$$ES_2 = P_{21}p_1 + P_{22}p_2 + \cdots + P_{2j}p_j$$
$$. \cdots \cdots \cdots \cdots$$
$$ES_i = P_{i1}p_1 + P_{i2}p_2 + \cdots + P_{ij}p_j$$

(Equation 3–5)

where $\quad p_1 + p_2 + p_3 + \cdots + p_j = 1$

In the first equation, the notation for payoff P_{11} stands for the first row and first column, P_{12} stands for the first row and second column, and so forth, while $p_1, p_2, \ldots, p_j$ are the associated probabilities. Using past or objective probabilities of .25, .50, and .25 for N_1, N_2, and N_3 states of nature, respectively, in Equation 3–5, we can calculate the expected payoff for each of the three strategies ($i = 1, 2, $ and 3):

$ES_1 = \$40,000 \ (.25) + \$60,000 \ (.50) + \$10,000 \ (.25) = \$42,500$

$ES_2 = \$50,000 \ (.25) + \$40,000 \ (.50) + \$15,000 \ (.25) = \$36,250$

$ES_3 = \$60,000 \ (.25) + \$20,000 \ (.50) + \$12,000 \ (.25) = \$28,000$

Since the expected payoff is greatest for the first strategy, that is the strategy to select.

Suppose the probabilities in our problem are different; say they are .50, .25, and .25, respectively, for the three states of nature. The new expected payoffs would then be:

$ES_1 = \$40,000 \ (.50) + \$60,000 \ (.25) + \$10,000 \ (.25) = \$37,500$

$ES_2 = \$50,000 \ (.50) + \$40,000 \ (.25) + \$15,000 \ (.25) = \$38,750$

$ES_3 = \$60,000 \ (.50) + \$20,000 \ (.25) + \$12,000 \ (.25) = \$38,000$

The largest expected payoff is the second strategy and not the first strategy. It should be obvious by now that different probabilities for the various states of nature, particularly a very high probability factor for N_1, would result in selecting the third strategy. Thus the critical factors are the objective probabilities assigned within the problem.

Decision Criteria under Uncertainty   The third type of decision criteria deals with *decision making under uncertainty*. This means that the probabilities of occurrence for the various states of nature are not known. Business problems of this type arise where there is no past experience for determining the probabilities of occurrence for the various states of nature. Problems associated with a new product, increasing plant capacity, and floating a new stock issue are examples of decision making under uncertainty. The approach to this type of decision making is different from decision making under certainty and risk.

The four basic approaches to decision making under uncertainty can best be illustrated by the following example. A firm is contemplating an introduction of a revolutionary new product with all new packaging to replace an existing product at a much higher price (S_1), or a moderate change in the ingredients of the existing product with new packaging at a small increase in price (S_2), or a small change in the ingredients of the existing product and only changing the packaging to include the word "new" with a negligible increase in price (S_3). The three possible states of nature are: expansion of the economy (N_1), no expansion or contraction of the economy (N_2), and contraction of the economy (N_3). The market research department has calculated the outcomes in terms of yearly net profits before federal income taxes to be as follows:

		States of Nature		
		N_1	N_2	N_3
	S_1	$500,000	$100,000	($ 50,000)
Strategies	S_2	300,000	250,000	0
	S_3	100,000	100,000	100,000

Based upon this data, there is one basic difference between this case and the previous example for decision making under risk. There are no probability factors for the various states of nature. Decision makers have no way to calculate an expected payoff for the three strategies. In theory, then, there is no best criterion for selecting a strategy for the firm. Instead of one criterion, there are several different criteria. Each of these criteria has its own rationale to justify its utilization. The choice of a specific criterion is determined by the size of the firm, the firm's objectives and policies, the feelings of decision makers, or some other logical basis. As one might suspect, varying conditions can affect the selection of different strategies. This is somewhat analogous to the situation with changing probability factors for decision making under risk. Four criteria for decision making under uncertainty are discussed below.

THE HURWICZ DECISION CRITERION The *Hurwicz decision criterion* is one of optimism based upon the idea that we do get some favorable or lucky breaks. Since nature can be good to us, decision makers should select that state of nature which will yield the highest payoff for the strategy selected. The procedure in our example is to look at the various payoffs for each strategy and select the highest amount for each strategy. The figures would be as follows:

Strategy	Largest Payoff
1	$500,000
2	300,000
3	100,000

Since the firm feels that nature will be favorable to it, the largest payoff of $500,000 would be chosen. This payoff is often referred to as a *maximax* (maximum maximum), which is the largest of the maxima for each strategy.

Hurwicz did not suggest that decision makers be completely optimistic in all cases. This would be like living in a utopian state, not the real world. To overcome this complete optimism, he introduced the concept *coefficient of optimism*. This means that decision makers take into consideration both the largest and smallest payoffs and weigh their importance according to some probability factors (values range from zero where the decision maker is completely pessimistic to one where the individual is completely optimistic). The probabilities assigned to largest and smallest payoffs (which must total 1.0) are based upon how the decision maker feels about optimistic conditions. If the firm in our example has a coefficient of optimism of .667, it would be satisfied to receive a maximum payoff which has a probability of occurrence of $\frac{2}{3}$ in a lottery and a minimum payoff which has a probability of occurrence of $\frac{1}{3}$. In order to select the highest payoff among all these strategies, it is necessary to make the following calculations:

Strategy	Maximum Payoff	Minimum Payoff	Expected Payoff
1	$500,000	($ 50,000)	$500,000(.667) + ($ 50,000)(.333) = $316,667
2	$300,000	$0	$300,000(.667) + $0 (.333) = $200,000
3	$100,000	$100,000	$100,000(.667) + $100,000 (.333) = $100,000

Using the Hurwicz criterion, the firm should select strategy 1—the introduction of a revolutionary new product with all new packaging to sell at a higher price.

If a small firm utilizes this approach, it is possible that nature would not be favorable to it, resulting in a loss of $50,000 if strategy 1 is selected. A small firm must take a second look before pursuing the Hurwicz criterion since such an approach could result in severe financial setbacks and possible bankruptcy for the firm. On the other hand, a medium firm and a large firm might consider this approach since a loss of this amount could be written off against its other profitable operations. However, full utilization of this approach for all projects by medium and large firms could result in substantial overall losses, as in the case of small firms. This approach, then, is readily applicable to business firms of all sizes, but it must be used with good judgment.

THE WALD DECISION CRITERION The *Wald decision criterion* is the opposite of that of Hurwicz. Wald suggested that decision makers should always be pessimistic or conservative, resulting in a *maximin* criterion. This maximin payoff approach means that decision makers should base their decisions on the constant malevolence of nature. Under these continually adverse circumstances, they should select the strategy that will give them as large a minimum payoff as possible. In our example, the worst state of nature would be a contraction or a recession in the economy (N_3). If strategy 1 or strategy 2 were selected, the payoff would be a loss of $50,000 or zero profits, respectively. If strategy 3 were selected, the payoff would be $100,000 for N_3 as well as for the other two states of nature. In essence, the worst state of nature that could happen would give a payoff of $100,000, shown as follows:

Strategy	Minimum Payoff
1	($ 50,000)
2	0
3	100,000

Wald's criterion dictates that strategy 3 be selected as the largest of the minimum payoffs—the maximum minimum (maximin).

Small businessmen, due to the very size of their business, must adopt this conservative approach. Since they have all or most of their assets invested in one location, they must be careful not to lose them. A safe and certain return allows the small business firm to survive while one wrong move (such as undertaking a project at the wrong time) can be detrimental to it. This approach must also be practiced by medium sized and large firms to a certain degree if they are to survive. A completely optimistic approach must be tempered by a conservative approach to provide a cushion for projects that may go bad due to unforeseen problems. Both the Hurwicz criterion and the Wald criterion are applicable to the business world.

THE SAVAGE DECISION CRITERION   A somewhat different criterion is that of Savage. He points out that decision makers might experience regret after the decision has been made and the state of nature has occurred. They may have wished they had selected a completely different strategy. The *Savage decision criterion* attempts to minimize the regret before actually selecting a particular strategy. Savage does this by initially constructing a *regret matrix*. Referring to N_1 state of nature, Savage suggests that the amount of regret can be measured by the difference between the payoff one actually may receive and the payoff one could have received. The highest payoff for the N_1 column is $500,000. If N_1 occurred and strategy 1 was selected, the decision maker would have experienced no regret. Hence a value of zero is assigned in the regret matrix. Suppose the decision maker had selected strategy 2 and N_1 had occurred; there would be a regret of $200,000 ($500,000 − $300,000). In a similar manner, if the individual had selected strategy 3 and expansion of the economy (N_1) had come about, a regret of $400,000 ($500,000 − $100,000) would have existed. The remaining values are calculated in a similar fashion for the following regret matrix:

		States of Nature		
		N_1	N_2	N_3
	S_1	0	$150,000	$150,000
Strategies	S_2	$200,000	0	100,000
	S_3	400,000	150,000	0

Decision makers can ensure against experiencing extreme regrets by selecting the strategy that has the minimum of such maximum, the *minimax*. To state it another way, decision makers will first select the highest regret value from each possible strategy based upon the above regret matrix and construct a new table which appears as follows:

Strategy	Maximum Regret
1	$150,000 (appear twice)
2	200,000
3	400,000

In order to assure a minimum of regret, decision makers would then select that strategy which would give them a minimum of regret, or strategy 1, based upon the preceding data. The minimax regret is $150,000, which is the maximum regret the decision makers need experience. It should be noted that they may experience less regret than this, but by using strategy 1, this is the most regret they should experience.

An individual (or firm) taking this approach to decision making under uncertainty might be called a bad loser. Depending upon the values contained in a payoff matrix, the strategy selected will tend toward the optimistic criterion or pessimistic criterion. In our example, this criterion of regret tended toward optimism. As far as small, medium, or large firms go, it has less application than the prior two criteria. Great use can be made by applying this criterion to individual projects in the long run so as to minimize regrets on the average for each project.

THE LAPLACE DECISION CRITERION   The preceding criteria have been of relatively recent origin compared to the *Laplace decision criterion,* which dates back over 2,500 years. This approach assumes that the various states of nature all have an equal chance of occurring, or every state of nature is as likely to occur as another. For each payoff, the expected amount is calculated and the strategy with the highest expected payoff is selected. Thus, this criterion is one of rationality and is based on the "principle of insufficient reason"—one state of nature is as likely to occur as another. The principle of insufficient reason, when used with probabilities, is connected with the name of Bayes. His famous hypothesis states that if we know of no reason for probabilities to be different, we should consider them to be equal.

One of the better-known arguments for the principle of insufficient reason was given during the Middle Ages. In the fourteenth century, Jean Buridan invented an imaginary ass, known today as Buridan's Ass, which was supposed to be placed in the middle (exactly) of two identical bales of hay. He stated that since the ass had no good reason to go to one bale versus the other bale, it would starve to death. Another interesting application of this principle is the toss of a fair coin. How do we know that a fair coin has a probability of .5 showing heads and a probability of .5 showing tails? One answer is the principle of insufficient reason. Since there is no logical reason for a coin coming up one way versus another, the probabilities must be equal, or .5, for there are only two possibilities. This principle is as applicable to business problems as any other principle if used properly within its limits.

Application of the rationality criterion is not complex. Since we have three separate states of nature in our illustration and each has an equal chance of occurring or .333 probability, the calculations for each strategy are given below:

Strategy	Expected Payoff
1	$\frac{1}{3} \times \$500,000 + \frac{1}{3} \times \$100,000 + \frac{1}{3} \times (\$50,000) = \$183,333$
2	$\frac{1}{3} \times \$300,000 + \frac{1}{3} \times \$250,000 + \frac{1}{3} \times \ \ \ \ \$0 \ \ \ \ = \$183,333$
3	$\frac{1}{3} \times \$100,000 + \frac{1}{3} \times \$100,000 + \frac{1}{3} \times \$100,000 = \$100,000$

The largest expected payoffs apply to strategies 1 and 2. Generally only one strategy will be selected since there is only one value that is the largest.

The question can again be asked: How can rationality be utilized by the various sized firms in the real world? In many cases, the states of nature may be fairly well known in advance. For example, a recession generally follows a war that has operated under a combination guns-and-butter economy. Periods of contraction or dips in economic activity are followed by periods of expansion. An extensive examination of the economy for our illustration may favor one of the three states of nature. In reality, each state of nature, for the most part, does not have an equal chance of occurring. An examination of historical data might disclose that the economy expands more than it contracts. If the states of the economy do not have an equal chance of happening, the various sized firms should recognize this factor in their selection of an appropriate strategy. The small firm is forced to take a conservative approach since economic conditions can change quickly. Again, such a firm must pursue a cautious strategy. The medium and larger firms can better utilize this approach if the economic outlook (or states of nature) could go any way. Thus the Laplace decision criterion is better applied to firms that are not small.

The foregoing examination of the four criteria under uncertainty indicates that every strategy was selected one or more times. Strategy 1 was selected for two of the decision criteria—Hurwicz and Savage. Strategy 3 was selected by the Wald criterion. Strategy 1 and 2, having the same value, were selected for the Laplace criterion. Obviously, there appears to be no best criterion. Therefore the choice of criterion must be left up to the decision makers, who are guided by their firm's size, company objectives and policies, their feelings, or some other rational criterion. Individuals or firms are free to select that criterion which reflects the value system to which they adhere. However, this chapter will assume a criterion of rationality unless otherwise stated.

No matter what criteria under uncertainty is employed, *sensitivity analysis* is an important element in reaching a final answer for decision theory problems. Decision makers, having made a preliminary test of estimates, make variations in these estimates. If the variations do not change the answer, they need go no further. On the other hand, if the answer is sensitive to these changes, they may redefine their preliminary estimates before finalizing their decision.

Decision Trees

Basically, decision trees are graphic representations of probability logic applied to decision alternatives. A *decision tree* is so named because it looks like a tree, although for convenience it is a horizontal one. The base of the tree is the beginning decision point. Its branches begin at the first chance event. Each chance event produces two or more possible effects, some of which lead to other chance events and subsequent decision points. Figures on which the tree's values are based come from careful analysis.

Suppose your firm wants to decide whether to continue regional distribution of a product or expand to national distribution. This represents a decision point for the firm. The chance events affecting the national distribution decision are whether there will be a large national demand for the product, an average national demand, or a limited national demand. If there is a large demand, you can expect to make $4 million, while $2 million and $0.5 million can be expected in profits for average and limited national demand, respectively. The probability factors are .5, .25, and .25, respectively. Three more payouts can be predicted if the firm continues with regional distribution. If regional demand is large, the firm can realize $2 million. On the one hand, if regional demand is average, an estimated profit of $1.8 million will result. On the other hand, if the regional demand is limited, an estimated profit of $1.5 million will result. This is shown in Figure 3–3. The addition of the expected profits (conditional profits × marginal probabilities) reveals that it would be better for the firm to distribute nationally.

Capital Investment Using a Decision Tree While the preceding problem illustrates the basic concept of what decision trees are, the following example will be more indicative of the real world problems confronting the manager. Consider a manufacturer of component parts in a growing industry. Presently, five automatic machines are operating at full capacity for one of its products. Sales demand has been rising for this product. The problem now confronting management is whether to install another automatic machine or to place its employees on overtime. After a careful analysis of market conditions, the consensus was there is a .667 probability that sales would increase 25 percent for this one product within a year. There is a .333 probability that sales might drop by as much as 5 percent.

Presently, the firm, due to its growth, has strained its working capital, resulting in a difficult cash position. It was decided to state all figures in terms of net cash flow to the firm. A careful analysis of the data showed that a 25 percent increase in sales would result in a $350,000 cash flow for the new equipment versus a $325,000 cash flow for overtime. Similar analysis showed a 5 percent sales drop would generate a $200,000 cash flow for new equipment versus $280,000 for the overtime alternative. It is obvious that if sales rose, the decision to go with new equipment would be the best. However, with a sales decrease, it would be more painful to the firm than the elimination of overtime. The solution to the problem is to construct a decision tree and multiply each event's values by the probability for that event (Figure 3–4). For the next year, the better choice is to utilize overtime.

Management need not stop here with a one-year basis but may look several years ahead. In this problem, we shall limit ourselves to two years. After management conferred on the prospects of sales, it concluded that even if sales dropped by 5 percent in the first year, the probability is .8 that sales would increase by 25 percent in the second year. There is also a probability factor of .2 that sales would increase by 12.5 percent in the second year even if the first year had a sales decrease. Management agreed that if sales rose by 25 percent in the first year, there was a 50-50 chance that they would increase further in the second year by either 25 or 12.5 percent. The data, including the calculated expected cash flows or payouts for the second year, are presented in Figure 3–5. It is apparent that a new automatic machine in the first year and overtime in the second year is the best solution on a two-year basis.

Figure 3–3
Decision tree for firm contemplating national distribution of products.

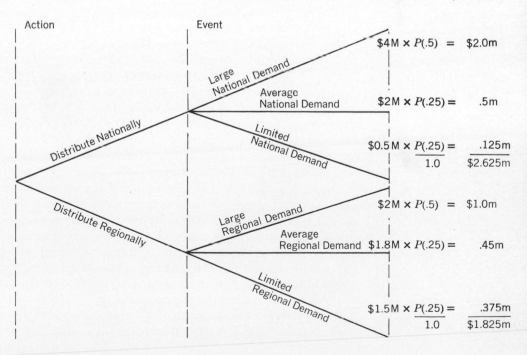

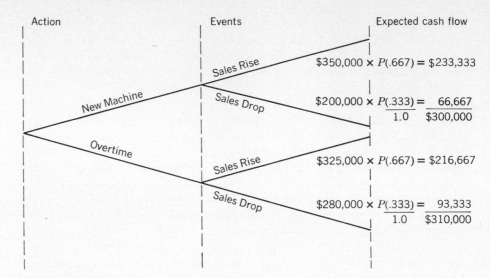

Figure 3–4
Decision tree for one year to determine the best path—new machine or overtime.

Decision Trees Versus Probability Trees Decision trees are basically an extension of probability trees. However, there are several basic differences, the first being that the decision tree utilizes the concept of "rollback" to solve a problem. This means starting at the right-hand terminus with the highest expected value of the tree and working back to the current or beginning decision point to determine the decision or decisions that should be made. Most decisions require trees with numerous branches and more than one decision point. It is the multiplicity of decision points that make the rollback process necessary.

A comparison of Figures 3–1 and 3–5 reveals that the former contains only events while the latter contains both actions and events. Another difference is that the probability tree is primarily concerned with calculating the correct probabilities, whereas the decision tree utilizes probability factors as a means in arriving at a final answer.

A most important feature of the decision tree, not found in probability trees, is that it takes time differences of future earnings into account. This can be substantial. At any stage of the decision tree, it may be necessary to weigh differences in immediate cost or revenue against differences in value at the next stage. Even though not stated, discounted cash flow was utilized in the capital investment and overtime problem since the time factor was two years.

There are several useful techniques for pruning bushy decision trees. One is the use of common sense, that is, eliminating possible actions which are not initially promising. For example, the firm can do nothing about prices or raise prices slightly, moderately, or greatly. The raising of prices to a great degree would probably encourage new competition, who would ultimately have a depressing effect upon this firm. Another method for thinning a tree would be to reduce the number of branches, say from six to two or three more promising ones. With careful analysis of the data, it is possible to trim a decision tree down to its principal branches before presenting it to management for review. In contrast, a probability tree cannot be pruned since it must contain all events in order to be collectively exhaustive.

Figure 3–5
Decision tree for two years to determine the best path—new machine(s) or overtime.

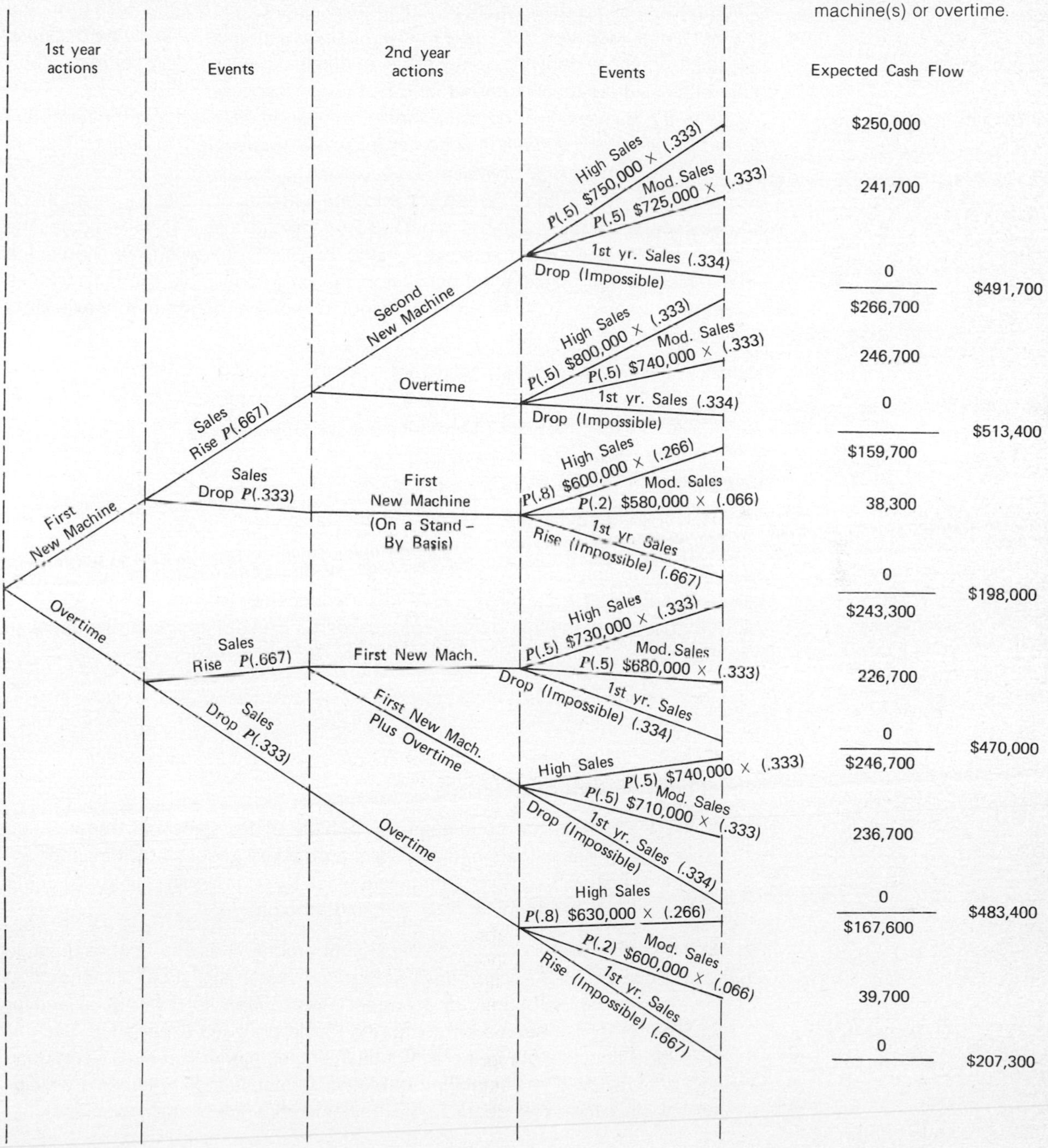

1st year actions	Events	2nd year actions	Events	Expected Cash Flow

High Sales P(.5) $750,000 × (.333) — $250,000

Mod. Sales P(.5) $725,000 × (.333) — 241,700

1st yr. Sales (.334) Drop (Impossible) — 0

Second New Machine — $266,700 / $491,700

High Sales P(.5) $800,000 × (.333) — 246,700

Mod. Sales P(.5) $740,000 × (.333)

Overtime

1st yr. Sales (.334) Drop (Impossible) — 0

$513,400

Sales Rise P(.667)

High Sales P(.8) $600,000 × (.266) — $159,700

Sales Drop P(.333)

First New Machine (On a Stand-By Basis)

Mod. Sales P(.2) $580,000 × (.066) — 38,300

1st yr. Sales Rise (Impossible) (.667) — 0

$198,000

First New Machine

$243,300

Overtime

High Sales P(.5) $730,000 × (.333)

Mod. Sales P(.5) $680,000 × (.333) — 226,700

First New Mach.

1st yr. Sales Drop (Impossible) (.334) — 0

$470,000

Sales Rise P(.667)

First New Mach. Plus Overtime

High Sales P(.5) $740,000 × (.333) — $246,700

Mod. Sales P(.5) $710,000 × (.333) — 236,700

1st yr. Sales Drop (Impossible) (.334) — 0

$483,400

Sales Drop P(.333)

Overtime

High Sales P(.8) $630,000 × (.266) — $167,600

Mod. Sales P(.2) $600,000 × (.066) — 39,700

1st yr. Sales Rise (Impossible) (.667) — 0

$207,300

119

Chapter Summary

The use of probability theory in conjunction with other quantitative methods will be evident throughout the text. Many applications of probability have been reported, including those for pricing, new product introductions, and market research. In a similar manner, decision trees have made substantial inroads in resolving business problems. For those decision theory applications that are large and complex, computer processing is recommended for accuracy and speed.

Within the framework of decision theory, it must be stressed that the terms *expected payoff, profit,* or *cash flow* do not refer to a single event or project. The expected value is an average of what would happen if such occurrences were repeated over and over again. The expected value for the outcome of a biased die might be 3.5. We know that it is impossible to get a 3.5 on a single toss. The 3.5 indicates the average value that is expected to occur in the long run. Thus, within the chapter the selection of the highest expected payoff from the various possible alternatives does not refer to a one-time basis, but to a condition over the long term to maximize a firm's profits.

Questions

1. How do probability formulas differ under statistical independence and dependence?
2. What important contribution did Bayes make to probability theory?
3. Explain and evaluate the four criteria under uncertainty.
4. What are the essential differences between a probability tree and a decision tree?

Model Formulation Exercises

1. Using the formula for conditional probability under statistical dependence (Equation 3–3) and the formula for joint probability under statistical independence (Equation 3–2), formulate the equation for conditional probability under statistical independence such that $P(A/B)$ equals $P(A)$.

2. In the section of the chapter on revision of probabilities, the final calculation (per Equation 3–3 — conditional probability under statistical dependence) determines the probability of a correct setup, given so many good and/or bad parts. The value is then compared to the previous experience, namely, 0.75 for a decision of whether to continue or stop manufacturing. Based upon this brief review of revision of probabilities, formulate a complementary method to obtain the same decision of whether to continue or stop manufacturing.

3. In formulating a payoff matrix where the payoffs for specific strategies and states of nature are zero or minus, should an individual or firm cross them out? Give reasons for supporting your point of view.

4. Within the chapter, the selection of the best criterion dealt with decision making under (1) certainty, (2) risk, and (3) uncertainty. For a more complete presentation of this subject, what other category could have been added that would result in expanding the field of decision theory?

5. Examine the last decision tree presented in the chapter (Figure 3–5) to determine whether or not probabilities have been employed in calculating expected outcomes. If they have been included, how were the probabilities used? If they were not included, what recommendation(s) would you make to include them?

Mathematical Exercises

1. Mr. Johnson has total cash of $100,000 for investing in various projects and cannot raise any additional capital during this month or next month. He is offered the opportunity of participating immediately in the first of the two separate projects A and B. Project A is equally likely to result in a profit of $12,000 or a loss of $5,000 on an investment of $50,000. Assuming that the principal plus the profit or minus the loss is available one month hence, project B is equally likely to result in a profit of $18,000 or a loss of $12,000 on an investment of $48,000. Ignore the computations for return on excess cash funds for the entire problem. It should be remembered that Mr. Johnson is offered the opportunity of investing in projects of this kind periodically. What is the greatest expected profit for Mr. Johnson?

   For the same information as above, the total cash available is now $50,000. What should Mr. Johnson do under this changed condition? Contrast the type of probability used in determining your answer with that used to find your original answer.

2. The Jamson Company has total excess cash funds of $60,000 for investing during this month and next month in various projects, according to the cash flow statement prepared by the accounting department. The firm has been offered the following investment opportunities. It can participate immediately (start of this month) in a project by investing $60,000, which is equally likely to result in a net profit of $20,000 or a loss of $10,000 within this month. In effect, the company will have its principal along with a profit or loss back by the end of this month. At the same time, the firm is informed that one month hence, it will be given the opportunity of investing $55,000 in another investment which is equally likely to result in a net profit of $15,000 or a net loss of $5,000. The assumption in this problem is that the Jamson Company examines its

cash position every two months to determine the feasibility of investing excess cash.

(a) What should the firm do regarding the four alternatives?

(b) What type of probability is found in the answer to (a)?

Suppose the firm is informed one month hence that the second investment will require only $45,000 rather than the $55,000 as originally stated. Answer (a) and (b) above.

3. The Hartwood Manufacturing Company has $100,000 available to invest in machinery and equipment. If business conditions continue as they are, the investment will return 15 percent, but if there is a mild recession, it will return only 3 percent. The money can also be invested in certificates of deposit for a certain return of 5 percent. What probability must the firm assign to a recession to make the two investments have the same expected monetary value?

4. The Cincinnati Chemical Company has found from experience that 20 percent of its setups for combining chemicals have been unacceptable. It has also found that the chemical process will produce 95 percent acceptable chemical batches if it is correctly set up and 10 percent acceptable chemical batches will be produced if errors have been made in the setup. The setup is made for combining chemicals and the first four batches are tested for acceptability. The batches were found to be acceptable, acceptable, unacceptable, and acceptable.

(a) Should the line personnel continue manufacturing?

(b) Suppose the batches were found to be unacceptable, acceptable, unacceptable, and unacceptable. Should manufacturing continue?

5. The Gulf Machinery Co. has a group of six semiautomatic machines used in the production of part No. 1250. The firm has decided to develop a table that can be used by its machine operators to determine the advisability of rechecking the setup. It has compiled from past experience the following data. The probability that a machine is correctly set up is .9; if correctly set up, the probability of a good part is .95. On the other hand, if the machine is not correctly set up, the probability of a good part is .2.

(a) Develop a table that can be read by the machine operators for testing four parts.

(b) What type of probabilities are used in developing this table?

6. The Ranco Manufacturing Company has sufficient capital on hand to invest in new machinery and equipment that can be used in the production of one new product only. Since the firm has three proposed products—X, Y, and Z—under consideration, only one of these products can be placed into production. In view of the capital constraint, the firm's marketing managers have been asked to estimate sales and their probability of occurrence. They are as follows:

Proposed Product	Estimated Annual Sales	Probability of Occurrence
X	$600,000	.6
	400,000	.3
	200,000	.1
Y	$600,000	.4
	300,000	.4
	200,000	.2
Z	$700,000	.1
	500,000	.3
	400,000	.6

Estimated fixed and variable costs for these products were obtained from the engineering and cost accounting departments. For all practical purposes, their costs are identical. Thus, the expected sales become the focal point in deciding which product should be placed into production.

Based on the foregoing data, what product can be expected to produce the highest expected profits for the firm? Assume in the problem that the firm utilizes this approach periodically in determining which new products they should market.

7. The Ritter Machine Company can purchase a certain small casting from three different vendors. The casting is an integral part of the firm's best selling prod uct. Currently, the prices being paid for the rough castings are:

Vendor	Price/Unit
A	$.50
B	.55
C	.60

Total machining costs by the firm's lathe department is $0.90 per casting. Based on buying in 1,000 lots from three vendors over the last several months, the firm has compiled scrappage probability data (on the 1,000 lots) which is:

Vendor	Scrappage Probability
A	.15
B	.07
C	.05

These values are considered representative of future scrappage probabilities. Given the foregoing data, what vendor should be selected to supply the rough castings in order to minimize the firm's future expected costs?

8. The controller of the Regis Corporation has asked you to determine the expected sales level based on the marketing department's projections for the coming year. The firm is typified by a small number of relatively large sales projects versus a product line reflecting many small dollar sales. The following data represents the sales projects as submitted to the controller.

Sales Project	Amount (000)
A	$ 362
B	447
C	443
D	540
E	319
F	180
G	1,343
	$3,634 Total Sales Forecast

The following additional data was supplied by the marketing department.

Project	Probability of Project Being Let During Coming Fiscal Year	Probability of Regis Being Awarded the Project If Let
A	.7	.5
B	.9	.6
C	.8	.8
D	.6	.7
E	.9	.7
F	1.0	1.0
G	1.0	1.0

(a) What sales level can the Regis Corporation expect for the coming fiscal year?

(b) What type of probability is illustrated in the problem?

9. The New Products Group of the Henderson Manufacturing Company is about to present the profit feasibility of a new product to management. The firm has experienced problems in determining long-range profitability and the manager of this group knows this will be one of the main interests of management in the presentation. Sales estimates that three separate volumes can be maintained depending on the amount of discount allowed. The following table has been developed by marketing to show sales volumes at each price level as well as the probability of selling these units.

Selling Price	Units	Prob.	Units	Prob.	Units	Prob.
$9	100,000	1.0	150,000	.75	200,000	.50
8	–	–	50,000	.25	100,000	.25
7	–	–	–	–	100,000	.25
Cumulative Probability		1.0		1.00		1.00
Volume Plans	100,000		200,000		400,000	

Presently, material costs are $5 per unit. However, engineering personnel are working on future modifications to reduce costs which will be incorporated in the presentation. Reduction in material costs are expected to be $0.25 per unit. Variable manufacturing costs, in addition to materials, are $1.75 per unit. Yearly fixed costs, primarily equipment investment needed at the three levels, are $125,000, $150,000, and $240,000 respectively. Marketing, general, and administrative costs are estimated to be $1.50 per unit at the 100,000 unit level, $1.25 per unit at the 200,000 unit level, and $1 per unit at the 400,000 unit level.

(a) On a profit per unit basis, what sales volume should the manager recommend?

(b) Does this volume provide the highest profits?

10. The Texas Company has received a request to bid on 250,000 special transistors. It should be noted that the firm receives many bids of this nature throughout the year for its various products — standard and special. The firm estimates the following machinery is necessary to take on this order:

Manufacturing Method	Total Cost of Machinery	Variable Cost per Unit
A	$100,000	$1.55
B	175,000	1.40
C	200,000	1.25

Since this may be the first and last contract of this kind, the entire amount of machinery costs should be allocated to this bid. Manufacturers of this equipment have agreed to accept cancellation of the machinery if the Texas Company fails to get the contract since all machinery will be shipped from their present stock. Great importance is placed on prices, which are as follows:

Price/Unit	Probability of Getting Contract
Bid $2.50	$\frac{1}{3}$
Bid $2.30	$\frac{2}{3}$
Bid $2.20	$\frac{3}{4}$

Of the several alternatives available to the Texas Company, what price should the firm quote and what method of manufacture should be used? This is an example of what type of probability?

11. The North America Corporation is submitting a proposal to the U.S. Navy for the development of an advanced carrier-based reconnaissance aircraft. It has asked three electronic manufacturers to submit bids on two phases of development (described by specification) for a new airborne navigational computer. The bids are as follows:

	Phase I	Phase II
DCA	$1,100,000	$1,000,000
Rollins	1,250,000	950,000
Central Electric	1,200,000	1,000,000

Since the Navy is very sensitive to cost overruns, it has asked that the proposed price include probable cost overruns, if any. The following information was supplied regarding cost overruns:

	Phase I		Phase II	
	Amount of Overrun	Probability of Overrun	Amount of Overrun	Probability of Overrun
DCA	$150,000	.15	$150,000	.5
	85,000	.35	100,000	.4
	0	.50	0	.1
Rollins	$100,000	.25	$200,000	.25
	50,000	.25	100,000	.25
	25,000	.25	50,000	.25
	0	.25	0	.25
Central Electric	$100,000	.25	$200,000	.333
	50,000	.50	100,000	.333
	0	.25	0	.333

Given the foregoing data, which proposal should be accepted for lowest development cost? Assume in the problem that the North America Corporation conducts bidding of large contracts on this basis regularly.

Bibliography

M. H. Agee, R. E. Taylor, and P. E. Torgersen, *Quantitative Analysis for Managerial Decisions*, Englewood Cliffs, N.J.: Prentice-Hall, 1976.

H. Bierman, C. P. Bonini, and W. H. Hausman, *Quantitative Analysis for Business Decisions*, Homewood, Ill.: Richard D. Irwin, 1973.

G. J. Brabb, *Introduction to Quantitative Management,* New York: Holt, Rinehart and Winston, 1968.

A. L. Edwards, *Probability and Statistics,* New York: Holt, Rinehart and Winston, 1971.

G. Hadley, *Introduction to Probability and Statistical Decision Theory,* San Francisco: Holden-Day, 1967.

F. S. Hillier and G. J. Lieberman, *Operations Research,* San Francisco: Holden-Day, 1974.

H. J. Larson, *Introduction to Probability Theory and Statistical Inference,* New York: John Wiley & Sons, 1969.

J. J. Martin, *Bayesian Decision Problems and Markov Chains,* New York: John Wiley & Sons, 1967.

C. M. Paik, *Quantitative Methods for Managerial Decisions,* New York: McGraw-Hill Book Company, 1973.

W. S. Peters and G. W. Summers, *Statistical Analysis for Business Decisions,* Englewood Cliffs, N.J.: Prentice-Hall, 1968.

H. Raiffa, *Decision Analysis,* Reading, Mass.: Addison-Wesley, 1968.

S. Ross, *Introduction to Probability Models,* New York: Academic Press, 1972.

R. Schlaifer, *Analysis of Decisions Under Uncertainty,* New York: McGraw-Hill Book Company, 1969.

C. H. Springer, R. E. Herlihy, R. T. Mall, and R. I. Beggs, *Probabilistic Models,* Homewood, Ill.: Richard D. Irwin, 1968.

M. K. Starr and I. Stein, *The Practice of Management Science,* Englewood Cliffs, N.J.: Prentice-Hall, 1976.

R. L. Winkler, *Introduction to Bayesian Inference and Decisions,* New York: Holt, Rinehart and Winston, 1972.

Chapter 4

Decision Making
with a Variable Demand

Chapter Objectives
- [ ] To develop appropriate decision methods for future demand that is representative of past demand.
- [ ] To formulate different methods for decision making where there are discrete and random distributions of values.
- [ ] To develop a method for decision making where there are continuous and random distributions of values.

Chapter Outline

This chapter presents two basic approaches for determining an optimum number of products to stock based upon a future variable demand. The first part will explore a problem with a limited demand. Expected profit and loss tables will be developed. Marginal analysis will also be used to solve the proper stocking of inventory for a discrete distribution. The last part of the chapter will discuss a continuous probability distribution. Appropriate quantitative methods, then, will be discussed for the proper stocking of inventory where past variable demand is considered representative of future demand. This is fundamentally true of products that are purchased frequently.

Requirements for
Decision Making With a Variable Demand

Management cannot know in advance what the exact demand for its products will be nor can it know precisely what its costs and profits will be, based upon a variable demand. Under these circumstances, management must develop the best forecasts for sales and costs, thereby making a decision based on these estimates. However, the situation is not as hopeless as it might seem, particularly in the area of potential demand, if probability is utilized as discussed in the preceding chapter.

For the two basic approaches of decision making with a variable demand which will be presented in this chapter, there are several important requirements concerning future potential demand. First, potential demand must be determinable based upon past or present sales data. Second, this demand must be compatible with the future, that is, the data can be modified to be representative of future sales patterns. In this manner, probabilities can be assigned to future sales demand. Third, the sales, cost, and salvage values (if any) of future demand must be determinable with a high degree of accuracy. The final solution is highly contingent upon the correctness of all input variables. Thus, for optimum results, these requirements must be followed when treating decision making with a variable demand.

Discrete Probability Distribution

To help understand the subject matter in this section, consider a problem dealing with a discrete probability distribution that has a future variable demand. A small doughnut shop buys its doughnuts from a local bakery for $0.50 per dozen delivered to the shop and sells them for $0.80 per dozen. Doughnuts left at the end of the day are sold at $0.40 per dozen. Demand for doughnuts is relatively constant over time, but varies from day to day. The results of recent daily demand for the small shop are given below. The problem now facing the doughnut shop is: What is the optimum quantity to stock in order to maximize expected profits? It should be noted that the shop buys only on a dozen basis from the bakery.

No. Days Sold	Daily Demand (dozens)	Relative Frequency (probability)
5	40	.05
10	41	.10
10	42	.10
20	43	.20
20	44	.20
15	45	.15
15	46	.15
5	47	.05
100 days		1.00

An inspection of the data used in compiling demand indicates that a random variable is present. A *random variable* can be defined as a value that changes, occurrence (or event) after occurrence (or event), in no predictable sequence. In the problem, this means we have no definite way of predicting tomorrow's sales of doughnuts. However, we do know the value of the random variable ranges from 40 dozens to 47 dozens daily. Not only is the data a random distribution of past sales with an increment of one unit, but also the information is a *discrete distribution* since the sales volume can take on only a limited number of values. Thus, the distribution for the doughnut shop is discrete and random; there are only eight possible values in the example for sales volume and there is no way of knowing which one quantity customers will buy on a certain day. For this type of problem, four methods are given below to solve for an optimum quantity and maximum expected profits.

Method 1—Conditional Profits

The term *conditional profit* means the amount that will result based upon a certain combination of supply and demand quantities. To state it another way, the firm can anticipate profits based upon the condition of selling so many units and stocking so many units. One way of attacking the doughnut sales problem is to construct a conditional profits table which shows the results of all combinations of possible sales and inventories. Profits can be either positive or negative and are conditioned upon a combination of a specific stocking action and a specific sales demand. Table 4–1 is a conditional profits table for the problem under study.

Table 4–1
Conditional Profits Table

Possible Sales Demand (dozens)	Possible Inventory Action (dozens)							
	40	41	42	43	44	45	46	47
40	$12.00	$11.90	$11.80	$11.70	$11.60	$11.50	$11.40	$11.30
41	12.00	12.30	12.20	12.10	12.00	11.90	11.80	11.70
42	12.00	12.30	12.60	12.50	12.40	12.30	12.20	12.10
43	12.00	12.30	12.60	12.90	12.80	12.70	12.60	12.50
44	12.00	12.30	12.60	12.90	13.20	13.10	13.00	12.90
45	12.00	12.30	12.60	12.90	13.20	13.50	13.40	13.30
46	12.00	12.30	12.60	12.90	13.20	13.50	13.80	13.70
47	12.00	12.30	12.60	12.90	13.20	13.50	13.80	14.10

An examination of the first column in Table 4–1 reveals that the stocking of 40 dozens each day will always result in a profit of $12 or 40 dozens stocked times $0.30 per dozen ($0.80 selling price per dozen minus $0.50 cost per dozen). Even though customers might want 41 through 47 dozens on different days, the doughnut shop can sell only those items it has in stock, 40 dozens. Moving over to the next column, the stocking of 41 dozens and selling of 41 dozens results in a profit of $12.30 ($0.30 times 41 dozens). The profits below this equal combination of stocking and demand is also $12.30. The same rationale applies: you can sell only those items in stock. The figures to the left of the diagonal in Table 4–1 are computed in like manner and the same reasoning applies.

Moving to the right of the diagonal in Table 4–1, consideration must now be given to the salvage value of the unsold items. Conditional profit for stocking 41 units when the demand is 40 units can be computed in two ways:

Profit on the 40 dozens (40 × $0.30 per dozen)	$12.00	Profit on the 40 dozens (40 × $0.30 per dozen)	$12.00
Less cost of the 1 dozen unsold	(0.50)	Less cost on 1 dozen unsold ($0.50 cost less $0.40 salvage value)	(0.10)
	$11.50		
Plus salvage value of 1 dozen unsold	0.40		
Conditional Profit	$11.90	Conditional Profit	$11.90

Referring to the last column where 47 dozens are stocked, the calculation for a sales demand of 41 dozens is as follows:

Profit on the 41 dozens
   (41 × $0.30 per dozen) $12.30
Less: Loss on 6 dozens
   unsold ($0.10 × 6)   (0.60)
Conditional Profit $11.70

The remaining calculations to the right of the diagonal in Table 4–1 are made in a similar fashion.

No conditional profit table can tell management how many items to stock each and every day in order to have the highest possible profits. It only shows what kind of profit or loss is available to the firm if a certain number of items are stocked and a specific number of items are sold. With an uncertain demand, as in many of the situations in the real world, the manager must decide the number of items to stock before demand is known. Only under conditions of certainty, which rarely exist in inventory, does the conditional profit table show the largest profit for stocking a certain number of units.

Optimum Quantity and Expected Profits with a Variable Demand Having determined the conditional profits table (Table 4–1) for the doughnut shop problem, the next step is to determine the optimum number of dozens to buy daily. This can be done by assigning probabilities to the possible outcomes or conditional profits. These probability factors and conditional profits are brought together to compute the expected monetary profit for any possible inventory action. The expected monetary profit is defined as the highest profit the firm can expect to make over a long period of time, assuming the probabilities of demand remain the same for specific inventory quantities. In Table 4–2, the expected profits from stocking 43 and 45 dozens are calculated.

Table 4–2
Expected Profits from
Stocking 43 and 45
Dozens

Sales Demand (dozens)	Conditional Profit— Stock 43 dozens	Prob.	Expected Profit 43 doz.	Sales Demand (dozens)	Conditional Profit— Stock 45 dozens	Prob.	Expected Profit 45 doz.
40	$11.70 ×	.05 =	$ 0.585	40	$11.50 ×	.05 =	$ 0.575
41	12.10 ×	.10 =	1.210	41	11.90 ×	.10 =	1.190
42	12.50 ×	.10 =	1.250	42	12.30 ×	.10 =	1.230
43	12.90 ×	.20 =	2.580	43	12.70 ×	.20 =	2.540
44	12.90 ×	.20 =	2.580	44	13.10 ×	.20 =	2.620
45	12.90 ×	.15 =	1.935	45	13.50 ×	.15 =	2.025
46	12.90 ×	.15 =	1.935	46	13.50 ×	.15 =	2.025
47	12.90 ×	.05 =	0.645	47	13.50 ×	.05 =	0.675
		1.00	$12.720			1.00	$12.880

Applications—Decision Making With a Variable Demand

- **Manufacturing of seasonal products**—Assists the manufacturer in determining the number of production runs for a firm's seasonal products.
- **Stocking of perishable items**—Determines the quantity of perishable items to stock on a periodic basis to optimize profits.
- **Processing of table products**—Optimizes for the producer of home-consumption products the quantity to process on a periodic basis.
- **Stocking of nonperishable items**—Analyzes the quantity of nonperishable items to stock in order to maximize profits.
- **Manufacturing of fashion goods**—Assists the firm in specifying the quantity of fashion goods to be produced to maximize expected profits.
- **Determining potential of new products**—Evaluates the potential of new products that are subject to an uncertain demand.
- **Determining likelihood of new markets**—Assists marketing management in determining the profitability of entering new markets.

A summary of all possible inventory stockings is given in Table 4–3. The optimum stock action is 45 dozens since it results in the greatest expected profit. This action will result in the highest daily profits and maximum total profits over a period of time. It is important to remember that we have not removed variable demand from the problem, but have called upon past experience to determine the best possible inventory action. Also, we still do not know exactly how many dozens will be requested on any specific day. In fact, we are not sure of making exactly $12.88 from the stocking of 45 dozens the day after this study has been completed; but we will average profits of that amount over time if past sales demand is representative of future demand.

Possible Inventory Quantities (dozens)	Expected Profit
40	$12.00
41	12.28
42	12.52
43	12.72
44	12.84
45	12.88
46	12.86
47	12.78

Table 4–3
Expected Profits for All
Possible Inventory
Quantities

Method 2 — Conditional Losses

An alternative method to any problem that makes use of a conditional profits table is a *conditional losses* table, shown in Table 4–4. Notice that no profits or losses exist on the diagonal since these levels represent the best possible conditional profits available to the firm. For example, if 44 dozens are stocked and demanded, supply equals demand for the greatest conditional profits with no losses occurring. The figures to the left of the diagonal represent *opportunity* losses or those sales lost by being out of inventory when demand is present. On the other hand, the figure to the right of the diagonal represent *obsolescence* losses. These losses are caused by having too much inventory.

Table 4–4
Conditional Losses Table

Possible Sales Demand (dozens)	Possible Inventory Action (dozens)							
	40	41	42	43	44	45	46	47
40	$0.00	$0.10	$0.20	$0.30	$0.40	$0.50	$0.60	$0.70
41	0.30	0.00	0.10	0.20	0.30	0.40	0.50	0.60
42	0.60	0.30	0.00	0.10	0.20	0.30	0.40	0.50
43	0.90	0.60	0.30	0.00	0.10	0.20	0.30	0.40
44	1.20	0.90	0.60	0.30	0.00	0.10	0.20	0.30
45	1.50	1.20	0.90	0.60	0.30	0.00	0.10	0.20
46	1.80	1.50	1.20	0.90	0.60	0.30	0.00	0.10
47	2.10	1.80	1.50	1.20	0.90	0.60	0.30	0.00

As stated above, the values to the left of the zeros are opportunity losses resulting from demands that cannot be met. If only 40 dozens are stocked while 41 dozens are demanded by customers, there is a loss of $0.30 ($0.80 selling price less $0.50 cost), as shown in the first column to the left. The subsequent figures below increase by an increment of $0.30 since the possible demand which cannot be met by the available supply of 40 dozens increases by one dozen each time. The obsolescence losses to the right of the zeros in Table 4–4 are calculated in a slightly different manner. The cost per dozen, $0.50, is reduced by the salvage value of $0.40 for a net obsolescence loss of $0.10 per dozen. The stocking of 41 dozens when demand is only 40 dozens results in an obsolescence loss of $0.10 on the 41st dozen.

The next step in the conditional loss method is to assign probabilities to the demand factors, ranging from 40 to 47 dozens. By applying the probabilities to the conditional losses, the expected losses can then be calculated. This is shown in Table 4–5 for stocking 43 and 45 dozens. The remaining expected losses are determined for the other six possible inventory actions, as shown in Table 4–6.

Again, the stocking of 45 dozens produces the lowest expected loss just as it produced the highest expected profit. The optimum stock level, then, is the one which minimizes the expected losses. This is obvious upon inspection of Table 4–7. Notice that all expected gains and losses total the same amount. The rationale is that the same conditional profit and loss tables plus assigned probabilities are used throughout the problem.

Sales Demand (dozens)	Condi-tional Loss— Stock 43 dozens	Prob.	Expected Loss 43 doz.	Sales Demand (dozens)	Condi-tional Loss— Stock 45 dozens	Prob.	Expected Loss 45 doz.
40	$0.30 ×	.05 =	$0.015	40	$0.50 ×	.05 =	$0.025
41	0.20 ×	.10 =	0.020	41	0.40 ×	.10 =	0.040
42	0.10 ×	.10 =	0.010	42	0.30 ×	.10 =	0.030
43	0.00 ×	.20 =	0.000	43	0.20 ×	.20 =	0.040
44	0.30 ×	.20 =	0.060	44	0.10 ×	.20 =	0.020
45	0.60 ×	.15 =	0.090	45	0.00 ×	.15 =	0.000
46	0.90 ×	.15 =	0.135	46	0.30 ×	.15 =	0.045
47	1.20 ×	.05 =	0.060	47	0.60 ×	.05 =	0.030
		1.00	$0.390			1.00	$0.230

Table 4–5
Expected Losses from Stocking 43 and 45 Dozens

Possible Inventory Quantities (dozens)	Expected Losses
40	$1.11
41	0.83
42	0.59
43	0.39
44	0.27
45	0.23
46	0.25
47	0.33

Table 4–6
Expected Losses for All Possible Inventory Quantities

Table 4–7
Expected Profits and Losses with a Variable Demand

	Possible Inventory Action (dozens)							
	40	**41**	**42**	**43**	**44**	**45**	**46**	**47**
Expected profits (per Table 4–3)	$12.00	$12.28	$12.52	$12.72	$12.84	$12.88	$12.86	$12.78
Expected losses (per Table 4–6)	1.11	0.83	0.59	0.39	0.27	0.23	0.25	0.33
Totals	$13.11	$13.11	$13.11	$13.11	$13.11	$13.11	$13.11	$13.11

Optimum Quantity and Expected Profits with Perfect Information Completely reliable information about the future, referred to as perfect information, removes all uncertainty from the problem. This condition allows demand to vary from day to day, yet the individual knows in advance how many units are going to be bought by customers. In essence, he has the proper level of stock on hand at all times. Under these idealistic conditions, the conditional profits on the diagonal in Table 4–1, multiplied by their respective probabilities, produce the greatest expected profits shown in Table 4–8. The maximum expected profit for the illustrative problem is $13.11. If the corresponding conditional loss table is used, all zeros on the diagonal times their respective probabilities are zero. This makes sense because the total $13.11 agrees with the totals for the various levels of inventory in Table 4–7.

Assuming that the manager of the doughnut shop could obtain perfect information regarding the future, what would the value of such data be? It would be necessary to compare the cost of obtaining this data with the additional profits realized as a result of perfect information. In the illustration, the maximum average daily profit is $13.11 with perfect information, whereas the best expected daily profit with a variable demand is $12.88. The difference of $0.23 (Table 4–7) is the highest amount the manager would be willing to pay per day for a perfect forecast of daily demand. This difference is referred to as the *EVPI—expected value of perfect information*. To pay more than $0.23 for the perfect forecast would lower the daily expected profits.

Table 4–8
Expected Profit under Certainty

Sales Demand (dozens)	Conditional Profit	Probability	Expected Profit
40	$12.00	.05	$ 0.600
41	12.30	.10	1.230
42	12.60	.10	1.260
43	12.90	.20	2.580
44	13.20	.20	2.640
45	13.50	.15	2.025
46	13.80	.15	2.070
47	14.10	.05	0.705
		1.00	$13.110

Method 3—Marginal Analysis

In the preceding illustrative problem, the use of conditional and expected profits and losses tables could have become unwieldy if the distribution of demand had ranged over a large number of values rather than just 40 through 47 dozens. The number of calculations would have been too numerous with a high chance of error. Besides, the wide range of demand could represent but one of many hundreds and thousands of products which would require similar computations. The marginal approach avoids the problems of excessive calculations.

The starting point for *marginal analysis* is to remember that the sum of the probabilities of two events must be 1.0; that is, the probability of selling an additional unit (last unit added) is a specific figure (say .7) and the probability of not selling an additional unit (last unit added) is the complement of this figure (say .3) If we let p be the probability of selling one additional item, the probability of not selling it is $1 - p$. If the last unit added can be sold, an increase in the conditional profit can be made with a resulting increase in expected profits. This is called *marginal profit, MP*. In the problem, the marginal profit from the sale of an additional unit is $0.80 (selling price) minus $0.50 (cost) or $0.30 per dozen. The construction of the conditional profits table (Table 4–1) made use of this marginal approach.

The effect of stocking an additional unit and not selling it, on the other hand, reduces conditional profits, as was demonstrated in Table 4–1. The amount of reduction in profits from stocking an item that is not sold is referred to as *marginal loss, ML*. The calculation for *ML* is the cost of the unsold unit less the salvage value if applicable. In the problem, the cost of $0.50 is reduced by a salvage value of $0.40 for a net marginal loss of $0.10. It should be noted that salvage value is generally associated with products that have a short shelf life, such as perishable goods and fashion goods. However, salvage value for items that have a long shelf life, say five years and more, is generally ignored. The rationale is that the present value of their salvage value is small or nil. Thus, for all practical purposes, their salvage value is ignored in the *ML* calculation.

The basic rule to follow regarding the addition of the last unit is: the expected *MP* must be greater than the expected *ML* from stocking that unit. The reason we are using "greater than" rather than "equal to" is that an equal condition results in an even exchange of dollars for the last unit and does not maximize the firm's return on its total assets (which include inventory). Hence the general rule is: additional units should be stocked so long as the probability of selling the additional unit is greater than the calculated *p*. An exception to the rule, where the equality condition would be rightfully applicable, is a department store that is trying to maximize profits as well as the customers' satisfaction—knowing items are available in the store when requested. If too many items in the various departments are not available when customers want them, they will shop elsewhere. This ultimately will have a direct effect on the firm's return on total assets.

In an equation for the marginal approach, the left side of the equation is the expected marginal profit from stocking and selling an additional unit. This can be written as *p(MP)* or the probability that the unit will be sold times the marginal profit of the unit. The right side of the equation is $(1 - p)$ *(ML)*, the expected marginal loss from stocking an additional unsold unit. To state it another way, it is the probability that the unit will not be sold $(1 - p)$ times the marginal loss incurred if the unit is unsold *(ML)*. The equation to maximize profit for the optimum quantity to stock is:

$$p(MP) = (1 - p)(ML)$$
$$p(MP) = ML - p(ML) \qquad \text{(Equation 4–1)}$$
$$p(MP) + p(ML) = ML$$
$$p(MP + ML) = ML$$

$$p = \frac{ML}{MP + ML} \qquad \text{(Equation 4–2)}$$

In Equation 4–2, *p* is the minimum probability of selling an additional inventory item in order to justify the stocking of that additional item. Using the rule set forth above, we should stock additional inventory items as long as the probability of selling these additional items is greater than the calculated p.

Use of Equation 4–2 can best be shown by referring to the illustration. First, a value for p must be determined. The marginal profit per dozen is $0.30 (selling price less cost) and the marginal loss per dozen is $0.10 (cost less salvage value). A value for p is calculated as follows:

$$p = \frac{ML}{MP + ML} = \frac{\$0.10}{\$0:30 + \$0.10} = \frac{\$0.10}{\$0.40} = .25$$

Next, a cumulative probability distribution schedule of sales needs to be constructed, as in Table 4–9. The cumulative probabilities in the last column are the probabilities that sales will reach or exceed each of the eight sales levels. For example, the cumulative probability value of .35 assigned to sales of 45 dozens or more can be calculated in the following manner:

Probability of selling 45 dozens   .15

Probability of selling 46 dozens   .15

Probability of selling 47 dozens   <u>.05</u>

            .35 probability of selling 45 dozens or more

Having determined a value for p of .25 and a cumulative probability of sales schedule, we can apply the marginal analysis rule for stocking an additional unit. Additional dozens should be stocked so long as the probability of selling an additional dozen is greater than p. In our illustration, the cumulative probability for stocking 45 dozens is .35, which is greater than p (.25). This comparison satisfies our rule. To ensure that no better answer exists, comparison is now made for the next higher level of sales, 46 dozens. The cumulative probability of stocking and selling 46 dozens is .20, which is less than .25. Thus the answer must be 45 dozens and not 46 dozens, according to our rule. Suppose the cumulative probability of selling 46 dozens was .25. Here we would have an equality in our comparison. The rule states that the cumulative probability must be greater than p. Therefore we would stock 45 and not 46 dozens. The marginal analysis method gives the same answer as the previous methods.

Table 4–9
Cumulative Probabilities
of Sales

Sales (dozens)	Probability of Sales Level	Cumulative Probability for Sales Will Be at this Level or Greater
40	.05	1.00
41	.10	.95
42	.10	.85
43	.20	.75
44	.20	.55
45	.15	.35
46	.15	.20
47	<u>.05</u>	.05
	1.00	

Method 4 — Alternative Marginal Analysis

An alternative method to marginal analysis is comparing the expected marginal profit $[(cum\ p)(MP)]$ and the expected marginal loss $[(1-cum\ p)(ML)]$ where *cum* is the cumulative probability that sales will be at this level or greater. The basic rule for this fourth method is: the expected marginal profit from stocking a unit must be greater than the expected marginal loss from stocking it. The values for the various expected marginal profits and marginal losses are given in Table 4–10. Again, the quantity to be stocked is 45 dozens since the expected marginal profit (0.35 $\times$ \$0.30 = \$0.105) is greater than the expected marginal loss (0.65 $\times$ \$0.10 = \$0.065). The reader will observe that this greater than condition applies to selling 40 through 45 dozens. However, the rule (starting with a maximum stock condition) is concerned with the first greater than condition after passing a less than or equal to condition. This assumption is in agreement with the foregoing rule since we are interested in the first time the expected marginal profit from selling an additional unit is greater than the expected marginal loss of not selling that additional unit.

Sales (dozens)	(cum p)(MP)	(1 − cum p)(ML)
40	$.300	$.000
41	.285	.005
42	.255	.015
43	.225	.025
44	.165	.045
45	.105	.065
46	.060	.080
47	.015	.095

Table 4–10
Expected Marginal Profits and Expected Marginal Losses

Relationship of Methods Of the foregoing four methods (summarized in Figure 4–1), only the first method allows for calculating expected profits given a discrete probability distribution problem. However, each method has a different way of viewing the same problem. For example, in Method 4 above, the difference of \$0.12 between the expected marginal profit of \$0.165 and the expected marginal loss of \$0.045 at the 44th level per Table 4–10 is the same increase appearing in total expected profits per Table 4–3 (Method 1) from the 43rd inventory level of \$12.72 to the 44th level of \$12.84. Also, the \$0.12 increase is the cause of falling expected losses in Table 4–6 (Method 2) from the 43rd inventory level of −\$0.39 to the 44th level of −\$0.27. Likewise, the \$0.04 difference between the expected profit of \$0.105 and the expected loss of \$0.065 in Table 4–10 is the same difference appearing in Tables 4–3 and 4–6 when going from the 44th inventory level to the 45th level. All other values, then, in Tables 4–3, 4–6, and 4–10 can be related in a similar manner for Methods 1, 2, and 4.

Continuous Probability Distribution

Four different methods for dealing with problems of a discrete probability distribution of sales (limited values) and an even increment between sales were presented above. However, in many inventory problems, the distribution of sales is not limited to a few values and the increment of item values is not constant. When a distribution of this kind occurs, it is called a *continuous distribution*. The use of the previous methods is neither feasible nor practical. Another method is necessary at this point in conjunction with the use of p in Equation 4–2. This method incorporates *standard deviation*.

Step 1. Calculate the Arithmetic Mean The continuous probability distribution method will be illustrated by enlarging upon the data (selling price = $0.80 per dozen, cost = $0.50 per dozen, salvage value = $0.40 per dozen, and $p = .25$) given in the preceding example. The data for the problem is found in Table 4–11, which represents data for 50 days. This data can, in turn, be approximately graphed as shown in Figure 4–2 in the form of a bell-shaped curve after drawing a line through the points. The average sales or *arithmetic mean* $(\overline{X})$ is 48.4 dozens per day, based upon the following equation:

$$\overline{X} = \frac{\Sigma X}{N}$$

(Equation 4–3)

$$= \frac{2420}{50} = 48.4 \text{ dozens}$$

where X represents each data value and N is the number of entries.

Table 4–11
Sales in Dozens for 50 Days

47	67	49	55	40	50	48	49	49	49
48	46	43	51	51	62	41	50	62	45
50	55	48	33	41	45	46	45	60	39
49	32	49	47	47	48	60	51	43	51
50	47	43	50	48	65	48	46	49	55

Step 2. Compute the Standard Deviation An examination of the bell-shaped curve in Figure 4–2 reveals that most of the values tend to cluster around the average. Intuitively, this is as one would expect; the instances of days with very high sales or very low sales are few. In the field of statistics, a measure of the tendency for the data to disperse in a regular manner around the average is termed *standard deviation*. The approach for calculating the standard deviation which will be of help in making inferences about our past data in Table 4–11 consists of the following procedures. The first is to subtract the arithmetic mean $(\overline{X} = 48.4)$ from each of the values (X ranges from 32 to 67) and square each of these differences. Consideration must be given to the frequency (f) for each X value. The squared differences are totaled. Finally, it is necessary to calculate the square root of the answer found

by dividing the sum of the squared differences ($\Sigma fd^2 = 2{,}358$) by the number of entries ($N = 50$). The calculations for standard deviation are found in Table 4–12. The standard deviation, denoted by σ (sigma), is 6.87 dozens.

Now that the standard deviation of 6.87 dozens has been determined by Equation 4–4, what can be done with this standard deviation value? Of what value is it

Summary—Methodology of
Discrete Probability Distribution with a Variable Demand

Method 1—Conditional Profits Construct a conditional profits table showing the possible sales and inventory actions. For each level of inventory, multiply the conditional profits times the probability factors and sum these values for total expected profits. Select the inventory level that gives the highest expected profit.

Method 2—Conditional Losses Construct a conditional losses table showing the possible sales and inventory actions. For each level of inventory, multiply the conditional losses times the probability factors and sum these values for total expected losses. Select the inventory level that gives the lowest expected loss.

Method 3—Marginal Analysis Calculate minimum probability of selling an additional unit (units) or p per the following equation:

$$p = \frac{ML}{MP + ML} \qquad \text{(Equation 4–2)}$$

Next, compare the cumulative probability for sales to calculated p. The optimum quantity to stock is that point where the first cumulative probability for sales is still greater than the calculated p. This cutoff point is based on the rule that additional units should be stocked so long as the probability of selling the additional units is greater than the calculated p. It should be noted that this method does not provide for calculating the expected profits.

Method 4—Alternative Marginal Analysis Calculate the expected marginal profits and expected marginal losses for each level of stock, as follows:

Expected Profit	Expected Loss
cum p(MP)	(1 − cum p)(ML)

The highest stock level where the expected profit is still greater than the expected loss is the desired inventory level. As with Method 3, this approach does not provide a means for calculating expected profits.

Figure 4–1
Available methods for solving a discrete probability distribution problem with a variable demand.

141

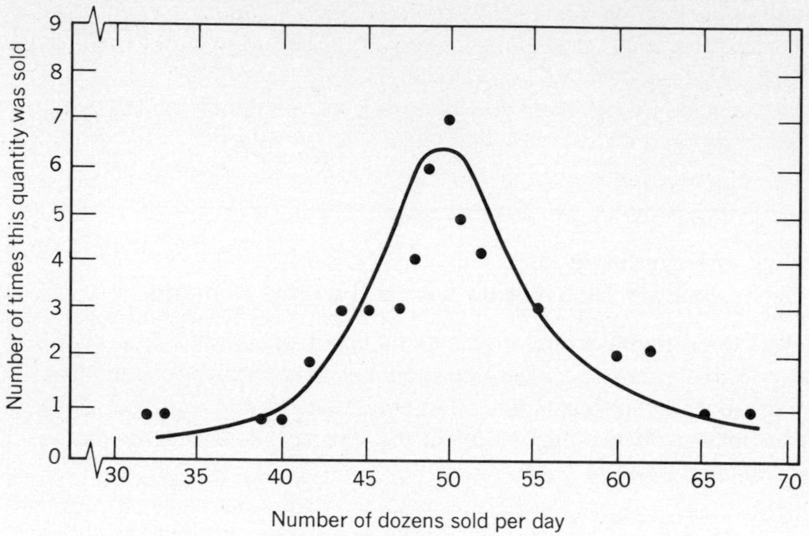

Figure 4-2
The bell-shaped curve—
continuous probability
distribution of past sales
for 50 days.

Table 4-12
Computations for
Standard Deviation

Values of X	Arith. Mean $\bar{X}$	Square Each of the Differences (d^2)	Frequency f	Squared Differences (fd^2)
32	— 48.4 =	$(-16.4)^2$ ×	1 =	269
33	— 48.4 =	$(-15.4)^2$ ×	1 =	237
39	— 48.4 =	$(-9.4)^2$ ×	1 =	88
40	— 48.4 =	$(-8.4)^2$ ×	1 =	71
41	— 48.4 =	$(-7.4)^2$ ×	2 =	110
43	— 48.4 =	$(-5.4)^2$ ×	3 =	87
45	— 48.4 =	$(-3.4)^2$ ×	3 =	35
46	— 48.4 =	$(-2.4)^2$ ×	3 =	17
47	— 48.4 =	$(-1.4)^2$ ×	4 =	8
48	— 48.4 =	$(-0.4)^2$ ×	6 =	1
49	— 48.4 =	$(0.6)^2$ ×	7 =	3
50	— 48.4 =	$(1.6)^2$ ×	5 =	13
51	— 48.4 =	$(2.6)^2$ ×	4 =	27
55	— 48.4 =	$(6.6)^2$ ×	3 =	131
60	— 48.4 =	$(11.6)^2$ ×	2 =	269
62	— 48.4 =	$(13.6)^2$ ×	2 =	370
65	— 48.4 =	$(16.6)^2$ ×	1 =	276
67	— 48.4 =	$(18.6)^2$ ×	1 =	346
			50	2,358

$$\sigma = \sqrt{\frac{\Sigma fd^2}{N}} = \sqrt{\frac{2358}{50}} = \sqrt{47.2} = 6.87 \text{ dozens} \qquad \text{(Equation 4-4)}$$

to us? Standard deviation is a unit of measurement for dispersion just as an inch is a unit of measurement of length. It has been statistically proven that in a perfect bell-shaped curve, approximately 68.27 percent of all values fall within plus or minus one standard deviation from the arithmetic mean. Similarly, it has been found that approximately 95.45 percent of all values lie within two standard deviations plus or minus from the average while over 99.73 percent of all the values are within three standard deviations plus or minus from the arithmetic mean. Applying these facts to the problem, where the arithmetic mean for past sales is 48.4 dozens, approximately 68 percent of future demand will be between 55.27 dozens (48.4 + 6.87) and 41.53 dozens (48.4 − 6.87) if the curve is perfectly bell-shaped as in Figure 4–2. In a similar manner, about 95 percent of future sales will be between 62.14 dozens (48.4 + 6.87 × 2) and 34.66 dozens (48.4 − 6.87 × 2). The future sales for approximately 99 percent of the time will range between 69.01 dozens (48.4 + 6.87 × 3) and 27.79 dozens (48.4 − 6.87 × 3). To solve this type of problem more easily, tables are available that show the expected positions of all values in a distribution and the number of points contained at any value of the standard deviations (σ) from the average.

Step 3. Determine a Value for *p* Having answered the first question regarding what can be done with the calculated standard deviation value, we will answer shortly the second question—its value to us. Previously, the value for *p* was calculated to be .25, which means that additional dozens should be stocked as long as the probability of selling the additional unit is greater than *p*. The value for *p* can also be represented as .25 of the area under the normal distribution curve, which is shown in Figure 4–3. The vertical line going through the center of the bell-shaped curve is the arithmetic mean of 48.4 dozens. As we move to the right of this vertical line representing the arithmetic mean, the probability that a certain quantity can be sold decreases. Thus we will stock additional dozens until just before we reach point *A*. To stock a quantity up to the point represented by point *A* would represent an equal to condition. However, we will use point *A* in determining the answer, then adjust for a greater than condition.

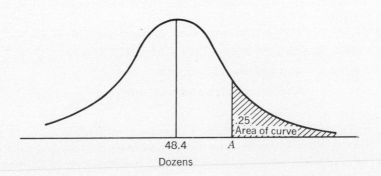

Figure 4–3
Continuous probability
distribution curve where
p = .25.

143

Step 4. Calculate Standard Deviation from the Arithmetic Mean In order to locate point A, refer to Appendix C for areas under the curve. This table indicates how many standard deviations it takes to include any part of the area under the curve, starting from the left-hand end of the curve and going to the right. In our problem, the open area must be .75 (1.00 − .25) of the total area under the curve since the shaded area is .25. Even though .75 does not appear per se in the table, the closest value is .74857 for a standard deviation value of .67. This means that the .75 area under the curve is located between the left-hand end of the bell-shaped curve and a point .67 standard deviation to the right of the arithmetic mean. Point A, then, is .67 standard deviation to the right of the arithmetic mean of 48.4 dozens.

Step 5. Determine the Inventory Level Having previously calculated one standard deviation to be 6.87 to the right (or left) of the arithmetic mean (Table 4–12), the value of .67 times 6.87 equals 4.6 dozens. Point A is located 4.6 dozens to the right of the arithmetic mean of 48.4. The value at point A is 53 dozens (48.4 + 4.6). This brings us to the vertical line for point A for an equal to condition, that is, additional quantities should be stocked as long as the probability of selling that unit is equal to p. To change the answer in our problem to a greater than condition, the value at point A should be changed from 53 to 52 dozens so as to move out of the shaded area into the open area. This is basically the same approach utilized in the marginal analysis method for a greater than condition.

Suppose the value of p in our problem was not .25 but some other value, say .80. Again, this revised problem can be illustrated by using a normal distribution curve. This time we shall start from the right-hand end of the curve, as shown in Figure 4–4. Now point A lies to the left of the arithmetic mean, whereas in the preceding problem it was to the right of the average. The procedure for reading the area under the curve from the appendix is simplified in the revised problem. When the optimum inventory level is smaller than the arithmetic mean, the distance between point A and the arithmetic mean can be taken directly from the table in the appendix. Looking for .8 in the table, the closest value is .79955, which is interpreted as .84 for the distance being measured in terms of standard deviation from the arithmetic mean.

Having determined values for p and the distance between point A and the arithmetic mean (.84), we can now solve for point A in terms of an equal to condition initially:

.84 × standard deviation = .84 × 6.87 = 5.77 dozens

Point A = 48.4 dozens −5.77 dozens

= 42.63 dozens (equal condition)

The optimum inventory position (must be in whole dozens) would not be rounded to 43 dozens. Going into the shaded area of the bell-shaped curve results in a less than condition for p. Thus the *optimum inventory level* is 42 dozens.

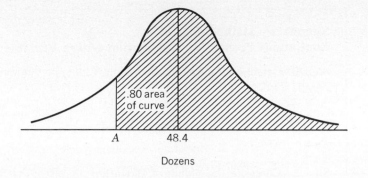

Figure 4–4
Continuous probability
distribution curve where
$p = .80$.

The foregoing steps involved in solving a problem with a continuous probability distribution are found in Figure 4–5. For fast and accurate results, these steps can be easily computerized.

What was stated previously for discrete distribution of demand also holds true for continuous distribution. Although probability cannot assure that the best decision will be made each and every day, it does allow for optimum profits in the long run for decision making with a variable demand, i.e. random day-by-day demand fluctuations. A word of caution is necessary: since business data may not be distributed in a bell-shaped (normal) manner, other quantitative methods may be required for an optimum solution.

Chapter Summary

The methods presented in this chapter for decision making with a variable future demand apply to conditions where demand is discrete or continuous. Although the calculations involved are not particularly complex, they can be time consuming. When such a condition arises, a computer should be employed to minimize the laborious task of analyzing past sales data and producing a usable solution.

Decision making with a variable demand is not restricted to inventory problems. This approach is rightfully applicable to areas such as new product potential and new market profitability. In fact, individuals and firms can handle their decision problems as ones dealing with a variable demand. An understanding of the fundamentals of probability theory for the states of nature or uncertainty about the future should be of help to decision makers in that it makes them quantify the problem. Instead of operating in the dark, the assignment of probability factors, based upon subjective and/or objective probabilities and tempered with expected changes, can help improve the quality of managers' decisions.

Summary—Methodology of
Continuous Probability Distribution with a Variable Demand

Step 1—Calculate the Arithmetic Mean Calculate the arithmetic mean $(\overline{X})$ per the formula:

$$\overline{X} = \frac{\Sigma X}{N}$$ (Equation 4–3)

Step 2—Compute the Standard Deviation Subtract the arithmetic mean from values within the problem and square their differences. Next, multiply these differences (d^2) times their frequencies (f), resulting in fd^2 values. The sum of these values (Σfd^2) and the number (N) of frequency values are entered in the following equation for determining standard deviation:

$$\sigma = \sqrt{\frac{\Sigma fd^2}{N}}$$ (Equation 4–4)

Step 3—Determine a Value for p Determine the p value (minimum probability of selling an additional unit or units in order to justify the stocking of that additional unit or units) per the equation:

$$p = \frac{ML}{MP + ML}$$ (Equation 4–2)

Step 4—Calculate Standard Deviation from the Arithmetic Mean Calculate the standard deviation from the arithmetic mean. If calculated p (per Step 3) is less than .5, subtract from 1.0 to obtain the complimentary value; otherwise, leave calculated p as is. In either case, refer to Appendix C—Areas Under the Curve, interpolating as necessary to find the standard deviation value from the arithmetic mean. If calculated p is less than .5, the standard deviation will lie to the right of the arithmetic mean. On the other hand, if calculated p is greater than .5, the standard deviation will lie to the left of the arithmetic mean.

Step 5—Determine the Inventory Level Calculate the number of units to the right (p is less than .5) or left (p is greater than .5) of the arithmetic mean. Thus, multiply the standard deviation value from the arithmetic mean (per Step 4) by the standard deviation (per Step 2). Where p is less than .5, add this calculated unit value to the arithmetic mean; where p is greater than .5, subtract this new unit value from the arithmetic mean. In either case, round the value down to stay out of the shaded area (for a greater than condition).

Figure 4–5
Steps involved in solving a continuous probability distribution problem with a variable demand.

Questions

1. Distinguish between conditional profits and expected profits.
2. Of the several methods for solving a problem that has a discrete distribution with a variable demand, which one results in the least amount of computations?
3. When solving a problem that has a continuous distribution with a variable demand, how can the concept of standard deviation help in the problem's solution?

Model Formulation Exercises

1. In the formulation of an inventory problem treating a variable demand (utilizing one of the methods found in the chapter), how sensitive is future expected performance to current data that was used in solving the problem, but which may not be representative of the future?

2. The basic rule in economics for stocking additional units is that additional units should be stocked so long as the marginal revenue equals the marginal cost. However, in this chapter, the basic rule has been changed to stocking additional units up to the point where the marginal revenue is greater than the marginal cost. Reconcile the differences between the two approaches (economics and operations research) so that they are comptatible.

3. In the formulation of a problem dealing with a variable demand, why is the salvage value ignored for those products that have a long shelf life, say five to ten years?

4. In the marginal analysis method (Method 3) for a discrete probability distribution problem with a variable demand, reformulate Equation 4–2

$$\left(p = \frac{ML}{MP + ML}\right)$$

so that it complements this equation. Using this new formula, what procedures must be changed within Method 3 to accommodate the reformulation?

5. In the alternative marginal analysis method (Method 4) for a discrete probability distribution problem with a variable demand,
    (a) Why is it necessary to multiply the cumulative probability ($cum\ p$) times marginal profit (MP); that is, why not use just the simple probability at a particular demand level?
    (b) Why is it necessary to multiply one minus the cumulative probability ($1 - cum\ p$) times marginal loss (ML); that is, why not use the simple probability at a particular demand level?

Mathematical Exercises

1. Given is the following distribution of unit sales and relative probability factors:

Units Sold	Probability of Selling these Units
50	.10
51	.35
52	.40
53	.15
	1.00

Cost per unit is $10 and sales price is $15 per unit.
(a) Prepare a conditional profits table and a conditional losses table.
(b) Prepare expected profits and losses tables for a variable demand.
(c) Determine the expected value of perfect information.

2. The French Baking Company operates many retail outlets it has decided to apply probability in order to determine whether or not profits can be improved, looking first at white bread. White bread is baked in units of 20. The following data was compiled for white bread from the load sheets of the firm's delivery trucks.

Delivery Truck Daily Demand	Relative Frequency
1,060	.055
1,080	.100
1,100	.100
1,120	.150
1,140	.200
1,160	.175
1,180	.125
1,200	.075
1,220	.020
	1.000

White bread sells for $0.25 a loaf on an average and costs (fixed and variable) $0.19 per loaf delivered to its retail outlets. Bread left over at the end of the day is returned to the baking plant and is sold for $0.10 per loaf to institutions.
(a) Determine the optimum quantity to bake in terms of the firm's delivery trucks.
(b) What are the maximum expected profits with a variable demand in the future?
(c) What would be the maximum expected profits under certainty if this were possible?

3. Bohr Bros., Inc., operates a small floral shop adjoining one of its eight large greenhouses. It specializes in the raising of mums, which are sold to other florists. However, it stocks mums for sale in its small floral shop for customers in its immediate market area. Mums are sold for $3 per dozen and cost $2 per dozen to grow and cut. Unsold mums left at the end of the second day after cutting are sold at $0.75 per dozen to other flower shops in the lower-income markets. Demand for mums during the winter months is relatively constant over a period of time but varies from day to day. Given is the following tabulation of recent demand:

Daily Demand	Relative Frequency
20	.05
22	.10
24	.25
26	.30
28	.20
30	.10
	1.00

(a) What is the optimum quantity to stock?
(b) What is the maximum expected profit with a variable future demand based upon the given schedule?

4. The Jones Company buys a certain nonperishable item which sells for $16 and cost $12. Due to the item's long shelf life, its salvage value will be ignored. A tabulation of recent demand for the product appears as follows:

Quantities Sold	Number of Days
80	14
81	36
82	70
83	30
84	20
85	10

Future demand for this product during the next 30 days should be comparable to past demand.
(a) What is the expected marginal profit and marginal loss from stocking the 83rd unit?
(b) Should the 83rd unit be stocked? If not, what level of inventory in units should be carried daily?

5. The Adam Shoe Company specializes in the manufacture of men's shoes. Its lowest price shoe, which sells for $10 per pair and costs $8 per pair (total fixed

and variable costs), is an important sales volume leader. All unsold shoes at the end of each season for this lowest price shoe are sold to discount houses at $6 per pair. The estimated demand and their probabilities for the coming season are as follows:

Seasonal Demand (pairs)	Probability
100,000	.10
90,000	.15
80,000	.25
70,000	.25
60,000	.15
50,000	.10
	1.00

(a) What quantity should the company manufacture for the coming season?
(b) What is the maximum expected profit based on the variable demand for the coming season?

6. Cosmetics, Inc., has under consideration the production of a new shampoo for women. The proposed selling price is $1.25 per bottle. The projected variable cost is $0.90 per bottle. An investment of $80,000 in fixed costs is necessary to undertake this project. The new product is expected to have a product life of five years. The market research group has estimated yearly demand to be as follows:

Yearly Demand	Probability
25,000	.05
50,000	.10
75,000	.20
100,000	.30
110,000	.35

(a) Based upon the facts given in the problem, should the new product be placed into production?
(b) What additional factors, not given in the problem, should be considered before making a final decision?

7. The main product of the Orlando Manufacturing Company sells for $20 each and costs $16. Analysis of past sales data indicates that sales average 40 units per day with a standard deviation of 10 units. What level of inventory should the firm carry?

8. Byrnes Sales, Inc., is contemplating the use of quantitative methods to determine the optimum level of inventory for its principal product. They have come to you with the following facts. The product sells for $22 and costs $12 from the wholesaler plus $6 for fixed and variable costs for the firm itself. A tabulation of recent demand which should be typical of future demand is as follows:

34	36	26
26	18	38
26	18	36
20	20	20
26	34	34
16	40	26
14	38	44
20	10	18
16	36	14
26	34	34

What optimum level of inventory would you recommend to management?

Bibliography

H. Bierman, C. P. Bonini, and W. H. Hausman, *Quantitative Analysis for Business Decisions*, Homewood, Ill.: Richard D. Irwin, 1973.

W. D. Brinkloe, *Managerial Operations Research*, New York: McGraw-Hill Book Company, 1969.

E. S. Buffa and W. H. Taubert, *Production-Inventory Systems: Planning and Control*, Homewood, Ill.: Richard D. Irwin, 1972.

T. R. Dyckman, S. Smidt, and A. K. McAdams, *Management Decision Making Under Uncertainty*, New York: The Macmillan Company, 1969.

F. S. Hillier and G. J. Lieberman, *Operations Research*, San Francisco: Holden-Day, 1974.

R. I. Levin and C. A. Kirkpatrick, *Quantitative Approaches to Management*, New York: McGraw-Hill Book Company, 1975.

C. M. Paik, *Quantitative Methods for Managerial Decisions*, New York: McGraw-Hill Book Company, 1973.

H. Raiffa, *Decision Analysis*, Reading, Mass.: Addison-Wesley, 1968.

R. Schlaifer, *Analysis of Decisions Under Uncertainty*, New York: McGraw-Hill Book Company, 1969.

Chapter 5

PERT/Time and PERT/Cost

Chapter Objectives
☐ To demonstrate how a Gantt chart can be converted to a PERT network.
☐ To present the steps for a PERT network that will maximize the employment of a company's resources.
☐ To show the procedures for condensing a PERT project from its normal time and cost to its crash time and cost.
☐ To demonstrate the relative merits of using PERT versus not using it.

Chapter Outline

PERT (Program Evaluation Review Technique) was born of sheer desperation in 1956. During the early stages of the Navy's Polaris submarine-missile development program, a Special Projects Office was set up to manage this large, complex project. The men in charge found that all the conventional managerial methods were hopelessly inadequate to keep track of the schedule. Superimposed on the job of coordinating the efforts of 11,000 contractors was a degree of uncertainty as to when crucial research and development stages might be completed. Willard Fazar of the Special Projects Office, with the help of Lockheed's Missile and Space Division and consultants from Booz, Allen & Hamilton, devised PERT as a network flowchart with built-in uncertainty. Instead of assigning a single-time estimate to each task, as is normally done with the Critical Path Method, Fazar called for three estimates: optimistic, normal, and pessimistic. Such multiple estimating made the computations somewhat more difficult, but they were still well within the capability of a high-speed computer. PERT worked well from the time it was put into operation in 1958. Polaris chief Vice Admiral W. F. Raborn, Jr., has given the technique much credit for the development of the first Polaris missile in two years' less time than originally estimated.

Requirements for
Transforming a Gantt Chart to a PERT Network

The Gantt milestone chart, a forerunner of PERT, is a chart depicting the work to be done. It has a time scale across the bottom of the chart that depicts the specific tasks relative to the entire project. The Gantt chart shows the relationships among the milestones within the same task, but not the relationships among the milestones contained in different tasks. This can best be illustrated by Figure 5–1. Each of the circles (milestones) represents the accomplishment of a specific phase of the total undertaking and each rectangle represents a task.

Modification of Gantt's milestone chart to show the interrelationships among all milestones in a project is achieved in three steps. The first is removal of the rectangles. These are replaced by arrows connecting the milestones (Figure 5–2).

The second step involves adding the relationships among the milestones for the various tasks (Figure 5–3). Here several milestones must precede other milestones. For example, milestone 5 cannot be started before milestones 1 and 3 are completed. This type of relationship is true for all other cases in the illustration. It should be noted that milestone 1 is the starting point while milestone 6 is the ending point of the project.

In the final step (Figure 5–4), the term *task* is dropped since all the relationships, irrespective of the task involved, are shown by arrows. Further, the horizontal time scale of the Gantt chart is dropped and replaced by individual time on each of the arrows. The transformation from the Gantt chart to a PERT network is now complete. The major advantage of this change should be evident. We now have all the interrelationships among the milestones. The project is viewed as an integrated whole (not a number of tasks) and each leg of the network has its own time value. In addition, this transformation permits the use of a network for large and complicated projects whereby estimates are used for determining completion dates.

Figure 5–1
Gantt milestone chart.

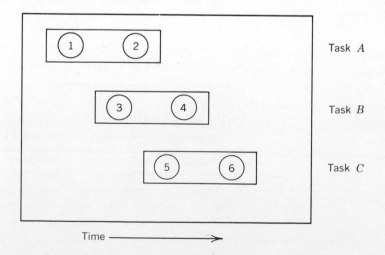

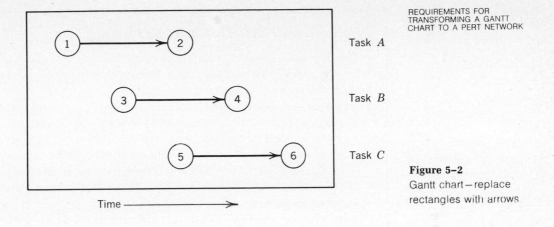

Task *A*

Task *B*

Task *C*

Time ⟶

Figure 5–2
Gantt chart—replace
rectangles with arrows

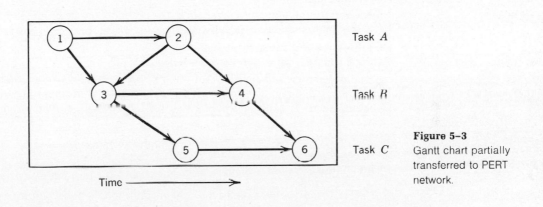

Task *A*

Task *B*

Task *C*

Time ⟶

Figure 5–3
Gantt chart partially
transferred to PERT
network.

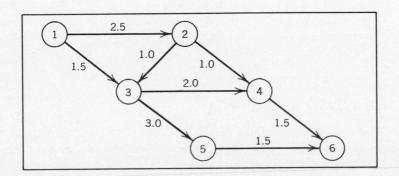

Figure 5–4
Complete transformation
of Gantt chart to PERT
network.

Applications—PERT/Time and PERT/Cost

- **Construction**—helps in planning construction projects, particularly large structures, and controls construction activities to keep highly paid workmen busy, thereby minimizing total project costs.
- **Research and development**—useful in overseeing complex research and development projects that are oriented toward pure or applied research, allowing management to keep actual R & D costs within budgeted amounts.
- **New products**—controls the development and launching of new products in the future. (Construction and R & D have been the most extensive areas of PERT usage in the past.)
- **Large government contracts**—utilized to keep overall time and costs under control for work on large government contracts; certain contracts may even require that PERT be employed in the preparation of bids.
- **Installation of equipment**—useful in planning a series of highly integrated activities when equipment is installed, including computers and major equipment.
- **First production runs**—controls initial production runs on a manufacturing line, including the necessary debugging, testing, and revisions.
- **Systems and procedures installation**—utilized to install new systems and procedures, either simple or complex.
- **Maintenance and turnaround**—helps solve maintenance problems, particularly in the steel, chemical, petroleum, glass, and paper industries.

PERT/Time

The PERT technique is a method of minimizing trouble spots—production bottlenecks, delays, and interruptions—by determining critical activities before they occur so various parts of an overall job can be coordinated. It is basically a *planning* and *control* technique that utilizes a network to complete a predetermined project or schedule. This technique helps facilitate the communications function in a firm by reporting favorable as well as unfavorable developments before they happen. In effect, PERT tries to keep managers appraised of all critical factors and considerations that bear on their decisions. From this standpoint, it can be a valuable managerial tool in decision making.

PERT/Time Problem

The six steps utilized in a PERT/Time project for planning and control are developed below. Throughout, basic terms are defined as they are needed. A sample problem is illustrated in the discussion to highlight the methodology of PERT/Time.

A summary of the important steps involved in solving a PERT/Time problem concludes the presentation.

Step 1. Prepare PERT Network A PERT network (Figure 5–5) has some differences from that of the Gantt chart. The first to be considered is terminology. A PERT network is concerned with developing a logical sequence of its activities that are undertaken to carry out the project and the interrelationships of these activities over time. The term *activity* (job) is defined as one work step in the total project and is represented by an arrow. The tail of the arrow represents the beginning of the activity and the head represents its completion. The length, shape, or position of the arrow is unimportant. The important thing is the way the activities, represented by arrows, are linked together in a time sequence for an operational network.

In constructing an arrow diagram, the planner should think through the activities required and their respective time relationships. This can be accomplished by developing a list of the project's activities. In a very complex project, it may not seem possible to list all the activities initially. However, additional activities will come to light as the arrow diagram is developed. Next, the planner should determine the logical order of the activities, that is, how does one activity fit in with other activities? Does a particular activity precede or follow, or is it concurrent with another activity? Finally, it is necessary to draw the arrow diagram to show how the activities are interrelated over time. The planner should watch for activities that are too large or too small. It is possible that a large activity can be treated as more than one activity or many small activities can be combined into a single activity.

The starting and ending points of activities, shown in Figure 5–5 as circled numbers, are called *events* (nodes). Events are points in time as contrasted with activities which have a time length or duration. Events are numbered serially from start to finish of a project. The general rule for numbering is that no event can be numbered until all preceding events have been numbered. Referring to Figure 5–5, this means that no event can be numbered until we have first numbered the tail of each arrow whose head points to the next event. The number at the head of an arrow is always larger than that at its tail.

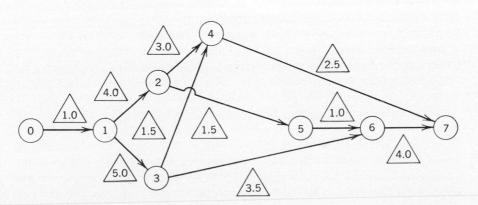

Figure 5–5
PERT network.

The term *network* relates to the activities and events that are combined together, resulting in a diagram such as Figure 5–5. Within this network, we can see that event 0 is the network beginning event while event 7 is the network ending event. Upon inspection of event 6, we notice that activities 3–6 and 5–6 lead to it, which means that event 6 is the ending event for these two activities. In a similar manner, event 2 begins two activities, 2–4 and 2–5, which indicates that event 2 is the beginning event for two activities. The same type of reasoning is applicable to the other activities and events in the PERT network.

The preceding PERT network shows simple relationships in time sequence. Often the relationships are more complex. In some cases, these require the use of nonactivity arrows inserted to clarify the activity pattern. These are called *dummy arrows*. They are represented by dotted line arrows. Figure 5–6 gives an example of a dummy arrow. *C* is dependent only on *A* being completed while *D* is dependent on both *A* and *B* being completed. Thus, *A* and *B*, being concurrent activities, as are *C* and *D*, indicate that *C* is dependent only on *A* being completed, not on *B* being completed. A dummy arrow in any situation does not represent an activity and thus has no time duration. It can be used effectively in those situations where activities can be overlapped to accelerate a project or can be used to bring activities to a formal close.

Figure 5–6
Example of a dummy arrow.

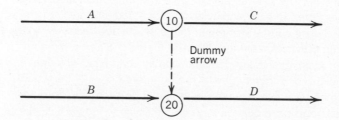

Step 2. Calculate Expected Times Assigning time to individual activities is essential in order to complete a PERT network. Should this be done on the basis of the lowest possible cost, irrespective of the time required; the shortest possible time, regardless of costs; some compromise between the two; or some other basis? To answer, it is necessary to utilize statistics, in particular the bell-shaped curve and the beta distribution. As you will recall from statistics, most groups of data tend to form a bell shape when plotted (Figure 5–7). However, some variables are not normally distributed and do not form a bell shape. Instead, the variables are unsymmetrical in one direction, as shown in Figure 5–7.

Since data from the business world reflect basically one of the three curves in Figure 5–7, the designers of PERT were faced with finding a particular kind of distribution that would satisfy the conditions of the shortest (optimistic), longest (pessimistic), and most likely times. We do not have the space to relate all the complicated statistics and algebra necessary to prove the validity of the weighted average used in the final formula for PERT. It should be somewhat obvious that the most likely time (*m*) should be weighted much heavier than the most optimistic (*a*) and the most pessimistic (*b*). There is certainly more of a chance that the project will be completed closer to the most likely time than the other two extreme times. The approximation formula developed for the *expected time* of an activity (t_e) is

$$t_e = \frac{a + 4m + b}{6}$$ (Equation 5–1)

When using this formula for a normal bell-shaped curve, the calculated value for t_e represents the midvalue of the bell-shaped curve, which is what we desire for this type of curve. Let us take a look at two examples for curves that are unsymmetrical and plot them for a *beta distribution*. The first time estimates for a beta distribution showing expected time (in weeks) lying to the right of the most likely time are: $a = 4$ (most optimistic), $m = 6$ (most likely), and $b = 15$ (most pessimistic). Using Equation 5–1, the value for t_e equals 7.2 weeks. The values for this example are plotted in Figure 5–8. The 15 weeks' pessimistic estimate pulled the expected time t_e farther to the right on the distribution.

In our second example of a beta distribution, it is unsymmetrical in the other direction. This time t_e lies to the left of the most likely time. The three time estimates are: $a = 4$, $m = 12$, and $b = 15$. This results in an elapsed time of 11.2 weeks, as shown in Figure 5–9. This example indicates that the estimator is a bit optimistic since t_e lies to the left of the most likely time.

The expected time t_e represents the particular time value (hours, days, weeks, or some other basis). If we erect a perpendicular line for the value t_e (as shown in Figures 5–8 and 5–9), about half of the area under the curve will be to either side of this line. In a normal bell-shaped curve, as stated previously, the most likely time is the average or expected time. However, in the beta distribution, skewed to the right or left, the expected time will lie to the right or left of the most likely value depending upon the three time figures. Studies have been made regarding the accuracy of t_e in a beta distribution. They all seem to indicate the error in calculating the expected time was too small to have any material effect in most business and industrial applications.

Figure 5–7
Bell-shaped curve and beta distribution curves: (*a*) normal bell-shaped curve, (*b*) and (*c*) beta distribution, unsymmetrical in one direction.

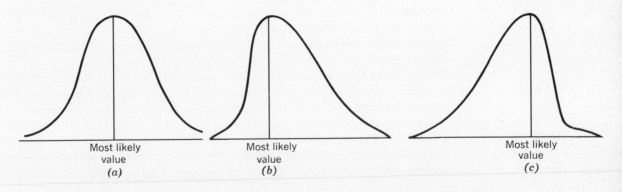

Most likely value
(*a*)

Most likely value
(*b*)

Most likely value
(*c*)

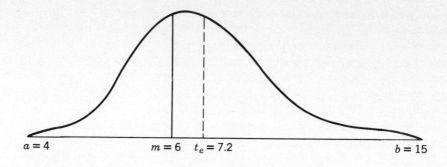

Figure 5–8
Beta distribution—t_e to the right of most likely time due to the time factor m.

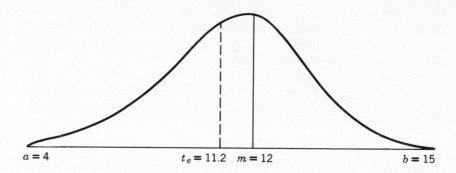

Figure 5–9
Beta distribution—t_e to the left of most likely time due to the time factor m.

Step 3. Determine Earliest Expected and Latest Allowable Times   Before determination can be made of the critical path, we must know more about the event time, that is, the aggregate time required to reach a certain event in a project. An event can have one or more values depending on activity-time relationships. Many events have a range of possible event times. In order to determine the event time, we need to know the earliest expected time as measured from the start of the project and a latest allowable time as measured from the finish of the project. Or to put it another way, it is necessary to know the earliest time at which the activities originating from an event can be started. This is the earliest expected time. Similarly, it is necessary to know the latest time at which activities terminating at an event can be completed and still permit the entire project to be finished on schedule. This is called the latest allowable time.

The *earliest expected time* (T_E) can be illustrated by using Figure 5–5 as revised in Figure 5–10 for insertion of earliest expected times (shown in squares). The earliest expected time for event 0 is zero since no activity time has preceded it. The zero event time becomes the base time to which all subsequent times are added. The earliest expected time for event 1 is the sum of the base time 0 and the duration of the activity 0–1 (1 week), or zero plus one equals 1 week. The earliest expected time for event 2 is the sum of the earliest expected time for event 1 (1 week) plus the duration of activity 1–2 (4 weeks), which is 5 weeks. Up to this point, the procedure is a simple summation.

When an event has two or more activities flowing into it, the earliest expected time for this particular event requires a choice. In our illustration, the earliest expected time for event 4 requires a choice: either the sum of the earliest expected time for event 2 (5 weeks) plus the duration of the activity 2–4 (3 weeks), equaling 8 weeks, or the earliest expected time for event 3 (6 weeks) plus the duration of activity 3–4 (1.5 weeks), equaling 7.5 weeks. Since activity 4–7 cannot begin until both activities 2–4 and 3–4 are completed, it is necessary to select the maximum time of 8 weeks as the earliest expected time for event 4. The basic rule to follow for determining earliest expected times is: when there is a choice of event times, take the maximum time.

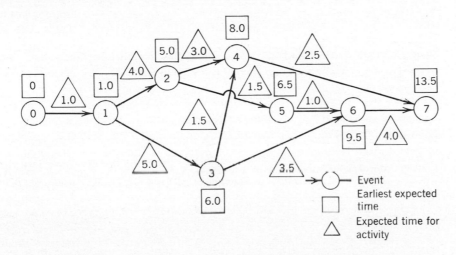

Figure 5–10
PERT network—earliest
expected time T_E.

The *latest allowable time* (T_L), as previously stated, is the latest time at which each activity can be completed and still permit the entire project to be completed on time. In computing latest allowable times (shown in circles), we begin at the end of the project with a latest expected time of 13.5 weeks for event 7 as in Figure 5–11. The latest allowable time for event 4 is the difference between the latest allowable time for event 7 (13.5 weeks) and the duration of activity 4–7 (2.5 weeks), or 13.5 minus 2.5 equals 11 weeks. The latest allowable time for event 3 is the latest allowable time for event 4 (11 weeks) minus the duration of activity 3–4 (1.5 weeks), or 9.5 weeks. Likewise, the latest allowable time for event 3 is also the latest allowable time for event 6 (9.5 weeks) minus the duration of activity 3–6 (3.5 weeks), or 6 weeks. We now have to make a choice between the two latest allowable times (9.5 weeks and 6 weeks). The choice must be 6 weeks since the latest allowable time is the latest time at which activities terminating in that event may be completed. This allows activities following the event to terminate with the earliest project completion date of 13.5 weeks. The basic rule to remember here for determining latest allowable times is: when there is a choice of event times, take the minimum time.

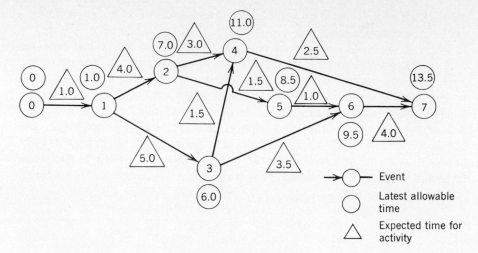

Figure 5–11
PERT network—latest
allowable time T_L.

Step 4. Locate Critical Path(s)   Having determined earliest expected and latest allowable times, these now can be brought together in a single network as shown in Figure 5–12. The *critical path* in the network is the longest time path throughout the network or 0–1–3–6–7. Observe that for each of the events on the critical path, its earliest event time T_E is equal to its latest event time T_L. This means that the latest allowable time in which each event can be completed is equal to the earliest date on which we can expect each event to be completed. Thus there is no spare (slack) time and the events must be completed exactly as scheduled to meet our completion time of 13.5 weeks. Although not illustrated in this example, it is possible to have more than one critical path.

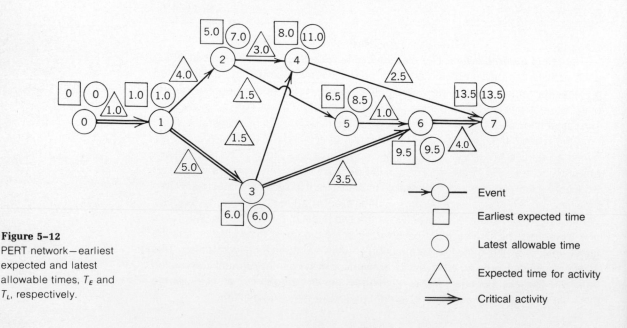

Figure 5–12
PERT network—earliest
expected and latest
allowable times, T_E and
T_L, respectively.

Step 5. Calculate Slack Observing events 2 and 4 which are not on the critical path, we could fall behind on activity 1–2 as much as 2 weeks and on activity 2–4 as much as 3 weeks and still not jeopardize finishing the network in 13.5 weeks. Thus, the network enables one to see where time can or must be saved and where the schedule can slide for a while if it is advantageous.

The time to spare in a PERT network, commonly referred to as *slack,* can be defined in two ways. *Total slack* is the length of time an activity may be delayed from its earliest start without affecting the completion time of the entire project. *Free slack* of an activity is the amount of time an activity may be delayed from its earliest start without affecting the earliest start of succeeding activities. It is possible that an activity may have total slack, but no free slack.

The formula for slack S (total) is the difference between the latest allowable time T_L and the earliest expected time T_E, defined as:

$$S = T_L - T_E \qquad\qquad \text{(Equation 5–2)}$$

In addition to slack at events 2 and 4 in Figure 5–12, there is slack at event 5 in the amount of 2 weeks. Knowing the amount of slack related to the different events, it may be possible to switch resources — workers, machinery, and materials — to the critical path in order to shorten the total project time. This is one of the basic reasons for using PERT.

The events and related times that appear in Figure 5–12 can be scheduled in terms of events and amount of slack time. This is done on the basis of event numbering, as in Table 5–1. Note that there is zero slack for the events on the critical path.

Preceding Event	Event	t_e	T_L	T_E	Slack $T_L - T_E$
—	0	0	0	0	0
0	1	1.0	1.0	1.0	0
1	2	4.0	7.0	5.0	2.0
1	3	5.0	6.0	6.0	0
2	4	3.0	11.0	8.0	3.0
2	5	1.5	8.5	6.5	2.0
3	4	1.5	11.0	8.0	3.0
3	6	3.5	9.5	9.5	0
4	7	2.5	13.5	13.5	0
5	6	1.0	9.5	9.5	0
6	7	4.0	13.5	13.5	0

Table 5–1
Summary of Expected Time (t_e), Latest Allowable Time (T_L), Earliest Expected Time (T_E), and Slack ($T_L - T_E$) for the PERT/Time Project

Step 6. Evaluate PERT Network Once the network has been drawn, all time values calculated (t_e, T_L, T_E, and slack), and the critical path(s) determined, the real job of PERT has actually just begun. This is where *sensitivity analysis* plays an important role. Activities whose times have been estimated may have no effect on the critical path even if they fall behind schedule. However, other estimated timed activities may be on the critical path or may be critical at a later date. The effect of these initial path activities must be assessed. Hence, adjustments and revisions of the original plans may be necessary to assure that the PERT network is completed within a scheduled end date.

If overall times are unsatisfactory, several methods of adjustment are available to the planner, one being the interchanging of workers, machines, and materials (if they are comparable) from the noncritical path(s) to the critical path(s). Another network adjustment is reducing the technical specifications of the project, such as reducing the amount of testing required. If activities can be rearranged, it may be possible to speed up the completion of a project. The overlapping of concurrent activities may be available to the planner. Moreover, the use of overtime provides additional flexibility for network replanning and adjustment. Thus, the planner has several alternatives available for adjusting the critical path(s) in order to improve completion dates throughout the project.

The foregoing steps for developing a final PERT project are summarized in Figure 5–13. As indicated above in the final step, the user has the capability of redoing the PERT network if need be to meet a specified completion date. Generally, any "trading off" of resources, revision in standards, and/or specifications will necessitate a recomputation of times—expected, earliest expected, latest allowable, slack, and critical path(s).

Computer PERT/Time Packages

When a network consists of very few activities and events or when one person has knowledge regarding the whole project, decisions regarding the initial network's critical path(s), rearrangement, and rescheduling should not be too difficult. However, in the development of complex networks where many workers, machines, and materials are involved, the use of a computer becomes a necessity. A computer, employing a PERT/Time packaged routine, provides a method of checking actual progress against the schedule. It can determine the slack time in the network as of a certain time, say this week. This allows the manager to shift resources if possible, rearrange subnetworks and like items, in an attempt to complete the project in the shortest feasible time. Also, it can print an event report (starting from the first event to the last), latest allowable time report, and departmental reports for events.

What is the cutoff point for a manual versus a computer approach to a PERT/Time network? Obviously, a network of 1,000 activities could not be handled properly using manual methods since one error could mean the wrong critical path was selected. Approximately 100 activities is a lower limit for a computer application with a weekly updating of changes to produce a new critical path and related reports. Since many firms have a computer available, the problem of accuracy with a manual approach can be solved by a computer approach. Furthermore, most projects do not follow original plans, and revisions must take place each time an activity exceeds its planned time or is completed in less than its planned time. These con-

Summary—Methodology of PERT/Time

Step 1—Prepare PERT Network Prepare the PERT/Time network without considering activity times or completion dates. Connect the succession of interrelationships through the use of event symbols (circled numbers) and activity flows (arrows).

Step 2—Calculate Expected Times Calculate the expected time (t_e) for each activity by inserting three time estimates—optimistic (a), most likely (m), and pessimistic (b)—in the following equation:

$$t_e = \frac{a + 4m + b}{6} \qquad \text{(Equation 5-1)}$$

As each t_e is calculated, it is entered on the network (shown in a triangle below the appropriate activity arrow).

Step 3—Determine Earliest Expected and Latest Allowable Times Determine earliest expected times (T_E—shown in squares above the appropriate events) by adding the expected times, starting with the first event and going from left to right. However, when an event has two or more activities flowing into it, take the maximum time.

Determine latest allowable times (T_L—shown in circles above the appropriate events) by subtracting the expected times, starting with the last event and going from right to left. However, when an event has two or more activities flowing out of it, take the minimum time.

Step 4—Locate Critical Path(s) Locate the critical path(s) by determining the longest time path(s) throughout the network. This is accomplished by observing the events on the critical path—their earliest expected times are equal to their latest allowable times.

Step 5—Calculate Slack Calculate the amount of slack for each activity by taking the time difference between the latest allowable time (T_L) and the earliest expected time (T_E) for the same event, utilizing the following equation:

$$S = T_L - T_E \qquad \text{(Equation 5-2)}$$

Step 6—Evaluate PERT Network Evaluate the PERT network from an overview standpoint. If total time is unsatisfactory, realign resources, add personnel from noncritical activities, utilize overtime, and use comparable schemes to improve completion dates throughout the project. Redo the PERT network employing the preceding steps. Any "trading off" of foregoing items will generally necessitate a recomputation of network times.

Figure 5-13
Steps employed in developing a final PERT project.

stant revisions can play havoc with manual methods. The computer has the ability to produce orderly reports faster and more accurately for those involved, especially those who want their reports yesterday. Complexity, accuracy, length of the project, number of events, and the frequency of output desired are determinants of whether a computer should be used.

PERT/Cost

PERT/Cost, developed in 1962 as an expansion of PERT/Time, integrates time data with cost data. It incorporates both time and cost into a network so that their trade-offs can be calculated. This technique shifts the focus from volume, such as cost per piece produced, to cost for each activity. It cuts across the traditional accounting boundaries of departments and accounting periods. PERT/Cost requires a high degree of coordination of engineering, estimating, control, and accounting activities.

Time-Cost Relationship   To explain the nature of PERT/Cost, it is essential to understand certain terms. Two time and cost estimates are indicated for each activity in the network. They are a normal estimate and a crash estimate. The *normal time estimate* is analogous to the expected time estimate. Normal cost is the cost associated with finishing the project in the normal time. The *crash time estimate* is the time that would be required if no costs were spared in trying to reduce the project time. The project manager would do whatever was necessary to speed up the work. Crash cost is the cost associated with doing the job on a crash basis in order to minimize completion time.

Time-cost relationships can take on many forms, as pictured in Figure 5–14. Case A is a time-cost relationship in which a reduction of time can be effected with a modest increase in cost. On the other hand, case B is a time-cost relationship in which a reduction in time can be effected with a large increase in cost. The more usual kind of cost-time relationship is the straight line drawn between case A and case B, which is a reasonably accurate linear approximation of the true relationship. To demonstrate a modest increase in cost for case A and a large increase in cost for case B, several lines have been drawn in Figure 5–14. Lines D, E, F, and H are applicable to case A, while lines, C, E, G, and H are related to case B.

The principal reason for using linear approximations in place of the true time-cost curves is to determine quickly the cost of expediting any one of the activities in a network without getting bogged down in complicated accounting concepts, such as the reallocation of costs on some accounting basis. However, the true time-cost curve can be determined and employed. Experience with this scheduling technique has shown that the extra expenditure to determine what these precise relationships are is not warranted. Since we have noted the rationale for treating a time-cost as a straight line, each unit reduction in time produces an equal increase in cost. The *incremental cost* I_c is the crash cost C_c minus normal cost N_c divided by the normal time N_T minus crash time C_T. This is shown as:

$$I_c = \frac{C_c - N_c}{N_T - C_T}$$ (Equation 5–3)

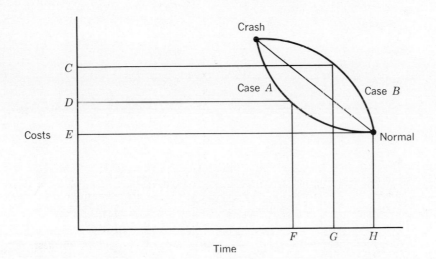

Figure 5–14
Time-cost relationships.

PERT/Cost Problem

We are now in a position to demonstrate how the incremental costs for each activity can be used to reduce the total project time at the least additional cost. Table 5-2 shows time and cost for each activity on a normal basis and a crash basis. Incremental costs for each activity also are shown, calculated by Equation 5–3. The PERT network on a normal time-cost basis in Figure 5–15 is based upon this table. It can be seen that the normal time for the illustration is 14 weeks at a cost of $53,000. When the same problem is crashed in terms of time and cost, the time is 10 weeks at a cost of $80,000. However, we should consider whether it is necessary to crash every activity in order to meet the time requirements of 10 weeks. The answer to this question will become apparent at the end of the problem.

The network found in Figure 5–15 is the starting point for crashing the program down to 10 weeks. The first and last activities cannot be crashed since an incremental cost cannot be computed. The starting point in our compression process is to determine the critical path which is 0–1–2–3–4–5. In order to shorten the time factor by 1 to 13 weeks, it is clear that one of the activities (on the critical path) must be shortened, since they determine the total project time. Reviewing the incremental costs for the critical activities in Figure 5–15, activity 2–3 has the lowest incremental cost, or $1,000. This is our selection to reduce the project time at the least additional cost. The revised PERT network is found in Figure 5–16.

Activity	Normal Time (N_T)	Crash Time (C_T)	Normal Direct Cost (N_c)	Crash Direct Cost (C_c)	Weekly Incremental Cost (I_c)
0–1	1	1	$ 5,000	$ 5,000	Not applicable
1–2	3	2	5,000	12,000	$7,000
1–3	7	4	11,000	17,000	2,000
2–3	5	3	10,000	12,000	1,000
2–4	8	6	8,500	12,500	2,000
3–4	4	2	8,500	16,500	4,000
4–5	1	1	5,000	5,000	Not applicable
			$53,000	$80,000	

Table 5–2
Normal and Crash Time-Cost Values Plus Incremental Costs

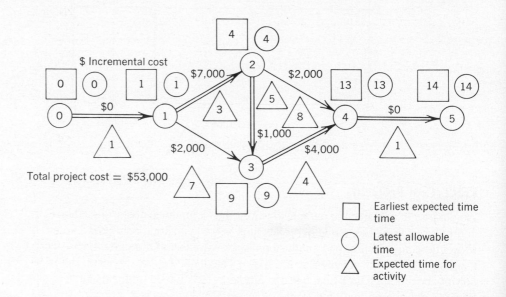

Figure 5–15
Normal time-cost PERT network for 14 weeks.

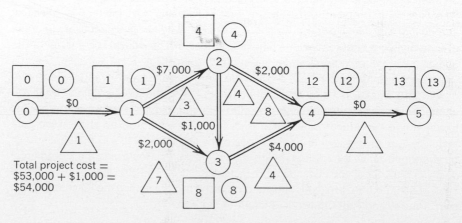

Figure 5–16
Time-cost PERT network for 13 weeks.

Inspection of Figure 5–16 reveals there are three critical paths (0–1–2–3–4–5, 0–1–2–4–5, and 0–1–3–4–5). In effect, all the activities have now become critical. It is now necessary to shorten certain critical activities in order to reduce total project time to 12 weeks. There are three combinations of two activities to choose from: 1–2 and 1–3 with a total increment cost of $9,000; 1–2 and 3–4 with a combined incremental cost of $11,000; and 2–4 and 3–4 with a total increment cost of $6,000. The last provides the lowest cost of the three combinations of two activities. There is another possibility, the combination of three activities. Here 1–3, 2–3, and 2–4 total a combined $5,000, a figure that clearly is preferable. The revised PERT network for 12 weeks is shown in Figure 5–17.

Based upon the crash time initially given, it is evident that activity 2–3 has reached its limiting crash point in terms of time (3 weeks) and cannot be shortened further. The combination of three activities cannot be used again in reducing the project completion time from 12 weeks. We now are forced to use the combinations of two activities which were set forth earlier. With all activities still being critical, the least costly combination is the 2–4 and 3–4 activities for a total cost of $6,000. This change is effected in Figure 5–18.

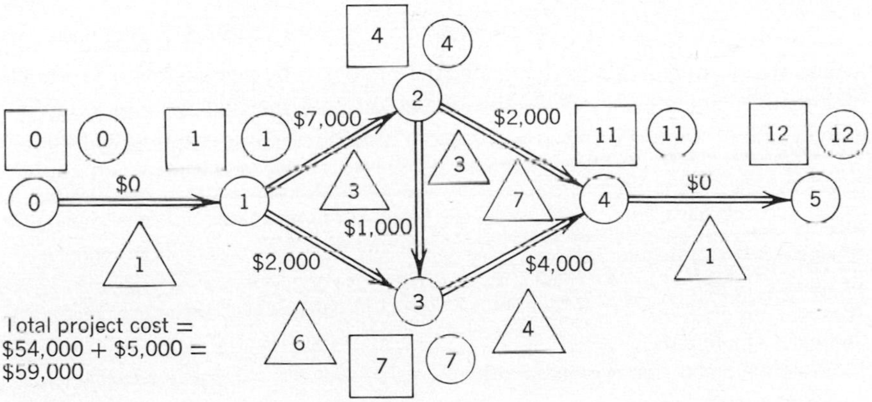

Figure 5–17
Time-cost PERT network for 12 weeks.

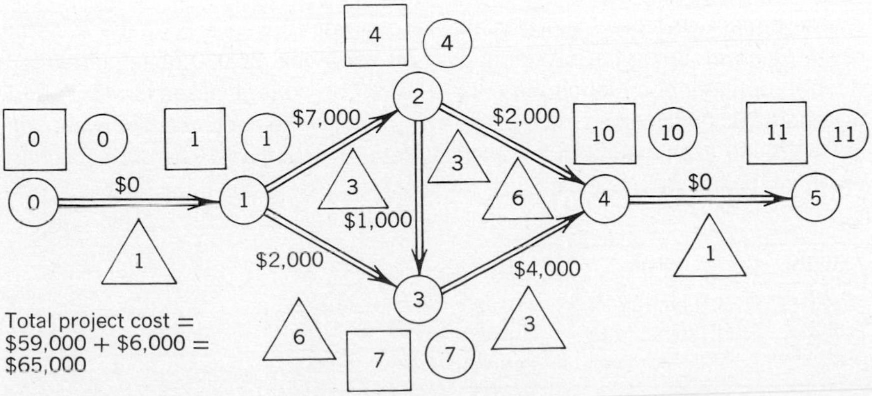

Figure 5–18
Time-cost PERT network for 11 weeks.

169

It was noted earlier that activity 2–3 had reached its limiting crash duration. The same now holds true for activity 2–4. Again we are confronted with all activities being critical and the combinations of two activities, either 1–2 and 1–3 or 1–2 and 3–4. The least cost combination is $9,000 for the first combination, which is reflected in Figure 5–19.

Figure 5–19
Time-cost PERT network for 10 weeks.

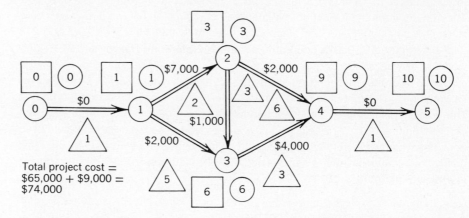

Total project cost =
$65,000 + $9,000 =
$74,000

Now that activities 1–2, 2–3, and 2–4 have reached their crash time, and all activities are still critical, we have crashed the project as far as possible. The reduction process is complete except for the question about the necessity to crash every activity in the project. Table 5–3 will serve as a basis for answering this question.

Table 5–3
Comparison of Normal and Crash Time-Cost Values

Project Time	Least Additional Cost	Project Cost
14 weeks (normal) (Figure 5–15)	—	$53,000
13 weeks (Figure 5–16)	$1,000	54,000
12 weeks (Figure 5–17)	5,000	59,000
11 weeks (Figure 5–18)	6,000	65,000
10 weeks (modified crash—Figure 5–19)	9,000	74,000
10 weeks (crash)	6,000	80,000

The project cost of $74,000 for a crash time of 10 weeks is called a *modified crash program*. Since the expenditure of an additional $6,000 does not further reduce the project completion time, there would be no logical reason for spending the entire $80,000. Instead of crashing every activity, we need crash only the critical activities. An examination of the original data reveals that it was not necessary to crash the following activities:

Activity	Week	Cost
1–3	1 (from 5 to 4)	$2,000
3–4	1 (from 3 to 2)	4,000
		$6,000

Computer PERT/Cost Packages

The PERT/Cost illustration is intended to demonstrate the principles and procedures followed in reducing a project. Even in this relatively simple example, there were some complexities in searching the various combinations of activities to obtain the least additional cost for the project being compressed. Obviously, to approach a PERT/Cost problem manually is difficult; generally a computer program is required. The original statement regarding the size of a PERT/Time network for using a computer (approximately 100 activities) needs to be revised substantially lower for a PERT/Cost network. Searching all the possible combinations can prove to be tedious and time consuming, not to mention the possibility of errors. For these reasons, a computer PERT/Cost program should be used in a network of approximately 25 or more activities which are closely interconnected.

Like other control techniques, PERT/Cost is no panacea since its usefulness is directly dependent upon the data fed into the computer system. This, in turn, depends upon the efficiency of the operating personnel. If unreliable data is fed into the computerized PERT/Cost program, the same type of information will be its output. However, efforts have been under way to improve the PERT/Cost system in order to alleviate the difficulties in the areas of cost. Perhaps more attention should be devoted to increasing the capabilities of the operating personnel who are responsible for the day-to-day functions of a PERT/Cost system.

Probability of Finishing a PERT Project

The preceding PERT approaches can be augmented by determining the probability of finishing a project which necessitates calculating the standard deviation for an activity. By way of review, *standard deviation* is a measure of the relative dispersion of a probability distribution about its mean. Since three time estimates (*a*, *m*, and *b*) have been determined, the distance between the *a* time and the *b* time represents the distance from the extreme left-hand end to the extreme right-hand end of a distribution of possible activity times. This distance can be represented by approximately ± 3 standard deviations (σ) which can be expressed mathematically as:

$$6\sigma = b - a$$

$$\sigma = \frac{b - a}{6} \qquad \text{(Equation 5–4)}$$

Thus, one standard deviation for an activity equals $(b - a)/6$.

In order to determine the probability of finishing a PERT network, the first step is to calculate the activity and expected times per Figure 5–20. For this simple PERT network, the individual standard deviations which represent dispersion of activities around their most likely times must also be calculated (Figure 5–20). The next step is to calculate the earliest expected time (T_E) for the network-ending event on the critical path(s). In the illustration, T_E is calculated to be 17.0 weeks (5.0 + 6.0 + 6.0) for the final event 40 on the critical path.

| Activity | Activity Time (weeks) | | | Expected Time (weeks) | Standard Deviation of Activity (weeks) |
	a	m	b	t_e	$\dfrac{b-a}{6}$
10–20[a]	2.0	5.0	8.0	5.0	1.0
10–40	9.0	15.0	21.0	15.0	2.0
20–30[a]	3.0	6.0	9.0	6.0	1.0
30–40[a]	4.5	6.0	7.5	6.0	.5

[a]Critical path.

Figure 5–20

Calculation of expected (t_e) and standard deviation (σ) for activities in a simple PERT network.

Now that T_E has been calculated for event 40, the standard deviation for this event must be determined, which is the square root of the sum of standard deviations squared for each activity. The formula is given as:

$$\sigma_E \text{ (network ending event)} = \sqrt{\Sigma\sigma_1{}^2 + \sigma_2{}^2 + \ldots \sigma_n{}^2} \qquad \text{(Equation 5–5)}$$

In the example, the standard deviation for the ending event on the critical path calulates to be 1.5 weeks as follows:

$$\begin{aligned}\sigma_E \text{ (event 40)} &= \sqrt{(1.0)^2 + (1.0)^2 + (.5)^2} \\ &= \sqrt{1 + 1 + .25} \\ &= \sqrt{2.25} \\ &= 1.5 \text{ weeks}\end{aligned}$$

At this point, two important measures of this PERT network have been determined; (1) $T_E = 17.0$ weeks and (2) $\sigma_E = 1.5$ weeks for event 40.

If the times are assumed to be distributed symmetrically around 17.0 weeks in Figure 5–21, half of the time we can expect to finish the PERT project before 17.0 weeks, and half of the time we can expect to finish the project later than 17.0 weeks. A question can be raised: What are the chances of finishing the project some time after 17 weeks (T_E), say within 20 weeks (A_E or point A, Figure 5–21)? It would be necessary to calculate the number of standard deviations from the mean to point A which is:

$$\frac{A_E - T_E}{\sigma_E} = \sigma_n \text{ (number of standard deviations)} \qquad \text{(Equation 5–6)}$$

$$\frac{20.0 - 17.0}{1.5} = 2.0 \text{ std. dev.}$$

Referring to Appendix C for areas under the curve 2.0 standard deviations to the right of the mean, we locate the value .97725. This means that we have better than a 97 percent chance of completing the PERT project within 20 weeks.

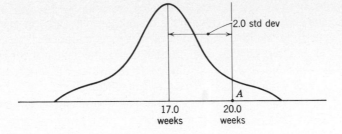

Figure 5–21
Normal distribution curve
for illustrative PERT
problem.

PERT Advantages

Some of the advantages of PERT should be evident after reviewing the preceding material. From a management point of view, PERT specifies how planning is to be done. It provides management with an approach for keeping planning up to date as the various events are accomplished and as conditions change. PERT permits management to foresee quickly the impact of deviations from the plan and thus to take corrective action in anticipation of potential trouble spots rather than after the fact. A general rule of experience is that only 10 percent of the activities in a project will be critical at any one time. Probably PERT's principal value is in helping management achieve an objective or complete a project with minimum time and cost expenditures.

Under the PERT approach, all managers of activities know the precise starting time for their work. They know they have a coordinating responsibility with other managers of activities and are aware of the results expected. Management responsibilities are precisely and empirically designated. PERT helps remove vagueness from the assignment of responsibility. It assists in eliminating one of the major blocks in relating planning to day-to-day operations. Although thus far we have dealt basically with the planning values of PERT, operating values are similarly applicable. Many managers have reported improved management control, identification of problem areas, improved communications, improved management of resources, improved decision making, improved progress reporting, and savings of time.

Regarding the last operating value — savings of time — several studies have indicated that PERT time savings for most firms have ranged from 5 to 20 percent, which can be translated directly into dollar savings even though the savings might not be on a one-for-one basis. Aside from the direct savings to the firm, there are other benefits, such as earlier generation of revenue and the introduction of a new product or process ahead of competition. It is conceivable that these indirect PERT savings could outweigh those that are directly apparent.

In addition to the benefits available to management, PERT provides a way of thinking through all the steps and interrelationships for a project in a methodical manner to reduce oversight of certain activities and events. Another important advantage of PERT is that it provides a number of checks and safeguards against going astray in developing a plan; that is, in making the network, the arrow diagram must show exactly which activities immediately precede and follow each one of the component activities in the project. Even though this quantitative technique has its origin in higher mathematics, its execution requires only simple arithmetic. This is in sharp contrast with some other mathematical techniques. Another valuable characteristic is its flexibility, which allows varying degrees of refinement and the use of costing procedures depending on the needs of the project. PERT can be useful as a simulation device. It allows the formulation and evaluation of alternative plans before actual implementation.

PERT Disadvantages

Despite the many advantages just set forth, there are some shortcomings to the PERT network. Surveys made by several reputable firms have pinpointed some noteworthy problems, the first dealing with securing realistic time and cost estimates. This is particularly true when a new and different type of project is undertaken and little previous experience exists. Securing both operating and management acceptance is termed a serious problem. This stems from the natural reluctance of people to accept and effect changes. Training of personnel can be a major problem. This comes from the resistance to change and the time required to learn PERT effectively. Developing a clear, logical network is another troublesome area. There appears to be no way to assure that the network accurately reflects the best thinking of those planning the work. This difficulty comes from the fact that PERT is no better than the persons who provide the input. One of the most mentioned trouble areas of PERT is determining the correct level of network detail. This is actually a matter of judgment and experience. Many companies tend to vary the detail of the networks, depending upon the management level and the usage to which they are placed.

There are certain kinds of projects in which PERT may not be useful; for example, projects which are too nebulous or changeable to allow any kind of methodical planning, and simple, even though large, projects involving only an uncomplicated succession of end-to-end activities. Integrating network techniques with existing budgeting and cost accounting procedures, and padding of original estimates by personnel who know that times and costs will be reviewed closely are other difficulties. There may be a problem of juggling resources to accommodate several programs at once. There can be the further difficulty of integrating "PERTed" and "non-PERTed" projects.

Cost of Using PERT

The variety of conditions present in firms makes it difficult to say precisely what it may cost to apply PERT. A few firms regard its costs too high, whereas others consider it moderate or minimal. The cost of PERT/Time networks has ranged from 0.5 to 2 percent of total project costs. For PERT/Cost networks, costs are 1 to 5 percent of project costs. The general consensus of firms using PERT indicates that its costs are not a major deterrent to its use. This is understandable since there are direct and indirect cost savings from using this technique, as was pointed out earlier. Since there are planning costs associated with other non-PERTing techniques, one should consider only the extra costs for using PERT over some other planning technique. The marginal cost for using PERT should be compared to its marginal savings. Such an analysis generally favors the implementation of PERT. This is readily understandable since reduction of workers' time, the major cost for most projects, means large cost savings.

Chapter Summary

Discussion of PERT in this chapter has included the methods of constructing networks using time and cost figures, the benefits of the technique, the problems involved, and the requirements for effective usage. Increased experience by business and government has demonstrated its management value. The technique has been applied to a variety of situations with beneficial results. Since PERT has proven to be an effective managerial tool that can be utilized by most companies in almost every industry, management, instead of asking its cost, should ask: "Can we afford not to use PERT now that it is available?"

Questions

1. Discuss the similarities and differences between the Gantt chart and a PERT/time network.
2. Distinguish among a normal time plan, a crash plan, and a modified crash plan in a PERT/cost network.
3. What are the principal difficulties with PERT? How can they be overcome?

Model Formulation Exercises

1. In the transformation of the Gantt chart to a PERT network, certain steps were performed. With the computerization of PERT, what step has been changed that makes it comparable to the Gantt chart? Also state the rationale for making this change back to the Gantt chart.

2. In the formulation of expected time, i.e., $t_e = \dfrac{a + 4m + b}{6}$, complex statistics and mathematics were used to prove the accuracy of this formula (Equation 5-1). In place of using this formula, when would it be proper to utilize the m value only (for expected time) and, at the same time, have a PERT network which depicts a critical path (paths) that is (are) accurate?

3. Although not stated in the chapter, the formulation for slack as presented in Equation 5–2, i.e., $S = T_L - T_E$, is in terms of *positive* slack. However, it is possible to talk about *negative* slack, which was not presented in the chapter. Define what negative slack is, and give an example in a typical PERT network.

4. Although many authors ignore the final PERT step given in the chapter (evaluate PERT network), relate its importance to sensitivity analysis.

5. To simplify the formulation of Equation 5–3 for incremental costs, i.e.,

$$I_c = \frac{C_c - N_c}{N_T - C_T},$$

what changes should be made? It should be noted that the calculations for incremental costs must result in the same values as in the original Equation 5–3.

Mathematical Exercises

1. Mr. Ralph Meeker is currently evaluating five different types of franchises that have varying levels of risk. Since the value of a franchise is determined by future income which the franchise will generate, the projected income statement is used as the starting point, which in turn is adjusted for cash flow under optimistic, most likely, and pessimistic conditions. After cash flow projections have been determined for a stated number of years into the future, their present values are ascertained by discounting back to the current time for optimistic, most likely, and pessimistic conditions. The discount rate employed considers the risk level for each type of franchise. Once the present values of each potential franchise are ascertained, they are grouped, shown as follows:

Franchise Opportunity	Optimistic Net Present Value	Most Likely Net Present Value	Pessimistic Net Present Value
1	$ 30,000	$12,000	($50,000)
2	100,000	25,000	(5,000)
3	25,000	12,000	(10,000)
4	70,000	40,000	(100,000)
5	25,000	(10,000)	(80,000)

Based on the foregoing facts, rank the five proposals according to their "expected value" estimates.

2. The National Business Machine Corporation has computed the values below which are the times for a power frame that is used in the manufacturing process of the Model C Executive typewriter.

Event	Preceding Events	Times (Days)		
		Optimistic	Most Likely	Pessimistic
1	—	1	1	1
2	1	1	2	3
3	1	2	6	10
4	1	2	3	4
5	2	3	4	5
6	3	1	2	3
7	4	1	3	5
8	6,7	2	4	6
9	5,8	3	4	8
10	9	1	3	5

(a) Draw the PERT network.
(b) Find the critical path in the network.

3. A new computer system for the Lawrence Company has to be installed now that the order for an IBM 370 (Model 138) has been finalized. Management wants to know how long it would take to install the new computer system, keeping in mind that the present system employs an IBM 360 (Model 30) computer. Since a change of this type can cause many personnel problems if it is not handled properly, it was decided to use PERT in order to ensure a smooth installation of the computer equipment. You have been appointed to develop the PERT network of events and activities as well as the most critical path. In order to determine the most critical path, the events have been given a serial number and shown in terms of sequence, that is, event 6 can be completed only after event 5 is completed. You have been asked to make recommendations based upon the results of your PERT network. The time for each event is in weeks.

Event	Preceding Event	Optimistic Time a	Most Likely Time m	Pessimistic Time b
1	0	0.1	1.0	2.0
2	1	1.0	3.0	4.0
3	2	4.0	6.0	12.0
4	2	0.1	2.0	4.0
5	4	1.0	1.5	3.0
6	5	1.0	4.0	8.0
7	5	1.0	3.0	4.0
8	7	1.0	2.0	4.0
9	6	0.1	1.0	4.0
9	7	0.1	2.0	3.0
10	6	0.1	1.0	3.0
10	7	0.1	1.0	2.0
11	2	0.1	1.0	2.0
12	11	6.0	13.0	30.0
13	12	10.0	12.0	40.0
14	9	0	0	0
14	10	0	0	0
14	11	0	0	0
14	13	0	0	0
14	3	0	0	0
14	8	0	0	0

4. A maintenance project for the Argo Manufacturing Company consists of the following jobs, which are identified by their respective activities.

Job Name	Activities	Expected Time (t_e)—Days
a	1–2	2
b	2–3	3
c	2–4	5
d	3–5	4
e	3–6	1
f	4–6	6
g	4–7	2
h	5–8	8
i	6–8	7
j	7–8	4

(a) Draw a PERT network showing the earliest expected and latest allowable times for each event.
(b) What is the slack time for events 5, 6, and 7?
(c) What is the critical path(s)?
(d) If event 3 took six days instead of three days to complete, would the end completion date be the same?

(e) Based upon the change in (d) above, what event(s) has (have) slack time remaining?

5. The President of Ricardo Manufacturing Company has an opportunity to participate in a project that has a sales price of $90,000 but must be completed within 8 weeks. This letter of intent was received Friday afternoon. Late the same afternoon, both the superintendent of production and the cost accountant completed the appropriate time and costs for you, based upon past jobs. Since the president needs an answer at 8:30 A.M. on Monday (start of the 8 weeks), you have been requested to work Saturday and determine the profitability of the project on an 8-week basis. An answer at 8:30 A.M. Monday allows the firm to start the production order at 10:00 A.M. in order to stay within the 8 weeks requested by the customer. The time and cost under normal conditions without crashing the project are based upon an 11-week basis. What answer should the president give the customer on Monday morning? A table of times and costs is listed below.

| | Preceding | Normal | | Crash | |
Event	Event	t_e (wks.)	Cost	Weeks	Cost
4	1	2	$ 8,000	1	$13,000
2	1	3	7,000	1	19,000
3	1	6	11,000	5	13,500
4	2	4	6,000	3	10,000
3	2	2	9,000	1	10,000
5	2	7	8,500	6	11,500
5	4	4	10,500	3	16,000
5	3	3	5,000	?	7,000

6. Several departmental managers of Ryan Aircraft, Inc., have been given the task of determining the times and costs of a new component that the firm may manufacture. Top management wants accurate time and cost estimates since this will be a fixed fee contract with no provision for renegotiating in case of modifications. Rather than give the departmental managers the time requirements of the customer and amount per component, top management feels more accurate answers will be forthcoming if this information is kept secret. You, one of the departmental managers, have been given one week to supply answers regarding the following: the critical path initially, modified crash plan in terms of time and cost for the various weeks, and total crash cost. After three days of analysis, the following time (in weeks) and costs were developed:

Activity	Activity Description	Opti-mistic Time a	Most Likely Time m	Pessi-mistic Time b	Normal Cost N_c	Time to Crash Activity C_T	Crash Cost C_C
1–2	Special component study	3.0	3.5	4.5	$ 8,000	2.6	$10,000
1–3	Layouts	4.0	5.0	6.0	15,000	3.0	20,000
1–4	Subsystem design	3.5	4.5	6.0	25,000	3.6	32,500
2–5	Vendor evaluation	2.0	2.2	3.5	4,000	1.4	6,000
3–5	Subcontract specs.	3.0	3.5	4.5	6,000	2.6	7,500
4–6	Subsystem tests	8.0	9.0	12.5	45,000	8.4	60,000
5–7	Subcontract work	7.5	8.5	11.5	35,000	6.8	50,000
3–6	Final drawings	6.0	7.5	12.0	30,000	6.0	40,000
6–7	Fabrication	7.5	9.0	12.5	35,000	7.33	42,500

7. The Arcose Machinery Company has been offered a contract to build and deliver nine extruding presses to the Homestead Bottling Company. The contract price is contingent on meeting a specified delivery time, a bonus being given for early delivery. The marketing department has established the following cost and time information.

Activity	Normal Time (weeks) a	b	$m(t_c)$	Cost	Crash Time (weeks)	Cost
1–2	1	5	3	$ 5,000	1	$ 9,000
2–3	1	7	4	8,000	3	14,000
2–4	1	5	3	4,000	2	6,000
2–5	5	11	8	5,000	7	6,000
3–6	2	6	4	3,000	2	5,000
4–6	5	7	6	2,000	4	3,600
5–7	4	6	5	10,000	4	14,000
6–7	1	5	3	7,000	1	10,600

The normal delivery time is 16 weeks for a contract price of $62,000.
(a) Based on the calculated profitability for each specified delivery time below, recommend the delivery schedule that the Arcose Machine Company should follow.

Contract Delivery Time (Weeks)	Contract Amount
15	$62,500
14	65,000
13	70,000
12	72,500

(b) Based on the foregoing data, what are the chances of completing the contract sometime after the normal delivery time, say one week later?

Bibliography

R. L. Ackoff and M. W. Sasieni, *Fundamentals of Operations Research,* New York: John Wiley & Sons, 1968.

R. D. Archibald and R. L. Villoria, *Network-Based Management Systems,* New York: John Wiley & Sons, 1967.

F. S. Hillier and G. J. Lieberman, *Operations Research,* San Francisco: Holden-Day, 1974.

A. Iannone, *Management Program Planning and Control with PERT, MOST & LOB,* Englewood Cliffs, N.J.: Prentice-Hall, 1971.

R. Levin and C. Kirkpatrick, *Planning and Control with PERT/CPM,* New York: McGraw-Hill Book Company, 1966.

K. G. McLaren and E. L. Buesnel, *Network Analysis in Project Management,* London: Cassell & Co., 1969.

R. Miller, *Schedule, Cost, and Profit Control with PERT: A Comprehensive Guide for Program Management,* New York: McGraw-Hill Book Company, 1963.

J. H. Mize, C. R. White, and G. H. Brooks, *Operations Planning and Control,* Englewood Cliffs, N.J.: Prentice-Hall, 1971.

J. J. Moder and C. R. Phillips, *Project Management with CPM and PERT,* New York: Van Nostrand, 1970.

New Uses and Management Implications of PERT, Booz, Allen & Hamilton, 1964.

J. J. O'Brien, *Scheduling Handbook,* New York: McGraw-Hill Book Company, 1969.

J. D. Wiest and F. K. Levy, *A Management Guide to PERT/CPM,* Englewood Cliffs, N.J.: Prentice-Hall, 1969.

Part IV

Operations Research Models — Matrix Algebra

Chapter 6

Linear Programming — Graphic and Simplex Methods

Chapter Objectives

□ To state the basic requirements for formulating a linear programming problem.

□ To present the graphic method of linear programming for solving a two- or a three-product problem.

□ To present a generalized approach, i.e., the simplex method, to solve a wide range of problems that can be formulated within the framework of linear programming.

□ To show how production bottlenecks can be uncovered and resolved by employing linear programming.

Chapter Outline

Many executive decisions hinge on the question of how to make the most of the company's resources — time, money, raw materials, manpower, production facilities, and shipping capabilities. For example, a manager may have to decide how many of several products the company should produce. The first item must be painstakingly assembled by hand; the second needs a great deal of machining; the third is bulky; and so forth. If the company were to concentrate on any one item, it would run short of labor, machines, or warehouse space. The OR technique called *linear programming* can tell the manager precisely the most profitable combination of the products to manufacture.

Linear programming had its beginnings in the input-output method of analysis developed by the economist W. W. Leontief. The present-day version is of more recent origin. Hitchcock first interpreted a "transportation type problem" in 1941, while Koopmans studied the same topic in 1947. In 1945, Stigler studied the "diet problem" (concerned with separate entities that can be selected and used in diversified quantities by choosing, combining, or mixing them with the purpose of obtaining an expected result). As to the current state of the art, the mathematical procedure most frequently used to find optimal solutions is the *simplex method,* invented in 1947 by George Dantzig, then with the U.S. Air Force. The method is essentially a trial-and-error approach. However, the groping for a solution is entirely methodical because it guarantees finding a better solution at each step and an optimal solution in a finite number of steps. Most practical linear-programming problems would take months, even years, to solve by hand, but a computer usually solves them in a few minutes or hours.

Requirements for Formulating a Linear Programming Problem

Before setting forth the requirements for formulating a linear programming problem, it would be helpful to define linear programming. The adjective *linear* is used to describe a relationship among two or more variables which are directly and precisely proportional. For example, if we say $x = f(y)$ where f is a linear function, then any change in x results in a constant proportional change in y. If this were graphed, the relationship would be expressed by a straight line—hence, linear. The term *programming* makes use of certain mathematical techniques to arrive at the best solution utilizing the firm's limited resources. Another word for programming could be computing, since it stands for calculating some unknown from a set of equations and/or inequalities under certain conditions expressed mathematically.

By gathering together the underlying concepts for both words, linear programming can be defined as a mathematical technique for determining the best allocation of a firm's limited resources. A mathematician might be more technical in defining linear programming by stating that it is a method of solving problems in which an objective function must be maximized or minimized when considering certain constraints. An economist might define linear programming as a method for allocating limited resources in a manner that satisfies the laws of supply and demand for the firm's products. In a similar manner, a businessman might look upon linear programming as one of management's tools for solving problems that are in conformity with the firm's clearly defined objectives.

Regardless of the way one defines linear programming, five basic requirements are necessary before this technique can be employed in solving business problems. They are:

1. Well-Defined Linear Objective Function A well-defined linear objective must be stated; this objective may serve to maximize contribution by utilizing the available resources, or it may produce the lowest possible cost by using a limited amount of productive factors, or it may determine the best distribution of the productive factors within a certain time period. It should be remembered that sales volume is linearly related not to profits but to total contribution (selling price minus variable cost per unit times the number of units sold). This first requirement, then, is that a linear objective function be clearly defined mathematically.

Applications—Linear Programming

- **Advertising media evaluation**—analyzes the effectiveness of advertising space and time based on the available advertising media.
- **Blast furnace operation**—aids production management in scheduling blast furnaces far more accurately and efficiently than possible with other analytical methods.
- **Blending of raw materials**—helps in blending the various ingredients of a particular mix in order to meet specified requirements and assists manufacturing management by proportioning raw materials subject to quality restrictions.
- **Inventory scheduling**—allows for the arrangement of raw materials and semifinished goods to minimize the firm's capital investment while maximizing efficient production flow.
- **Manpower management planning**—allows personnel management to analyze personnel policy combinations in terms of their appropriateness for maintaining a steady-state flow of people into, through, and out of the firm.
- **Physical distribution**—determines the most economic and efficient manner of locating manufacturing plants and distribution centers for physical distribution management.
- **Production scheduling**—determines for manufacturing management the most profitable combination of products to manufacture for facilities possessing a wide range of production capabilities and the most efficient method for machine loading.
- **Raw material allocation**—optimizes for buyers potential raw material sources for production and minimizes transportation costs.
- **Site location**—helps top management in deciding which location is best for new plants, warehouses, and branch offices and how to eliminate existing facilities.
- **Time standards determination**—assists time study personnel in determining standard times for those type of jobs in which the discrete work elements are essentially the same but vary in number.
- **Vendor quotation analysis**—aids buyers in analyzing vendor quotations in cases where a number of products are quoted by many vendors.

2. Alternative Courses of Action Second, there must be alternative courses of action. For example, it may be possible to make a selection between various combinations of manpower and automatic machinery. Or it may be possible to allocate manufacturing capacity in a certain ratio for the manufacture of a firm's products.

3. Linear Objective Function and Linear Constraints Must Be Expressed Mathematically   Another requirement is that equations and inequalities must describe the problem in linear form. Linearity in linear programming is a mathematical term used to describe systems of simultaneous equations of the first degree which satisfy the objective function and constraints. Just as the linear objective function must be expressed by an equation, so too must the linear constraints (restraints) be expressed mathematically by equations or inequalities. In essence this requirement dictates that the firm's objective and its constraints be expressed mathematically as linear equations or inequalities.

4. Variables Must Be Interrelated   Another necessary condition is that it be possible to formulate mathematical relationships among the variables describing the problem. To state it another way, variables in the problem must be interrelated.

5. Resources Must Be In Limited Supply   The resources must be finite and economically quantifiable. For example, each plant has a limited number of hours available—labor hours are finite. Since the cost of direct labor has an impact on profit, it is also economic. The allocation of this resource will be demonstrated in the next sections.

Graphic Method of Linear Programming

The *graphic method* of linear programming focuses on the intersection of lines for a two-dimensional approach. The intersection of planes in three dimensions or the use of one dimension, which is trivial, are not treated here. It should be noted that the four steps of the graphic method can be used only where no more than three variables are involved since we cannot draw in more than three dimensions.

In order to relate the fundamentals of linear programming throughout this chapter, the following example will be used. The Revco Corporation has one small plant located in a large city. Its production is limited to two industrial products, Alpha (A) and Beta (B). The unit contributions (unit selling price minus unit variable costs) for each product have been computed by the firm's accounting department as $10 for product Alpha and $12 for product Beta. Each product passes through three departments of the plant. The time requirements for each product and total time available in each department are as follows:

	Hours Required		Available Hours this Month
Department	Product Alpha	Product Beta	
1	2.0	3.0	1,500
2	3.0	2.0	1,500
3	1.0	1.0	600

Stating these requirements in mathematical terms, Revco wishes to maximize the objective function:

Z (total contribution) $= \$10A + \$12B$

subject to the following constraints:

$2A + 3B \leq 1{,}500$	Department 1
$3A + 2B \leq 1{,}500$	Department 2
$A + B \leq 600$	Department 3

where

$A =$ the number of units for product Alpha

$B =$ the number of units for product Beta

The first equation above, dealing with total contribution, is an equality. However, the next three equations are inequalities where the sign $\leq$ means "is equal to or less than." In all three equations, the firm can produce any combination of products that will be equal to or less than the available stated hours in each department. In this sense, an inequality is less restrictive than a corresponding equality. Inequalities can also have a sign $\geq$ which means "is equal to or greater than." Most constraints in a linear programming problem are expressed as inequalities which set upper and lower limits but do not express exact equalities. The equal to condition is not required in the expression of inequalities. The step-by-step procedures for solving the foregoing system equality and the three inequalities are given below.

Step 1. Define the Problem Mathematically The first step in the graphic method is stating the collected information in mathematical form, as shown above. The objective function ($Z = 10A + 12B$) shows the relationship of output to contribution. (Z for a two-product problem refers to the third dimension for plotting contribution.) The three inequalities refer to the time used making one unit of products Alpha and Beta on the left-hand side of the inequality and the total time available in the departments on the right-hand side. The hours needed to make one unit of product Alpha times the number of units produced for Alpha plus the hours required to make one unit of product Beta times the number of units produced for Beta must be equal to or less than the time available in each department. It should be noted that all three inequalities represent capacity restrictions regarding output and not contribution.

The values calculated for products Alpha and Beta must be positive since one either produces a unit of a product or does not. Thus, all elements in the solution of a linear programming problem must be greater than or equal to zero ($A \geq 0$ and $B \geq 0$). These two additional constraints mean the solution must lie in the positive quadrant of the graph (X and Y are positive). Summarizing the first step in terms of equations and inequalities, the sample problem stated mathematically is:

Maximize $Z = \$10A + \$12B$

Subject to these constraints:

$2A + 3B \leq 1,500$

$3A + 2B \leq 1,500$

$A + B \leq 600$

$A \geq 0$

$B \geq 0$

Step 2. Graph the Constraint Inequalities Next the constraint inequalities are graphed. In the problem, product Alpha is shown on the X axis and product Beta on the Y axis. Any of the three inequalities can be drawn on the graph by locating their two terminal points and joining these points by a straight line. Referring to the first inequality ($2A + 3B \leq 1,500$), the two terminal points can be found in the following manner. If all the time in department 1 is used in making product Alpha and if no units of product Beta are made, then 750 units of product Alpha can be made. This is calculated as follows:

$2A + 3(0) \leq 1,500$

$2A \leq 1,500$

$A \leq 750$ (maximum number of Alpha units)

The first point (750 units of product Alpha and zero units of product Beta) is graphed in Figure 6–1. The second point is computed in the same manner, only this time all the hours available are used in making the maximum units (500) of product Beta and zero units of product Alpha. The calculations are as follows:

$2(0) + 3B \leq 1,500$

$3B \leq 1,500$

$B \leq 500$ (maximum number of Beta units)

The second point (zero units of product Alpha and 500 units of product Beta) is graphed in Figure 6–1.

After locating the two terminal points, a straight line can be drawn (Figure 6–1). The same procedure is used for the other two inequalities which are plotted in Figure 6–2. In order to complete products Alpha and Beta, all three departments must be utilized. This means that the feasible solution area is the striped area in Figure 6–2. It contains all possible combinations of products satisfying the original inequalities.

What happens when a combination of output for products Alpha and Beta results in a solution outside the striped area? This means that we have violated one or more of the given constraints. For example, if management decided to make 100 units of product Alpha and 550 units of product Beta with a total contribution of $7,600 (100 × $10 + 550 × $12) as shown by point K in Figure 6–2, the time required to make these units falls within the time available in department 2, but exceeds the time available in departments 1 and 3. Based upon the existing constraints, the solution is not feasible.

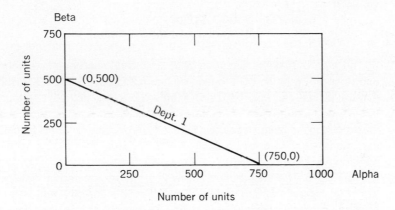

Figure 6–1
Graph of Equation
$2A + 3B = 1,500$.

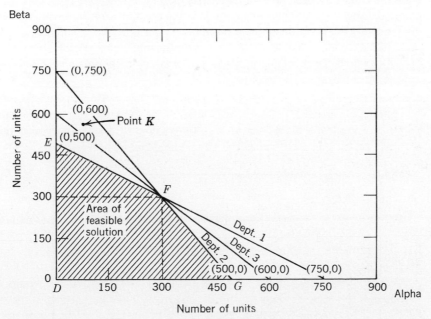

Figure 6–2
Graph of problem
constraints (Step 2).

Step 3. Plot the Objective Function   The third step is to plot the objective function, which is given as $Z = \$10A + \$12B$. This can be done by first letting total contribution equal some minimum dollar amount, say $1,200, an amount easily attainable per the given constraints. The objective function can be rewritten as $\$1,200 = \$10A$

191

+ $12B$. In order to plot this equation (Figure 6–3), two terminal points must be located and joined with a straight line. The calculations are:

When $A = 0$:
$$\$1,200 = \$10(0) + \$12B$$
$$B = 100 \text{ units (of product Beta)}$$

When $B = 0$:
$$\$1,200 = \$10A + \$12(0)$$
$$A = 120 \text{ units (of product Alpha)}$$

The area of feasible solutions (D, E, F, and G) has been taken from Figure 6–2 and is shown with the contribution equation $\$1,200 = \$10A + \$12B$ in Figure 6–3. A parallel line can now be drawn from the original objective function line to the farthest point in the area of feasible solution. Another method for reaching the farthest point in the feasible solution area is to use higher amounts for contribution and calculate new values for products Alpha and Beta. In effect, a series of objective function lines can be drawn to determine the farthest point from the origin, as shown in Figure 6–3. The contribution line which can be located farthest from the origin (point D) contains all the combinations of products Alpha and Beta that will generate the greatest possible contribution. As long as at least one point on this maximum contribution line is still within the feasible solution area, that point represents the most profitable combination of products. In our problem, point F is the farthest point in the area of feasible solutions and represents the most profitable combination of products. Dotted lines indicate this best combination, namely 300 units of product Alpha and 300 units of product Beta.

Figure 6–3
Objective function plotted (Step 3).

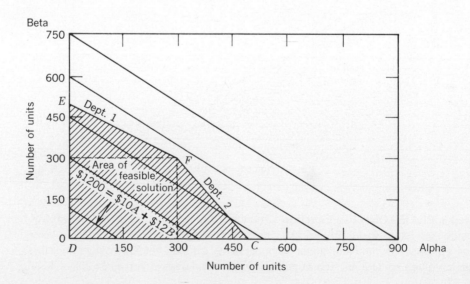

Summary—Methodology of the Graphic Method

Step 1—Define the Problem Mathematically   Determine the *objective function* (an equality) and the *constraints* (inequalities) in the problem. It should be noted that the values calculated for products to be manufactured must be positive. Thus, all values found in the solution of a linear programming problem must be greater than (if they are to be manufactured) or equal to zero (if they are not to be manufactured).

Step 2—Graph the Constraint Inequalities   Draw a constraint line for each of the constraint inequalities (say departments) by locating its two terminal points and joining these points by a straight line. Each of the two terminal points is determined by dividing the total time (say hours) available by the time necessary (say hours) to manufacture a unit of one product only. For example, if all the time within a department is used in making the first product only versus a second product, then so many units of the first product can be made, resulting in the determination of one of the two terminal points. The same type of calculation is made for the second product, thereby establishing the other terminal point.

Step 3—Plot the Objective Function   Determine two terminal points that represent physical quantities whose total contribution is easily attainable. Next, join these terminal points with a straight line which represents an initial objective function line. Draw one or more parallel lines from the original objective function line to the farthest point out in the feasible solution area. That point (could be a series of points) on the maximum objective function line which still lies within the feasible solution area represents the most profitable combination of products.

Step 4—Solve Using Simultaneous Equations   Determine the quantities to be manufactured by solving simultaneously the equations of the two lines for the farthest point (or points) determined in step (3) above. Also, place these resulting quantities to be manufactured in the contribution equation for determining total contribution.

Figure 6–4
Steps employed in the two-dimensional graphic method of linear programming.

Step 4. Solve Using Simultaneous Equations   The final step is to solve simultaneously the equations of the two lines which intersect at point *F* in Figure 6–3. The two equations for departments 1 and 2 are common to point *F*. As noted in Step 3, the numerical values for both products were read off the graph. However, in most cases, there is difficulty in reading a precise answer for real-world problems. The equations for departments 1 and 2 are solved simultaneously as follows:

193

$$2A + 3B = 1{,}500 \text{ (dept. 1)} \qquad 2A + 3B = 1{,}500$$
$$3A + 2B = 1{,}500 \text{ (dept. 2)} \underline{- 2A - \tfrac{4}{3}B = -1{,}000}$$
$$B = 300$$

Substituting 300 for B into the equation for department 2, the value for A equals 300 $(3A + 600 = 1{,}500)$. Using the total contribution equation, $Z = \$10A + 12B$, the total contribution is \$6,600 $(\$10 \times 300 + \$12 \times 300)$.

The foregoing steps used in the graphic method of linear programming are set forth in Figure 6–4 for a two-dimensional approach. For three-product analysis, the same procedures can be employed.

Testing the Corners Method Another approach to the graphic method of linear programming is "testing the corners." For the sample problem, this means to test the four points (D, E, F, and G) of Figure 6–3 that delineate the striped area to determine which yields the highest contribution. Basically, this is the comparison of the heights of the contribution lines at the corners in the two-product problem. (Had we been working a problem with three or more products, we could not graph the additional dimension for contribution.) A graphing of contribution for points D through G in Figure 6–3 would indicate that point F has the highest contribution (Z) in three-dimensional space based on the following data:

$$\text{Point } D \ (0,0) = \$10(0) + \$12(0) = 0$$
$$\text{Point } E \ (0,500) = \$10(0) + \$12(500) = \$6{,}000$$
$$\text{Point } F \ (300,300) = \$10(300) + \$12(300) = \$6{,}600$$
$$\text{Point } G \ (500,0) = \$10(500) + \$12(0) = \$5{,}000$$

This approach can replace Steps 3 and 4 of the traditional graphical method. However, more simultaneous equations are used in order to determine the proper quantities for each product.

Importance of Related Dual Program In 1949, Albert W. Tucker and Harold W. Kuhn of Princeton University and David Gale of Brown University proved that every linear programming problem has a *shadow*, called its "dual program." When mathematicians set up a linear program to achieve one objective, they can solve for the dual program and, thereby achieve a different objective. For example, an original linear programming problem might find a production schedule that minimizes costs for a fixed labor force and consumption of raw materials. The dual program would determine a system of pricing that would maximize the value of net output while balancing the direct costs of labor and raw material. Looking at the solutions of both the original program and its dual gives managers another degree of flexibility in making decisions. In addition to learning how to make the most profit with the machines at hand, they may be able to tell how to increase profits by installing more or different machines. Hence, managers learn what would happen if some of the variables were to change slightly. Such an analysis also reveals how critical an error in the data might affect the final solution. The significance of this additional information is that it enables nonmathematical executives to ask "what if" questions they would naturally want to ask, as well as those that may not have occurred to them when the linear program was begun. Also, they are able to use this analysis to increase the realism of this technique by blending hunches and judgments with applied mathematics.

For the sample problem illustrated in the chapter, a graphical representation of the dual program is found in Figure 6–5. An examination of the graph indicates that the answers complement those found originally.

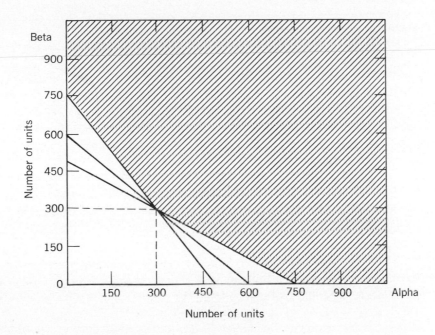

Figure 6–5
Graphic representation of the dual program.

Simplex Method—Maximization Problem

Most production mix problems reach a level of complexity involving a dozen products and the same number of departments, for example, which necessitates a new approach, called the *simplex method* of linear programming. The computational procedure used is an iterative process, sometimes referred to as an *algorithm,* that is, the same basic computational routine is used over and over again. This results in a series of successively improved solutions until the best one is found. A basic characteristic of the simplex method is that the last solution yields a contribution as large as or larger than the previous solution in a maximization problem. In a minimization problem, the simplex method determines a cost that is the same or lower than the previous one. This feature assures that the optimal answer can finally be reached.

The simplex method, consisting of four steps, utilizes matrix algebra as found in Appendix A of this book. Also found in this appendix is background material on vectors and determinants which will be useful for this chapter and succeeding chapters. A reader who is unfamiliar with these subjects should read this appendix before proceeding any further in this chapter. In the simplex method, an inverse of a matrix to solve a set of simultaneous equations is formed. The formation of the inverse will not be accomplished in the same manner as that found in Appendix A; however, it is still an inverse.

The preceding example, which will be used to demonstrate the simplex method of linear programming, is

Maximize $Z = \$10A + \$12B$

Subject to:

$$2A + 3B \leq 1,500 \quad \text{(department 1)}$$
$$3A + 2B \leq 1,500 \quad \text{(department 2)}$$
$$A + B \leq 600 \quad \text{(department 3)}$$
$$A \geq 0, B \geq 0$$

In order to use the simplex method, it is necessary first to convert the three inequalities into equations for the departments. This can be performed by adding a *slack variable* for each department, that is, add to each inequality a variable that will take up the slack or time not used in a department. The following slack variables (in hours) will be used:

$S_1 =$ unused time in department 1

$S_2 =$ unused time in department 2

$S_3 =$ unused time in department 3

It should be noted that the foregoing slack variables are positive, caused by the departmental constraints being equal to or less than ($\leq$). However, if the department constraints were greater than or equal to ($\geq$), *surplus variables* would have been introduced, sometimes referred to as negative slack variables. An example of the surplus variable is the situation in which a contract assures a supplier of an order for at least so many units per month.

The slack variable S_1 is equal to the total amount of time available in department 1 or 1,500 hours minus any hours used in processing products Alpha and Beta. The same type of reasoning is applicable to S_2 and S_3. The original inequalities for the three departments now can be expressed by writing equations for the slack variables as follows:

$$S_1 = 1,500 - 2A - 3B \quad \text{(Equation 6–1)}$$
$$S_2 = 1,500 - 3A - 2B \quad \text{(Equation 6–2)}$$
$$S_3 = 600 - A - B \quad \text{(Equation 6–3)}$$

The value of these equations is that they show the relationship among the variables in the first solution (S_1, S_2, and S_3 or unused time) and the other variables. However, to state the objective function and these three equations in an acceptable format for the simplex algorithm, they must be written as:

Maximize $Z = \$10A + \$12B + \$0S_1 + \$0S_2 + \$0S_3$ (Equation 6–4)

Subject to:

$$1{,}500 \text{ hours} = 2A + 3B + S_1 + 0S_2 + 0S_3 \qquad \text{(Equation 6–5)}$$
$$1{,}500 \text{ hours} = 3A + 2B + 0S_1 + S_2 + 0S_3 \qquad \text{(Equation 6–6)}$$
$$600 \text{ hours} = A + B + 0S_1 + 0S_2 + S_3 \qquad \text{(Equation 6–7)}$$

In addition to converting the inequalities into equations by adding slack variables, the simplex method requires that any unknown which appears in one equation must appear in all equations. However, the unknowns that do not affect an equation are written with zero coefficients. In the sample problem, the objective function shows zero coefficients for S_1, S_2, and S_3. Similarly, the equation for department 1 shows zero coefficients for slack time in departments 2 and 3.

In order to simplify handling the equations in the problem, they can be placed in a tabular form, known as a *tableau*—refer to Tableau I. Appendix A shows how a system of equations can be solved by working only with the coefficients; thus, the variables need not be written.

Tableau I
Linear Programming
Maximization Problem

C_j	Product Mix	Quantity	$10 A	$12 B	$0 S_1	$0 S_2	$0 S_3	Contribution per Unit Variables
$0	S_1	1,500	2	3	1	0	0	⎫
$0	S_2	1,500	3	2	0	1	0	⎬ Coefficients
$0	S_3	600	1	1	0	0	1	⎭
			__Body__ Matrix		__Identity__ Matrix			
	Z_j	$0	$0	$0	$0	$0	$0	Contribution lost per unit
	$C_j - Z_j$		$10	$12	$0	$0	$0	Net contribution per unit

Starting with the left-hand column in Tableau I, the C_j column contains the contribution per unit for the slack variables S_1, S_2, and S_3. The zero indicates that the contribution per unit is zero. The rationale is that profits are not made on unused time in a department, but on time used. The second column, product mix, contains the variables in the solution which are used to determine total contribution. In the initial solution, no products are being made. The values for S_1, S_2, and S_3 must contain all of the unused time in the problem, which is found in the third column—quantity. The starting solution will be zero contribution since no units of products

Alpha and Beta are being manufactured. This is represented by $0 ($0 × 1,500 + $0 × 1,500 + $0 × 600) in the Z_j row for the third column. Since no units of Alpha and Beta are being manufactured, the first solution is:

$A = 0$

$B = 0$

$S_1 = 1,500$

$S_2 = 1,500$

$S_3 = 600$

This is essentially represented by the first three columns of Tableau I.

The *body matrix* consists of the coefficients for the real product variables in the first tableau. Referring to the first row and A column, the coefficient 2 means that if we wanted to bring one unit of product Alpha into the solution, we would have to give up two hours of S_1 in department 1. To state it another way, it takes two hours to make product Alpha in department 1. Likewise, the element 3 in the B column, first row, indicates that production of one unit of product Beta would require us to give up three hours in department 1. In reality, what we have in the coefficients of the body matrix is the rate of substitution.

The *identity matrix* in the first simplex tableau represents the coefficients of the slack variables that have been added to the original inequalities to make them equations. As stated previously, any unknown that occurs in one equation must appear in all equations but with a zero coefficient so as not to affect the equation.

Referring to the element in the S_1 column, first row, the 1 indicates that in order to make one hour of S_1 available, it would be necessary to give up one of the 1,500 hours in the initial solution. The zero in the S_2 column, first row, indicates that making one hour in department 2 available for other purposes has no effect on S_1 (slack time of department 1). The logic used for S_2 is also applicable to the S_3 column, first row.

The same type of rationale is applicable to the next two rows (S_2 and S_3) in Tableau I. Basically, we are dealing with substitution rates, that is, the addition of products Alpha and Beta into the solution and the withdrawal of time from the three departments' slack time S_1, S_2, and S_3.

The last two rows of the first simplex tableau are used to determine whether or not the solution can be improved. Evaluation of the last row or the $C_j - Z_j$ row is the first step in the simplex method and therefore will not be treated in this section. However, the second to last row or the Z_j row is explained here. The Z_j row value under the quantity column indicates an initial solution of zero contribution for the firm. The other five values of $0 are the amounts by which contribution would be reduced if one unit of the variables (A, B, S_1, S_2, and S_3) were added to the mix. Another way of defining the Z_j row for the five variables is the contribution lost per unit. For example, if we desire to make one unit of product Alpha, the coefficients $\begin{pmatrix} 2 \\ 3 \\ 1 \end{pmatrix}$ in the body matrix tell us we must give up two hours of S_1 (department 1) unused time, three hours of S_2 (department 2) unused time, and one hour of S_3 (department 3) unused time. Since slack time is worth $0 per hour, there can be no reduction in contribution. The calculation for how much contribution is lost by adding one unit of product Alpha to production is:

Number of hours of S_1 given up   2
   × Contribution per unit of S_1 × $0 = $0

Number of hours of S_2 given up   3
   × Contribution per unit of S_2 × $0 = $0

Number of hours of S_3 given up   1
   × Contribution per unit of S_3 × $0 = $0

Total contribution given up $0

TABLEAU I TO TABLEAU II   In order to understand the interworkings of Tableau I and all subsequent tableaus, the four steps employed in the simplex method will be treated in detail. However, in the next section, only the steps involved in going from Tableau I to Tableau II are discussed.

Step 1. Select the Column with the Highest Plus Value   Evaluation of the last row in the initial tableau represents the first step in our computational procedure for the sample maximization problem. The final row is the net contribution that results from adding one unit of a variable (product) to production. As shown in Tableau I, if one unit of product Alpha is added to the solution, the contribution to the solution is $10. The contribution is $12 for one unit of product Beta and $0 for S_1, S_2, and S_3. An examination of the figures in the $C_j - Z_j$ row reveals that the largest positive value is $12. A plus value indicates that a greater contribution can be made by the firm. A negative value would indicate the amount by which contribution would decrease if one unit of the variable for that column were brought into the solution. The largest positive amount in the last row is selected as the optimum column or $12 per unit for product Beta since we want to maximize total contribution. When no more positive values remain in the $C_j - Z_j$ row and values are zero or minus in a maximization problem, total contribution is at its greatest value.

Step 2. Determine the Replaced (old) Row   Once the initial simplex tableau has been constructed and the variable (optimum column) has been selected (first step) which contributes the most per unit ($12 per one unit of product Beta), the second step is to determine which variable should be replaced. To state it another way, inspection of the optimum column ($12 for product Beta) indicates that the variable B should be added to the product mix, replacing row S_1, S_2, or S_3. To determine which variable will be replaced, divide the value in the quantity column by the corresponding coefficient in the optimum column. Select the row with the smallest positive quantity as the row to be replaced. As in the previous method, the firm would like to produce the largest quantity, but consideration must be given to the constraints in the problem. The possible units are computed as follows:

S_1 row $\dfrac{1{,}500 \text{ hours} - \text{unused time}}{3 \text{ hours required per unit of product Beta}}$

$= 500$ units of product Beta

S_2 row $\dfrac{1{,}500 \text{ hours} - \text{unused time}}{2 \text{ hours required per unit of product Beta}}$

$= 750$ units of product Beta

S_3 row $\dfrac{600 \text{ hours} - \text{unused time}}{1 \text{ hour required per unit of product Beta}}$

$= 600$ units of product Beta

Based on these calculations for product Beta, row S_1 will be replaced in the second tableau by 500 units of product Beta; it is called the *replaced row*. The elements common to the optimum column and three rows $\begin{pmatrix} 3 \\ 2 \\ 1 \end{pmatrix}$ are called intersectional elements. Having picked the optimum column and the replaced row, we are now ready to work on an improved solution, found in Tableau II.

Step 3. Compute Values for the Replacing (new) Row In the third step, the first row to determine in the second tableau is the new B row (replacing row) for the S_1 row (replaced row). The B row is computed by dividing each value in the replaced row (S_1) by the intersectional element (3) of the replaced row. The results for the new B row are: $\frac{1500}{3} = 500$ (quantity column), $\frac{2}{3} = \frac{2}{3}$ (A column), $\frac{3}{3} = 1$ (B column), $\frac{1}{3} = \frac{1}{3}$ (S_1 column), $\frac{0}{3} = 0$ (S_2 column), and $\frac{0}{3} = 0$ (S_3 column). These become the values for the first row (B) in Tableau II.

Tableau II
Linear Programming
Maximization Problem

C_j	Product Mix	Quantity	$10 A	$12 B	$0 S_1	$0 S_2	$0 S_3	
$12	B	500	$\frac{2}{3}$	1	$\frac{1}{3}$	0	0	replacing row
$ 0	S_2	500	$1\frac{2}{3}$	0	$-\frac{2}{3}$	1	0	remaining row with new values
$ 0	S_3	100	$\frac{1}{3}$	0	$-\frac{1}{3}$	0	1	remaining row with new values
	Z_j	$6,000	$8	$12	$4	$0	$0	
	$C_j - Z_j$		$2	$ 0	$-4	$0	$0	

Step 4. Calculate New Values for Remaining Rows The fourth and final step in our computational procedures is to calculate all new values for the remaining rows (S_2 and S_3). The formula for calculating these new rows is

$$\begin{pmatrix} \text{Former} \\ \text{element} \\ \text{in the} \\ \text{remaining} \\ \text{row} \end{pmatrix} - \left[\begin{pmatrix} \text{Former} \\ \text{intersectional} \\ \text{element of} \\ \text{remaining} \\ \text{row} \end{pmatrix} \times \begin{pmatrix} \text{New} \\ \text{corresponding} \\ \text{element in} \\ \text{replacing} \\ \text{row} \end{pmatrix} \right] = \begin{pmatrix} \text{New value} \\ \text{for} \\ \text{remaining} \\ \text{row} \end{pmatrix}$$

Based upon this formula, the values in Tableau II for the new S_2 and S_3 rows are:

Row S_2:

$$1,500 - (2 \times 500) = 500$$

$$3 - \left(2 \times \frac{2}{3}\right) = 1\frac{2}{3}$$

$$2 - (2 \times 1) = 0$$

$$0 - \left(2 \times \frac{1}{3}\right) = -\frac{2}{3}$$

$$1 - (2 \times 0) = 1$$

$$0 - (2 \times 0) = 0$$

Row S_3:

$$600 - (1 \times 500) = 100$$

$$1 - \left(1 \times \frac{2}{3}\right) = \frac{1}{3}$$

$$1 - (1 \times 1) = 0$$

$$0 - \left(1 \times \frac{1}{3}\right) = -\frac{1}{3}$$

$$0 - (1 \times 0) = 0$$

$$1 - (1 \times 0) = 1$$

The procedure for calculating the last two rows in Tableau II has been explained previously. The computations for the Z_j row are:

Z_j (total contribution) $= \$12(500) + \$0(500) + \$0(100) = \$6,000$

Z_j for $A = \$12\left(\frac{2}{3}\right) + \$0\left(1\frac{2}{3}\right) + \$0\left(\frac{1}{3}\right) = \$8$

Z_j for $B = \$12(1) + \$0(0) + \$0(0) = \$12$

Z_j for $S_1 = \$12\left(\frac{1}{3}\right) + \$0\left(-\frac{2}{3}\right) + \$0\left(-\frac{1}{3}\right) = \$4$

Z_j for $S_2 = \$12(0) + \$0(1) + \$0(0) = \$0$

Z_j for $S_3 = \$12(0) + \$0(0) + \$0(1) = \$0$

The calculations for the $C_j - Z_j$ row are:

A (variable), $10 C_j$ (contr./unit) $- \$8 Z_j$ (contr. lost/unit)

$$= \$2 \ C_j - Z_j \text{ (net contr./unit)}$$

B, $12 - \$12 = \$0$

S_1 $\$0 - \$4 = -\$4$

S_2 $\$0 - \$0 = \$0$

S_3 $\$0 - \$0 = \$0$

These steps complete the second tableau. The total contribution is now $6,000 versus $0 in the first tableau. The presence of a positive $2 in the last row of the A column denotes a better overall contribution is available to the firm; thus it is necessary to complete a third tableau.

It might be helpful at this point to examine the coefficients of the variables in Tableau II, particularly in row B and row S_2, to understand what they mean. The logic applicable to row S_2 will be also applicable to row S_3. The value ($\frac{2}{3}$) in the A column, row B means that for every unit of product Alpha processed in department 1, $\frac{2}{3}$ unit of product Beta must be given up to provide the required two hours. The 1 in the B column, row B indicates that we have a one-for-one substitution, or each unit of product Beta added to production replaces one unit of product Beta in the solution. The third item ($\frac{1}{3}$) in the B row requires that every hour of S_1 added to the solution reduces the production of product Beta by $\frac{1}{3}$ unit. The coefficients of zero for S_2 and S_3 in the B row indicate that adding one unit of S_2 or S_3 has no effect (0) on product Beta. Returning to the quantity column, the value of 500 means 500 units of product Beta should be produced.

Dropping down to the next row (S_2), the value in column A indicates that adding one unit of product Alpha replaces $1\frac{2}{3}$ hours of S_2. The next column (B) with a zero value has this meaning: adding one unit of B has no effect on S_2. The same is true for column S_3 in this row. The coefficient ($-\frac{2}{3}$) in the S_1 column can be explained by the following:

Units of B now in the solution	500
If 1 unit of S_1 is added to the solution, B is reduced by	$-\frac{1}{3}$
New quantity of B	$499\frac{2}{3}$
2 hours per unit of B required in department 2	$\times 2$
Total hours required to make	
$499\frac{2}{3}$ units of B in department 2	$999\frac{1}{3}$
Total hours required to make 500 units of B (2×500)	1,000
Total hours freed by adding 1 unit of S_1	$-\frac{2}{3}$

The 1 in the S_2 column of the S_2 row indicates if we add one hour of S_2, we must subtract one hour of S_2 in order not to exceed 1,500 hours. The value of 500 in the quantity column for this row indicates the number of unused hours for department 2.

TABLEAU II TO TABLEAU III   Returning to the computational procedures used in the simplex method, the first step is to determine the optimum column. This is the A column of Tableau II. Units of product Alpha will be added to the solution, replacing one of the variables B, S_2, or S_3, since an additional contribution of \$2 per unit is available. The replaced row is found as the second step in the simplex method. Again, the values in the quantity column are divided by the corresponding intersectional elements in the optimum column as follows:

B row:

$$\frac{500}{\frac{2}{3}} = 750$$

S_2 row:

$$\frac{500}{1\frac{2}{3}} = 300$$

S_3 row:

$$\frac{100}{\frac{1}{3}} = 300$$

The foregoing calculations show a condition of *degeneracy* exists since there is a tie between the S_2 and S_3 rows, that is, the quantity (300) is common to both. In this problem, the simplex method will give the correct answer if we choose either of the two rows in Tableau III. Hence, the S_3 row will be arbitrarily designated as the replaced row.

C_j	Product Mix	Quantity	$10 A	$12 B	$0 S_1	$0 S_2	$0 S_3
$12	B	300	0	1	1	0	−2 remaining row with new values
$ 0	S_2	0	0	0	1	1	−5 remaining row with new values
$10	A	300	1	0	−1	0	3 replacing row
	Z_j	$6,600	$10	$12	$2	$0	$6
	$C_j - Z_j$		$ 0	$ 0	−$2	$0	−$6

Tableau III
Linear Programming
Maximization Problem

For larger problems, the simplex algorithm will generally give the correct answer if any of the two (or more) tied rows is chosen. However, the remaining tied row (or rows) may have to be selected if the first choice does not produce a solution. Thus, the general rule for degeneracy is: if the selected row does not lead to a solution, that is, the simplex tableaus begin to repeat themselves, then choose the other tied row (or one of the other tied rows) at the point where the degeneracy was discovered.

In addition to the foregoing degeneracy condition, a tie can also occur in the $C_j - Z_j$ row. However, such a condition is not called degeneracy since either of the tied variables can be chosen to enter the next tableau. The variable selected may affect the number of tableaus required in the problem but never the final outcome.

Returning to the third step in the simplex method, a new replacing row is computed in Tableau III. The replacing row is calculated by dividing each number in the replaced row by the intersectional element of the replaced row, which is

$$\frac{100}{\frac{1}{3}} = 300; \quad \frac{\frac{1}{3}}{\frac{1}{3}} = 1; \quad \frac{0}{\frac{1}{3}} = 0; \quad \frac{-\frac{1}{3}}{\frac{1}{3}} = -1; \quad \frac{0}{\frac{1}{3}} = 0; \quad \frac{1}{\frac{1}{3}} = 3$$

The replacing row (A) has the following values: 300, 1, 0, −1, 0, and 3.

The last step is concerned with calculating new values for row B (300, 0, 1, 1, 0, and −2) and row S_2 (0, 0, 0, 1, 1, and −5). These have been entered in the third tableau (see earlier procedure and formula). The last two rows are determined in the manner set forth previously. The total contribution in the third tableau is $6,600 versus $6,000 in Tableau II. The completed third tableau indicates no further improvements in contribution can be made since all $C_j - Z_j$ row values are zero or minus. The optimum is the same as for the previous method: 300 units each of products Alpha and Beta should be produced with no unused time remaining.

It is suggested that the calculated values derived in the problem be placed back in the original constraint inequalities for the three departments to test whether or not the values are within the constraints. The original equations are:

$$2A + 3B \leq 1,500$$
$$3A + 2B \leq 1,500$$
$$A + B \leq 600$$

Substituting the appropriate values for A and B in the preceding equations, the results show that we are within the constraints of the problem:

$$2(300) + 3(300) \leq 1,500$$
$$600 + 900 \leq 1,500$$
$$1,500 = 1,500$$
$$3(300) + 2(300) \leq 1,500$$
$$900 + 600 \leq 1,500$$
$$1,500 = 1,500$$
$$(300) + (300) \leq 600$$
$$600 = 600$$

In many cases, there may be unused time in a problem. The time used for production plus unused time must equal the original constraints or an error has been made.

An important feature of the simplex method involves the inversion of the original body matrix. Many times an optimum solution utilizing the simplex method will be reached before a complete inversion of the body matrix ($2 \times 2, 3 \times 3, \ldots$). The inversion of the original body matrix is part of the computational procedures for the simplex method. In the sample problem, a complete inversion was not possible since we did not have a square matrix in the beginning. Notice the location of 0s and 1s in the body matrix of Tableau III.

A summary of the foregoing iterative steps is set forth in Figure 6–6 for a maximization problem. The three simplex tableaus to solve this sample problem are recapped in Figure 6–7, which shows the steps used in developing Tableaus I to III.

Summary—Methodology of the Simplex Method

Step 1—Select the Column With the Highest Plus Value Calculate the values for the final row in the simplex tableau, that is, the $C_j - Z_j$ row and select that column which has the largest positive value for $C_j - Z_j$. If no more positive values remain in the $C_j - Z_j$ row, that is, only zero or minus values remain, total contribution is at its greatest. The iterative steps are complete.

Step 2—Determine the Replaced (old) Row Determine the replaced (old) row by dividing the values in the quantity column of the simplex tableau for each row by the intersectional elements in the optimum column (selected per Step 1 above). Select the row with the smallest positive quantity as the row to be replaced.

Step 3—Compute Values for the Replacing (new) Row Compute values for the replacing (new) row in the next tableau—takes the place of the replaced (old) row in the prior tableau. New values for the replacing row are calculated by dividing each value in the replaced (old) row by the intersectional element of the replaced row. Also, the variable in the product mix column for the new row must be changed to that found in the optimum column per Step 1 above.

Step 4—Calculate New Values for Remaining Rows Calculate new values for all remaining rows in the tableau started in Step 3 above. The formula for calculating these new row values, other than the Z_j and $C_j - Z_j$ rows, is:

$$\begin{pmatrix} \text{Former} \\ \text{element} \\ \text{in the} \\ \text{remaining} \\ \text{row} \end{pmatrix} - \left[\begin{pmatrix} \text{Former} \\ \text{intersectional} \\ \text{element of} \\ \text{remaining} \\ \text{row} \end{pmatrix} \times \begin{pmatrix} \text{New} \\ \text{corresponding} \\ \text{element in} \\ \text{replacing} \\ \text{row} \end{pmatrix} \right] = \begin{pmatrix} \text{New value} \\ \text{for} \\ \text{remaining} \\ \text{row} \end{pmatrix}$$

while the variables in the product mix column remain unchanged. The last two rows (Z_j and $C_j - Z_j$) are calculated. The iterative procedure loops back to Step 1 above in order to determine if there is need for developing another tableau.

Simplex Method—Minimization Problem

The preceding material (graphic and simplex methods) has been concerned exclusively with a maximization problem. These computational procedures are readily applicable to a minimization problem whose main objective is to minimize costs. However, only the simplex method will be illustrated.

The Toms River Chemical Corporation must produce 1,000 pounds of a special mixture for a customer which consists of ingredients $01X$, $02X$, and $03X$. Ingredient $01X$ costs $5 per pound, $02X$ costs $6 per pound, and $03X$ costs $7 per pound. No more than 300 pounds of $01X$ can be used and at least 150 pounds of $02X$ must be used. In addition, at least 200 pounds of $03X$ is required. Since the firm desires to minimize costs, the problem is determining what amount of each ingredient the firm should include in the mixture.

The problem first must be stated in mathematical form. Based on data given, the equality and inequalities are:

Minimize cost $= \$5X_1 + \$6X_2 + \$7X_3$

Subject to:
$$X_1 + X_2 + X_3 = 1{,}000 \text{ pounds}$$
$$X_1 \leq 300 \text{ pounds}$$
$$X_2 \geq 150 \text{ pounds}$$
$$X_3 \geq 200 \text{ pounds}$$

where
$X_1 =$ number of pounds for ingredient $01X$
$X_2 =$ number of pounds for ingredient $02X$
$X_3 =$ number of pounds for ingredient $03X$

The statement that no more than 300 pounds of X_1 can be used means that we can use any amount up to and including 300 pounds. This can be written as $X_1 \leq 300$ pounds. The second (and third) restriction above means that we may use more than 150 (200) pounds, but not less than 150 (200) pounds since $X_2 \geq 150$ ($X_3 \geq 200$) pounds.

Just as a starting point was necessary in the maximization problem, the same holds true for a minimization problem. The initial solution for the previous problem resulted in no contribution, which is actually an unrealistic solution. However, it did furnish us with a basis for getting started and moving toward a better solution. Again, we need a mathematical starting point. However, this time the cost will be very high, which will permit us to search for the lowest cost mixture.

The second constraint in the problem is $X_1 \leq 300$ pounds. For this restriction, a slack variable (S_1) is added since X_1 in the optimum solution might be less than 300. The S_1 slack variable represents the difference between the possible 300 pounds of X_1 and the actual number of pounds of X_1. This inequality now can be written as an equation: $X_1 + S_1 = 300$ pounds.

Tableau I
Linear Programming
Maximization Problem

Tableau II
Linear Programming
Maximization Problem

Tableau III
Linear Programming
Maximization Problem

Figure 6–7
The three tableaus use
to solve the sample
maximization problem
are the steps related t
specific columns and
rows (simplex method

Summary—Methodology of Tableau I through Tableau III

	C_j	Product Mix	Quantity	$10 A	$12 B	$0 S_1	$0 S_2	$0 S_3	Contribution per Unit Variables	Solution Optimal?
Steps 2 and 3→	$0	S_1	1,500	2	(3)	1	0	0	Coefficients	
Step 4 →$0		S_2	1,500	3	(2)	0	1	0		
→$0		S_3	600	1	(1)	0	0	1		
					Body Matrix		Identity Matrix			No
	Z_j		$0	$0	$0	$0	$0	$0	Contribution lost per unit	
	$C_j - Z_j$			$10	$12	$0	$0	$0	Net contribution per unit	

Intersectional elements

↑ Step 1

	C_j	Product Mix	Quantity	$10 A	$12 B	$0 S_1	$0 S_2	$0 S_3
Step 4 →$12		B	500	($\frac{2}{3}$)	1	$\frac{1}{3}$	0	0 replacing row
→ $0		S_2	500	($1\frac{2}{3}$)	0	$-\frac{2}{3}$	1	0 remaining row with new values
Steps 2 and 3→ $0		S_3	100	($\frac{1}{3}$)	0	$-\frac{1}{3}$	0	1 remaining row with new values
	Z_j		$6,000	$8	$12	$4	$0	$0
	$C_j - Z_j$			$2	$0	$4	$0	$0

Intersectional elements

Solution Optimal? No

↑ Step 1

C_j	Product Mix	Quantity	$10 A	$12 B	$0 S_1	$0 S_2	$0 S_3
$12	B	300	0	1	1	0	−2 remaining row with new values
$0	S_2	0	0	0	0	1	1 −5 remaining row with new values
$10	A	300	1	0	−1	0	3 replacing row
	Z_j	$6,600	$10	$12	$2	$0	$6
	$C_j - Z_j$		$0	$0	−$2	$0	−$6

Solution Optimal? Yes

Step 1—Since there are zero and minus values in the $C_j - Z_j$ row, the final solution has been reached.

In the first solution X_1, X_2, and X_3 can equal zero in the first constraint equation. But instead of using a slack variable, an artificial variable (A_1) which represents a new ingredient with a very high cost M (say $100 a pound) will be utilized. The resulting equation is $X_1 + X_2 + X_3 + A_1 = 1{,}000$. Having a very high cost assures us that it will not be present in the final solution. The first tableau will show a quantity of 1,000 pounds for the A_1 artificial variable. The *artificial variable* is a computational device; it is used for an "equality" constraint (such as the first constraint in this problem) and for "greater-than-or-equal-to constraints" (such as the third and fourth constraints in this problem). However, it is not needed for "less-than-or-equal-to" constraints.

The third and fourth constraints must be converted into equations by adding negative slack variables. The resulting equations are:

$$X_2 - S_2 = 150 \text{ pounds}$$
$$X_3 - S_3 = 200 \text{ pounds}$$

The slack variable, S_2, represents the amount by which X_2 will exceed 150 pounds in the final solution. (The same type of rationale applies to S_3 and 200 pounds.) For example, if X_2 is 500 pounds in the last tableau, then S_2 must be 350 pounds for the equation to be valid ($500 - 350 = 150$). However, it is possible that X_2 equals 150 pounds in an optimum solution, which means the value of S_2 would be zero ($150 - 0 = 150$).

Going one step further, we must ask what happens if X_2 equals zero in the initial solution. The first solution would be $0 - 150 = -150$ or $S_2 = -150$ pounds. This cannot be, since -150 pounds makes no more sense than -300 units of product Alpha or Beta. Thus we must prevent S_2 from appearing in the initial solution. This can be done by letting S_2 equal zero. If both X_2 and S_2 are zero in the initial solution, then we must introduce a new ingredient that will be an acceptable substitute for X_2 in the first solution. This new ingredient can be thought of as a very expensive substance, say $100 ($M$) per pound or the artificial variable mentioned earlier for a greater-than-or-equal-to condition. The high price of A_2 reassures us that it will never appear in the final solution. The third and fourth constraint equations above can be written to include these aritificial variables as follows:

$$X_2 - S_2 + A_2 = 150 \text{ pounds}$$
$$X_3 - S_3 + A_3 = 200 \text{ pounds}$$

Although the artificial variable was not demonstrated for a maximization problem, it can be used in such cases. A maximization problem may require minimum sales requirements to be produced. Hence, both artificial and slack variables must be introduced. For example, if the minimum sales requirements for Product X_{20} is 500 units, the equation to express this condition is: $X_{20} - S_{20} + A_{20}$ where the subscript 20 refers to the appropriate variable for Product 20. The C_j value for these variables are: current contribution for Product 20, zero, and $-M$, respectively.

In order to insert the proper values in the first minimization tableau, it is necessary to state the cost function and constraint equations. For the cost function, a zero cost must be shown for the slack variables (S_1, S_2, and S_3) and M cost for the artificial variables (A_1, A_2, and A_3). For the constraint equations, it will be recalled that any unknown in one constraint equation must appear in all equations. The appropriate variable must be inserted with zero coefficients. The final cost function and constraint equations, applicable to the first tableau, are:

$$\text{Minimize cost} = \$5X_1 + \$6X_2 + \$7X_3 + \$MA_1 + \$0S_1 + \$0S_2 + \$MA_2 + \$0S_3 + \$MA_3 \qquad \text{(Equation 6–8)}$$

Subject to:

$$X_1 + X_2 + X_3 + A_1 + 0S_1 + 0S_2 + 0A_2 + 0S_3 + 0A_3 = 1{,}000 \qquad \text{(Equation 6–9)}$$

$$X_1 + 0X_2 + 0X_3 + 0A_1 + S_1 + 0S_2 + 0A_2 + 0S_3 + 0A_3 = 300 \qquad \text{(Equation 6–10)}$$

$$0X_1 + X_2 + 0X_3 + 0A_1 + 0S_1 - S_2 + A_2 + 0S_3 + 0A_3 = 150 \qquad \text{(Equation 6–11)}$$

$$0X_1 + 0X_2 + X_3 + 0A_1 + 0S_1 + 0S_2 + 0A_2 - S_3 + A_3 = 200 \qquad \text{(Equation 6–12)}$$

Upon inspection of the foregoing equations and Tableau IV, it should be apparent why A_1, S_1, A_2, and A_3 were selected as the beginning product mix. The artificial variables (A_1, A_2, and A_3) enable us to keep the starting equations in balance. The same can also be said for the slack variable S_1. The artificial variables, by having a very high cost, assure us that they will not appear in the final solution. The computational procedures for a minimization problem are identical to those used for the previous maximization problem, except for modifying Step 1.

Tableau IV
Linear Programming
Minimization Problem

Intersectional elements

	C_j	Product Mix	Quantity	$5 X_1	$6 X_2	$7 X_3	$M A_1	$0 S_1	$0 S_2	$M A_2	$0 S_3	$M A_3
Step 4 →$M		A_1	1,000	1	(1)	1	1	0	0	0	0	0
Step 4 →$0		S_1	300	1	(0)	0	0	1	0	0	0	0
Replaced row Steps 2 and 3→$M		A_2	150	0	(1)	0	0	0	−1	1	0	0
Step 4 →$M		A_3	200	0	(0)	1	0	0	0	0	−1	1
	Z_j		$1,350M	$M	$2M	$2M	$M	$0	−$M	$M	−$M	$M
	$C_j - Z_j$			$5 − M	$6 − 2M ↑ Step 1	$7 − 2M	$0	$0	$M	$0	$M	$0

Since the optimum solution is concerned with minimizing costs, the optimum column is found by choosing the one that has the largest negative value in the $C_j - Z_j$ row and not the largest plus value as in a maximization problem. The most negative column is selected because this value will decrease costs the most. Upon inspection of Tableau IV, the most negative value (assuming that M equals $100) is $6 −

$2M$; thus X_2 is the optimum column (first step). Note the relatively high cost of the solution, $1,350M$.

Calculations for the last two rows in Tableau IV that were needed in this first step are:

$$\underline{Z_j \text{ row}}$$

Z Total $= \$M(1{,}000) + \$0(300) + \$M(150) + \$M(200) = \$1{,}350M$

$\quad ZX_1 = \$M(1) + \$0(1) + \$M(0) + \$M(0) = \$M$

$\quad ZX_2 = \$M(1) + \$0(0) + \$M(1) + \$M(0) = \$2M$

$\quad ZX_3 = \$M(1) + \$0(0) + \$M(0) + \$M(1) = \$2M$

$\quad ZA_1 = \$M(1) + \$0(0) + \$M(0) + \$M(0) = \$M$

$\quad ZS_1 = \$M(0) + \$0(1) + \$M(0) + \$M(0) = \$0$

$\quad ZS_2 = \$M(0) + \$0(0) + \$M(-1) + \$M(0) = -\$M$

$\quad ZA_2 = \$M(0) + \$0(0) + \$M(1) + \$M(0) = \$M$

$\quad ZS_3 = \$M(0) + \$0(0) + \$M(0) + \$M(-1) = -\$M$

$\quad ZA_3 = \$M(0) + \$0(0) + \$M(0) + \$M(1) = \$M$

$$\underline{C_j - Z_j \text{ row}}$$

$CX_1 - ZX_1 = \$5 - \$M = \$5 - \$M$

$CX_2 - ZX_2 = \$6 - \$2M = \$6 - \$2M$

$CX_3 - ZX_3 = \$7 - \$2M = \$7 - \$2M$

$CA_1 - ZA_1 = \$M - \$M = \$0$

$CS_1 - ZS_1 = \$0 - \$0 = \$0$

$CS_2 - ZS_2 = \$0 - (-\$M) = \$M$

$CA_2 - ZA_2 = \$M - \$M = \$0$

$CS_3 - ZS_3 = \$0 - (-\$M) = \$M$

$CA_3 - ZA_3 = \$M - \$M = \$0$

In the second step, the replaced row is found by dividing the values in the quantity column by their corresponding intersectional elements in the optimum column and selecting the row with the smallest number of units. These values are calculated as follows:

$$A_1 \text{ row} = \frac{1{,}000}{1} = 1{,}000$$

$$S_1 \text{ row} = \frac{300}{0} = \text{Not defined; therefore it is ignored}$$

$$A_2 \text{ row} = \frac{150}{1} = 150$$

$$A_3 \text{ row} = \frac{200}{0} = \text{Not defined; therefore it is ignored}$$

The A_2 row, the smaller value of the two, is designated as the replaced row.

For the third step, the replacing row (X_2) is determined by dividing each value in the replaced row (A_2) by the intersectional element of the replaced row (A_2). Since the intersectional element is 1, the values remain the same. Only the variable A_2 needs to be changed to X_2.

In the fourth and final step, new values for the A_1, S_1, and A_3 rows must be calculated for Tableau V. The formula is

Former element in the remaining row − (Former intersectional element of remaining row × New corresponding element in replacing row) =

New value for remaining row

The calculations for the new rows are:

A_1 Row	S_1 Row	A_3 Row
$1,000 - (1 \times 150) = 850$	$300 - (0 \times 150) = 300$	$200 - (0 \times 150) = 200$
$1 - (1 \times 0) = 1$	$1 - (0 \times 0) = 1$	$0 - (0 \times 0) - 0$
$1 - (1 \times 1) = 0$	$0 - (0 \times 1) = 0$	$0 - (0 \times 1) = 0$
$1 - (1 \times 0) = 1$	$0 - (0 \times 0) - 0$	$1 - (0 \times 0) = 1$
$1 - (1 \times 0) = 1$	$0 - (0 \times 0) = 0$	$0 - (0 \times 0) = 0$
$0 - (1 \times 0) = 0$	$1 - (0 \times 0) = 1$	$0 - (0 \times 0) = 0$
$0 - (1 \times - 1) = 1$	$0 - (0 \times - 1) = 0$	$0 - (0 \times - 1) = 0$
$0 - (1 \times 1) = - 1$	$0 - (0 \times 1) = 0$	$0 - (0 \times 1) - 0$
$0 - (1 \times 0) = 0$	$0 - (0 \times 0) = 0$	$- 1 - (0 \times 0) = - 1$
$0 - (1 \times 0) - 0$	$0 - (0 \times 0) - 0$	$1 - (0 \times 0) = 1$

When the intersectional element is zero, such as for the S_1 row and the A_3 row, the values of the new row are the same as the old row. This condition is true of all succeeding tableaus in which an intersectional element of a row is zero.

Inspection of Tableau V reveals the optimum column to be X_3. The replaced row is A_3 and the replacing row is X_3 in the next tableau. Notice that the total cost has decreased from $\$1,350M$ to $\$1,050M + \$900$ between the first two tableaus. The optimum column in Tableau VI is X_1 and the replaced row is S_1. These changes are reflected in Tableau VII, the fourth tableau in the problem. Again the cost has decreased from the preceding tableaus.

In Tableau VII, there is presently $\$350M$ in the total cost function. Nevertheless, total cost is still declining. The optimum column is S_2. When the calculation is made for the replaced row, the value for the X_2 row is -150 $[150/(-1)]$. This is not a feasible solution since we cannot have a minus quantity in the final solution. Therefore it is discarded as a possibility for the replaced row. The only positive quantity for the replaced row is $A_1(350)$. Again, new rows are determined, as in Tableau VIII.

Inspection of the $C_j - Z_j$ row reveals that no negative values remain. The optimum solution has been reached. Moreover, the total cost solution no longer contains an artificial variable (M). In addition, it is necessary to make certain that the values for the variables X_1, X_2, X_3, and S_2 in the tableau satisfy the original restrictions. Reviewing the original constraint equations, they are:

$$X_1 + X_2 + X_3 + A_1 = 1{,}000 \qquad \text{(Equation 6–9)}$$
$$X_1 + S_1 = 300 \qquad \text{(Equation 6–10)}$$
$$X_2 - S_2 + A_2 = 150 \qquad \text{(Equation 6–11)}$$
$$X_3 - S_3 + A_3 = 200 \qquad \text{(Equation 6–12)}$$

Substituting the values into the equations, it will be seen that we still are within the constraints of the problem when $X_1 = 300$, $X_2 = 500$, $X_3 = 200$, and $S_2 = 350$. All other variables have a value of zero.

$$300 + 500 + 200 = 1{,}000 \qquad \text{(Equation 6–9)}$$
$$1{,}000 = 1{,}000$$

$$300 + 0 = 300 \qquad \text{(Equation 6–10)}$$
$$300 = 300$$

$$500 - 350 + 0 = 150 \qquad \text{(Equation 6–11)}$$
$$150 = 150$$

$$200 - 0 + 0 = 200 \qquad \text{(Equation 6–12)}$$
$$200 = 200$$

Sensitivity Analysis After a linear programming problem has been solved, it is useful to study the effect of discrete changes in the problem's parameters on the current optimal solution. Hence, it is usually advisable to perform *sensitivity analysis* or *postoptimality analysis*. If the objective function solution is relatively sensitive to changes in certain parameters, special attention must be given to these parameters so that the final solution gives consideration to most of their likely values. For such situations, it is not necessary to solve the problem from the very beginning each time a minor change is made. Using the previous optimal solution and the corresponding set of equations, it is usually possible to check whether or not the basis is optimal and, if not, to utilize it as a beginning point for solving the new optimal solution.

Tableau V
Linear Programming
Minimization Problem

Intersectional elements

	C_j	Product Mix	Quantity	$5 X_1	$6 X_2	$7 X_3	$M A_1	$0 S_1	$0 S_2	$M A_2	$0 S_3	$M A_3
Step 4 →$M		A_1	850	1	0	(1)	1	0	1	−1	0	0
→$0		S_1	300	1	0	(0)	0	1	0	0	0	0
→$6		X_2	150	0	1	(0)	0	0	−1	1	0	0
Replaced row Steps 2 and 3→$M		A_3	200	0	0	(1)	0	0	0	0	−1	1
	Z_j		$1,050M +	$M	$6	$2M	$M	$0	$M − 6	−$M + 6	−$M	$M
	$C_j − Z_j$		$900	$5 − $M	$0	$7 − 2M	$0	$0	−$M + 6	$2M − 6	$M	$0

↑
Step 1

Tableau VI
Linear Programming
Minimization Problem

Intersectional elements

	C_j	Product Mix	Quantity	$5 X_1	$6 X_2	$7 X_3	$M A_1	$0 S_1	$0 S_2	$M A_2	$0 S_3	$M A_3
Step 4 ———→$M		A_1	650	1	0	0	1	0	1	−1	1	−1
Replaced row Steps 2 and 3→$0		S_1	300	1	0	0	0	1	0	0	0	0
Step 4 ⎰ →$6		X_2	150	0	1	0	0	0	−1	1	0	0
⎱ →$7		X_3	200	0	0	1	0	0	0	0	−1	1
		Z_j	$650M +	$M	$6	$7	$M	$0	$M − 6	−$M + 6	$M − 7	$M + 7
		$C_j − Z_j$	$2,300	−$M + 5	$0	$0	$0	$0	−$M + 6	$2M − 6	−$M + 7	$2M − 7

↑
Step 1

Tableau VII
Linear Programming
Minimization Problem

Intersectional elements

	C_j	Product Mix	Quantity	$5 X_1	$6 X_2	$7 X_3	$M A_1	$0 S_1	$0 S_2	$M A_2	$0 S_3	$M A_3
Replaced row Steps 2 and 3→$M		A_1	350	0	0	0	1	−1	1	−1	1	−1
⎰ →$5		X_1	300	1	0	0	0	1	0	0	0	0
Step 4 ⎰ →$6		X_2	150	0	1	0	0	0	−1	1	0	0
⎱ →$7		X_3	200	0	0	1	0	0	0	0	−1	1
		Z_j	$350M +	$5	$6	$7	$M	−$M + 5	$M − 6	−$M + 6	$M − 7	−$M + 7
		$C_j − Z_j$	$3,800	$0	$0	$0	$0	$M − 5	−$M + 6	$2M − 6	−$M + 7	$2M − 7

↑
Step 1

Tableau VIII
Linear Programming
Minimization Problem

C_j	Product Mix	Quantity	$5 X_1	$6 X_2	$7 X_3	$M A_1	$0 S_1	$0 S_2	$M A_2	$0 S_3	$M A_3
$0	S_2	350	0	0	0	1	−1	1	−1	1	−1
$5	X_1	300	1	0	0	0	1	0	0	0	0
$6	X_2	500	0	1	0	1	−1	0	0	1	−1
$7	X_3	200	0	0	1	0	0	0	0	−1	1
	Z_j	$5,900	$5	$6	$7	$6	−$1	$0	$0	−$1	$1
	$C_j − Z_j$		$0	$0	$0	$M − 6	$1	$0	$M	$1	$M − 1

Step 1—
since there are zeros and plus values in the $C_j − Z_j$ row, the final solution has been reached.

Advantages of Linear Programming Methods

Several important advantages of linear programming are self-evident. Among these is the optimum use of productive factors within the firm. Linear programming indicates how managers can most effectively employ their productive factors by more efficient selection and distribution. The more efficient use of manpower and machines can be obtained by solving a well-structured linear programming problem.

Another advantage is the improved quality of decisions. Managers become more objective (through the use of information obtained by the process of linear programming) and less subjective (relying on their feelings about existing conditions). Individuals who utilize linear programming methods must analyze business problems as they actually are and collect only the data pertinent to the mathematical formulation. Managers, having a clear picture of the relationships within the basic equations and inequalities or constraints, can better understand the problem and its related solution.

Consideration must be given to the fact that linear programming gives possible and practical solutions since there might be other constraints operating outside of the problem which must be taken into account, for example, sales demands. Just because a company can produce so many units does not mean that they can be sold. On the other hand, it might be necessary to restrict a certain amount of production volume for less profitable items which are necessary for a complete product line. Unless these less profitable items are made and included in the product line, customers will buy elsewhere. This latter situation can be handled easily by taking the time available initially and subtracting the time necessary for the minimum sales requirements (profitable and less profitable products) and solving for the mixture of products based upon the remaining time available in the various departments. The fact that the method of linear programming allows modification of its mathematical solution for the sake of convenience must, in itself, be considered an advantage.

The simplex method gives the user an opportunity to calculate *shadow prices* (see the earlier discussion of the dual program). The use of shadow prices provides relevant information for decisions concerning the acquisition of additional resources needed to meet some objective, such as maximizing contribution. The shadow price shows the additional contribution generated by relaxing a constraint and thus sets an upper limit on the cost to acquire one more unit of a constraining factor. To state it another way, the shadow price is a form of sensitivity analysis since it measures the value or worth of relaxing a constraint by acquiring an additional unit of that factor of production. The value of additional resources can be compared to the actual cost of acquiring these resources, thereby allowing decisions to be made on the basis of these comparisons.

Although the foregoing advantages are somewhat obvious, a frequently overlooked advantage (which refutes the accountant's point of view in selecting those products with the highest contribution) is one that relates to the identification of production bottlenecks. Consider the following problem where the marketable products A, B, C, and D of the Sawbrook Company, Inc., have a contribution of $4,

$3.75, $3.60, and $3 respectively. The production requirements and time available are as follows:

	Time Required per Product (hours)				Time Available Next Week (hours)
	A	B	C	D	
Dept. 1	0.3	0.3	0.3	0.2	250
Dept. 2	0.7	0.6	0.7	0.8	1,000
Dept. 3	0.35	0.3	0.3	0.2	250
Dept. 4	0.2	0.25	0.25	0.22	250

A quick inspection of this problem indicates that the most profitable items should be promoted and the less profitable ones not promoted. The marketing, accounting, and production managers, using this premise, came up with the quantities to be produced and sold. The assumption in this problem is that the customer can be made to switch among the four products since all are identical type products. The rate of substitution of one product for another is unusually high.

Inasmuch as the firm's managers wanted to take full advantage of the highest contribution rate and the sales demands of customers, they decided to allocate production in this manner: 60 percent to product A, 25 to product B, 10 to product C, and 5 to product D. The minimum sales requirements needed for each product take up 5 percent of total production. This is the reason for 5 percent of total weekly production time being allocated to product D. The calculations for allocated production time are depicted in Table 6–1.

Using the rationale set forth previously for linear programming, that is, selecting the lowest of the values calculated for the various products in each of the departments (circled figures in Table 6–1), the production schedule (60 percent for product A, 25 for product B, 10 for product C, and 5 for product D) and contribution expected are as follows:

Product A: 429 units × $4.00 = $1,716.00
Product B: 208 units × $3.75 =   780.00
Product C: 83 units × $3.60 =   298.80
Product D: 57 units × $3.00 =   171.00
              Total contribution $2,965.80

When applying the simplex method to this problem, the initial production for minimum sales requirements must be calculated, as in Table 6–2. The minimum sales requirements (based on production) are:

Product A: 36 units × $4.00 = $144.00
Product B: 42 units × $3.75 = 157.50
Product C: 42 units × $3.60 = 151.20
Product D: 57 units × $3.00 = 171.00
      Total contribution for minimum sales requirements
                            (based on production) $623.70

215

Now that the minimum sales requirement and its related contributions have been computed, it is necessary to calculate the remaining time available for production of A, B, C, and D or some combination of these products. This is determined in Table 6–3.

Table 6–1

Allocated Production
Time

	Product A (60% of production)	Product B (25% of production)	Product C (10% of production)	Product D (5% of production)	Time Available Next Week (hours)
Dept. 1	$\dfrac{150 \text{ hr}}{0.3 \text{ hr/unit}} = 500$	$\dfrac{62.5 \text{ hr}}{0.3 \text{ hr/unit}} = \boxed{208}$	$\dfrac{25 \text{ hr}}{0.3 \text{ hr/unit}} = \boxed{83}$	$\dfrac{12.5 \text{ hr}}{0.2 \text{ hr/unit}} = 63$	250
Dept. 2	$\dfrac{600}{0.7} = 857$	$\dfrac{250}{0.6} = 417$	$\dfrac{100}{0.7} = 143$	$\dfrac{50}{0.8} = 63$	1,000
Dept. 3	$\dfrac{150}{0.35} = \boxed{429}$	$\dfrac{62.5}{0.3} = \boxed{208}$	$\dfrac{25}{0.3} = \boxed{83}$	$\dfrac{12.5}{0.2} = 63$	250
Dept. 4	$\dfrac{150}{0.2} = 750$	$\dfrac{62.5}{0.25} = 250$	$\dfrac{25}{0.25} = 100$	$\dfrac{12.5}{0.22} = \boxed{57}$	250

Table 6–2

Production for Minimum
Sales Requirements

	Product A (5% of production)	Product B (5% of production)	Product C (5% of production)	Product D (5% of production)	Time Required for Minimum Sales Requirements (hours)
Dept. 1	$\dfrac{12.5 \text{ hr}}{0.3 \text{ hr/unit}} = 42$	$\dfrac{12.5 \text{ hr}}{0.3 \text{ hr/unit}} = \boxed{42}$	$\dfrac{12.5 \text{ hr}}{0.3 \text{ hr/unit}} = \boxed{42}$	$\dfrac{12.5 \text{ hr}}{0.2 \text{ hr/unit}} = 63$	50
Dept. 2	$\dfrac{50}{0.7} = 71$	$\dfrac{50}{0.6} = 83$	$\dfrac{50}{0.7} = 71$	$\dfrac{50}{0.8} = 63$	200
Dept. 3	$\dfrac{12.5}{0.35} = \boxed{36}$	$\dfrac{12.5}{0.3} = \boxed{42}$	$\dfrac{12.5}{0.3} = \boxed{42}$	$\dfrac{12.5}{0.2} = 63$	50
Dept. 4	$\dfrac{12.5}{0.2} = 63$	$\dfrac{12.5}{0.25} = 50$	$\dfrac{12.5}{0.25} = 50$	$\dfrac{12.5}{0.22} = \boxed{57}$	50

Table 6–3

Remaining Time
Available for Production

	Available Time	−	(Product A)	−	(Product B)	−	(Product C)	−	(Product D)	=	Rem T
Dept. 1	250 hr		36 units × 0.3 = −10.8 hr		42 units × 0.3 = −12.6 hr		42 units × 0.3 = −12.6 hr		57 units × 0.2 = −11.4 hr		20
Dept. 2	1,000 hr		36 units × 0.7 = −25.2 hr		42 units × 0.6 = −25.2 hr		42 units × 0.7 = −29.4 hr		57 units × 0.8 = −45.6 hr		87
Dept. 3	250 hr		36 units × 0.35 = −12.6 hr		42 units × 0.3 = −12.6 hr		42 units × 0.3 = −12.6 hr		57 units × 0.2 = −11.4 hr		20
Dept. 4	250 hr		36 units × 0.2 = − 7.2 hr		42 units × 0.25 = −10.5 hr		42 units × 0.25 = −10.5 hr		57 units × 0.22 = −12.5 hr		20

The first tableau can be determined for this linear programming maximization problem now that the remaining time has been computed (Tableau IX).

The final tableau for this problem is Tableau X. The total contribution from the last tableau ($2,930.60) plus the contribution based upon the minimum sales requirements ($623.70) is $3,554.30. The original contribution was $2,965.80. The improved solution of linear programming represents an increase in weekly contribution of $588.50, a significant one.

ADVANTAGES OF LINEAR PROGRAMMING METHODS

C_j	Product Mix	Quantity	$4.00 A	$3.75 B	$3.60 C	$3.00 D	$0 S_1	$0 S_2	$0 S_3	$0 S_4
$0	S_1	202.6	0.3	0.3	0.3	0.2	1	0	0	0
$0	S_2	874.6	0.7	0.6	0.7	0.8	0	1	0	0
$0	S_3	200.8	0.35	0.3	0.3	0.2	0	0	1	0
$0	S_4	209.3	0.2	0.25	0.25	0.22	0	0	0	1
	Z_j		$0	$0	$0	$0	$0	$0	$0	$0
	$C_j - Z_j$		$4.00	$3.75	$3.60	$3.00	$0	$0	$0	$0

Tableau IX
Linear Programming Maximization Problem (First Tableau)

Tableau X
Linear Programming Maximization Problem (Final Tableau)

C_j	Product Mix	Quantity	$4.00 A	$3.75 B	$3.60 C	$3.00 D	$0 S_1	$0 S_2	$0 S_3	$0 S_4
$0	S_1	4.0	0	0.017	0.017	0	1	0	− 0.7	− 0.28
$0	S_2	119.8	0	− 0.3	− 0.2	0	0	1	0.15	− 3.77
$4	A	70.4	1	0.43	0.43	0	0	0	5.93	− 0.54
$3	D	883.0	0	0.755	0.755	1	0	0	− 5.38	9.43
	Z_j	$2,930.60	$4	$3.985	$3.985	$3	$0	$0	$7.58	$26.13
	$C_j - Z_j$		$0	−$0.235	−$0.385	$0	$0	$0	−$7.58	−$26.13

In the example, product D, originally produced only to meet the minimum sales requirements (based on 5 percent of total production time), or 57 units, is the biggest volume product with 940 (883 + 57) units. A comparison of the original and improved solution is as follows:

	Original Solution	Improved Solution
Product A	429 units × $4.00 = $1,716.00	106.4 units × $4.00 = $ 425.60
Product B	208 units × $3.75 = 780.00	42 units × $3.75 = 157.50
Product C	83 units × $3.60 = 298.80	42 units × $3.60 = 151.20
Product D	57 units × $3.00 = 171.00	940 units × $3.00 = 2,820.00
Total Contribution	$2,965.80	$3,554.30

Although product A did show a high unit contribution, it was a bottleneck in Department 3. Why is this department a bottleneck for product A? This question can be answered by examining Tableau X for unused department time. Variables S_1 and S_2, representing Departments 1 and 2, have remaining time. Since the variables S_3 and S_4 do not appear in this final tableau, time in Departments 3 and 4 must have been exhausted. Analysis of Tableau X clearly indicates that Department 2 is not a bottleneck department due to the 119.8 remaining hours. However, Department 1, which has 4.0 remaining hours has, for all practical purposes, no remaining time. Based on the foregoing evaluation of used time for Departments 1, 3, and 4, it is necessary to examine the first tableau (IX) for product A. Time to produce this product is .3, .35, and .2 in Departments 1, 3, and 4, respectively. Since there is zero time available in these departments, and the time factor to manufacture product A in Department 3 is the highest, Department 3 is the present bottleneck.

When bottlenecks occur, some machines cannot meet demand while other equipment stands idle part of the time. As a result, imbalance is an important cost factor which more then offsets the gains from high unit contribution. Thus a foremost advantage (perhaps the most significant to many companies) is the highlighting of bottlenecks in their present operations. Ignoring bottlenecks can result in promoting the wrong product(s). Experience gained from periodic linear programming analysis will help management determine where new equipment should be installed for those departments limiting overall plant capacity.

Cautions of Linear Programming Methods

There are some cautions or difficulties associated with every mathematical method; linear programming is no exception. The objective function and constraints can change overnight due to internal as well as external factors. There is the necessity of keeping data current. Obviously, the more rigidly the data adheres to the reality of the situation, the more reliable will be the solution.

Managers who contemplate using this technique must be sure that they have a practical application for the selected method of linear programming. Another way of stating it is that even though the problem is correctly stated and formulated mathematically, there may be some limiting factors from a practical point of view. For example, if not enough time has been allotted to the proper collecting of data, garbage-in, garbage-out will result. To cite another example, if the computed program available cannot handle all the constraints, constraints will have to be dropped which could render the output basically unusable.

Where the objective function and constraints are nonlinear, extreme caution must be used when applying linear programming. The misapplication of linear programming under nonlinear conditions usually results in an incorrect solution.

The last limitation is the cost related to maintaining linear programming solutions. As stated previously, cost factors, constraints, and similar data are continually changing. By the time the initial data have been collected and properly formulated, they may be out of date. Thus there is a maintenance cost for the factors necessary in problems of this type. It may be questionable whether the cost of introducing new data is worth the change. When the results are worth the total expenses involved in reprocessing the current data, this apparent limitation no longer applies.

Chapter Summary

Linear programming has made an impressive impact on solving many recurring business problems. Problems once thought to be unsolvable can be formulated in terms of an objective function and constraints. Many successes of operations research can be attributed to the simplex method.

Like other OR techniques, the methods of linear programming have not been finalized at this time. More modifications of the basic simplex method will result in extending it to other difficult business problems, especially those that have non-linear functions and constraints. Also, the more rigorous use of computers will bring new developments to the forefront. Linear programming, then, is viewed as a management tool and an analytical process that offers many advantages to the user.

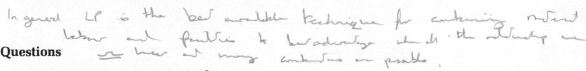

Questions

1. (a) What is linear programming?
   (b) What are its essential requirements?
2. Discuss the relationship of the graphic method to the simplex method of linear programming.
3. Discuss the similarities and differences between a maximization problem and a minimization problem using the simplex method of linear programming.
4. What are the advantages and disadvantages of linear programming?

Model Formulation Exercises

1. After formulating a two-product problem, what criteria should be used to determine whether the "conventional graphic" method or "testing the corners" method is better suited to solve the linear programming problem?

2. In the formulation of a problem using the graphic method of linear programming, it is possible to determine whether or not the solution will have multiple answers by examining the slope of the constraints and the slope of the objective function. If the slope of one of the constraints is the same as that for the objective function, the solution is not unique. When using the simplex method of linear programming for a multiproduct problem, is it safe to conclude that the slope of at least one constraint which is the same as the objective function will always result in a multiple-point solution?

3. In the mathematical formulation of a linear programming problem, what are the controllable and uncontrollable variables for a maximization problem using the simplex method? Similarly, what are the controllable and uncontrollable variables for a minimization problem?

4. An important feature of linear programming is that production bottlenecks can be identified without too much difficulty. However, when the problem is being formulated, that is, when the objective function and constraint equations are completed, is it possible at that time to pinpoint potential production bottlenecks for a typical multiproduct problem?

5. Referring to the problem presented in the chapter, formulate its dual for the simplex method of linear programming.

Mathematical Exercises

1. The Dumont Company, a manufacturer of test equipment, has three major departments for its manufacture of S-1000 Model and S-2000 Model. Manufacturing times and monthly capacities are given as follows:

	Per Unit Time Requirements (hours)		
	S-1000 Model	S-2000 Model	Hours Available This Month
Main frame dept.	4.0	2.0	1,600
Electrical wiring dept.	2.5	1.0	1,200
Assembly dept.	4.5	1.5	1,600

The contribution of the S-1000 Model is $40 each and the contribution of the S-2000 Model is $10 each. Assuming that the company can sell any quantity of either product due to favorable market conditions, determine the optimal output for both models, highest possible contribution for this month, and slack time in the three departments. Use the graphic method. Prove your answer by using the simplex method.

2. The Kenmore Corporation, a progressive manufacturer of military and civilian devices, is currently manufacturing a line of civilian hardware with a present daily production of 30 units for Model Z-1200 and 120 units of Model Z-1500. The vice president of manufacturing wants to know if profits could be increased by changing the product mix between the two models. The following information was compiled on the hours required to build each model and the capacities of the departments in the plant.

	Man-Hours Required		Department Capacity (Hours per day)
	Model Z-1200	Model Z-1500	
Department 1	2	0	300
Department 2	0	3	540
Department 3	2	2	440
Department 4	$1\frac{1}{3}$	$1\frac{1}{2}$	300
Contribution/unit	$50	$40	

(a) Determine the optimum product mix assuming the quantities can be sold. Use the graphic method.

(b) By how much would the optimum mix increase the contribution to fixed costs and profit?

(c) Suppose the price of Model Z-1200 is reduced by $10; what will the optimum product mix be? Use the graphic method.

The firm is contemplating a third product, Model Z-1800, which will utilize the same facilities as the two models for the military market. The departmental capacities will remain the same. The requirements for Model Z-1800 are: Department 1, 0.1 hour; Department 2, 3.6 hours; Department 3, 2.2 hours; and Department 4, 1.2 hours. The contribution for the new model is $55 each (use the original contribution for the other two models).

(d) Assuming the firm can sell any combination of quantities that it can produce, what is the optimum product mix and the highest daily contribution? Use the simplex method.

(e) Is the answer to (d) unique? Prove your answer. (*Hint:* graph the problem.)

3. The sales manager of the Rose Manufacturing Company has budgeted $120,000 for an advertising program for one of the firm's products. The selected advertising program consists of running advertisements in two different magazines. The advertisement for Magazine 1 costs $2,000 per run while the advertisement for Magazine 2 costs $5,000 per run. Past experience has indicated that at least 20 runs in Magazine 1 and at least 10 runs in Magazine 2 are necessary to penetrate the market with any appreciable effect. Also, experience has indicated that there is no reason to make more than 50 runs in either of the two magazines. Based on the foregoing data, how many runs (X) should be made in Magazine 1, and how many runs should be made in Magazine 2 to satisfy the foregoing restrictions and still not exceed the $120,000 budget?

4. The Henderson Food Products Company has established a new products division to develop and test market new snack-food items. The manager of this division is considering three promising products: *A, B,* and *C.* He feels that linear programming (simplex method) offers the best means for determining an optimum production schedule that allows producing these products simultaneously. The firm has three basic manufacturing departments: mixing, frying,

and packing. The time requirements for each product and total available monthly hours are:

Product	Department		
	Mixing	Frying	Packing
A	.1 hr	.2 hr	.1 hr
B	.2 hr	.4 hr	.1 hr
C	.4 hr	.2 hr	.1 hr
Available monthly hours	5,000	5,500	4,500

It is estimated that the contribution for Product A is $0.30, Product B is $0.40, and Product C is $0.50.

Based on the monthly time available in each department and product contribution, what is the optimum quantity for each product and total contribution?

5. The Cincinnati Chemical Company must produce 10,000 pounds of a special mixture for a customer. The mix consists of ingredients X_1, X_2, and X_3. X_1 costs $8 per pound, X_2 costs $10 per pound, and X_3 costs $11 per pound. No more than 3,000 pounds of X_1 can be used and at least 1,500 pounds of X_2 must be used. Also, at least 2,000 pounds of X_3 is required.
   (a) Calculate the number of pounds for each ingredient to use in order to minimize total costs for 10,000 pounds.
   (b) Calculate the lowest total possible cost.
   (c) Are there any slack pounds in the problem?

6. Gas Turbine Incorporated is starting production of a polymeric composite blade. The blade consists of three basic components: resin, fiber, and glass cloth. The maximum resin content is 40 percent by weight, the minimum fiber content is 40 percent by weight, and the minimum glass cloth content is 20 percent by weight. Resin cloth costs $20 per pound while fiber costs $80 per pound and glass cloth costs $40 per pound.
   (a) What is the optimum percent composition of materials for minimum production cost per pound of this polymeric composite blade?
   (b) What is the lowest cost composition per pound for producing this blade?

7. The test kitchen of Iowa Packing Company is experimenting with a new formula for "summer sausage." The basic ingredients, besides salt and spices, are (1) lean cow meat, (2) blade beef, and (3) pork trimmings. The costs per pound are $0.50, $0.30, and $0.40 respectively. Sausage is made in batches of one hundred pounds.

The basic ingredients have the following limitations as to quantities:

	Maximum	Minimum
Lean cow meat		40 pounds
Blade beef	20 pounds	
Pork trimmings	30 pounds	

(a) Determine the quantity of each ingredient to minimize cost.

(b) Determine the minimum cost for each batch of 100 pounds.

8. Of the many products manufactured by the Arco Manufacturing Company, only products C, D, E, and F pass through the following departments: planner (small), milling (vertical), drilling (small), and assembly (small parts). The requirements per unit of product in hours and contribution are as follows:

	Department				
	Planner	**Milling**	**Drilling**	**Assembly**	**Contr./Unit**
Product C	0.5	2.0	0.5	3.0	$8
Product D	1.0	1.0	0.5	1.0	$9
Product E	1.0	1.0	1.0	2.0	$7
Product F	0.5	1.0	1.0	3.0	$6

The available capacities this month for products C, D, E, and F and minimum sales requirements are:

	Capacities (hours)		Minimum Sales Requirements
Planner	1,800	Product C	100 units
Milling	2,800	Product D	600 units
Drilling	3,000	Product E	500 units
Assembly	6,000	Product F	400 units

(a) Determine the number of products C, D, E, and F to manufacture this month to maximize contribution.

(b) Determine the total maximum contribution for products C, D, E, and F this month.

(c) Determine the slack time in the four departments.

Bibliography

D. R. Anderson, D. Sweeney, and T. A. Williams, *Linear Programming for Decision Making: An Application Approach,* St. Paul: West Publishing, 1976.

E. K. Bowen, *Mathematics, With Applications in Management and Economics,* Homewood, Ill.: Richard D. Irwin, 1972.

L. Cooper and D. Steinberg, *Methods and Applications of Linear Programming,* Philadelphia: W. B. Saunders Company, 1974.

H. G. Dallenbach and E. J. Bell, *User's Guide to Linear Programming,* Englewood Cliffs, N.J.: Prentice-Hall, 1970.

N. J. Driebeek, *Applied Linear Programming,* Reading, Mass.: Addison-Wesley, 1969.

S. I. Gass, *Linear Programming: Methods and Applications,* New York: McGraw-Hill Book Company, 1969.

F. S. Hillier and G. J. Lieberman, *Operations Research,* San Francisco: Holden-Day, 1974.

N. K. Kwak, *Mathematical Programming with Business Applications,* New York: McGraw-Hill Book Company, 1973.

R. I. Levin and R. P. Lamone, *Linear Programming for Management Divisions,* Homewood, Ill.: Richard D. Irwin, 1969.

T. H. Naylor, E. T. Byrne, and J. M. Vernon, *Introduction to Linear Programming: Methods and Cases,* Belmont, California: Wadsworth Publishing, 1971.

M. Simmonnard, *Linear Programming,* Englewood Cliffs, N.J.: Prentice-Hall, 1966.

D. M. Simmons, *Linear Programming for Operations Research,* San Francisco: Holden-Day, 1972.

R. S. Stockton, *Introduction to Linear Programming,* Homewood, Ill.: Richard D. Irwin, 1971.

J. E. Strum, *Introduction to Linear Programming,* San Francisco: Holden-Day, 1972.

H. A. Taha, *Operations Research, An Introduction,* New York: The Macmillan Company, 1971.

C. D. Throsby, *Elementary Linear Programming,* New York: Random House, 1970.

S. Zionts, *Linear and Integer Programming,* Englewood Cliffs, N.J.: Prentice-Hall, 1974.

Chapter 7

Transportation Methods

Chapter Objectives
☐ To specify the basic requirements for formulating a transportation problem.
☐ To present a manually oriented approach, the stepping-stone method, for solving transportation problems.
☐ To enlarge upon the simplex method presented in the prior chapter for solving transportation problems that are computer oriented.
☐ To show other uses of transportation methods, such as the placement of orders on machines.

Chapter Outline

The origin of transportation methods dates back to 1941 when F. L. Hitchcock presented a study entitled *The Distribution of a Product from Several Sources to Numerous Localities*. This presentation is considered to be the first important contribution to the solution of transportation problems. In 1947, T. C. Koopmans presented a study, not related to Hitchcock's, called *Optimum Utilization of the Transportation System*. These two contributions helped in the development of transportation methods which involve a number of shipping sources and a number of destinations.

Requirements for Formulating a Transportation Problem

The requirements for formulating a transportation problem are identical to those for linear programming, as set forth in Chapter 6. By way of review, they include: (1) a well-defined linear objective function, (2) alternative courses of action, (3) linear objective function and linear constraints expressed mathematically, (4) interrelated variables, and (5) resources in limited supply. Within this framework for formulating a transportation problem, an iterative process (transportation method) allocates limited resources, e.g., factory capacity, among competing activities, e.g., warehouses, to keep overall shipping costs at a minimum. The objective function is to minimize transportation costs within the constraints of the individual factories and the individual warehouses plus the normal nonnegativity constraints found in business problems. The final solution, then, is the determination of the optimal shipping schedule with its lowest transportation costs.

Although transportation methods determine optimal shipping patterns, many types of problems having nothing to do with transportation may be solved using these methods. This will be apparent later in the chapter and in the application section on the next page.

Stepping-Stone Method — Using the Northwest Corner Rule and Inspection

There are several methods for solving the transportation problem, including the stepping-stone method and the simplex method. We will deal with the stepping-stone method first. The stepping-stone method, in its initial solution, can make use of the *northwest corner rule*. This rule states that the quantities shipped from the factories to the warehouses must begin in the upper left-hand corner of the table used in the method. When this route is fully used, that is, the factory capacity or warehouse (sales) requirements are totally utilized, depending on which number is lower, the remainder of either the factory capacity or warehouse requirement is then assigned to the new row(s) or column(s) until it is fully used. Using this procedure, the table is filled from the upper left cell down to the lower right cell, fully using the warehouse requirement, then factory capacity, etc. In Table 7–1, the first shipping route, *RA,* satisfies the warehouse requirement of *A* for 1,000 units, and the second shipping route, *RB,* satisfies the warehouse requirement of *B* for 2,000 units. However, for route *RC,* 4,000 of the 4,500 units satisfies *R*'s factory capacity of 7,000 (1,000 + 2,000 + 4,000). This means 500 units (4,500 − 4,000) are available for route *SC,* which now takes care of *C*'s warehouse requirements. This same procedure is followed until all rim requirements, the limiting values for the factory capacity column and the warehouse storage requirements row, are fully satisfied.

If the factory capacity is in excess of warehouse (sales) requirements, this is known as *slack* for the factories. No cost is assigned to slack since there is no transportation cost involved. It is either excess capacity of a factory(s) or excess inventory at a factory(s). The slack column allows for the rim requirements of the factories to equal the warehouse requirements or the rows to equal the columns.

A faster initial starting point for the stepping-stone method is to use *inspection* in conjunction with the northwest corner rule, illustrated in Table 7–2 (the initial table for the stepping-stone method). The inspection method means that the quantities to be shipped are positioned in cells according to the northwest corner rule in order to have many of the lowest transportation costs associated with the filled cells (quantities to be shipped). As can be seen from Table 7–2, this means moving the columns around. The same procedure can also be applied to the rows, but is not used in this problem. The total shipping costs of Table 7–1 are $116,000 versus $94,500 for Table 7–2. It should be apparent that other possibilities for an initial solution exist. The use of inspection in the initial table for the stepping-stone method reduces the number of tables required for the lowest cost transportation schedule.

Step 1. Test for Degeneracy Once the initial table has been determined using the northwest corner rule and inspection or some other initial solution method, the first step is to check whether or not the solution (quantities to ship) is degenerate.

Applications—Transportation Methods

- **Assignment of workers**—optimizes the allocation of workers based upon test scores so that the right individual is placed in the right job. The assumption is that an individual's score is directly proportional to the profit that the company would make if the individual were placed in the right job.
- **Assignment of machines**—provides a means for assigning machines to those factory orders that are best suited for the respective machines to minimize costs and/or to meet specific delivery dates.
- **Allocation of fixed assets**—determines the proper allocation of fixed assets, such as trucks, to those regions of the country where each type operates best based upon loading and/or climatic conditions.
- **Determination of freight carriers**—proves a means for management to determine which freight carriers are the lowest priced for hauling the firm's finished products.
- **Assignment of freight equipment**—allows a firm to determine what tractor trucks should be sent to which plants in order to minimize total distance between its terminals and plants.
- **Efficient utilization of a transportation system**—optimizes not only the lowest shipping costs from the firm's plants to its warehouses, but also can keep overall transportation costs from its warehouses to customers at a minimum.
- **Determination of optimum contribution**—optimizes not only in terms of minimizing costs, but also can be used in maximizing contribution for a firm's products.

Table 7–1
Stepping-Stone Method
Using the Northwest
Corner Rule in the Initial
Solution

Warehouse:	A	B	C	D	E	F	G	Slack	Factory Capacity
Factory: R	$6 1,000	$7 2,000	$5 4,000	$4 − $2	$8 + $3	$6 − $3	$5 + $1	$0 $0	7,000
S	$10 + $5	$5 − $1	$4 500	$5 3,500	$4 $0	$3 − $5	$2 $1	$0 + $1	4,000
T	$9 + $3	$5 − $2	$3 − $2	$6 500	$5 2,000	$9 3,500	$4 3,000	$0 1,000	10,000
Warehouse Requirements	1,000	2,000	4,500	4,000	2,000	3,500	3,000	1,000	21,000

Total transportation costs $116,000.

Degeneracy is a condition in which it is not possible to evaluate all empty (unused) cells due to a smaller number of cells used, i.e., filled, than the rim requirements (rows and columns) minus one. Also, degeneracy is caused by too many filled cells. The formula (Equation 7–1) to test for degeneracy is $m + n - 1$, where m is the rows and n is the columns. In the example, $3 + 8 - 1 = 10$. The number of filled cells is 10. Therefore the problem is not degenerate. The method for handling a degenerate condition is explained in a subsequent section.

Warehouse:	D	C	F	G	E	B	A	Slack	Factory Capacity
Factory: R	$4 4,000	$5 3,000	$6 + $2	$5 + $6	$8 + $8	$7 + $7	$6 + $2	$0 + $5	7,000
S	$5 + $2	$4 1,500	$3 2,500	$2 + $4	$4 + $5	$5 + $6	$10 + $7	$0 + $6	4,000
T	$6 − $3	$3 − $7	$9 1,000	$4 3,000	$5 2,000	$5 2,000	$9 1,000	$0 1,000	10,000
Warehouse Requirements	4,000	4,500	3,500	3,000	2,000	2,000	1,000	1,000	21,000

Total transportation costs $94,500.

Step 2. Evaluate all Unfilled Cells   The second step is to determine a better shipping schedule by evaluating the unfilled cells or those cells which do not have scheduled shipments. Each cell that is not used must be evaluated. This evaluation method shows the net total cost effect of adding one unit to the cell route. Unfilled cells *SD* and *TD* of Table 7–2 will be used to illustrate this procedure.

If one unit is added to cell *SD*, it will cost the firm $5. Since rim requirements (rows and columns) must be satisfied, if one unit is added to cell *SD*, a unit must be subtracted from *RD* in order that the *D* column cells still total 4,000 units. The unit subtracted from *RD* saves the firm a shipping cost of $4. Likewise, as a unit is subtracted from *RD*, a unit must be added to *RC* in order that the shipments of factory *R* still equal 7,000 units. This costs the firm $5. Now that column *C* has one too many units, one unit must be subtracted from *SC*, which saves the firm $4. This is shown in Table 7–3. In effect, a unit has been added to *SD*, subtracted from *RD*, added to *RC*, and subtracted from *SC*, thereby satisfying the rim requirements. If this change did take place, the cost factor is of utmost importance since $5 has been added (*SD*), $4 has been subtracted (*RD*), $5 has been added (*RC*), and $4 has been subtracted (*SC*) for net cost of $2 per unit ($+$5 - $4 + $5 - $4 = +$2$) to the firm. This means that every unit added to route *SD* will cost the firm an additional $2 per unit. It would certainly not be worthwhile for the firm to use this route if this were the only choice available.

An evaluation of cell *TD* in Table 7–2 is longer than the previous example. Adding one unit to cell *TD* costs the firm $6. In order to satisfy the rim requirements, one unit must be subtracted from cell *RD* for savings of $4. Similarly, for warehouse *C*, one unit must be added to cell *RC* (cost of $5) and one unit must be subtracted from cell *SC* (savings of $4). For warehouse *F*, one unit must be added to cell *SF* (cost of $3) and one unit must be subtracted from cell *TF* (savings of $9). The net result is a savings of $3 per unit ($+\$6 - \$4 + \$5 - \$4 + \$3 - \$9 = -\$3$). It would pay the firm to use this route, shown in Table 7–4.

Warehouse:	D	C	All Other	Slack	Factory Capacity
Factory: R	$4 3,999 ⟶	$5 → 3,001			7,000
S	$5 ↑ 1 ←	$4 ↓ 1,499	2,500		4,000
T			9,000	1,000	10,000
Warehouse Requirements	4,000	4,500	11,500	1,000	21,000

Table 7–3
Movement of One Unit
Involving Four Cells

The two examples show that it is necessary to have three filled cells to evaluate unfilled cell *SD* and five filled cells to evaluate unfilled cell *TD*. Why is this so? Because the rim (row and column) requirements must be met. If, for example, we moved one unit from *RD* to *RC*, the row requirement of 7,000 units would be met, but not the column requirements of 4,000 for warehouse *D* and 4,500 for warehouse *C*. Thus we have moved at right angles or at 90-degree angles in order to satisfy the rim requirements of the problem.

It should be apparent how this approach got the name stepping-stone method. Only filled cells or stepping-stones can be used in the evaluation of an unfilled cell. Later, it will be shown that an epsilon (ϵ) in a cell is considered a filled cell. It should be pointed out that it is allowable to jump over cells (filled or unfilled) when forming a closed route to evaluate an unfilled cell.

The computations for the unused cells in Table 7–2 are as follows:

Warehouse:	D	C	F	All Other	Slack	Factory Capacity
Factory: R	$4 3,999	$5 →3,001				7,000
S	↑	$4 ↓ 1,499	$3 2,501			4,000
T	$6 1 ←		$9 ↓ 999	8,000	1,000	10,000
Warehouse Requirements	4,000	4,500	3,500	8,000	1,000	21,000

Table 7–4
Movement of One Unit
Involving Six Cells

		Cost	
Unfilled Cells		**Penalty**	**Savings**
$SD = + \; 5 - 4 + 5 - 4$ (per above) $\quad =$		$+2$	
$TD = + \; 6 - 4 + 5 - 4 + 3 - 9$ (per above) $=$			-3
$TC = + \; 3 - 4 + 3 - 9 \qquad\qquad\quad =$			-7
$RF = + \; 6 - 3 + 4 - 5 \qquad\qquad\quad =$		$+2$	
$RG = + \; 5 - 4 + 9 - 3 + 4 - 5 \qquad =$		$+6$	
$SG = + \; 2 - 4 + 9 - 3 \qquad\qquad\quad =$		$+4$	
$RE = + \; 8 - 5 + 9 - 3 + 4 - 5 \qquad =$		$+8$	
$SE = + \; 4 - 5 + 9 - 3 \qquad\qquad\quad =$		$+5$	
$RB = + \; 7 - 5 + 9 - 3 + 4 - 5 \qquad =$		$+7$	
$SB = + \; 5 - 5 + 9 - 3 \qquad\qquad\quad =$		$+6$	
$RA = + \; 6 - 9 + 9 - 3 + 4 - 5 \qquad =$		$+2$	
$SA = +10 - 9 + 9 - 3 \qquad\qquad\quad =$		$+7$	
R Slack $= + \; 0 - 0 + 9 - 3 + 4 - 5 \qquad =$		$+5$	
S Slack $= + \; 0 - 0 + 9 - 3 \qquad\qquad\quad =$		$+6$	

Step 3. Select Unfilled Cell with Largest Negative Value   Now that the evaluation of the cost values are complete (a plus sign denotes a cost penalty or higher transportation costs, whereas a negative sign denotes additional cost savings or lower transportation costs), the third step is to select the highest negative figure. This will enable the firm to ship at lower costs. Based upon the values found in Table 7–2, cell TC offers the best opportunity to reduce transportation costs further. Thus, this cell with a negative value of 7 is selected.

Step 4. Move as Many Units as Possible into Selected Cell   The fourth and final step of the stepping-stone method is moving as large a quantity as possible into the selected unfilled cell. Based upon the quantities shown in Table 7–2, the largest quantity is 2,500 in the three filled cells that were used to evaluate unfilled cell TC. The following example will demonstrate the feasibility or nonfeasibility of moving 2,500 units:

	Before		**After**	
Warehouse:	**C**	**F**	**C**	**F**
Factory:				
S	1,500	2,500	$-1,000$	$+5,000$
T		1,000	$+2,500$	$-1,500$

Based on this analysis, it is not feasible to move 2,500 units into cell TC since two negative figures would appear in the adjoining cells. This is not possible in the real world since we cannot move minus units. The same condition results in trying to move the second largest quantity or 1,500 units. Thus only 1,000 units can be moved into cell TC, as reflected in Table 7–5 (second table).

STEPPING-STONE METHOD—OPTIMUM SOLUTION The first step in all subsequent tables is to test for degeneracy, that is, does $m + n - 1$ (Equation 7–1) equal the number of filled cells? The number of filled cells, 10, equals $3 + 8 - 1$. Since degeneracy is not applicable, the next step is to re-evaluate all unfilled cells in the manner shown for Table 7–2. The results are shown in Table 7–5. If an unfilled cell can be evaluated by more than one set of routes, the highest minus or lowest plus amount is inserted. However, this was not the case in the first or second

Table 7–5

Stepping-Stone Method (Second Table)

Warehouse:	D	C	F	G	E	B	A	Slack	Factory Capacity
Factory: R	$4 / 4,000	$5 / 3,000	$6 / +$2	$5 / −$1	$8 / +$1	$7 / $0	$6 / −$5	$0 / −$2	7,000
S	$5 / +$2	$4 / 1,500 − 1,000 / 500	$3 / 2,500 +1,000 / 3,500	$2 / −$3	$4 / −$2	$5 / −$1	$10 / $0	$0 / −$1	4,000
T	$6 / +$4	$3 / +1,000 / 1,000	$9 / 1,000 − 1,000 / +$7	$4 / 3,000	$5 / 2,000	$5 / 2,000	$9 / 1,000	$0 / 1,000	10,000
Warehouse Requirements	4,000	4,500	3,500	3,000	2,000	2,000	1,000	1,000	21,000

Total transportation costs $87,500.

Table 7–6

Stepping-Stone Method (Third Table)

Warehouse:	D	C	F	G	E	B	A	Slack	Factory Capacity
Factory: R	$4 / 4,000	$5 / 3,000 − 1,000 / 2,000	$6 / +$2	$5 / −$1	$8 / +$1	$7 / $0	$6 / +1,000 / 1,000	$0 / −$2	7,000
S	$5 / +$2	$4 / 500	$3 / 3,500	$2 / −$3	$4 / −$2	$5 / −$1	$10 / +$5	$0 / −$1	4,000
T	$6 / +$4	$3 / 1,000 + 1,000 / 2,000	$9 / +$7	$4 / 3,000	$5 / 2,000	$5 / 2,000	$9 / 1,000 − 1,000 / +$5	$0 / 1,000	10,000
Warehouse Requirements	4,000	4,500	3,500	3,000	2,000	2,000	1,000	1,000	21,000

Total transportation costs $82,500.

table. Selecting the highest minus value in all of the unfilled cells results in moving products to cell *RA* for lower transportation costs. Again, the largest quantity will be moved into the unfilled cell as in Table 7–6 (third table).

Again, the first step in succeeding tables is to test for degeneracy (not applicable) in Table 7–6. The unfilled cells are evaluated, resulting in cell *SG* with the largest minus value. The movement of units is shown in Table 7–7 (fourth table).

Table 7–7
Stepping-Stone Method
(Fourth Table)

Warehouse:	D	C	F	G	E	B	A	Slack	Factory Capacity
Factory: R	$4	$5	$6	$5	$8	$7	$6	$0	
	4,000	2,000	−$1	−$1	+$1	$0	1,000	−$2	7,000
	$5	$4 (500 − 500)	$3	$2 (+500)	$4	$5	$10	$0	
S	+$5	+$3	3,500	500	+$1	+$2	+$8	+$2	4,000
	$6	$3 (2,000 + 500)	$9	$4 (3,000 − 500)	$5	$5	$9	$0	
T	+$4	2,500	+$4	2,500	2,000	2,000	+$5	1,000	10,000
Warehouse Requirements	4,000	4,500	3,500	3,000	2,000	2,000	1,000	1,000	21,000

Total transportation costs $81,000.

Table 7–8
Stepping-Stone Method
(Fifth Table)

Warehouse:	D	C	F	G	E	B	A	Slack	Factory Capacity
Factory: R	$4	$5 (2,000 − 1,000)	$6	$5	$8	$7	$6	$0 (+1,000)	
	4,000	1,000	−$1	−$1	+$1	$0	1,000	1,000	7,000
S	$5 +$5	$4 +$3	$3 3,500	$2 500	$4 +$1	$5 +$2	$10 +$8	$0 +$4	4,000
	$6	$3 (2,500 + 1,000)	$9	$4	$5	$5	$9	$0 (1,000 − 1,000)	
T	+$4	3,500	+$4	2,500	2,000	2,000	+$5	+$2	10,000
Warehouse Requirements	4,000	4,500	3,500	3,000	2,000	2,000	1,000	1,000	21,000

Total transportation costs $79,000.

232

Following the same steps as for the previous tables results in allocating units to an unfilled cell, R slack, per Table 7–8 (fifth table). Inspection of this table indicates two minus amounts of the same value. Unfilled cell RG was randomly selected since either cell RF or RG could have been used.

Table 7–9
Stepping-Stone Method
(Sixth Table)

Warehouse:	D	C	F	G	E	B	A	Slack	Factory Capacity
Factory:	$4	$5	$6	$5	$8	$7	$6	$0	
		1,000 − 1,000		+ 1,000					
R	4,000	+ $1	$0	1,000	+ $2	+ $1	1,000	1,000	7,000
	$5	$4	$3	$2	$4	$5	$10	$0	
S	+ $4	+ $3	3,500	500	+ $1	+ $2	+ $7	+ $3	4,000
	$6	$3	$9	$4	$5	$5	$9	$0	
		3,500 + 1,000		2,500 − 1,000					
T	+ $3	4,500	+ $4	1,500	2,000	2,000	+ $4	+ $1	10,000
Warehouse Requirements	4,000	4,500	3,500	3,000	2,000	2,000	1,000	1,000	21,000

Total transportation costs $78,000.

The optimal solution is reached in Table 7–9 (sixth table) since there are no minus signs to denote further cost savings. The final shipping schedule is:

Route	No. of Units	Cost per Unit	Total Monthly Transportation Costs
RD	4,000	$4	$16,000
RG	1,000	5	5,000
RA	1,000	6	6,000
R Slack	1,000	0	—
SF	3,500	3	10,500
SG	500	2	1,000
TC	4,500	3	13,500
TG	1,500	4	6,000
TE	2,000	5	10,000
TB	2,000	5	10,000
	21,000		$78,000

The shipping schedule is not a unique solution since at least one zero appears in the final solution. A zero in an unfilled cell means another alternative is available with the same total cost. In Table 7–8 there was another unfilled cell, *RF*, with the same minus value that could have been used in place of the unfilled cell *RG*.

Degeneracy

One method for saving computation time is to start with the existing shipping schedule. When using this initial basis, there is a chance of *degeneracy*. When an attempt is made to evaluate the unfilled cells, some of the cells cannot be evaluated because the number of filled cells does not equal the answer per Equation 7–1 $(m + n - 1)$ for the rim requirements.

The problem of degeneracy is apparent when using Table 7–1 as the basis for a second table. Evaluation of the unfilled cells reveals that cell *SF* has the largest negative value, thereby resulting in the greatest unit cost savings. If units are moved into this cell, the following movement of units takes place:

Warehouse:	D	F
Factory:		
S	$3{,}500 - 3{,}500 = \quad 0$	$+3{,}500$
T	$500 + 3{,}500 = 4{,}000$	$3{,}500 - 3{,}500 = 0$

An examination of the above indicates that what started out as three filled cells is now two filled cells. This movement of goods is reflected in Table 7–10.

The first step in Table 7–10 is to test for degeneracy. Using Equation 7–1, we find the solution is degenerate at this stage. For computation purposes in degeneracy, one unfilled cell is considered artificially used where necessary, that is, an ϵ (epsilon) is placed in the cell as though it represented a very small quantity to be shipped through that cell route. The value of ϵ is actually zero when used in the movement of units from one cell to another.

Table 7–10
Stepping-Stone Method Utilizing the Northwest Corner Rule in First Table (Table 7–1)

Warehouse:	A	B	C	D	E	F	G	Slack	Factory Capacity
Factory: R	$6 1,000	$7 2,000	$5 4,000	$4 − $2	$8 + $3	$6 + $2	$5 + $1	$0 $0	7,000
S	$10 + $5	$5 − $1	$4 500	$5 ε	$4 $0	$3 3,500	$2 − $1	$0 + $1	4,000
T	$9 + $3	$5 − $2	$3 − $2	$6 4,000	$5 2,000	$9 + $5	$4 3,000	$0 1,000	10,000
Warehouse Requirements	1,000	2,000	4,500	4,000	2,000	3,500	3,000	1,000	21,000

Total transportation costs $98,500.

The next step in Table 7–10 is to evaluate all unfilled cells. Due to degeneracy, several unfilled cells cannot be evaluated. Hence, it is necessary to place ϵ in a low-cost empty cell that allows evaluation of the remaining cells. The rationale for the placement of epsilon in a low-cost cell is that units are generally moved into a low-cost cell as opposed to a high-cost cell. Thus, the placement of ϵ in cell SD allows us to evaluate all unused cells, which was not possible previously.

It is possible to have more than one epsilon in a transportation problem at the same time. Generally, this is caused by long paths where several filled cells become empty cells when the movement of units takes place. This is an extension of the preceding example for factories S and T and warehouses D and F. Once the ϵ is inserted it stays in the table until it is no longer needed. For example, if the addition of 50 units to a cell that has ϵ contained therein $(50 + \epsilon)$, the resulting figure is 50 units. If one or more ϵs remain in the final solution, they are ignored.

Also, it is possible not only to have too few filled cells, but also too many filled cells when applying the formula $m + n - 1$. In this case, a reduction in the number of used cell routes is necessary. This can be accomplished by finding four (six, eight, . . .) used cell routes which form a closed system in moving units. This is shown by making a shift of 25 units, starting with cell $A2$. The choice for the switch is based upon costs factors or on a random basis to obtain an acceptable solution.

From Four Filled Cells			To Three Filled Cells		
Warehouse:	1	2	Warehouse:	1	2
Factory:			*Factory:*		
A	100	25	A	125	0
B	50	200	B	25	225

If for some reason a cell route is not feasible, that is, a factory cannot make the product or management wishes to eliminate the possibility of its use, a very high cost of M can be used for that cell. A cell with a value of M means that it will never enter the final solution. Another way of handling this problem is to cross out the cell in question and never use or evaluate it.

One last comment on the stepping-stone method using the northwest corner rule, as in Tables 7–1 and 7–10, is that the shipping costs are $116,000 and $98,500, respectively. When these tables are compared to Table 7–2 for the same method using inspection, the total monthly transportation costs are $94,500. Hence the use of inspection in the initial solution reduces the number of tables needed for a final solution.

The iterative steps involved in the stepping-stone method after setting up the first table are set forth in Figure 7–1.

Simplex Method of Linear Programming

In Chapter 6, the minimization problem using the simplex method of linear programming was presented. The transportation problem is of the same type. Linear programming searches for the optimum quantities of units to ship from each factory to each warehouse for a least cost solution.

Returning to our original problem (Table 7–1), we shall let a series of Xs represent the quantities to be shipped from the factories to the warehouses as follows:

Let X_1 represent that quantity shipped from R to A

Let X_2 represent that quantity shipped from R to B

Let X_3 represent that quantity shipped from R to C

Let X_4 represent that quantity shipped from R to D

Let X_5 represent that quantity shipped from R to E

Let X_6 represent that quantity shipped from R to F

Let X_7 represent that quantity shipped from R to G

Let X_8 represent that quantity shipped from S to A

Let X_9 represent that quantity shipped from S to B

Let X_{10} represent that quantity shipped from S to C

Let X_{11} represent that quantity shipped from S to D

Let X_{12} represent that quantity shipped from S to E

Let X_{13} represent that quantity shipped from S to F

Let X_{14} represent that quantity shipped from S to G

Let X_{15} represent that quantity shipped from T to A

Let X_{16} represent that quantity shipped from T to B

Let X_{17} represent that quantity shipped from T to C

Let X_{18} represent that quantity shipped from T to D

Let X_{19} represent that quantity shipped from T to E

Let X_{20} represent that quantity shipped from T to F

Let X_{21} represent that quantity shipped from T to G

Let X_{22} represent slack for Factory R

Let X_{23} represent slack for Factory S

Let X_{24} represent slack for Factory T

The foregoing variables appear in Table 7–11. The optimum solution must satisfy the column requirements, which are an equal condition, and the row requirements, which are equal or less than conditions. With the addition of the slack variables (X_{22}, X_{23}, and X_{24}), we have an equal to condition for the rows. All that remains is to add artificial variables (X_{25}, X_{26}, X_{27}, X_{28}, X_{29}, X_{30}, and X_{31}) to the column equations in order to generate an initial solution.

Summary—Methodology of Stepping-Stone Method

Step 1—Test for Degeneracy Test for degeneracy focuses on Equation 7–1. The degeneracy test formula is $m + n - 1$ (m is the rows and n is the columns) while the resultant value of this equation should equal the number of filled cells. If the equation fails the equality test, too few filled cells mean that one or more epsilons must be added in step (2) below. Too many filled cells mean that their number must be reduced.

Step 2—Evaluate All Unfilled Cells Calculate the net total cost or saving of adding one unit to the unfilled cell. This means finding a closed route of filled cells that can be used to evaluate the unfilled cell and recognizing that the rim (row and column) requirements cannot be violated. Hence, evaluation of an unfilled cell means moving at right angles or making 90-degree turns at filled cells only to form a closed route. It is allowable to jump over cells (filled or unfilled) when forming a closed route to evaluate an unfilled cell. In those cases where there are too few filled cells based on the test in step (1), one or more epsilons must be placed in the table in order to evaluate the unfilled cells. Similarly, too many filled cells require reducing the number of these cells.

Step 3—Select Unfilled Cell With Largest Negative Value Select from the unfilled cells that one which has the largest negative value. In those cases where two minus values are equal, select that one which will result in moving as many units as possible into the selected unfilled cell. When all unfilled cell values are plus or zero, an optimal solution to the problem has been found.

Step 4—Move As Many Units As Possible Into Selected Cell Move as many units as possible into the selected unfilled cell. One word of caution—no negative quantities are allowed in the problem. Thus, filled cells cannot have values deducted from them that exceed their quantities.

Figure 7–1
Iterative steps in the stepping-stone method.

Table 7–11
Shipments from Factories to Warehouses

Warehouse:	A	B	C	D	E	F	G	Slack	Factory Capacity
Factory: R	X_1	X_2	X_3	X_4	X_5	X_6	X_7	X_{22}	7,000
S	X_8	X_9	X_{10}	X_{11}	X_{12}	X_{13}	X_{14}	X_{23}	4,000
T	X_{15}	X_{16}	X_{17}	X_{18}	X_{19}	X_{20}	X_{21}	X_{24}	10,000
Warehouse Requirements	1,000	2,000	4,500	4,000	2,000	3,500	3,000	1,000	21,000

Note: Xs represent shipments from factories to warehouses (X_1 to X_{21}) and slack variables (X_{22} to X_{24}).

The equations for the first tableau appear as follows:

$$X_1 + X_2 + X_3 + X_4 + X_5 + X_6 + X_7 + 0X_8 + 0X_9 + 0X_{10}$$
$$+ 0X_{11} + 0X_{12} + 0X_{13} + 0X_{14} + 0X_{15} + 0X_{16} + 0X_{17} + 0X_{18}$$
$$+ 0X_{19} + 0X_{20} + 0X_{21} + X_{22} + 0X_{23} + 0X_{24} + 0X_{25} + 0X_{26}$$
$$+ 0X_{27} + 0X_{28} + 0X_{29} + 0X_{30} + 0X_{31} = 7{,}000$$

$$\cdots + X_8 + X_9 + X_{10} + X_{11} + X_{12} + X_{13} + X_{14} \cdots \qquad + X_{23} \cdots = 4{,}000$$

$$\cdots + X_{15} + X_{16} + X_{17} + X_{18} + X_{19} + X_{20} + X_{21} \cdots \qquad + X_{24} \cdots = 10{,}000$$

$$X_1 + 0X_2 + 0X_3 + 0X_4 + 0X_5 + 0X_6 + 0X_7 + X_8 + 0X_9$$
$$+ 0X_{10} + 0X_{11} + 0X_{12} + 0X_{13} + 0X_{14} + X_{15} + 0X_{16} + 0X_{17}$$
$$+ 0X_{18} + 0X_{19} + 0X_{20} + 0X_{21} + 0X_{22} + 0X_{23} + 0X_{24} + X_{25}$$
$$+ 0X_{26} + 0X_{27} + 0X_{28} + 0X_{29} + 0X_{30} + 0X_{31} = 1{,}000$$

$$0X_1 + X_2 + 0X_3 + 0X_4 + 0X_5 + 0X_6 + 0X_7 + 0X_8 + X_9$$
$$+ 0X_{10} + 0X_{11} + 0X_{12} + 0X_{13} + 0X_{14} + 0X_{15} + X_{16} + 0X_{17}$$
$$+ 0X_{18} + 0X_{19} + 0X_{20} + 0X_{21} + 0X_{22} + 0X_{23} + 0X_{24} + 0X_{25}$$
$$+ X_{26} + 0X_{27} + 0X_{28} + 0X_{29} + 0X_{30} + 0X_{31} = 2{,}000$$

$$\cdots + X_3 \cdots + X_{10} \cdots + X_{17} \cdots + X_{27} \cdots = 4{,}500$$

$$\cdots + X_4 \cdots + X_{11} \cdots + X_{18} \cdots + X_{28} \cdots = 4{,}000$$

$$\cdots + X_5 \cdots + X_{12} \cdots + X_{19} \cdots + X_{29} \cdots = 2{,}000$$

$$\cdots + X_6 \cdots + X_{13} \cdots + X_{20} \cdots + X_{30} \cdots = 3{,}500$$

$$\cdots + X_7 \cdots + X_{14} \cdots + X_{21} \cdots + X_{31} \cdots = 3{,}000$$

The preceding equations are shown in the first simplex tableau, Table 7–12. By using the procedures described in Chapter 6, the optimum shipping schedule results in a least cost solution of $78,000, the same result that appears in Table 7–9 (last table) for the stepping-stone method.

The simplex algorithm is useful for a wide range of factory and warehouse choices that are too numerous to handle by the stepping-stone or other manually oriented methods. A computer can be used either in a batch or a real-time pro-

Table 7–12
First Simplex Tableau for Transportation Problem

C_j	Shipping Mix	Quantity	$6 X_1	$7 X_2	$5 X_3	$4 X_4	$8 X_5	$6 X_6	$5 X_7	$10 X_8	$5 X_9	$4 X_{10}	$5 X_{11}	$4 X_{12}	$3 X_{13}	$2 X_{14}
$0	X_{22}	7,000	1	1	1	1	1	1	1	0	0	0	0	0	0	0
$0	X_{23}	4,000	0	0	0	0	0	0	0	1	1	1	1	1	1	1
$0	X_{24}	10,000	0	0	0	0	0	0	0	0	0	0	0	0	0	0
$M	X_{25}	1,000	1	0	0	0	0	0	0	1	0	0	0	0	0	0
$M	X_{26}	2,000	0	1	0	0	0	0	0	0	1	0	0	0	0	0
$M	X_{27}	4,500	0	0	1	0	0	0	0	0	0	1	0	0	0	0
$M	X_{28}	4,000	0	0	0	1	0	0	0	0	0	0	1	0	0	0
$M	X_{29}	2,000	0	0	0	0	1	0	0	0	0	0	0	1	0	0
$M	X_{30}	3,500	0	0	0	0	0	1	0	0	0	0	0	0	1	0
$M	X_{31}	3,000	0	0	0	0	0	0	1	0	0	0	0	0	0	1
	Z_j	$20,000$M$	M	M	M	M	M	M	M	M	M	M	M	M	M	M
	$C_j - Z_j$		$6-M$	$7-M$	$5-M$	$4-M$	$8-M$	$6-M$	$5-M$	$10-M$	$5-M$	$4-M$	$5-M$	$4-M$	$3-M$	$2-M$

cessing mode to arrive at a final solution. This is another reason why the linear programming method is widely used.

Placement of Orders on Machines

Modified methods of the transportation problem are available to solve other recurring business problems. One method solves for the placement of orders on different machines. In the illustration, three machines are capable of producing four different products. An accurate survey of the machines' capabilities reveals that the machines differ in type and degree of automation. The time required to produce these four products also differ for each machine.

The total time available each month is: machine 1, 320 hours; machine 2, 390 hours; and machine 3, 375 hours. The products to be manufactured are: 1,500 units of A, 1,800 units of B, 2,100 units of C, and 2,250 units of D. Since some machines do not have the capability of producing some items due to their technical characteristics, Table 7–13 shows the number of units that can be produced in one hour by each machine.

The selling prices for each unit are: $2.45 for A, $2.40 for B, $2.25 for C, and $2.10 for D. The variable costs of production are: product A, $0.83, $0.91, and $0.87 for machines 1, 2, and 3, respectively; product B, $0.79, $0.93, and $0.91 for machines 1, 2, and 3, respectively; product C, $0.60 for machine 2; and product D, $0.81 and $0.82 for machines 2 and 3, respectively. The objective is to maximize the total contribution by scheduling and assigning the appropriate work load to the three machines. The contribution for each product is shown in Table 7–14.

The efficiency of the three machines must be considered. One must be selected in such a way that all machine time can be measured. Upon inspection of Table 7–13, machine 1 is unable to produce units of C and D and is slower in producing units A and B when compared to machine 2. The same reasoning can be applied to machine 3, which means machine 2 is best in terms of output. Machine 2 will be the common unit of production measurement. Since machine 2 is the basic unit of mea-

Table 7–12 (continued)
First Simplex Tableau for
Transportation Problem

Shipping Mix	Quantity	$5 X_{16}	$3 X_{17}	$6 X_{18}	$5 X_{19}	$9 X_{20}	$4 X_{21}	$0 X_{22}	$0 X_{23}	$0 X_{24}	$M X_{25}	$M X_{26}	$M X_{27}	$M X_{28}	$M X_{29}	$M X_{30}	$M X_{31}
X_{22}	7,000	0	0	0	0	0	0	1	0	0	0	0	0	0	0	0	0
X_{23}	4,000	0	0	0	0	0	0	0	1	0	0	0	0	0	0	0	0
X_{24}	10,000	1	1	1	1	1	1	0	0	1	0	0	0	0	0	0	0
X_{25}	1,000	0	0	0	0	0	0	0	0	0	1	0	0	0	0	0	0
X_{26}	2,000	1	0	0	0	0	0	0	0	0	0	1	0	0	0	0	0
X_{27}	4,500	0	1	0	0	0	0	0	0	0	0	0	1	0	0	0	0
X_{28}	4,000	0	0	1	0	0	0	0	0	0	0	0	0	1	0	0	0
X_{29}	2,000	0	0	0	1	0	0	0	0	0	0	0	0	0	1	0	0
X_{30}	3,500	0	0	0	0	1	0	0	0	0	0	0	0	0	0	1	0
X_{31}	3,000	0	0	0	0	0	1	0	0	0	0	0	0	0	0	0	1
Z_j	$20,000M	$M	$M	$M	$M	$M	$M	$0	$0	$0	$M	$M	$M	$M	$M	$M	$M
$C_j - Z_j$		$5 - M	$3 - M	$6 - M	$5 - M	$9 - M	$4 - M	$0	$0	$0	$0	$0	$0	$0	$0	$0	$0

surement, its efficiency will be established at 100 percent. Based on data in Table 7–13, the efficiency of machines 1 and 3 is 75 and 80 percent, respectively.

Table 7–13
Production Rate per Hour for Each Machine

Machine:	1	2	3
Unit:			
A	7.5	10.0	8.0
B	9.0	12.0	9.6
C		6.0	
D		9.0	7.2

Table 7–14
Contribution per Unit

Machine:	1	2	3
Unit:			
A	$2.45 − $0.83 = $1.62	$2.45 − $0.91 = $1.54	$2.45 − $0.87 = $1.58
B	$2.40 − $0.79 = $1.61	$2.40 − $0.93 = $1.47	$2.40 − $0.91 = $1.49
C		$2.25 − $0.60 = $1.65	
D		$2.10 − $0.81 = $1.29	$2.10 − $0.82 = $1.28

In order to set up a table that utilizes the stepping-stone method, the hours of machine 2 (standard) are used to find the other total standard hours for machines 1 and 3. The calculation for the standard machine hours is obtained by dividing the total number of units to be produced monthly by the number of units produced in 1 hour for machine 2. The results are:

Unit A:

$$\frac{1,500 \text{ units}}{10 \text{ units produced per hour}}$$
= 150 standard hours needed to manufacture 1,500 units of A

Unit B:

$$\frac{1,800 \text{ units}}{12 \text{ units produced per hour}}$$
= 150 standard hours needed to manufacture 1,800 units of B

Unit C:

$$\frac{2,100 \text{ units}}{6 \text{ units produced per hour}}$$
= 350 standard hours needed to manufacture 2,100 units of C

Unit D:

$$\frac{2,250 \text{ units}}{9 \text{ units produced per hour}}$$
= 250 standard hours needed to manufacture 2,250 units of D

Having determined the column totals for Table 7–15, it is necessary to calculate the productive capacity of each machine by the same unit of measure. The effective available capacity in hours is calculated by taking the available time each month and multiplying by the efficiency factor. The standard hours for the rows are:

Machine 1: 320 available hours × 75% efficiency = 240 standard hours

Machine 2: 390 available hours × 100% efficiency = 390 standard hours

Machine 3: 375 available hours × 80% efficiency = 300 standard hours

The total standard hours for the rows are 930 hours (machine capacities) while the total standard hours for the columns are 900 hours (requirements for units A, B, C, and D) in Table 7–15. This necessitates the need for column E of 30 hours, representing a hypothetical item with a zero contribution, analogous to slack in the transportation problem.

Table 7–15
Production Requirements and Contribution Table for the Stepping-Stone Method

Unit:	A	B	C	D	E	Capacity of Machines (std. hrs.)
Machine: 1	$16.20 ($1.62 × 10)	$19.32 ($1.61 × 12)			$0	240
2	$15.40 ($1.54 × 10)	$17.64 ($1.47 × 12)	$9.90 ($1.65 × 6)	$11.61 ($1.29 × 9)	$0	390
3	$15.80 ($1.58 × 10)	$17.88 ($1.49 × 12)		$11.52 ($1.20 × 0)	$0	300
Units Requirements (std. hrs.)	150	150	350	250	30	930

The last data necessary for the initial stepping-stone table is the contribution per standard machine hour. The values are obtained by multiplying the contribution per unit, shown in Table 7–14, by the production rates in pieces on an hourly basis for machine 2 (standard), as in Table 7–13. These calculations are found in Table 7–15 for the stepping-stone method.

In order to simplify the problem, inspection is used in the initial solution. Rows and columns are interchanged in order to reduce the number of tables needed to reach a solution. This is done by arranging the row contributions in descending order, starting from the left. This results in arranging the rows in this order: machine 1, machine 3, and machine 2. An alternative method for determining the proper placement of the rows is to sum their respective contributions for comparable products, which are:

Machine 1: $16.20 + $19.32 = $35.52

Machine 3: $15.80 + $17.88 = $33.68

Machine 2: $15.40 + $17.64 = $33.04

241

Based upon inspection, columns are arranged in this sequence: B, A, D, C, and E. This rearrangement of rows and columns forms the first table for the stepping-stone method, using the northwest corner rule and inspection in Table 7–16.

Using the rules set forth under the stepping-stone method, the first table is not degenerate. The signs are to be treated differently, that is, a plus sign indicates further contribution is available, a minus sign indicates a decrease in contribution. The first table (Table 7–16) indicates more profits are available with the $0.09 in cell 3E. The second and final table for this problem is found in Table 7–17. The total monthly contribution from Table 7–16 is $11,649.90, based on standard hours of machine 2. Since 30 standard hours have been moved to increase profits by $0.09 per standard machine hour, this results in an increase in the contribution by $2.70. Adding this figure results in a total contribution of $11,652.60, the same figure shown in Table 7–17.

Table 7–16
Stepping-Stone Method Using the Northwest Corner Rule and Inspection (First Table)

Unit:	B	A	D	C	E	Capacity of Machines (hrs.)
Machine: 1	$19.32 / 150	$16.20 / 90			$0 / − $.31	240
3	$17.88 / − $1.04	$15.80 / 60	$11.52 / 240		$0 / + $.09	300
2	$17.64 / − $1.37	$15.40 / − $.49	$11.61 / 10	$9.90 / 350	$0 / 30	390
Unit Requirements (hrs.)	150	150	250	350	30	930

Total monthly contribution $11,649.90.

Table 7–17
Stepping-Stone Method (Second Table)

Unit:	B	A	D	C	E	Capacity of Machines (hrs.)
Machine: 1	$19.32 / 150	$16.20 / 90			$0 / − $.40	240
3	$17.88 / − $1.04	$15.80 / 60	$11.52 / 210		$0 / 30	300
2	$17.64 / − $1.37	$15.40 / − $.49	$11.61 / 40	$9.90 / 350	$0 / − $.09	390
Unit Requirements (hrs.)	150	150	250	350	30	930

Total monthly contribution $11,652.60.

Chapter Summary

near programming—were pre-
...ar problems. An important con-
...ortation problem cannot always
...ransportation is but one part of
...the best transportation program
...is area requires continuous up-
...sulting in a challenging task for

...olution using the stepping-stone

...een the simplex method and the
...ation problem.

...the stepping-stone method and
...n problem.

1. In the formulation of the first table using the stepping-stone method, how does the combined northwest corner rule and inspection (Table 7–2) approach produce a lower cost in the initial solution than the northwest corner rule (Table 7–1) by itself?

2. To test for degeneracy, the formula (Equation 7–1), $m + n - 1$, is used where m is the rows and n is the columns. Would it matter mathematically to change the meaning of these terms, so that m represents the columns and n represents the rows?

3. In a transportation problem using the stepping-stone method, is it possible to make more than one movement of units per Step 4 in one table? Give your reason for allowing or not allowing two or more movements of units within one table.

4. Since the transportation problem is one of minimizing total transportation costs, how can a computer package that utilizes the simplex method of linear programming be used to accommodate the cost factors in a transportation problem? In other words, what simple change can be noted in the instructions for a computer package that will distinguish certain values in a maximization problem from a minimization problem?

5. When formulating a transportation problem using the simplex method of linear programming, what variables are normally considered to be controllable and uncontrollable?

Mathematical Exercises

1. The Acme Corporation manufactures widgets in three factories: Orlando, Florida; New Orleans, Louisiana; and Reidsville, North Carolina. These factories ship widgets to four warehouses: Houston, Texas; Seattle, Washington; San Francisco, California; and Denver, Colorado. The requirements of each warehouse, the capacity of each factory, and the cost per unit from each factory to each warehouse are:

| | Factories | | | Warehouse |
Warehouse	Orlando	New Orleans	Reidsville	Requirements
Houston	$4	$3	$4	1,000
Seattle	8	8	9	800
San Francisco	7	8	7	2,100
Denver	5	4	4	1,200
Factory Capacity	2,000	1,700	1,400	5,100

Find the minimum cost transportation schedule using the stepping-stone method.

2. Three factories are operated by the Link Manufacturing Company of St. Louis, Missouri. Currently, the products manufactured are shipped to three different warehouses. The location and capacities of these warehouses are:

Warehouse	Capacity
Newark, New Jersey	1,200 units
Jacksonville, Florida	800 units
San Diego, California	1,000 units

The capacity of each factory together with the per unit freight rate from each factory to each warehouse are:

Factory	Capacity	Freight Rates To	Per Unit
1	600 units	Newark	$5
		Jacksonville	6
		San Diego	8
2	1,000 units	Newark	4
		Jacksonville	7
		San Diego	7
3	1,400 units	Newark	6
		Jacksonville	8
		San Diego	6

Determine what factories should ship what quantities to the three warehouses and total minimum freight costs.

3. The Jutson Manufacturing Company must ship from three factories to seven warehouses. The transportation cost per unit from factory to each warehouse, the requirements of each warehouse, and the capacity of each factory are:

Warehouse	Factories			Warehouse Requirements
	1	2	3	
A	$6	$11	$8	100
B	7	3	5	200
C	5	4	3	450
D	4	5	6	400
E	8	4	5	200
F	6	3	8	350
G	5	2	4	300
Factory capacity	700	400	1,000	

(a) Find the minimum cost transportation schedule using the stepping-stone method.
(b) If warehouse C is closed by the company, what procedures should be undertaken in order to find the minimum cost transportation schedule?
(c) How would you handle the case where the total warehouse requirements exceed total factory capacity?

4. The top management of the Austine Manufacturing Company is questioning whether its current shipping schedule is optimal. The firm has three factories and five warehouses. The necessary data in terms of transportation costs, factory capacities, and warehouse requirements are as follows:

Warehouse	Factories			Warehouse Requirements
	A	B	C	
1	$5	$4	$8	400
2	8	7	4	400
3	6	7	6	500
4	6	6	6	400
5	3	5	4	800
Factory capacity	800	600	1,100	2,500

Solve for an optimal shipping schedule in terms of lowest possible shipping costs using the simplex method of linear programming.

5. Building Products Company has a division made up of five separate plants scattered around the outskirts of a city. Railroad facilities are not available at any of the plant sites. The firm's own trucks carry all of the raw materials needed from suppliers. However, due to a strike of the firm's truck drivers, several trucking companies have bid on the amounts they can carry to various plants. The prices quoted for this temporary situation are per 1,000 pounds:

Plant	Requirements (weekly)	1,000 Pound Rates		
		Dalton	Doran	Riggs
A	800,000 pounds	$8	$6	$7
B	1,000,000 pounds	4	5	3
C	900,000 pounds	7	8	9
D	1,200,000 pounds	3	4	5
E	1,500,000 pounds	8	9	8
	5,400,000 pounds			

Hauling Capacities (weekly):	
Trucking firm Dalton	2,000,000 pounds
Trucking firm Doran	1,800,000 pounds
Trucking firm Riggs	2,000,000 pounds

Determine the least cost program for the Building Products Company during this temporary situation (one week).

6. Three classifications of workers (W_1, W_2, and W_3) can be used on three different jobs (J_1, J_2, and J_3) per an agreement with the union. Each man has a different cost for each job, which appears in the table below.

Worker:	W_1	W_2	W_3	Workers Needed
Jobs:				
J_1	$4.00	$3.60	$3.75	5
J_2	$4.40	$3.50	$4.00	20
J_3	$4.60	$4.40	$4.60	10
Workers available	10	15	10	35

What is the best allocation of workers to the various jobs in order to minimize costs?

7. The Clover Transportation Company has four terminals, A, B, C, and D. At the start of a particular day, there are 8, 8, 6, and 3 tractors available at terminals A, B, C, and D, respectively. During the previous night, at plants R, S, T, and U, 2, 12, 5, and 6 trailers were loaded, respectively. The company dispatcher has come up with the distances between the terminals and plants which appear as follows:

Plant:	R	S	T	U
Terminal:				
A	22	46	16	40
B	42	15	50	10
C	82	32	48	60
D	40	40	36	30

Based upon the foregoing information, what tractors should the dispatcher send to which plants in order to minimize total distances?

8. The Nielsen Printing Company has six orders for single-page advertising leaflets. The quantities are: 28,000, 15,000, 15,000, 20,000, 38,000, and 44,000. The three presses available can produce 50,000, 70,000, and 60,000 sheets per day, respectively. The variable costs, per thousand in running the orders on the various presses, are given as follows:

Order:	1	2	3	4	5	6
Press:						
1	$4.48	$5.60	$6.40	$5.40	$6.42	$4.88
2	4.40	5.44	6.70	4.82	7.52	5.44
3	4.63	4.80	6.20	5.26	6.18	5.26

Determine the optimal assignment of orders to presses 1, 2, and 3.

9. The Precision Products Company has certain products that can be produced on several machines. However, there are differences of running speeds, selling prices, and costs which are as follows:

	Machines (output per hour)			Selling Price	Number of Products
	1	2	3		
Products:					
A	—	9.0	7.2	$3.05	1,620
B	7.5	10.0	8.0	$3.00	2,000
C	—	8.0	6.4	$2.85	1,800
D	7.5	10.0	8.0	$2.90	1,750
Monthly available time	320 hrs	400 hrs	320 hrs		

	Variable Costs per Machine		
	1	2	3
Products:			
A	—	$1.15	$1.25
B	$1.50	1.25	1.40
C	—	1.05	1.30
D	1.35	1.20	1.45

Find the optimum allocation of products to the three machines for the coming month.

Bibliography

H. Bierman, C. P. Bonini, and W. H. Hausman, *Quantitative Analysis for Business Decisions,* Homewood, Ill.: Richard D. Irwin, 1973.

E. S. Buffa, *Operations Management: The Management of Productive Systems,* New York: John Wiley & Sons, 1976.

N. J. Driebeek, *Applied Linear Programming,* Reading, Mass.: Addison-Wesley, 1969.

F. S. Hillier and G. J. Lieberman, *Operations Research,* San Francisco: Holden-Day, 1974.

N. K. Kwak, *Mathematical Programming with Business Applications,* New York: McGraw-Hill Book Company, 1973.

S. B. Richmond, *Operations Research for Management Decisions,* New York: The Ronald Press Company, 1968.

G. M. F. di Roccaferrera, *Introduction to Linear Programming Processes,* Cincinnati, O.: South-Western Publishing Company, 1967.

M. Simonnard, *Linear Programming,* Englewood Cliffs, N.J.: Prentice-Hall, 1966.

Chapter 8

Dynamic Programming

Chapter Objectives
☐ To examine the great potential of dynamic programming due to its multistage process of decision making.
☐ To present the requirements for formulating a dynamic programming problem.
☐ To demonstrate how dynamic programming can be applied to a wide range of business problems.
☐ To show how dynamic programming is superior, at least in concept, to many other mathematical programming techniques.

Chapter Outline

Linear programming problems have one common characteristic: they are static. Problems are stated and solved in terms of a specific situation occurring at a certain moment. When a problem is concerned with variations over time, another OR technique must be utilized which includes the time element. Such a technique, called *dynamic programming,* is an extension of the basic linear programming technique. It was developed by Richard Bellman and G. B. Dantzig. Their important contributions on this quantitative technique were first published in the 1950s. Initially, dynamic programming was referred to as stochastic linear programming or linear programming problems dealing with uncertainty. Today, dynamic programming has been developed as a quantitative technique to solve a wide range of business problems.

Dynamic programming is based on the "principle of optimality" which states that an optimal policy consists of optimum sub-policies. It can be defined as a mathematical technique which solves for a series of sequential decisions, each of which affects future decisions. This is important since we rarely encounter an operational situation where the implications of a decision do not extend into the future. Executives face situations that require them to make a series of decisions with the outcome of each depending on the results of a previous decision(s) in the series. A production manager, for example, might neglect plant maintenance in order to obtain a higher output today rather than some time in the future. The total return resulting from all decisions may not be optimal if each decision is considered by itself. Instead, a sacrifice of some gain in making the first and subsequent decisions, resulting in the need of suboptimization for each decision, may produce a higher total return. The technique of dynamic programming, then, is used to determine the possibilities of modifying decisions that may exist over a period of time.

Similarly, dynamic programming is concerned with problems in which time is not a relevant variable. For example, a decision must be made which involves an allocation of a fixed quantity of resources among a number of alternative uses. This type of problem can be solved by breaking it down into several steps. In this manner, the final decision is handled as if it were a series of dependent decisions over time. Even though this type of problem is not concerned with the time factor per se, it still adheres to the fundamental characteristic of dynamic programming—a multistage process of decision making. Examples of each type are presented in this chapter.

Requirements for Formulating a Dynamic Programming Problem

Dynamic programming may be thought of as an approach for breaking large, complex problems into a series of smaller problems that are individually easier to solve. Unlike the previous allocation technique of linear programming, dynamic programming has no standard format, but rather is a general approach to problem solving. The format of any given dynamic-programming formulation can vary widely in nature and complexity, depending on the problem's structure. To illustrate its essential nature, several basic concepts, i.e., requirements, for formulating a dynamic programming problem are set forth.

The first concept is a *state variable* whose value specifies the condition of the process. The values of these variables tell us all we need to know about the system for the purpose of making decisions. For example, in a production problem, we might require state variables that relate to plant capacity and present inventory. Although the number of state variables can be large, the difficulty in solving a problem increases considerably as the number of these variables increase. It is to our advantage to minimize their number.

Included in the formulation of a dynamic programming problem is the concept of *decisions* or *decision variables*, which are opportunities to change the state variables (possibly in a probabilistic manner). The net change in the state variables over some time period is subject to considerable uncertainty. The returns generated by each decision depend on the starting and ending states for that decision, thereby adding up as a sequence of decisions. The task is to make decisions that maximize total return.

The last important concept for formulating a dynamic programming problem is the ability to make decisions about the problem at various *stages* or points in time. At each step in the problem, a decision is made to change the state and thereby maximize the gain. At the next stage, decisions are made using the values of the state variables that result from the preceding decision, and so forth. Thus the time component is considered in only two ways: the present and its immediate preceding period. This approach is shown as follows:

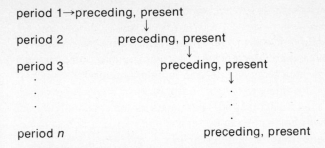

period 1 → preceding, present

period 2   preceding, present

period 3   preceding, present

period n preceding, present

The foregoing is based on the mathematical notion of *recursion,* found in continued fractions. A number plus a fraction in which the denominator is a number plus a fraction is called a continued fraction.

To illustrate, what is the minimum-cost production schedule for the next three months? If the *state variable* is inventory and the *decision variable* is the level of production—with each month being a *stage,* then the dynamic programming formulation for sequential decision making becomes:

Inventory 4 → Month 1   → Inventory 3 → Month 2   →
(Beginning)   Stage 3   Stage 2
              Decision 3   Decision 2

Inventory 2 → Month 3   → Inventory 1
              Stage 1   (Ending)
              Decision 1

One last point should be noted when formulating a dynamic programming problem. No matter what the initial state(s) and decision(s) were, the remaining decisions will constitute an optimal policy. For example, if wrong decisions have been made for the first week and second week, this does not prevent one from making the right decisions in the future—third week, fourth week, and remaining weeks. Thus, dynamic programming enables one to arrive at optimal decisions for the periods or stages that still lie ahead despite bad decisions made in the past.

Production Smoothing and Inventory Control

The first example of dynamic programming is a production scheduling and inventory control problem that determines the best plan for producing a seasonal product. The basic costs are those of production and storage for a nonperishable product. As always, management wants to minimize the total operational costs for the period.

The production smoothing aspect of the problem looks to a leveling of the valleys and peaks in the production process. The time period in this problem is well defined, as are demand, production (supply), and storage factors. The cost factors are known: (1) cost of production in terms of regular time and overtime and (2) cost of storage in terms of quantity stored. The task of dynamic programming is to minimize the sum of these two costs—those due to fluctuation and output and those due to inventories.

There are three basic approaches to the dynamic programming problem in which demand varies within a fixed period of time. The first approach manufactures the product in accordance with the amount desired in each time period. Sales requirements, production, and inventory are not the same for each time period, resulting in wide swings of volume for each period. Thus, costs for the seasonal product will be very high during the peak sales period unless major inventories were accumulated during prior periods. These high costs result from hiring and training short-term help, excessive overtime, and equipment purchases.

The second approach utilizes a constant production rate. When demand is light, inventory is accumulated. When demand is heavy, the inventory "cushion" minimizes its impact upon production. The difficulty with this approach is the determination of the beginning inventory. If the initial inventory is too small, stockouts will occur initially and stock overages eventually. If the initial inventory is too large, excess carrying costs will be experienced through the entire year. The value of this approach varies directly with the accuracy of prediction of the initial inventory and the general assumption that inventory carrying costs are relatively low.

The last approach compromises these two approaches, thereby allowing the production manager to plan production in a manner to meet demand and, at the same time, minimize both production and storage costs. This production smoothing problem utilizes linear programming to produce an optimum solution and allows for regular time and overtime.

Applications—Dynamic Programming

- **Smoothing employment**—helpful in smoothing production employment in an environment of widely fluctuating demand.
- **Scheduling equipment overhauls**—employed as a scheduling method for routine and major overhauls of machinery and equipment.
- **Determining equipment replacement policy**—useful in determining an optimal new equipment replacement policy.
- **Optimizing processes of varying efficiencies**—used successfully for computing the maximum output for production processes of varying efficiencies.
- **Maximizing expected sales**—determines the best combination of advertising media and frequency within a certain budget constraint to maximize expected sales.
- **Allocating capital funds**—assists in capital budgeting for allocating scarce resources to new ventures for maximizing profits over the long term.
- **Evaluating investment opportunities**—determines the most profitable investment of resources or alternative opportunities.
- **Determining dividend policies**—helpful in the proper determination of short- to long-range dividend policies.

For example, the production manager has a product, part #5050, which must be produced to meet a fluctuating demand. The monthly requirements are: 900 for the first month, 700 for the second month, 1,100 for the third month, and 1,000 for the fourth month. The part can be produced either on regular time or on overtime. However, two restrictions imposed by technical conditions are: regular production cannot exceed 900 items per month and overtime production cannot exceed 500 items per month. Manufacturing cost per item during regular hours varies each month: $3 in the first month, $4 in the second month, $2.50 in the third month, and $3 in the fourth month. This cost varies due to the anticipated volume for each month. The manufacturing costs for overtime are: $4 in the first month, $5 in the second month, $3.50 in the third month, and $4 in the fourth month. Monthly storage cost is $2 per unit. Items manufactured but not distributed during the month are stored for distribution in the following month. Since the time period is limited, no inventory is to remain at the end of the period (fourth month). The number of units produced must equal the number demanded and distributed.

Based on this information, the *state variables* are: monthly requirements, monthly plant capacities (regular and overtime), and zero inventory at the end of the period. The *stages* within the problem are the four monthly periods. *Decisions* concerning monthly production schedules must be made on a regular and an overtime basis.

Since the problem is to minimize the objective function in terms of production costs and storage costs, it can be approached as a transportation model. The unused capacity has a value of 1,900 items or $(900 \times 4) + (500 \times 4) - (900 + 700 + 1,100 + 1,000)$. The costs associated with unused capacity are zero. The costs of an item produced in a given month are its production cost (regular or overtime). However, the cost of the same item in subsequent months is its production cost plus its monthly storage costs. These figures appear in Table 8–1.

Since the costs increase progressively within each row, the lowest cost for the first row lies to the extreme left. Thus the northwest corner rule (modified) can be used. Table 8–2 is the initial table for this production smoothing problem. Using the basic formula for the rim requirements $(m + n - 1)$, the initial solution is degenerate since the rim requirements of $12(8 + 5 - 1)$ do not equal the filled cells. Thus, one artificial variable (ϵ) is needed for evaluation of all unused cells. Applying the

Table 8–1
Cost Factors for Production Smoothing (Scheduling) Problem

		Units	First Month	Second Month	Third Month	Fourth Month	Unused Capacity
First month	Regular production	900	$3	$5	$7	$9	$0
	Overtime production	500	4	6	8	10	0
Second month	Regular production	900	—	4	6	8	0
	Overtime production	500	—	5	7	9	0
Third month	Regular production	900	—	—	2.50	4.50	0
	Overtime production	500	—	—	3.50	5.50	0
Fourth month	Regular production	900	—	—	—	3	0
	Overtime production	500	—	—	—	4	0
Monthly Requirements			900	700	1,100	1,000	1,900

rules of the stepping-stone method, all pluses in the unused cells indicate the best solution in terms of costs has been reached in Table 8–2 and that the solution is unique. The total production cost plan during the next four months for part #5050 is computed as follows:

First month	900 items × $3 (R)	= $ 2,700
Second month	700 items × $4 (R)	= 2,800
Third month	900 items × $2.50 (R)	= 2,250
Third month	200 items × $3.50 (O)	= 700
Fourth month	900 items × $3 (R)	= 2,700
Fourth month	100 items × $4 (O)	= 400
	3,700 items	$11,550 total cost

where (R) = regular time and (O) = overtime. In this solution which minimizes total costs, the production manager can utilize the excess capacity for manufacturing other parts.

Table 8–2
Production Smoothing
Problem

	First Month	Second Month	Third Month	Fourth Month	Unused Capacity	Available Capacities
First month	$3 ⟨900⟩	$5 +$1	$7 +$3.50	$9 +$5	$0 ε	900
	$4 +$1	$6 +$2	$8 +$4.50	$10 +$6	$0 ⟨500⟩	500
Second month	−	$4 ⟨700⟩	$6 +$2.50	$8 +$4	$0 ⟨200⟩	900
	−	$5 +$1	$7 +$3.50	$9 +$5	$0 ⟨500⟩	500
Third month	−	−	$2.50 ⟨900⟩	$4.50 +$1.50	$0 +$1	900
	−	−	$3.50 ⟨200⟩	$5.50 +$1.50	$0 ⟨300⟩	500
Four month	−	−	−	$3 ⟨900⟩	$0 +$1	900
	−	−	−	$4 ⟨100⟩	$0 ⟨400⟩	500
Monthly requirement	900	700	1,100	1,000	1,900	5,600

Allocation of Salesmen to Various Marketing Areas

Initially this section will investigate the distribution of salesmen for two marketing areas and then extend this analysis to three marketing areas. The problem is how to allocate a given number of salesmen among marketing areas to achieve maximum profit. In Figure 8–1, the profit for two marketing areas is given as a function of sales effort expended. Inspection of this data indicates that sales actually drop since too many salesmen tend to antagonize the customers.

Using six salesmen in two sales areas produces seven possible combinations: allocate all six to sales area 1 and none to sales area 2, five salesmen to sales area 1 and one salesman to sales area 2, and so on. This is summarized in Table 8–3. The mathematical notation is: $f_1(x)$ denotes profit in sales area 1, $f_2(x)$ denotes profit in sales area 2, and x equals the number of salesmen employed in a sales area.

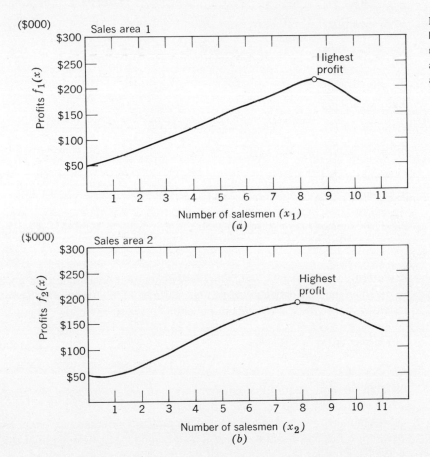

Figure 8–1
Profits as a function of sales effort for (a) sales area 1 and (b) sales area 2.

Table 8–3
Profits Available in Both Sales Areas

Number of Salesmen	x (area 1)	6	5	4	3	2	1	0
	x (area 2)	0	1	2	3	4	5	6
Profit in sales area	$f_1(x)$	$150,000	$130,000	$115,000	$105,000	$ 80,000	$ 60,000	$ 50,000
	$f_2(x)$	50,000	65,000	85,000	110,000	140,000	160,000	175,000
Total Profit		$200,000	$195,000	$200,000	$215,000	$220,000	$220,000	$225,000

The last row in Table 8–3 indicates the total profit for each of the seven alternatives. The best allocation is six salesmen in sales area 2 and none in sales area 1 for a maximum profit of $225,000. Data in Table 8–3 can be written in mathematical form as follows:

$$Z = f_1(x) + f_2(x) \qquad \text{(Equation 8–1)}$$

where Z equals total profit and x is the number of salesmen for one sales area. Hence, all possible profit combinations for two sales areas are:

$$Z = f_1(0) + f_2(6)$$
$$Z = f_1(1) + f_2(5)$$
$$Z = f_1(2) + f_2(4)$$
$$Z = f_1(3) + f_2(3)$$
$$Z = f_1(4) + f_2(2)$$
$$Z = f_1(5) + f_2(1)$$
$$Z = f_1(6) + f_2(0)$$

Based upon Equation 8–1, a generalized formula for obtaining the best allocation of salesmen in two sales areas for optimum profit is:

$$Z = F(A) = \max_{0 \leqslant x \leqslant A} \left[f_1(x) + f_2(A - x) \right] \qquad \text{(Equation 8–2)}$$

where $F(A)$ is the maximum profit that can be made if A salesmen are allocated in an optimum manner between the two sales areas. In this problem, A is defined as a state variable. Thus, the optimum equation for six salesmen is:

$$F(6) = \max_{0 \leqslant x \leqslant 6} \left[f_1(x) + f_2(6 - x) \right] \qquad \text{(Equation 8–3)}$$

It should be remembered that other values for the state variable, not just 6, could have been used in the preceding equation.

An alternative method is to compute the profit for a certain number of salesmen assigned to the first sales area and a given number of salesmen allocated to the second sales area. This is shown in Table 8–4, the source data being Figure 8–1. For example, if 4 salesmen are assigned to the first area and 1 salesman is assigned to the second area, the profit realized will be $180,000, or $115,000 for 4 salesmen in sales area 1 and $65,000 for 1 salesman in sales area 2. Another example for 11 salesmen is an optimum profit of $310,000, where profit from utilizing six men is $150,000 in the first sales area and profit from using five men in the second sales area is $160,000. Inspection of Table 8–4 reveals that optimum profits are starred (*) amounts on the diagonals for the various number of salesmen. This data is plotted in Figure 8–2. Thus $F(A)$, which is the maximum profit for a combined number of A salesmen assigned to two marketing areas, can be easily determined.

Having treated two marketing areas, we can now consider the interrelationship of profit and salesmen for three sales areas. Just as we plotted profit as a function of sales effort for the first two sales areas, the same method can be continued for sales area 3 as shown in Figure 8–3. However, solving for an optimum allocation of salesmen in three marketing areas requires a somewhat different point of view. For example, we could solve the problem of allocating the 6 salesmen with the understanding that 2 salesmen will be allocated to the first two sales areas and that the other 4 will be in sales area 3. Upon modification of Equation 8–1, we can say that the profit by using 2 salesmen in the first two sales areas is $F(2)$ and the profit from allocating 4 salesmen to the last sales area is $f_3(4)$. Therefore profit is:

$$Z = F(2) + f_3(4) \hspace{4cm} \text{(Equation 8–4)}$$

However, there is no logical reason to allocate exactly two salesmen to the first two areas. Since this is the case, it is necessary to drop this assumption and try to allocate 0 salesman, 1 salesman, and so forth, to the first two sales areas. The problem can now be seen as one of trying to select the largest of the following (based upon Equation 8–4):

$$Z = F(0) + f_3(6)$$
$$Z = F(1) + f_3(5)$$
$$Z = F(2) + f_3(4)$$
$$Z = F(3) + f_3(3)$$
$$Z = F(4) + f_3(2)$$
$$Z = F(5) + f_3(1)$$
$$Z = F(6) + f_3(0)$$

Table 8–4
Profits for Sales Efforts
in Two Sales Areas

			Sales Area 1										
Number of Salesmen			**0**	**1**	**2**	**3**	**4**	**5**	**6**	**7**	**8**	**9**	**10**	**11**
Profits		**($000)**	**$50**	**$60**	**$80**	**$105**	**$115**	**$130**	**$150**	**$165**	**$185**	**$200**	**$195**	**$185**
Number	0	$50	$100*	$110	$130	$155	$165	$180	$200	$215	$235	$250	$245	$235
of	1	$65	115*	125	145	170	180	195	215	230	250	265	260	
Salesmen	2	$85	135*	145	165	190	200	215	235	250	270	285		
Sales	3	$110	160*	170	190	215	225	240	260	275	295			
Area	4	$140	190*	200	220	245*	255	270	290	305				
2	5	$160	210*	220	240	265*	275	290	310*					
	6	$175	225*	235	255	280*	290	305						
	7	$190	240	250	270	295*	305							
	8	$200	250	260	280	305								
	9	$195	245	255	275									
	10	$193	243	253										
	11	$190	240											

*Profits are the maxima along each diagonal.

Equation 8–4 can be restated so that we can solve the problem in terms of optimum profit for three marketing areas, which is as follows:

$$F_3(A_3) = \max_{0 \leq A_2 \leq A_3} [F_2(A_2) + f_3(A_3 - A_2)] \qquad \text{(Equation 8–5)}$$

The term $F_3(A_3)$ in the equation is the maximum profit that can be realized by allocating a number of salesmen among the three marketing areas. On the other hand, $F_2(A_2)$ is the optimum profit for allocating salesmen among two marketing areas (refer to Equation 8–2).

The problem can be stated in a tabular form (as previously shown) by adding the profits of two sales areas to the profits of the third sales area. This is shown in

Figure 8–2
Maximum profits from optimum allocation of salesmen between two sales areas.

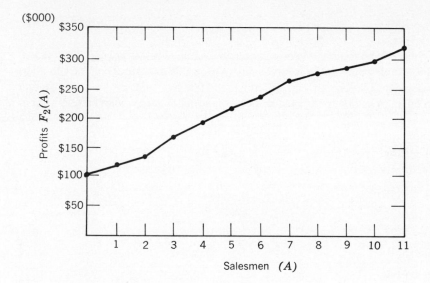

Figure 8–3
Profits as a function of sales effort for sales area 3.

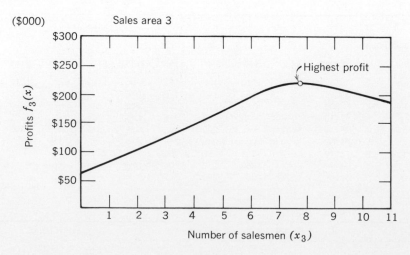

258

Table 8–5. The top row shows the combined number of salesmen in sales areas 1 and 2 while the second row indicates the maximum profit, $F_2(A_2)$, that can be realized by allocating the salesmen between the first two sales areas. This second row is from Table 8–4, the profits marked with asterisks on the diagonals. The columns to the left of Table 8–5 are the number of salesmen and profits for sales area 3. The second column (profits) is based upon the data found in Figure 8–3. The entire table shows the combined profits of all three salesmen. Again, we must follow the diagonals and select the maximum values, which are marked with asterisks. These maximum profits refer to the term $F_3(A_3)$ in Equation 8–5. Figure 8–4 shows a graphical representation of $F_3(A_3)$ or the maximum profit that can be realized when considering the three sales areas.

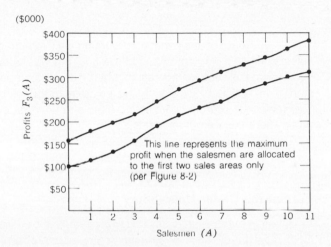

($000)

Figure 8–4
Maximum profits from optimum allocation of salesmen among three sales areas.

Table 8–5
Profits for Sales Efforts in Three Sales Areas

Number of Salesmen			Sales Areas 1 and 2											
			0	1	2	3	4	5	6	7	8	9	10	11
Profits		($000)	$100	$115	$135	$160	$190	$210	$225	$245	$265	$280	$295	$310
Number	0	$60	$160*	$175*	$195	$220*	$250*	$270*	$285	$305	$325	$340	$355	$370
of	1	$75	175*	190	210	235	265	285	300	320	340	355	370	
Salesmen	2	$100	200*	215	235	260	290*	310*	325	345*	365*	380		
	3	$120	220*	235	255	280	310*	330*	345*	365*	385*			
	4	$135	235	250	270	295	235	345*	360	380				
Sales	5	$150	250	265	285	310	340	360	375					
Area	6	$175	275	290	310	335	365*	385*						
3	7	$190	290	305	325	350	380							
	8	$205	305	320	340	365								
	9	$202	302	317	337									
	10	$200	300	315										
	11	$195	295											

*Profits are the maxima along each diagonal.

Referring to the earlier example where only six salesmen are available, the problem is how to allocate these six men in three sales areas for maximum profit. Inspection of Table 8–5 (on the diagonal) reveals that a profit of $290,000 is available with four salesmen in sales areas 1 and 2 plus two salesmen in sales area 3. Table 8–4 then determines the breakdown between sales areas 1 and 2. The maximum profit on the diagonal for four salesmen is $190,000, which results in allocating four salesmen to sales area 2 and none to sales area 1. Thus both tables had to be consulted for the proper allocation of salesmen.

The preceding maximum profit equations (Equation 8–2 for two sales areas and Equation 8–5 for three sales areas) can be written for any number of sales areas (where $n = 2$, 3, etc.) by using the following recursion formula:

$$F_n(A_n) = \max_{0 \le A_{n-1} \le A_n} \left[F_{n-1}(A_{n-1}) + f_n(A_n - A_{n-1}) \right]$$ (Equation 8–6)

This approach to the dynamic programming problem made use of an algorithm since a solution was not obtained at once, but was obtained step by step. Each successive step utilized the results obtained in the preceding steps. From the first step, the solution for the first two sales areas in the form of a table was obtained. This table was used in constructing a second table for determining the maximum profit where there are three sales areas.

Purchasing Under Uncertainty

An optimum purchasing policy that will minimize the cost of obtaining raw materials is solvable by dynamic programming. For example, suppose that during the next four weeks, raw material prices for a particular purchased item are expected to vary week by week per the following probability factors:

Price	Probability
$150	.25
170	.35
200	.40
	1.00

Utilization of these values is illustrated in Figure 8–5 for the alternatives faced weekly by purchasing. If the purchasing agent buys the raw material at the end of the first week, the price that is paid is the price that is prevailing in that week. However, if he decides to delay his purchase until one of the three remaining weeks, he must pay the prevailing price for that week. Should the purchasing agent not purchase the material prior to the fourth week, production requirements will force him to buy at the end of the fourth week.

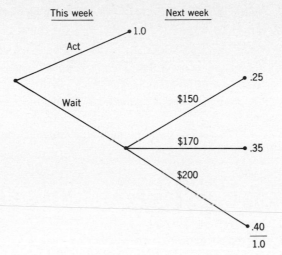

This week   Next week

Act   1.0

Wait $150   .25

$170   .35

$200

.40

1.0

Figure 8–5
Alternatives faced weekly
by the purchasing agent
during the four-week
period.

An approach for this problem is to start with the fourth or final week and work our way back to the first week since the material must be purchased before the end of the fourth week. The fourth-week decision can be expressed as:

$$F_4(X_4) = X_4 \qquad \text{(Equation 8–7)}$$

where $F_n(X_n)$ = lowest expected cost if purchase price observed in week n is X_n
and an optimal policy is pursued for the four-week period
X_n = purchase price observed in week n
n = week number, that is 1, 2, 3, or 4

In Equation 8–7, n is referred to as the stage value while X is the state variable.
For the third week, an equation can be written which is:

$$F_3(X_3) = \min \; [\overset{Act}{X_3},\; \overset{Wait}{(\$150)\,(0.25) + (\$170)\,(0.35) + (\$200)\,(0.40)}\,] \qquad \text{(Equation 8–8)}$$

The foregoing equation has this meaning: in the third week, the purchasing agent can *Act* on the basis of price X_3 or *Wait* for the expected value of the price in the fourth week. Thus, Equation 8–8 can be expressed as:

$$F_3(X_3) = \min \; [\overset{Act}{X_3},\; \overset{Wait}{F_4(\$150)\,(0.25) + F_4(\$170)\,(0.35) + F_4(\$200)\,(0.40)}\,]$$
$$\text{(Equation 8–9)}$$

To determine a breakeven point between the *Act* and *Wait* alternatives, it is necessary to restate Equation 8–9 so that the values of these two alternatives are equal to each other. For a breakeven X_{3be} value, Equation 8–9 becomes:

261

$$X_{3be} = (\$150)\,(0.25) + (\$170)\,(0.35) + (\$200)\,(0.40) \qquad \text{(Equation 8–10)}$$
$$= \$37.50 + \$59.50 + \$80.00$$
$$= \$177.00$$

Thus, if the material price is below the expected purchase price of $177, that is, at $150 or $170, the purchasing agent should make the purchase. On the other hand, if the price is above this value of $177, the purchase should be delayed for the fourth week.

The calculation for the minimum expected cost in the third week (refer to Equation 8–7), then, is:

$$F_3(X_3) = \begin{bmatrix} \$150 \text{ if } X_3 = \$150 \\ \$170 \text{ if } X_3 = \$170 \\ \$177 \text{ breakeven} \end{bmatrix} \qquad \text{(Equation 8–11)}$$

For the second week, a comparable equation to Equation 8–9 is developed, which is:

$$\begin{array}{cc} Act & Wait \end{array}$$
$$F_2(X_2) = \min\,[\,X_2,\ F_3(\$150)\,(0.25) + F_3(\$170)\,(0.35) + F_3\,(\$177)\,(0.40)\,]$$
$$\text{(Equation 8–12)}$$

Substitution of the values from Equation 8–11 into the foregoing equation allows a calculation of a breakeven between the *Act* and *Wait* alternatives (as in the third week). The breakeven point for X_{2be} at which the two alternatives have equal value is:

$$X_{2be} = (\$150)\,(0.25) + (\$170)\,(0.35) + (\$177)\,(0.40)$$
$$= \$37.50 + \$59.50 + \$70.80 \qquad \text{(Equation 8–13)}$$
$$= \$167.80$$

If the purchase price in the second week is under the expected price of $167.80, that is, at $150, the purchasing agent should initiate an order. But if the price is greater than the calculated $167.80, the purchase can be delayed. Thus, the minimum expected cost for the second week is:

$$F_2(X_2) = \begin{bmatrix} \$150 \text{ if } X_2 = \$150 \\ \$167.80 \text{ breakeven} \end{bmatrix} \qquad \text{(Equation 8–14)}$$

In the first week, the problem can be expressed mathematically as:

$$\begin{array}{cc} Act & Wait \end{array}$$
$$F_1(X_1) = \min\,[\,X_1,\ F_2(\$150)\,(0.25) + F_2(\$167.80)\,(0.35) + F_2(\$167.80)\,(0.40)\,]$$
$$\text{(Equation 8–15)}$$

The breakeven value calculates to be:

$$X_{1be} = \$163.35 \qquad \text{(Equation 8–16)}$$

The lowest cost, then, in the first week is:

$$F_1(X_1) = \begin{bmatrix} \$150 \text{ if } X_1 = \$150 \\ \$163.35 \text{ breakeven} \end{bmatrix} \qquad \text{(Equation 8–17)}$$

An analysis of the foregoing values for an optimum purchasing policy under uncertainty indicates the following results: If the price in the first or second week is $150, the purchasing agent should acquire the materials; otherwise, he should wait. If the purchase price in the third week is either $150 or $170, the purchase should be made; otherwise, wait. If no purchase is made by the fourth week, the purchase must be made at the prevailing price in the fourth (final) week. It should be noted that generalized equations can be developed for this purchasing problem under uncertainty for any number of weeks, whereby they can be solved recursively by working backward.

Differences Between Dynamic Programming and Linear Programming

The preceding problems are not sophisticated examples of dynamic programming, but they do present some of its basic concepts. Generally, both linear programming and dynamic programming make use of an algorithm, although their mathematical procedures are different.

The basic characteristic of dynamic programming involves a multistage process of decision making where there are generally time intervals. However, these stages may be only an order in which the problem is solved. On the other hand, linear programming gives a solution as of one time period based upon certain capacity, quantity, and contribution (or cost) constraints.

Wrong decisions in the past, under dynamic programming, do not prevent the making of correct decisions now and in the future. In essence, regardless of earlier decisions, dynamic programming enables one to find optimal decisions for future periods. Conversely, linear programming requires constant updating that reflects the current constraints for an optimal answer.

Dynamic programming is more powerful in concept, but computationally less so than linear programming. This should be apparent in the sample problems. Dynamic programming is similar to calculus, whereas linear programming is analogous to solving sets of simultaneous linear equations. Tables 8–4 and 8–5 are examples of the similarity to calculus from the viewpoint of finite differences on the diagonals. Dynamic programming is quite different in form from linear programming. While certain rules must be followed in the iterative process of linear programming, dynamic programming utilizes the appropriate mathematics necessary for the problem's solution.

Chapter Summary

Dynamic programming is structured somewhat differently from other OR techniques because it divides the problem into a number of subproblems or decision stages. General recurrence relations between one stage and the next stage describe the problem. A stage usually refers to a time period but need not necessarily represent time. Also, the state of the system is described by one or more state variables. Within this structural framework, a dynamic programming approach is helpful in solving sequential decision problems where a sequence of decisions that affect future decisions must be made. Even though incorrect or less than optimal decisions have been made in the past, dynamic programming still enables one to make correct decisions for future periods.

This technique is one of the newer tools of operations researchers. As more researchers master the subject matter of dynamic programming, it will find wider application. Imaginative OR personnel are required if this technique is to reach its full potential.

Questions

1. What concepts should be understood before attempting to formulate a dynamic programming problem?
2. What is meant by the statement: "Dynamic programming divides the problem into a number of decision stages"?
3. Compare dynamic programming to linear programming.

Model Formulation Exercises

1. In formulating a dynamic programming problem, the various state variables, stages, and decisions must be specified. In terms of the classification of parameters given in the introduction of the text, state whether the foregoing items are objectives, variables (controllable or uncontrollable), or constraints, and give your reasons for selecting one over the others.

2. The allocation of salesmen problem in the chapter focused on two and three marketing areas. Formulate the mathematical equations for four and five sales areas based upon the criterion of optimizing profits. Also, state how the problem should be stated in tabular form on these bases.

3. When solving certain dynamic programming problems, like the purchasing under uncertainty problem in the chapter, why does the solution start with the last period and work back toward the beginning period? What important mathematical concept is involved?

4. Formulate the appropriate formulas for a fifth week for the purchasing under uncertainty problem in the chapter. What changes must be made to the equations (Equations 8–7 through 8–17) for the four remaining weeks?

5. In the formulation of dynamic programming problems, what is the rationale for employing various forms of mathematics to solve them? In other words, why does dynamic programming resort to different mathematical forms and structures for solving the problem under study?

Mathematical Exercises

1. The Newcomb Manufacturing Company has compiled the following data for future monthly production requirements and costs:

Month	Quantity	Regular Costs per Unit	Overtime Costs per Unit
January	820	$4	$6
February	1,000	5	7
March	1,000	5.50	7.50
April	920	5.20	7.20
May	800	5	7
June	500	5	7

On December 31, there are 400 units in stock at a cost of $5 each. Regular production cannot exceed 650 units, overtime production cannot exceed 300 units. Storage costs are $1.50 per month for each unit. What is the optimal production schedule and total related costs? Assume no inventory is desired at the end of six months.

2. The Monsot Manufacturing Corporation has nine salesmen who presently sell in three separate sales areas of the United States. The profitability for each salesman in the three sales areas is as follows:

		0	1	2	3	4	5	6	7	8	9
No. of Salesmen	Area 1	0	1	2	3	4	5	6	7	8	9
	Area 2	9	8	7	6	5	4	3	2	1	0
	Area 3	0	1	2	3	4	5	6	7	8	9
($000) Profitability	Area 1	$20	$32	$47	$57	$66	$71	$82	$90	$100	$110
	Area 2	135	125	115	104	93	82	71	60	50	40
	Area 3	50	61	72	84	97	109	120	131	140	150

Determine the optimum allocation of salesmen in order to maximize profits.

3. The Berry Manufacturing Company presently has seven salesmen who sell in two separate sales areas of eastern United States. The profitability for each salesman is as follows:

No. of {Area 1	0	1	2	3	4	5	6	7
Salesmen {Area 2	7	6	5	4	3	2	1	0
Profitability {Area 1	$50	$61	$73	$87	$97	$106	$112	$117
($000) {Area 2	107	101	94	86	75	62	45	30

(a) Determine the optimum allocation of all salesmen to two sales areas to maximize profits.
(b) What are the maximum profits for two sales areas?
The company is considering an expansion to three sales areas. The third sales area would comprise the states west of the Mississippi River. No additional salesmen would be hired. The profitability for each salesman in the third sales area is estimated as follows:

No. of Salesmen Area 3	0	1	2	3	4	5	6	7
Profitability ($000)		$70	$82	$93	$103	$112	$120	$127	$133

(c) Determine the optimum allocation of salesmen to all three sales areas to maximize profits.
(d) What would be the optimum allocation of salesmen for all three sales areas if six salesmen are employed?

4. The Dandy Diaper Delivery Company presently has seven delivery trucks. Based on a number of complaints about poor pickup and delivery service, the owner of the company has hired you to determine the proper distribution of the trucks within the four districts it serves. You have conducted a survey on the pickup rates per day that could occur in a given district for the various number of trucks. Given this survey data (shown below), you are to determine the distribution of seven trucks within the four districts that will result in the maximum number of pickups.

Survey Data

District		0	1	2	3	4	5	6	7
					Number of Trucks				
1	P	0	1,000	2,000	2,800	3,700	4,200	5,000	5,500
2	i	0	900	1,900	3,000	4,000	4,300	4,800	5,000
3	c	0	1,200	1,900	2,200	2,400	3,000	3,800	5,000
4	k	0	1,100	1,500	2,000	2,800	3,700	4,900	5,800
	u								
	p								
	s								

5. The Sperry Corporation has a problem of determining the number of units for each of three items to put in a military repair kit whose total cost cannot exceed $390. Part 23 costs $40; part 56, $60; and part 42, $100. The utility (usefulness) in the field for each part decreases as more are added, as shown in the schedule below. (The utility of the repair kit is based upon multiplying the value in use by the probability of use in the field.) The problem is to determine the number of each type of part (23, 56, and 42) to pack in a field kit to maximize its usefulness. At least one unit each of parts 23 and 56 must be contained in the repair kit.

No. of Parts In Kit	Utility of Part 23	Utility of Part 56	Utility of Part 42
1	60	140	200
2	120	200	300
3	180	250	380
4	230	290	440
5	275	320	480
6	310	345	510
7	345	365	540
8	375	380	560

6. An engineering executive wants to hire an engineer as soon as possible. From past experience, he can determine in the interview whether the applicant will be exceptional, good, or fair. He assigns the relative values of 3, 2, and 1 respectively. He knows that there is a .2 chance of interviewing an exceptional engineer, .5 chance of a good one, and .3 chance of a fair one. Since he wishes to interview only three engineers because of his demanding work schedule, he must decide whether to hire or not to hire at the end of each interview. From this view, determine an optimum decision process that the executive should follow.

7. The LaCrosse Manufacturing Company has $2 million in additional funds available for investing during the next five months. The return on each monthly investment is a random variable distributed according to the probabilities below:

Annual Return on Investment (%)	Probability
20	.5
30	.4
40	.1
	1.0

At the start of each month, the company's treasurer is presented an opportunity, which must be accepted or rejected, to invest the entire $2 million. If the investment is rejected, the opportunity is withdrawn. If the treasurer has not invested the money by the fifth month, it must be invested at the return available during that month. In what month(s) should the treasurer invest the $2 million?

Bibliography

R. E. Bellman and S. E. Dreyfus, *Applied Dynamic Programming*, Princeton, N.J.: Princeton University Press, 1962.

U. Bertele and F. Brioschi, *Nonserial Dynamic Programming,* New York: Academic Press, 1972.

H. Bierman, C. P. Bonini, and W. H. Hausman, *Quantitative Analysis For Business Decisions,* Homewood, Ill.: Richard D. Irwin, 1973.

E. V. Denardo, *Dynamic Programming: Theory and Application,* Englewood Cliffs, N.J.: Prentice-Hall, 1975.

S. E. Dreyfus, *Dynamic Programming and the Calculus of Variations*, New York: Academic Press, 1965.

G. Hadley, *Nonlinear and Dynamic Programming*, Reading, Mass.: Addison-Wesley Publishing Company, 1964.

F. S. Hillier and G. J. Lieberman, *Operations Research,* San Francisco: Holden-Day, 1974.

N. K. Kwak, *Mathematical Programming with Business Applications,* New York: McGraw-Hill Book Company, 1973.

G. L. Nemhauser, *Introduction to Dynamic Programming,* New York: John Wiley & Sons, 1966.

H. M. Wagner, *Principles of Operations Research with Applications to Managerial Decisions,* Englewood Cliffs, N.J.: Prentice-Hall, 1975.

D. J. White, *Dynamic Programming,* San Francisco: Holden-Day, 1969.

Chapter 9

Markov Analysis

Chapter Objectives
- [ ] To set forth the requirements for formulating Markov analysis problems.
- [ ] To demonstrate the methods for calculating probable future (short-run) market shares in Markov analysis problems.
- [ ] To present the methods for calculating probable equilibrium (long-run) conditions in Markov analysis problems.
- [ ] To contrast the structure of Markov chains of the first order with those of a higher order.

Chapter Outline

Markov analysis originated with the studies (1906–1907) of A. A. Markov on the sequence of experiments connected in a chain, and with the attempts to describe mathematically the physical phenomenon known as Brownian motion. The first correct mathematical construction of a Markov process with continuous trajectories was given by N. Wiener in 1923. The general theory of Markov processes was developed in the 1930s and 1940s by A. N. Kolmagorov, W. Feller, W. Doeblin, P. Levy, J. L. Doob, and others.

Currently, *Markov analysis* is defined as a *way of analyzing the current movement of some variable in an effort to forecast the future movement of that same variable.* This method has come into use as a marketing research tool for examining and forecasting the behavior of customers from the standpoint of their loyalty to one brand and switching to other brands. The basic assumption is that customers do not shift from one brand to another at random, but instead buy brands in the future which reflect their choices in the past. It should be noted, however, that applications of this technique are not limited to marketing.

Requirements for Formulating Markov Analysis Problems

Markov analysis problems are of different orders. The *first order* considers only the brand choices made during the current period for determining the probabilities of choice in the forthcoming period. A *second-order* Markov analysis assumes choices for a specific brand in the coming period depend upon the brand choices made by the customers during the last two periods. Similarly, a *third-order* Markov process looks to customers' preferences for the past three periods in order to forecast their behavior toward particular brands in the next period. In addition, even *higher-order* Markov chains can be formulated to forecast future customer shifts. However, many marketing research studies have shown that first-order assumptions are valid for forecasting purposes. The data indicate that customer choices of brands follow a fairly stable pattern.

Within the framework of Markov models, attention is focused on the "hard-core component" — the group that does not switch to competition — and on the "switching component" — the group that does switch to competitors. For the first group, it is necessary to compute the probabilities that the sellers will retain their customers. In a similar manner for the second group, it is necessary to calculate the gains and losses for customers who switch from one seller to another in order to complete the matrix of transition probabilities (to be explained below). Last, the state of the activities must be specified, such as competing firms or brands.

The matrix of transition probabilities for a first-order Markov analysis problem is then multiplied by present market shares to obtain future market shares. Depending upon the type of mathematical calculations, probable market shares for the next period, future periods, and the long run can be computed. The end result is the prediction of future market shares of one company versus its competitors, based upon the hard-core component and the switching component of customers.

Procedure 1 — Develop Matrix of Transition Probabilities

In order to illustrate the Markov process, a problem is presented in which the states of activities are brands and the transition probabilities forecast the likelihood of consumers moving from one brand to another. Assume that the initial consumer sample is composed of 1,000 respondents distributed over four brands, *A, B, C,* and *D.* One further assumption is that the sample is representative of the entire group from the standpoint of brand loyalty and switching patterns from one brand to another. Consumers switch from one brand to another due to advertising, special promotions, price, dissatisfaction, and similar causes.

Before treating the switching component, it is necessary to compute the probabilities of the hard-core component. Per Table 9–1, brand *A* lost 45 customers for a retention of 175 customers $(220 - 45)$. To determine the probability factor, the number of customers retained for the period under review is divided by the number of customers at the beginning of the period, resulting in a retention probability of .796 $\left(\frac{175}{220}\right)$ for brand *A.* The transition probabilities for *B, C,* and *D* are calculated to be .767, .891, and .860, respectively.

For those customers who switch brands, it is necessary to show gains and losses among the brands in order to complete the matrix of transition probabilities. In Table 9–2, it is possible to observe not only the net gains or losses for any of the four brands but also the interrelationships among the gains and losses of customers for each brand. Brand *A* gains most of its customers from brand *B* while losing many of its customers to the same brand. A more intelligent analysis of the facts, then, is available with Table 9–2 than with Table 9–1. In Table 9–2, zeros on the diagonals mean a brand incurs neither gains nor losses from itself.

Applications—Markov Analysis

- **Determining manpower needs**—helpful in determining future manpower needs, after considering resignations, retirements, and deaths, in order to recruit from within and outside the firm.
- **Estimating doubtful accounts**—determines the allowances for doubtful accounts in the accounting department—a popular application.
- **Introducing a new product**—valuable in determining how the customer's loyalty to a particular brand may be switched to a new product.
- **Evaluating market shares**—useful in determining a firm's short-run and long-run market shares for marketing management versus its competition.
- **Determining the appropriate marketing strategy**—reviews the results for promoting the "hard-core component" or the "switching component" to help marketing management obtain the best results for marketing expenditures.
- **Comparing advertising programs**—helpful in assessing the relative merits of one advertising program versus others by evaluating market shares at some future date.

From the data developed, the next step is to convert the customer switching of brands so that all gains and losses take the form of transition probabilities. This is represented in Figure 9–1, where the arrows flowing in indicate increases while arrows flowing out represent losses. However, a more convenient form for ease of mathematical calculations is the use of a *matrix of transition probabilities*. This is found in Table 9–3 with the probabilities calculated to three decimal places.

The rows in the matrix show the retention of customers and the gain of customers while the columns show the retention of customers and the loss of customers. In Table 9–3, the first matrix is in terms of actual number of customers, whereas the second matrix is stated in terms of transition probabilities. It should be remembered that these probabilities are applicable to all customers since this is a representative sample of 1,000 customers.

The calculations for the matrix probabilities in Table 9–3 are as follows:

	Brands			
	A	*B*	*C*	*D*
A	$\frac{175}{220} = .796$	$\frac{40}{300} = .133$	$\frac{0}{230} = 0$	$\frac{10}{250} = .040$
B	$\frac{20}{220} = .091$	$\frac{230}{300} = .767$	$\frac{25}{230} = .109$	$\frac{15}{250} = .060$
C	$\frac{10}{220} = .046$	$\frac{5}{300} = .017$	$\frac{205}{230} = .891$	$\frac{10}{250} = .040$
D	$\frac{15}{220} = .067$	$\frac{25}{300} = .083$	$\frac{0}{230} = 0$	$\frac{215}{250} = .860$

Examples of how to read the rows and columns are: row 1 indicates that brand *A* retains .796 of its customers while gaining .133 of *B*'s customers and .040 of *D*'s customers while gaining none of *C*'s customers; column 1 indicates that brand *A* retains .796 of its customers while losing .091, .046, and .067 of its customers to brands *B*, *C*, and *D*, respectively. The same approach can be used to read the remaining rows and columns. The basic gain and loss relationships can be easily observed. Brand *A* gains most of its customers from brand *B*, and, at the same time, loses more to brand *B* than to brands *C* and *D* individually.

Several advantages accrue to marketing management through utilizing the data shown in the matrix. It can assist management in analyzing its promotional efforts in terms of the effect they have on the gain or loss of its market share. This data can forecast the rate at which a brand will gain or lose its market share in the future and can show the possibility of some future market equilibrium.

Table 9–1
Exchanges of Customers for One Month

Brand	Period One, No. of Customers	Changes During Period Gain	Changes During Period Loss	Period Two, No. of Customers
A	220	50	45	225
B	300	60	70	290
C	230	25	25	230
D	250	40	35	255
	1,000	175	175	1,000

Table 9–2
Brand Switching— Gains and Losses

Brand	Period One, No. of Customers	Gains From A	Gains From B	Gains From C	Gains From D	Losses To A	Losses To B	Losses To C	Losses To D	Period Two, No. of Customers
A	220	0	40	0	10	0	20	10	15	225
B	300	20	0	25	15	40	0	5	25	290
C	230	10	5	0	10	0	25	0	0	230
D	250	15	25	0	0	10	15	10	0	255
	1,000									1,000

Figure 9–1
Brand switching by customers.

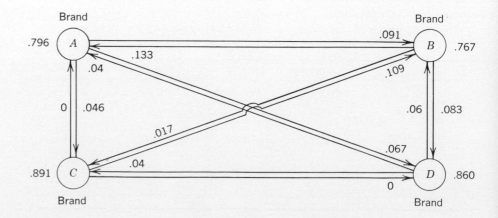

Procedure 2—Calculate Future Probable Market Shares

In the example, the market shares for brands A, B, C, and D are now 22, 30, 23, and 25 percent, respectively, for period one. Management would benefit if it knew what market shares will be at some future period. Calculating the probable market shares for brands A, B, C, and D in period two is a matter of multiplying the matrix of transition probabilities by the market shares in the first period:

$$
\begin{array}{c}
\textbf{Transition Probabilities} \\[4pt]
\begin{array}{ccccc}
 & A & B & C & D \\
A & .796 & .133 & .000 & .040 \\
B & .091 & .767 & .109 & .060 \\
C & .046 & .017 & .891 & .040 \\
D & .067 & .083 & .000 & .860 \\
\hline
 & 1.0 & 1.0 & 1.0 & 1.0
\end{array}
\end{array}
\times
\begin{array}{c}
\textbf{Period One,} \\
\textbf{Market} \\
\textbf{Shares} \\[4pt]
\begin{array}{c}
.22 \\ .30 \\ .23 \\ .25 \\ \hline 1.0
\end{array}
\end{array}
=
\begin{array}{c}
\textbf{Period Two,} \\
\textbf{Probable} \\
\textbf{Market Shares} \\[4pt]
\begin{array}{c}
.225 \\ .290 \\ .230 \\ .255 \\ \hline 1.0
\end{array}
\end{array}
$$

Brand A's calculations (first row × first column):

1. A's ability to retain its own customers times A's share of the market:
   $$.796 \times .22 = .175$$

2. A's ability to obtain B's customers times B's share of the market:
   $$.133 \times .30 = .040$$

3. A's ability to obtain C's customers times C's share of the market:
   $$0 \times .23 = 0$$

4. A's ability to obtain D's customers times D's share of the market:
   $$.040 \times .25 = \underline{.010}$$

   Brand A's share of market at period two: .225

Similar calculations are made for brands B, C, and D:

Brand B's calculation (second row × first column):
$$.091 \times .22 = .020$$
$$.767 \times .30 = .230$$
$$.109 \times .23 = .025$$
$$.060 \times .25 = \underline{.015}$$
Brand B's share of market at period two: .290

Table 9–3
Matrix of Transition
Probabilities

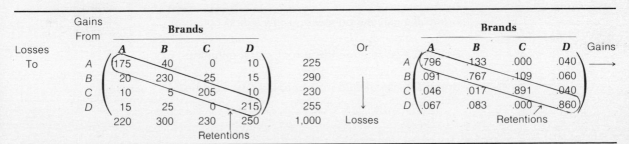

Losses To	Gains From	Brands A	B	C	D		Or		Brands A	B	C	D	Gains
	A	175	40	0	10	225		A	.796	.133	.000	.040	→
	B	20	230	25	15	290		B	.091	.767	.109	.060	
	C	10	5	205	10	230		C	.046	.017	.891	.040	
	D	15	25	0	215	255		D	.067	.083	.000	.860	
		220	300	230	250	1,000	Losses				Retentions		
				Retentions									

Brand C's calculation (third row × first column):
$$.046 \times .22 = .010$$
$$.017 \times .30 = .005$$
$$.891 \times .23 = .205$$
$$.040 \times .25 = \underline{.010}$$

Brand C's share of market at period two: .230

Brand D's calculation (fourth row × first column):
$$.067 \times .22 = .015$$
$$.083 \times .30 = .025$$
$$0 \ \ \times .23 = \ \ 0$$
$$.860 \times .25 = \underline{.215}$$

Brand D's share of market at period two: .255

After solving for period two, which takes into account starting market shares and the transition probabilities, period three can be determined in two ways. The first method is a continuation of the approach just set forth, that is, multiplication of the original matrix of transition probabilities by the second-period brand shares gives the results for the third period. The second method is squaring the matrix of transition probabilities for the desired number of periods and then multiplying the resultant matrix by the original market shares.

First Method (Computations) Using the first method, matrix multiplication is used to solve for the market shares of each brand for period three. The detailed calculations are shown only for the first row and the first column.

	Transition Probabilities					**Period Two, Probable Market Shares**		**Period Three, Probable Market Shares**
	A	*B*	*C*	*D*				
A	.796	.133	.000	.040		.225		.228
B	.091	.767	.109	.060	×	.290	=	.283
C	.046	.017	.891	.040		.230		.231
D	.067	.083	.000	.860		.255		.258
	1.0	1.0	1.0	1.0		1.0		1.0

Brand A's calculation (first row × first column):
$$.796 \times .225 = .179$$
$$.133 \times .290 = .039$$
$$0 \times .230 = \ \ \ 0$$
$$.040 \times .255 = \underline{.010}$$
$$ .228$$

Brand B's calculation (second row × first column):
.283

Brand C's calculation (third row × first column):
.231

Brand D's calculation (fourth row × first column):
.258

Second Method (Computations)   The advantage of the first method is that changes which occur from period to period can be observed. However, management might desire market shares of its particular brand for some specified future period. If this is the case, the second method would be preferred. This method basically makes use of raising the matrix of transition probabilities to a power that represents the number of periods in the future. For example, the probable market shares for period three, which is two periods in the future, are calculated as follows:

	Transition Probabilities					Period One, Market Shares		Period Three, Probable Market Shares
	A	*B*	*C*	*D*				
A	.796	.133	.000	.040	^{2}	.22		.228
B	.091	.767	.109	.060	$\times$	.30	$=$	.283
C	.046	.017	.891	.040		.23		.231
D	.067	.083	.000	.860		.25		.258
	1.0	1.0	1.0	1.0		1.0		1.0

Matrix multiplication is again used. The squaring of the matrix of transition probabilities means that new probabilities of retention, gain, and loss have to be calculated. The squared matrix of transition probabilities is multiplied by the original market shares. To illustrate, the various rows in the matrix of transition probabilities are multiplied by their corresponding columns to form a squared matrix of transition probabilities:

$$
\begin{array}{c}
\begin{array}{cccc} A & B & C & D \end{array} \\
\begin{array}{c} A \\ B \\ C \\ D \end{array}
\begin{pmatrix}
.796 & .133 & 0 & .040 \\
.091 & .767 & .109 & .060 \\
.046 & .017 & .891 & .040 \\
.067 & .083 & 0 & .860
\end{pmatrix}
\end{array}
\times
\begin{array}{c}
\begin{array}{cccc} A & B & C & D \end{array} \\
\begin{pmatrix}
.796 & .133 & 0 & .040 \\
.091 & .767 & .109 & .060 \\
.046 & .017 & .891 & .040 \\
.067 & .083 & 0 & .860
\end{pmatrix}
\end{array}
$$

$$
=
\begin{array}{c}
\begin{array}{cccc} A & B & C & D \end{array} \\
\begin{array}{c} A \\ B \\ C \\ D \end{array}
\begin{pmatrix}
.6484 & .2112 & .0145 & .0742 \\
.1513 & .6073 & .1808 & .1056 \\
.0818 & .0375 & .7957 & .0729 \\
.1185 & .1440 & .0090 & .7473
\end{pmatrix}
\end{array}
$$

Brand *A*'s calculation (first row × first column):

$$
\begin{pmatrix} A\text{'s ability to} \\ \text{retain its own} \\ \text{customers} \end{pmatrix}
\times
\begin{pmatrix} A\text{'s ability to} \\ \text{retain its own} \\ \text{customers} \end{pmatrix}
=
\begin{pmatrix} A\text{'s ability to retain its} \\ \text{original customers after} \\ \text{two periods} \end{pmatrix}
$$

$$\qquad .796 \qquad \times \qquad .796 \qquad = \qquad .6336$$

$$
\begin{pmatrix} A\text{'s ability to} \\ \text{gain customers} \\ \text{from } B \end{pmatrix}
\times
\begin{pmatrix} B\text{'s ability to} \\ \text{gain customers} \\ \text{from } A \end{pmatrix}
=
\begin{pmatrix} A\text{'s regain of its} \\ \text{own customers} \\ \text{from } B \end{pmatrix}
$$

$$\qquad .133 \qquad \times \qquad .091 \qquad = \qquad .0121$$

$$\begin{pmatrix} A\text{'s ability to} \\ \text{gain customers} \\ \text{from } C \end{pmatrix} \times \begin{pmatrix} C\text{'s ability to} \\ \text{gain customers} \\ \text{from } A \end{pmatrix} = \begin{pmatrix} A\text{'s regain of its} \\ \text{own customers} \\ \text{from } C \end{pmatrix}$$

$$0 \qquad \times \qquad .046 \qquad = \qquad 0$$

$$\begin{pmatrix} A\text{'s ability to} \\ \text{gain customers} \\ \text{from } D \end{pmatrix} \times \begin{pmatrix} D\text{'s ability to} \\ \text{gain customers} \\ \text{from } A \end{pmatrix} = \begin{pmatrix} A\text{'s regain of its} \\ \text{own customers} \\ \text{from } D \end{pmatrix}$$

$$.040 \qquad \times \qquad .067 \qquad = \qquad \underline{.0027}$$

The portion of A's original customers A retains
(sum of brand A's calculation) = .6484

The other 15 terms are calculated in a similar manner. The resulting squared matrix of transition probabilities is now multiplied by the original market shares. The results are:

	Squared Matrix of Transition Probabilities					**Original Market Shares for Each Period**		**Period Three, Probable Market Shares**
	A	B	C	D				
A	.6484	.2112	.0145	.0742		.22		.228
B	.1513	.6073	.1808	.1056	×	.30	=	.283
C	.0818	.0375	.7957	.0729		.23		.231
D	.1185	.1440	.0090	.7473		.25		.258
	1.0	1.0	1.0	1.0		1.0		1.0

The raising of a matrix to a much larger power is no easy task; however, computer programs are available.

Procedure 3 — Determine Equilibrium Conditions

The condition of equilibrium results only if none of the competitors alters the matrix of transition probabilities. It is reasonable to assume that a state of equilibrium might be reached in the future regarding market shares. The exchange of customers in terms of retentions, gains, and losses would be static at the moment equilibrium is reached. In terms of marketing, what are the final or equilibrium market shares?

Several matrices of transition probabilities can be used to illustrate equilibrium conditions. The matrix of transition probabilities where A gains no customers but loses to B and C is:

	A	B	C
A	.85	0	0
B	.10	.80	.25
C	.05	.20	.75
	1.0	1.0	1.0

It is quite apparent that eventually B and C will take away all of A's customers since A loses .10 to B and .05 to C. But, more importantly, A gains no customers from B or C.

Another type of equilibrium that might occur is the condition under which A never loses any of its customers:

$$
\begin{array}{c c c c}
 & A & B & C \\
A & 1.0 & .10 & .05 \\
B & 0 & .80 & .05 \\
C & 0 & .10 & .90 \\
\hline
 & 1.0 & 1.0 & 1.0
\end{array}
$$

Since A suffers no losses of its market, it is only a question of time until A has all of the customers of B and C. This is referred to as a "sink" or "basin of one state" since one firm eventually gets all the customers. The first illustration is referred to as a "sink" or "basin of two states" since two firms eventually share all the customers.

The more common illustration occurs when no one firm gets all the customers, that is, no one firm or two firms out of three capture the entire market. Some final condition of equilibrium develops and continues based upon a stable matrix of transition probabilities. This can be illustrated by an example in the following section.

Simultaneous Equations Solution   The Gordon Company has two competitors in one market segment of its business. At the present time (this year), the market shares are as follows: Gordon Company (G), 30 percent; first competitor (A), 20 percent; and second competitor (B), 50 percent. The matrix of transition probabilities (first order Markov chain), showing the flow of customers, is as follows:

	Gordon Co.	First Competitor	Second Competitor
	(G)	(A)	(B)
Gordon Co. (G)	.6	.2	.2
First Comp. (A)	.1	.6	.2
Second Comp. (B)	.3	.2	.6
	1.0	1.0	1.0

The equation for the Gordon Company's share of the market at equilibrium equals .6 times the share Gordon had in the period immediately preceding equilibrium (or eq. − 1 period) plus .2 times the share the first competitor had in equilibrium minus one period plus .2 times the share the second competitor had in equilibrium minus one period. This equation can be written as follows:

$$G_{eq. - 1} = .6G_{eq. - 1} + .2A_{eq. - 1} + .2B_{eq. - 1}$$

It should be noted that G's share of the market is labeled as some unspecified future period which we call the equilibrium period. The same type of equation can also be developed for both competitors.

In most Markov problems, the gains and losses are usually of a high magnitude in the early periods. However, as equilibrium is approached, the gains and losses become very small, as shown in Figure 9–2. The changes in the market shares between the equilibrium period and the period immediately preceding it are so small that they may be treated mathematically as equal. In the equation above, *eq.* equals *eq.* − 1. The three equations in the example can be written as follows:

$$G = .6G + .2A + .2B \qquad \text{(Equation 9–1)}$$
$$A = .1G + .6A + .2B \qquad \text{(Equation 9–2)}$$
$$B = .3G + .2A + .6B \qquad \text{(Equation 9–3)}$$
$$1.0 = G + A + B \qquad \text{(Equation 9–4)}$$

Figure 9–2
Changes become smaller and smaller as equilibrium is reached.

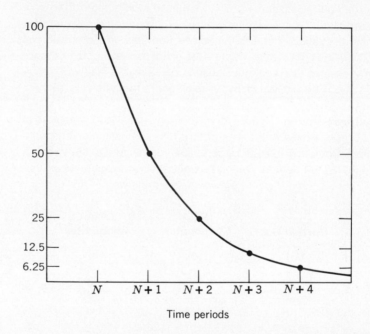

Time periods

A fourth equation is used to show that the total of the three market shares equals 1.0.

Since there are similar terms on both sides of the equation, the resulting equations which show the gains and losses for each firm are as follows:

$$0 = -.4G + .2A + .2B \qquad \text{(Equation 9–5)}$$
$$0 = .1G - .4A + .2B \qquad \text{(Equation 9–6)}$$
$$0 = .3G + .2A - .4B \qquad \text{(Equation 9–7)}$$
$$1.0 = G + A + B \qquad \text{(Equation 9–4)}$$

Having four equations and three unknowns, it is necessary to drop one equation (either Equation 9–5, 9–6, or 9–7, but not Equation 9–4) in order to have a one-to-one ratio between the number of equations and the number of unknowns. The reason one equation can be dropped is that the equations are mathematically interrelated, that is, the sum of $-.4G$ (Equation 9–5), $+.1G$ (Equation 9–6) and the $+.3G$ (Equation 9–7) equals zero. The ability to sum column G to zero is also applicable to columns A and B. Solving two equations (Equations 9–5 and 9–7) simultaneously and using Equation 9–4 for the equilibrium market shares is as follows:

(First set of simultaneous equations)

$$0 = -.4G + .2A + .2B \qquad \text{(Equation 9–5)}$$

$$\underline{0 = -.3G - .2A + .4B} \quad \text{(Change signs)} \qquad \text{(Equation 9–7)}$$

$$0 = -.7G + .6B$$

$$.7G = .6B$$

$$G = \frac{6}{7}B \quad \text{or} \quad .857B$$

(Second set of simultaneous equations)

$$0 = -.4G + .2A + .2B \qquad \text{(Equation 9–5)}$$

$$\underline{0 = +.4G + .267A - .533B} \quad \text{(Multiplied by } 1\tfrac{1}{3}) \qquad \text{(Equation 9–7)}$$

$$0 = .467A - .333B$$

$$.467A = .333B$$

$$A = \frac{333}{467}B \quad \text{or} \quad .715B$$

Substitute respective values for G and A:

$$1 = G + A + B$$

$$1 = .857B + .715B + 1.0B \qquad \text{(Equation 9–4)}$$

$$1 = 2.572B$$

$$B = .389 \quad (B \text{ at equilibrium})$$

Determine values for G and A:

$$G = \frac{6}{7}B = \frac{6}{7}(.389) = .333 \quad (G \text{ at equilibrium})$$

$$A = \frac{333}{467}B = \frac{333}{467}(.389) = .278 \quad (A \text{ at equilibrium})$$

An effective way to prove that we have solved for equilibrium is to multiply the matrix of transition probabilities by the equilibrium market shares. This can be calculated by using matrix algebra; the final results are:

	Matrix of Transition Probabilities			**Equilibrium Market Shares**	
	G	A	B		

$$
\begin{array}{l}
\text{Gordon } (G) \\
\text{First Comp. } (A) \\
\text{Second Comp. } (B)
\end{array}
\begin{pmatrix}
.6 & .2 & .2 \\
.1 & .6 & .2 \\
.3 & .2 & .6
\end{pmatrix}
\times
\begin{pmatrix}
.333 \\
.278 \\
.389
\end{pmatrix}
=
\begin{pmatrix}
.333 \\
.278 \\
.389
\end{pmatrix}
$$

$$
\begin{array}{ccc}
1.0 & 1.0 & 1.0 \\
\end{array}
\qquad 1.0 \qquad\quad 1.0
$$

Determinants Solution   When dealing with a 4 × 4 matrix of transition probabilities (four unknowns and five equations) and current market shares, it is sometimes easier to use determinants to solve for the answer. Returning to the previous problem given in the chapter, determinants are employed in this last illustration for equilibrium conditions. Restating the problem for convenience is:

$$
\begin{array}{c}
\begin{array}{cccc} A & B & C & D \end{array} \\
\begin{array}{c} A \\ B \\ C \\ D \end{array}
\begin{pmatrix}
.796 & .133 & 0 & .040 \\
.091 & .767 & .109 & .060 \\
.046 & .017 & .891 & .040 \\
.067 & .083 & 0 & .860
\end{pmatrix}
\times
\begin{pmatrix}
.22 \\
.30 \\
.23 \\
.25
\end{pmatrix}
= \text{Equilibrium Shares}
\end{array}
$$

Appendix A defines a determinant as an array of numbers, arranged in rows and columns, which has a numerical value. Expanding a determinant by a row simply means choosing any row, and then eliminating, in turn, each column which intersects that row. Likewise, expanding a column means choosing any column and eliminating, in turn, each row which intersects that column. This procedure will be shown in expanding the numerator and denominator to determine an equilibrium condition for A.

The algebraic sign of each step in the expansion depends upon the row and column eliminated. If the total of the row and column that are eliminated is an even number (for example, row 1 plus column 1 equals 2), the sign for that step is not changed. However, if the total of the row and column that are eliminated is an odd number (for example, row 1 plus column 2 equals 3), the sign is changed.

In using determinants, the value for each of the unknown variables — A, B, C, and D — is found by solving a particular set of two determinants which forms a fraction. The determinant that forms the denominator of the fraction remains the same and the determinant that forms the numerator of the fraction changes for each variable. The determinants which solve for A are given as follows:

$$
A = \cfrac{
\begin{vmatrix}
0 & .133 & 0 & .040 \\
0 & -.233 & .109 & .060 \\
0 & .017 & -.109 & .040 \\
1 & 1 & 1 & 1
\end{vmatrix}
}{
\begin{vmatrix}
-.204 & .133 & 0 & .040 \\
.091 & -.233 & .109 & .060 \\
.046 & .017 & -.109 & .040 \\
1 & 1 & 1 & 1
\end{vmatrix}
}
\begin{array}{l}
\text{(numerator)} \\[18pt]
= \text{Equilibrium position for } A \\[10pt]
\text{(denominator)}
\end{array}
$$

An inspection of the determinant in the denominator reveals that it is nothing more than the coefficients of the four unknowns arranged in the same form as they would have appeared in the revision to the original equations, analogous to what we did with Equations 9–4, 9–5, and 9–7. One equation has been dropped for the same reason as in the previous problem dealing with the Gordon Company.

The determinant which forms the numerator of the fraction for A is identical to the determinant for the denominator, except the first column has been replaced by the values to the left of the equality signs, as they would have appeared in the revision of the original equations. Similarly, the determinant for the numerator of the fraction for the variable B is formed by eliminating the column of coefficients for the unknown B and replacing it with the values to the left of the equality sign in the revision of the original equations. The same procedure is used for the column coefficients of C and D.

The determinants for B, C, and D are as follows:

$$
B = \frac{\begin{vmatrix} -.204 & 0 & 0 & .040 \\ .091 & 0 & .109 & .060 \\ .046 & 0 & -.109 & .040 \\ 1 & 1 & 1 & 1 \end{vmatrix}}{\begin{vmatrix} -.204 & .133 & 0 & .040 \\ .091 & -.233 & .109 & .060 \\ .046 & .017 & -.109 & .040 \\ 1 & 1 & 1 & 1 \end{vmatrix}} = \text{Equilibrium position for } B
$$

$$
C = \frac{\begin{vmatrix} -.204 & .133 & 0 & .040 \\ .091 & -.233 & 0 & .060 \\ .046 & .017 & 0 & .040 \\ 1 & 1 & 1 & 1 \end{vmatrix}}{\begin{vmatrix} -.204 & .133 & 0 & .040 \\ .091 & -.233 & .109 & .060 \\ .046 & .017 & -.109 & .040 \\ 1 & 1 & 1 & 1 \end{vmatrix}} = \text{Equilibrium position for } C
$$

$$
D = \frac{\begin{vmatrix} -.204 & .133 & 0 & 0 \\ .091 & -.233 & .109 & 0 \\ .046 & .017 & -.109 & 0 \\ 1 & 1 & 1 & 1 \end{vmatrix}}{\begin{vmatrix} -.204 & .133 & 0 & .040 \\ .091 & -.233 & .109 & .060 \\ .046 & .017 & -.109 & .040 \\ 1 & 1 & 1 & 1 \end{vmatrix}} = \text{Equilibrium position for } D
$$

Using the rules for expanding a determinant, the first step is to expand the numerator determinant for A by its first column. Note that in the 4 × 4 determinant, when a row and a column are deleted, a 3 × 3 determinant remains in each case. This is apparent in steps a, b, c, and d.

Step *a*:

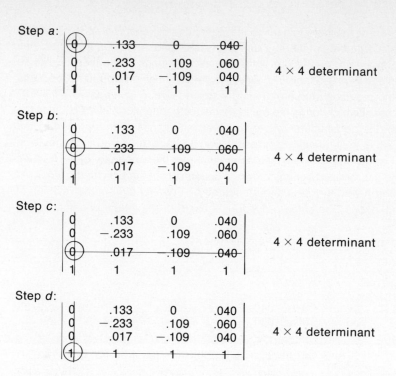

4×4 determinant

Step *b*:

4×4 determinant

Step *c*:

4×4 determinant

Step *d*:

4×4 determinant

In steps *a*, *b*, and *c*, the value of the 4×4 determinants must be zero since the value of the 3×3 determinants is multiplied by the circled element zero. However, this is not true of step *d*, whose value is determined as follows:

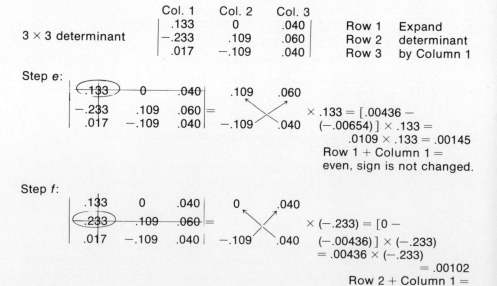

	Col. 1	Col. 2	Col. 3		
3×3 determinant	.133	0	.040	Row 1	Expand
	−.233	.109	.060	Row 2	determinant
	.017	−.109	.040	Row 3	by Column 1

Step *e*:

.133	0	.040
−.233	.109	.060
.017	−.109	.040

$= \begin{matrix} .109 & .060 \\ -.109 & .040 \end{matrix} \times .133 = [.00436 - (-.00654)] \times .133 = .0109 \times .133 = .00145$

Row 1 + Column 1 = even, sign is not changed.

Step *f*:

.133	0	.040
.233	.109	.060
.017	−.109	.040

$= \begin{matrix} 0 & .040 \\ -.109 & .040 \end{matrix} \times (-.233) = [0 - (-.00436)] \times (-.233) = .00436 \times (-.233) = .00102$

Row 2 + Column 1 = odd, sign is changed.

Step g:

$$\begin{vmatrix} .133 & 0 & .040 \\ -.233 & .109 & .060 \\ .017 & -.109 & .040 \end{vmatrix} = \begin{matrix} 0 & .040 \\ .109 & .060 \\ .017 & \end{matrix}$$

$$\begin{array}{c} 0 \quad .040 \\ \diagdown \diagup \\ .109 \quad .060 \end{array} \times .017 = [0 - (.00436)] \times$$

$$.017 = -.00436$$
$$\times .017 = -.00007$$

Row 3 + Column 1 =
even, sign is not changed.

Step d—sum of steps e, f, and $g = +.00145 + .00102 - .00007$
$$= .00240 \text{ (value of } 3 \times 3 \text{ determinant)}$$

Value of step $a = 0$
Value of step $b = 0$
Value of step $c = 0$
Value of step $d = -.00240$ (Sums of steps e, f, and $g = .00240 \times 1$)
Column 1 + Row 4 = odd, sign is changed.
_____
Value of determinant $-.00240$ (numerator for A)

Using the same procedure, the values for numerators B, C, and D are $-.00282$, $-.00249$, and $-.00281$, respectively. The same approach can be used for determining the denominator, its value being $-.01052$. A faster method is to expand the determinants using row 4, which amounts to adding determinant values for the numerators, A, B, C, and D $(-.00240 - .00282 - .00249 - .00281 = -.01052)$. The resulting equilibrium shares for brands A, B, C, and D are:

$$A = \frac{-.00240}{-.01052} = 22.8\%$$

$$B = \frac{-.00282}{-.01052} = 26.8\%$$

$$C = \frac{-.00249}{-.01052} = 23.7\%$$

$$D = \frac{-.00281}{-.01052} = 26.7\%$$
$$\overline{100.0\%}$$

The solution to the preceding problem can be proven by multiplying the original matrix of transition probabilities by the equilibrium market shares.

It should be apparent that the nearer the initial market shares are to the final or equilibrium market shares, the faster equilibrium will be reached. If the beginning market shares are one-third each and the equilibrium shares are 30, 37, and 33 percent, it is obvious that equilibrium will be reached faster than if the initial market shares are 15, 55, and 30 percent.

The preceding procedures for determining probable future market shares with Markov chains of the first order are summarized in Figure 9–3. Sometimes the equilibrium state for market shares is not needed. In those cases, the third procedure is dropped. The procedures employed, then, are discretionary.

Figure 9–3
Procedures utilized in
Markov analysis of the
first order.

Summary — Methodology of Markov Analysis

Procedure 1 — Develop Matrix of Transition Probabilities Determine the "hard-core component" or retentions (the groups that do not switch) and the "switching component" or gains and losses (the groups that do switch). In a matrix of transition probabilities, retentions are shown as values on the diagonal while gains become row values and losses become column values.

Procedure 2 — Calculate Future Probable Market Shares Calculate probable market shares for the next period (period two) by multiplying the original matrix of transition probabilities by the original market shares (period one). Similarly, multiplication of the original matrix of transition probabilities by period two market shares gives the results for period three. All remaining future probable market shares are calculated in a similar manner. An alternative method is raising the original matrix of transition probabilities to the desired power and multiplying by the original market shares. In such cases, computer programs are available for fast and accurate calculations.

Procedure 3 — Determine Equilibrium Conditions Changes in market shares between the equilibrium period and the period immediately preceding it are so small that they are treated mathematically as equal. Thus, equations can be developed for each row in the matrix of transition probabilities along with the addition of a final equation that sums all variables in the problem to 1.0. These equations can be solved simultaneously or by determinants.

Possible Market Shares — Higher Order

The foregoing Markov chain analysis was of the first order since the probability of the future event(s) depended upon the outcomes of the last period only. A higher-order Markov process depends upon the choices of consumers during the immediate preceding periods for predicting the probable future shares. Little or erratic brand loyalty patterns give rise to higher-order Markov chains. In essence, the degree of brand switching must be considered for predicting future periods more accurately.

A higher-order (third-order) Markov chain can be illustrated by utilizing the matrices of transition probabilities for three competing brands, shown during the last three time periods in Table 9–4. The matrices are considered representative of future market behavior. It should be noted that the transition probabilities are not equal since brand switching is taking place period by period. This is caused mainly by the introduction of slightly improved products, resulting in a state of disequilibrium. The problem is solvable by starting with period one market shares and employing matrix multiplication for each of the three periods, illustrated in Table 9–5. Thus, probable period three market shares are contingent on the past matrices of transition probabilities.

		A	B	C
Period one (third last period)	A	.4	.3	.3
	B	.3	.5	.3
	C	.3	.2	.4
		1.0	1.0	1.0
		A	B	C
Period two (second last period)	A	.3	.2	.3
	B	.5	.5	.4
	C	.2	.3	.3
		1.0	1.0	1.0
		A	B	C
Period three (first last period)	A	.3	.2	.3
	B	.4	.3	.3
	C	.3	.5	.4
		1.0	1.0	1.0

Table 9–4
Past Matrices of Transition Probabilities in a Higher-Order Chain Problem

		Transition Probabilities			Beginning of Period One, Market Shares	Ending of Period One, Probable Market Shares
		A	B	C		
Period one	A	.4	.3	.3	.3	.33
	B	.3	.5	.3	× .4 =	.38
	C	.3	.2	.4	.3	.29
		1.0	1.0	1.0	1.0	1.0

		Transition Probabilities			Beginning of Period Two, Probable Market Shares	Ending of Period Two, Probable Market Shares
		A	B	C		
Period two	A	.3	.2	.3	.33	.262
	B	.5	.5	.4	× .38 =	.471
	C	.2	.3	.3	.29	.267
		1.0	1.0	1.0	1.0	1.0

		Transition Probabilities			Beginning of Period Three, Probable Market Shares	Ending of Period Three, Probable Market Shares
		A	B	C		
Period three	A	.3	.2	.3	.262	.253
	B	.4	.3	.3	× .471 =	.326
	C	.3	.5	.4	.267	.421
		1.0	1.0	1.0	1.0	1.0

Table 9–5
Probable Market Shares at the End of Period Three in a Higher-Order Markov Chain Problem (Based on Table 9–4)

Chapter Summary

This chapter has concentrated primarily on Markov chains of the first order. The assumption of stationary transition probabilities is critical to Markov brand-switching theory of the first order. For the period during which the transition probabilities are stable, an equilibrium will result and can be calculated. However, if we know the transition probabilities will change due to internal or external conditions, these new figures can be used to calculate the equilibrium market shares. In this manner, Markov analysis can be used as a short-run, intermediate-run, or long-run marketing management tool.

Questions

1. What is Markov analysis?
2. Distinguish among Markov chains of the first order, the second order, and the third order.
3. Compare the procedures for solving Markov chains of the first order in the long run.

Model Formulation Exercises

1. In developing a matrix of transition probabilities, it is necessary to determine the "gains from" and "losses to" for the various competitors. In Table 9–2, the gains and losses for a typical situation are illustrated. These gains are shown as row values while losses are given as column values in Table 9–3 for the matrix of transition probabilities. What is the rationale for doing so? In other words, in Table 9–2, there are two sets of values (gains from and losses to) while in Table 9–3, there is one set of values (transition probabilities). Why?

2. In the development of period market shares from the short run to the long run, why do certain market shares initially decrease, then increase, or vice versa (increase, then decrease) as they approach equilibrium?

3. In the formulation of Markov analysis problems at equilibrium, which method—simultaneous equations or determinants—is preferred for what situations?

4. As shown in the chapter, all columns of a matrix of transition probabilities must add to 1.0. In addition, if the rows of a matrix of transition probabilities happen to add across to 1.0 when the problem has been formulated, what can be said about the market shares at equilibrium?

5. After examining the matrices of transition probabilities, determine the equilibrium market shares for each firm. Give the rationale for a certain firm or firms not having any market shares at equilibrium.

(a)

	Firm A	Firm B	Firm C
Firm A	1.0	.1	.3
Firm B	0	.8	0
Firm C	0	.1	.7

(b)

	Firm A	Firm B	Firm C
Firm A	.8	0	0
Firm B	.1	.8	.4
Firm C	.1	.2	.6

Mathematical Exercises

1. The Best-Cut Butcher Shop had 30 percent of the local fresh meat market at the end of last year. The two competitors—Jones Meats and Henry's Meats—had 50 percent and 20 percent respectively. A study by an independent marketing researcher has shown that over the last year, Best-Cut retained 90 percent of its customers while gaining 10 percent of Jones's customers and 5 percent of Henry's customers. The study also showed that Best-Cut lost 5 percent of its customers to each of its competitors and that both competitors lost 10 percent of their customers to each other. Based upon these trends for the last year, which the researcher expects to continue throughout the coming months of this year, what percent of the local market should the Best-Cut Butcher Shop expect to have at the end of this year?

2. On January 1 (this year), Klosman Bakeries had 40 percent of its local market while the other two bakeries, A and B, have 40 percent and 20 percent, respectively, of the market. Based upon a study by a marketing research firm, the following facts were compiled. Klosman Bakeries retains 90 percent of its customers while gaining 5 percent of competitor A's customers and 10 percent of B's customers. Bakery A retains 85 percent of its customers while gaining 5 percent of Klosman's customers and 7 percent of B's customers. Bakery B retains 83 percent of its customers and gains 5 percent of Klosman's customers and 10 percent of A's customers. What will each firm's share be on January 1 next year, and what will each firm's market share be at equilibrium?

3. The Ribicoff Manufacturing Company is planning an extensive advertising campaign to increase the company's market share. Its executive committee is faced with the job of choosing between two campaigns that have been recommended. The committee has decided to test each proposal in two areas where the initial market shares of the competing firms and the initial transition probability matrices are the same. Also, the market shares are close to their national average, which are: brand R (Ribicoff), 28 percent; brand A, 39 percent; and brand B, 33 percent. In the two test areas, the initial market shares are: brand R, 30 percent; brand A, 40 percent; and brand B, 30 percent. The matrix of initial transition probabilities for both test areas is:

	Brand R	Brand A	Brand B
Brand R	.6	.2	.1
Brand A	.3	.7	.1
Brand B	.1	.1	.8

At the finish of the two different advertising programs in the two test areas, the transition probabilities, which were determined, are:

	Test Area 1			Test Area 2		
	Brand R	Brand A	Brand B	Brand R	Brand A	Brand B
Brand R	.7	.1	.1	.8	.1	.2
Brand A	.2	.7	.1	.1	.7	.1
Brand B	.1	.2	.8	.1	.2	.7

(a) Using the initial matrix of transition probabilities, determine whether the test market shares at equilibrium for Ribicoff approach the national average.

(b) Assuming the advertising campaigns are equal in terms of cost, which advertising campaign gives the highest market share at equilibrium?

4. On July 1, the Hudson Chemical Company is competing with three other competitors in the area of a special chemical mixture. The market shares presently are: 24 percent for the Hudson Chemical Company, 29 percent for competitor A, 30 percent for competitor B, and 17 percent for competitor C. Over the past six months, the retentions and losses for the four firms are:

1. Hudson Chemical Company retains 70 percent of its customers while losing 20 percent to competitor A, 5 percent to competitor B, and 5 percent to competitor C.

2. Competitor A retains 65 percent of its customers while losing 15 percent to the Hudson Chemical Company, 10 percent to competitor B, and 10 percent to competitor C.

3. Competitor B retains 75 percent of its customers while losing 5 percent to the Hudson Chemical Company, 5 percent to competitor A, and 15 percent to competitor C.

4. Competitor C retains 70 percent of its customers while losing 10 percent to the Hudson Chemical Company, 10 percent to competitor A, and 10 percent to competitor B.

(a) What share of the total market is likely to be held by each company at the end of this year?

(b) Assuming no change in the rates of retention, gain, and loss, what is the long-run market share for the Hudson Chemical Company?

5. On January 1, the Kummins Engine Company is competing with two other companies in the manufacturing of lightweight diesel engines. The market shares presently are: 61 percent for the Kummins Engine Company (*A*), 14 percent for competitor *B*, and 25 percent for competitor *C*. The percentage of retentions and losses for the three firms are:

Companies	Customer Gains From			Customer Losses To		
	A	*B*	*C*	*A*	*B*	*C*
Kummins	0%	5%	8%	0%	9%	6%
B	9	0	6	5	0	8
C	6	8	0	8	6	0

Based upon the foregoing data, which is representative of future market movement, answer the following questions.

(a) What share of the total market is likely to be held by each company at the end of this year?

(b) Assuming no changes, what are the market shares for the three companies at the end of the following year?

6. The Racine Manufacturing Company has asked its advertising agency to develop two entirely different advertising programs to help one of the company's slow-moving product lines (floor wax). It was decided to use Columbus, Ohio, and Rochester, New York, as the test areas since both cities have a similar matrix of transition probabilities; that is, customer loyalty for the firm's product as well as gains and losses, for all practical purposes, are identical. The industry sales are $150 million. Racine has 30 percent of the market while its competitors have 40 percent (competitor *A*) and 30 percent (competitor *B*) of the total market. The net income as a percent of sales is a low 3 percent for Racine. The cost of advertising for test area number one (Columbus) is an additional $25,000 per year. Projected yearly sales in Columbus without additional advertising are $1.1 million. Cost of additional advertising in test area number two (Rochester) is $30,000. Comparable projected sales in Rochester without additional advertising are $1.2 million. The original matrix of transition probabilities for both test areas is:

$$
\begin{array}{cccc}
 & \text{Racine} & \text{Comp. }A & \text{Comp. }B \\
\text{Racine} & .75 & .15 & .10 \\
\text{Comp. }A & .15 & .80 & .10 \\
\text{Comp. }B & .10 & .05 & .80
\end{array}
$$

The new matrices of transition probabilities for several months which appear to be realistic for the entire year are:

	Columbus, Ohio			Rochester, N.Y.		
	Racine	**Comp. *A***	**Comp. *B***	**Racine**	**Comp. *A***	**Comp. *B***
Racine	.76	.20	.12	.75	.20	.11
Comp. *A*	.14	.77	.08	.13	.77	.07
Comp. *B*	.10	.03	.80	.12	.03	.82

Which of the two advertising programs appear best suited for the national market in terms of profits to Racine?

Bibliography

C. Derman, *Finite State Markov Decision Processes,* New York: Academic Press, 1970.

E. B. Dynkin, *Markov Processes,* Englewood Cliffs, N.J.: Prentice-Hall, 1965.

D. Freedman, *Markov Chains,* San Francisco: Holden-Day, 1971.

F. S. Hillier and G. J. Lieberman, *Operations Research,* San Francisco: Holden-Day, 1974.

R. A. Howard, *Dynamic Probabilistic Systems* (2 vol.), New York: John Wiley & Sons, 1971.

C. Kim, *Quantitative Analysis for Managerial Decisions,* Reading, Mass.: Addison-Wesley, 1976.

P. Kotler, *Marketing Decision Making, A Model Building Approach,* New York: Holt, Rinehart and Winston, 1971.

J. J. Martin, *Bayesian Decision Problems and Markov Chains,* New York: John Wiley & Sons, 1967.

C. H. Springer, R. E. Herlihy, R. T. Mall, and R. I. Beggs, *Probabilistic Models,* Homewood, Ill.: Richard D. Irwin, 1968.

T. H. Williams and C. H. Griffin, *Management Information, A Quantitative Accent,* Homewood, Ill.: Richard D. Irwin, 1967.

Part V

Operations Research Models— Simulation Techniques

Chapter 10

Queuing Models

Chapter Objectives

☐ To contrast the methods of handling uniform arrivals and service times with those that are random.

☐ To present single-channel queuing models that require random arrival and service times to conform to certain types of distributions.

☐ To formulate procedures for solving random arrival and service time problems that utilize the Monte Carlo method of queuing.

☐ To demonstrate that Monte Carlo procedures for single-channel and multichannel queuing problems are computer oriented.

Chapter Outline

The theory of queues, or waiting-line theory, has its origin in the work of A. K. Erlang, starting in 1909. He experimented on a problem dealing with the congestion of telephone traffic. During busy periods, intending callers experienced some delay because the operators were unable to handle the calls as rapidly as they were made. The original problem Erlang treated was the calculation of this delay for one operator, and in 1917 the results were extended to the case of several operators. This was the same year that Erlang published his well-known work, *Solution of Some Problems in the Theory of Probabilities of Significance in Automatic Telephone Exchanges*. Development in the field of telephone traffic continued largely along the lines initiated by Erlang, and the main publications were those of Molina in 1927 and Thornton D. Fry in 1928. It was not until the end of World War II that this early work was extended to other general problems involving queues or waiting lines.

Requirements for Formulating Queuing Problems

Queuing theory, like most mathematical techniques, has its own set of requirements. Queuing or waiting line discipline refers to the condition in which arrivals are selected for service. The procedure in this chapter is that arrivals take their place in the waiting line on a first-come, first-served basis. In the same manner, arrivals in line will be serviced on a next-in-line, next-served basis. Although some priority could change this pattern of servicing, the analysis does not consider this possibility.

Arrivals can be "uniform over a period of time" or they can be "at random." The arrival rate can take the form of employees arriving at the firm's tool crib or, in another situation, the number of customers arriving to eat. The *arrival rate* is generally stated as the number of arrivals per unit of time. If the arrival rate is random, the customers arrive in no logical pattern or order over time. This represents most cases in the business world. In situations where the arrivals are randomly distributed, their average can be used provided that the data was accumulated over a sufficiently long time period.

Similarly, the *service rate* treats the manner in which the servicing facility can handle the incoming demands and is expressed as a rate per unit of time. For instance, servicing rate might indicate the number of orders that are processed per hour. Service time may also be uniformly or randomly distributed. More cases of a uniform service rate will be found in business problems than a uniform arrival rate.

Utilizing the concept of random arrival and service rates, single-channel and multichannel models can be formulated (developed originally by Erlang). Due to their complexity, the derivations of these models are not presented. However, the use of single-channel models that employ certain assumptions about their arrival and service times is set forth in the chapter. In addition, the Monte Carlo method of queuing is set forth. Basically, it is a simulation technique in which statistical distribution functions are created by using a table of random numbers. Since it is useful for solving single-channel and multichannel waiting-line problems, the development of Monte Carlo models for both types will be presented. The chief advantage of the Monte Carlo method over the Erlang models is that the former can be formulated to handle any type of distributions for arrival and service times while the latter must conform to certain restrictions. Also, the Monte Carlo method is oriented toward computer processing.

Initially, in our presentation, the uniform arrival and service times approach to queuing is illustrated. Although there are very few real-world cases of this queuing approach, it does serve as a way of contrasting the concept of uniformity with randomness.

Uniform Arrival and Service Times Approach to Queuing

The handling of uniform arrival and service times in terms of solving for minimum cost can be illustrated. A manufacturing firm operates several tool rooms within one of its large plants. Currently one of these tool rooms, staffed by one attendant, is under observation by the systems analysis group to determine if additional staffing is justified. The machinists arrive for service at a uniform rate of one every six minutes while the tool room attendant handles these requests at a uniform rate of one every seven minutes. Would costs be reduced by increasing the number of attendants? The tool room attendant is paid $6 per hour and the machinists are paid $8 per hour. Both rates include fringe benefits.

The problem is calculated initially on a four-hour basis since the shop personnel work from 8 A.M. to 12 A.M. and then go to lunch. The final results are calculated on an eight-hour basis. Based upon the data—uniform arrival rate of one every six minutes and a uniform service rate of one every seven minutes—the problem can be solved by utilizing the formula for the sum of an arithmetic series. If the first man

Applications—Queuing Models

- **Checkout stations and personnel determination**—determines the number of checkout stations and personnel in supermarkets and department stores to ensure smooth and economic operation at various times of the day.
- **Delays at toll booths evaluation**—focuses on the number and scheduling of toll booths required on a 24-hour basis to minimize cost at a given level of service.
- **Airplane departure analysis**—used by airlines in scheduling the departures of their planes versus those of their competitors.
- **Manning of tool cribs**—assigning one or more attendants to tool cribs can actually reduce overall manufacturing costs since factory personnel will be working instead of waiting in line.
- **Construction of docks determination**—because both dock costs and demurrage costs can be high, the number of docks constructed should minimize the sum of these two costs.
- **Machine breakdowns and repairs analysis**—determines the number of repairmen to handle machine breakdowns and repairs to minimize overall costs.
- **Wage incentive plan study**—analyzes machine capabilities so that workers are paid fairly throughout the plant.
- **Material flow balancing**—effects the balancing of material flow in a plant.

arrives at 8 A.M., he has no waiting time. Before the first arrival has been serviced, the second machinist arrives and becomes the first person to wait in line. His waiting time is one minute (7 minutes − 6 minutes) before being serviced.

Once we know the waiting time for the first machinist, it is necessary to calculate the waiting time of the last man in the initial four hours. Since 40 (10 men per hour × 4 hours) machinists arrive and the first man does not wait, we can calculate the waiting time for this 39th machinist or 39 machinists times 1 minute equals 39 minutes. Because the increase in waiting time for each additional machinist is linear, we can average the waiting time of the second and fortieth arrival. Average waiting time per machinist equals 1 minute plus 39 minutes divided by 2, or 20 minutes. Table 10–1 summarizes this information. (The probability that the last arrivals will not wait in line, since the lunch hour is approaching, has not been considered, although normally it would be.) Inspection of the data reveals that using two attendants minimizes cost. In contrast to uniform rates, most business problems are concerned with random rates of arrival and service, the subject matter for the remainder of the chapter.

	Number of Attendants		
	1	**2**	**3**
Uniform arrival of machinists—4 hours	40	40	40
Average time each machinist			
spends waiting for service	20 min.	—	—
Total time lost by machinists during 4 hours	20 min. × 39 men =	—	—
	780 minutes		
Machinists' average hourly pay			
(including fringe benefits)	$8	$8	$8
Tool crib attendant's average hourly pay			
(including fringe benefits)	$6	$6	$6
Value of machinists' lost time during 4 hours	$104	—	—
Pay of tool crib attendants during 4 hours	24	$48	$72
Total cost for 4 hours	$128	$48	$72
	× 2	× 2	× 2
Total cost for 8 hours (machinists' lost time plus			
tool crib attendant's pay on an 8-hour basis)	$256	$96	$144

Table 10–1
Simulated Behavior of
Tool Crib Based Upon
Uniform Arrival and
Uniform Service Rates

Single-Channel Queuing Models

A single-channel queuing problem results from random arrival and service times at a single service station. The random arrival time can be described mathematically with a probability distribution. The probability distribution used depends upon the pattern of the arrivals as shown by observed data and the nature of the operation. One of the most common distributions found in queuing problems is the Poisson distribution. This is used in single-channel queuing problems for random arrivals where the service provided is exponentially distributed. Both of these distributions are explained below.

Model for Arrivals (Poisson Distribution)   A *Poisson distribution* is a discrete probability distribution that predicts the number of arrivals in a given time. The Poisson distribution involves the probability of the occurrence of an arrival and is independent of what has occurred in preceding observations. It is similar to a normal distribution but is skewed to one side (Figure 10–1). The Poisson assumption indicates the arrivals occur at random as represented by the constant λ. The constant λ is the number of arrivals per unit of time, or the mean arrival rate, while $1/\lambda$ is defined as the length of the time interval between two consecutive arrivals (t and $t + \Delta t$ where t is the time factor).

Since the single-channel queuing models make use of a Poisson distribution, one can test the assumption that arrivals do follow a Poisson distribution. This is accomplished by picking a fixed interval of time and counting the number of units arriving in an interval. This is performed for a sample of the arrivals where the mean number of arrivals is then computed. The observed data can be plotted to see how well the data fits a Poisson distribution.

Model for Service Time (Exponential Distribution) Service time is that interval between the beginning of service and its completion. The mean service rate (μ) is the number of customers served per time unit while average service time ($1/\mu$) is time units per customer. Service time delivered is given by an *exponential distribution* (referred to by many authors as a negative exponential distribution) when the servicing of a customer takes place (between the time t and $t + \Delta t$ where t is the time factor). It should be noted that the Poisson distribution cannot be applied to servicing. There is usually some idle time on the part of the attendant. The Poisson distribution holds for a fixed time interval of continuous servicing, but we can never be sure this will occur in all situations. For this reason, the (negative) exponential distribution is used. When graphed, it slopes downward and to the right from its maximum, as illustrated in Figure 10-2.

Like the arrival times, service times that are distributed exponentially can be verified; that is, the observed service time data can be collected through standard study methods and plotted to determine if it fits an exponential distribution.

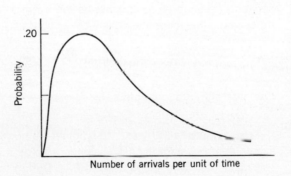

Figure 10-1
Poisson distribution (approximates a normal distribution but is skewed to one side) describes those cases in which there is a much greater probability of few arrivals per unit of time than there is of very many arrivals per unit of time.

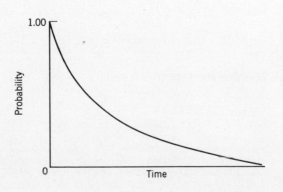

Figure 10-2
Exponential distribution (slopes downward and to the right) describes the probability distribution function of service times.

297

Single-Channel Poisson Arrivals with Exponential Service

A single-channel Poisson arrivals with exponential service problem treats a condition where one unit is delivering the service. The inputs, such as customers and jobs, are considered to arrive in a Poisson manner. The exponential servicing rate is independent of the number of elements in line. Arrivals are handled on a first-come, first-served basis. Also, a very important assumption is made about the arrival rate (λ) and the service rate (μ) — the service rate is greater than the arrival rate.

As indicated earlier, the single-channel queuing models are given without their mathematical derivation.[1] The formula for the average number of units (both waiting and being served) in the system is given as:

$$E(n) \text{ average number in the system} = \frac{\lambda}{\mu - \lambda} \qquad \text{(Equation 10-1)}$$

In order to determine the average number of customers waiting to be served, it is necessary to use a different notation from the $E(n)$ above. $E(w)$ will be used to designate the average number of customers in the system before entering the service facility. Because there can be only one unit in the service facility at any time, the average number of units (both waiting and in service), or $E(n)$ less the one being serviced (defined as λ/μ), must be the average number of customers waiting to be served. Thus the equation is:

$$E(w) = E(n) - \frac{\lambda}{\mu} = \frac{\lambda}{\mu - \lambda} - \frac{\lambda}{\mu}$$

$$E(w) \text{ average queue length} = \frac{\lambda^2}{\mu(\mu - \lambda)} \qquad \text{(Equation 10-2)}$$

From Equations 10-1 and 10-2, other waiting line models can be derived. For example, the average time a customer spends in the system can be determined. The mathematical notation used is $E(v)$. During the time period $E(v)$, the average number of customers arriving is $\lambda E(v)$. This is also the average number of customers in the system or $E(n)$. Equating these terms, the equation for the average time a customer spends in the system is:

$$E(n) = \lambda E(v)$$

$$E(v) = \frac{1}{\lambda}E(n) = \frac{1}{\lambda}\left(\frac{\lambda}{\mu - \lambda}\right)$$

$$E(v) \text{ average time in the system} = \frac{1}{\mu - \lambda} \qquad \text{(Equation 10-3)}$$

---

[1] For their mathematical derivation, refer to Robert J. Thierauf and Robert C. Klekamp, *Decision Making Through Operations Research*, 2d Ed., New York: John Wiley & Sons, 1975, pp. 416–24. Also, refer to pp. 429–34 for multichannel queuing models with Poisson arrivals and exponential service.

The last model for single-channel queuing relates to the average time a customer waits before being served. The notation for this condition is $E(y)$. The average time a customer spends in the system includes both his service and waiting time. $E(v)$, minus the average service time $(1/\mu)$, must equal the average time a customer spends before being served or his average waiting time. The model for this condition is:

$$E(y) = E(v) - \frac{1}{\mu} = \frac{1}{\mu - \lambda} - \frac{1}{\mu}$$

$E(y)$ average waiting time for service $= \dfrac{\lambda}{\mu(\mu - \lambda)}$ (Equation 10–4)

Applying Equations 10–1 through 10–4 to a sample problem, we will assume that the data is representative of customers arriving in a single station service facility. The mean arrival rate (λ) is one customer every 4 minutes and the means service time (μ) is $2\frac{1}{2}$ minutes. The calculations for arrival and service times in minutes and, on the basis of an hour, are as follows:

$\lambda = \dfrac{1}{4} = 0.25$ arrivals per minute or 15 arrivals per hour

$\mu = \dfrac{1}{2.5} = 0.4$ service time per minute or 24 service times per hour

1. Using Equation 10–1, the average number of customers in the system is:

$$E(n) = \frac{\lambda}{\mu - \lambda} = \frac{0.25}{0.4 - 0.25} = \frac{0.25}{0.15} = 1.66 \text{ customers}$$

$$\frac{15}{24 - 15} = \frac{15}{9} = 1.66 \text{ customers}$$

2. Using Equation 10–2, the average number of customers waiting to be served or average queue length is:

$$E(w) = \frac{\lambda^2}{\mu(\mu - \lambda)} = \frac{(0.25)^2}{0.4(0.4 - 0.25)} = \frac{0.0625}{0.06} = 1.04 \text{ customers}$$

$$\frac{(15)^2}{24(24 - 15)} = \frac{225}{216} = 1.04 \text{ customers}$$

Calculation for the average number being served:

1.66 (average number in system) − 1.04 (average queue length)
                         = 0.62 (average number being served)

Proof: 15 arrivals/hour ÷ 24 service times/hour = 0.62 customers

3. Using Equation 10–3, the average time a customer spends in the system is:

$$E(v) = \frac{1}{\mu - \lambda} = \frac{1}{0.4 - 0.25} = \frac{1}{0.15} = 6.66 \text{ minutes}$$

$$\frac{1}{24 - 15} = \frac{1}{9} = 0.111 \text{ hour}$$

4. Using Equation 10–4, the average time a customer waits before being served is:

$$E(y) = \frac{\lambda}{\mu(\mu - \lambda)} = \frac{0.25}{0.4(0.4 - 0.25)} = 4.16 \text{ minutes}$$

$$\frac{15}{24(24 - 15)} = \frac{15}{216} = 0.07 \text{ hour}$$

Proof: 6.66 minutes (average time in system)
  − 2.5 minutes (average service time) = 4.16 minutes

Single-Channel Minimum Cost Service Rate

The expected total cost is the sum of the expected waiting cost for the arrivals per period (WC) and the expected facility cost (basically salary and fringe benefits) of service personnel per period (FC). This can be written as follows (m = mean):

$$TC_m = WC_m + FC_m \qquad\qquad \text{(Equation 10–5)}$$

The expected waiting cost per period (WC_m) is the product of unit waiting cost (C_w) for an arrival per period and the mean number of units in the system $E(n)$ during the period:

$$WC_m = C_w[E(n)]$$

$$= \frac{C_w\lambda}{\mu - \lambda}$$

The expected service cost per period (FC_m) is the product of the cost of servicing one unit (C_f) and the service rate in units per period (μ):

$$FC_m = C_f(\mu)$$

Restating Equation 10–5, the expected total system cost per period becomes:

$$TC_m = \frac{C_w\lambda}{(\mu - \lambda)} + C_f(\mu)$$

A minimum cost service rate that solves for μ can be written as:

$$\mu = \lambda \pm \sqrt{\frac{\lambda C_w}{C_f}}$$

(Equation 10–6)

The calculus that was used in developing this minimum cost service rate is set forth in Appendix B. Note that a plus sign and a minus sign appear before the square root sign. A $-\mu$ is not a possible answer in the real world. This can be seen in the example where λ is 0.25 arrivals per minute and μ is 0.4 persons serviced per minute. The waiting cost is $0.05 per minute and the cost for servicing one unit is $0.04. Substituting these figures into Equation 10–6 results in the minimum cost service rate of 0.81 units per minute and not -0.31 units per minute, calculated as follows:

$$\mu = 0.25 \pm \sqrt{\frac{(0.25)\,(\$0.05)}{\$0.04}}$$

$$\mu = 0.25 \pm \sqrt{\frac{\$0.0125}{\$0.04}}$$

$$\mu = 0.25 \pm 0.56$$

$\mu = 0.81$ units per minute or $\mu = -0.31$ units per minute (not a feasible solution)

Monte Carlo (Random) Approach to Queuing

In many cases, the observed distributions for arrival and service times cannot be fitted to certain mathematical distributions (Poisson and exponential). In addition, the first-in-and-first-out assumption may not be valid for a particular queuing problem. Similarly, in multichannel queuing, departures from one queue may form the arrivals for another. Under these conditions, the Monte Carlo method is extremely useful since none of the previous queuing models perform adequately.

Basically, the *Monte Carlo method* is a simulation technique in which statistical distribution functions are created by using a series of random numbers. This approach can develop many months or years of data in a matter of a few minutes on a computer. It allows manipulation of those factors that are subject to control, such as adding another service station, without actually having to incur the expense of installing one. Changes can be tried without disrupting the actual process.

Single-Channel Arrival and Service Time Distributions   Even though Monte Carlo analysis does not require that the arrival and service time distributions obey certain theoretical forms, it does demand that the form and parameters of these distributions be set forth. The cumulative distributions which can then be developed are used as a means for generating arrival and service times. The following single-channel queuing problem illustrates Monte Carlo analysis.

A firm has a single-channel service station which has the following characteristics based upon empirical data: the time between arrivals has a mean of 6.0 minutes

(A_m) while the service time has a mean of 5.5 minutes (S_m). These arrival and service time distributions are found in Figure 10–3.

In Figure 10–3, the probabilities associated with each value of A_x and S_x are shown. In order to determine the cumulative arrival and service time distributions, the individual probabilities are totaled, starting from left to right. These cumulative distributions, shown in Figure 10–4, are the basis for generating arrival and service times in conjunction with a table of random numbers.

Figure 10–3
Arrival and service time distributions in minutes.

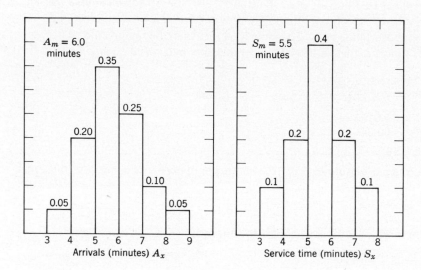

Figure 10–4
Cumulative arrival and service time distributions in minutes.

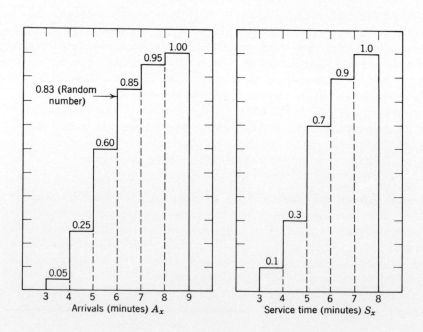

Single-Channel Monte Carlo Method Using Random Numbers

In the illustration, the queuing process begins at 8:00 A.M. and continues for approximately two hours. An arrival moves immediately into the service facility if it is empty. Otherwise, if the service station is busy, the arrival will wait in a queue. Units in the waiting line will enter the service facility on a first-come, first-served basis. Instead of using a computer program for solving the problem, a worksheet will serve the same purpose (Table 10–2).

The arrival and service times for the simulation worksheet of Table 10–2 are developed in the following manner. A table of random numbers (a group of numbers which occur in no order with no one number more likely to occur than any other number), found in Appendix D, is utilized. The random numbers for arrival times are taken arbitrarily from the second last group column (first two digits) and the service times are taken from the last group column (first two digits). The random numbers are related to Figure 10–4, (cumulative arrival and service time distributions). For example, the first random number for arrival time is 83. Inspecting Figure 10–4, 83

Table 10–2

Simulation Worksheet for Arrival Time, Service Time, and Waiting Time

Random Number	Time Till Next Arrival (Min.)	Arrival Time (A.M.)	Service Begins (A.M.)	Random Number	Service Time (Min.)	Service Ends (A.M.)	Waiting Time Attend. (Min.)	Waiting Time Cust. (Min.)	Length of Line
83	6	8:06	8:06	46	5	8:11	6	—	—
70	6	8:12	8:12	64	5	8:17	1	—	1
06	4	8:16	8:17	09	3	8:20	—	1	—
12	4	8:20	8:20	48	5	8:25	—	—	—
59	5	8:25	8:25	97	7	8:32	—	—	1
46	5	8:30	8:32	22	4	8:36	—	2	1
54	5	8:35	8:36	29	4	8:40	—	1	1
04	3	8:38	8:40	01	3	8:43	—	2	—
51	5	8:43	8:43	40	5	8:48	—	—	—
99	8	8:51	8:51	75	6	8:57	3	—	—
84	6	8:57	8:57	10	4	9:01	—	—	—
81	6	9:03	9:03	09	3	9:06	2	—	—
15	4	9:07	9:07	70	6	9:13	1	—	1
36	5	9:12	9:13	41	5	9:18	—	1	1
12	4	9:16	9:18	40	5	9:23	—	2	1
54	5	9:21	9:23	37	5	9:28	—	2	—
97	8	9:29	9:29	21	4	9:33	1	—	—
00	9	9:38	9:38	38	5	9:43	5	—	—
49	5	9:43	9:43	14	4	9:47	—	—	—
44	5	9:48	9:48	32	5	9:53	1	—	1
13	4	9:52	9:53	60	5	9:58	—	1	1
23	4	9:56	9:58	31	5	10:03	—	2	—
22	116				103		20	14	9

(or 0.83) lies between 0.60 and 0.85. The vertical line that intersects the x-axis for the value 0.83 indicates a simulated arrival time of six minutes. All simulated arrival and service times are determined in the same manner.

Having generated arrival and service times from a table of random numbers, the next step is to list the waiting time in the appropriate column. Since the first arrival comes in six minutes after the starting time, the clerk has waited six minutes. This time is written in the column, Waiting Time—Attendant while the column, Waiting Time—Customer is blank due to zero waiting time on the part of the first customer. The simulated service time for the first arrival is five minutes, which results in the service ending at 8:11. Looking at the next line, we see the next arrival comes at 8:12, which indicates no one has waited in line. Therefore the last column is blank for the first line.

The second arrival comes at 8:12 while the attendant has waited one minute from 8:11 to 8:12. The service time of five minutes results in the service ending at 8:17. Before the attendant can finish servicing the second arrival, a third arrival comes at 8:16, which means that a customer is waiting. The last column, Length of Line, indicates one person in line. When the attendant does service the third arrival, the individual has waited one minute. The column Waiting Time—Customer is used to indicate the one minute of waiting time from 8:16 to 8:17. The same procedures are used throughout Table 10–2.

Based upon the simulated period for about two hours, several questions can be asked: (1) What is the average length of the waiting line? (2) What is the average time a customer waits before being served? (3) What is the average time a customer spends in the system? (4) Would it pay to add another attendant? The first question can be answered by taking the number of customers in line for the two-hour period and dividing by the number of arrivals: 0.41 people (9 divided by 22) is the average length of the waiting line. The answer to the second question can be obtained by taking the waiting time of the customers (14 minutes) and dividing by the number of arrivals (22) for 0.64 minutes, the average time a customer waits before being served.

In order to answer the third question of how much time a customer spends in the system, it is necessary to calculate the average service time. Total service time of 103 minutes divided by 22 arrivals equals 4.68 minutes. It should be noted that this average service time is far short of the 5.5 minutes originally set forth in the problem. The sample is much too small; in fact, many weeks of simulated data would be needed to bring it back in line. (This is where the benefits of the computer are apparent.) Nevertheless, the average time a person spends in the system is the summation of average service time (4.68 minutes) and average waiting time (0.64 minutes) for 5.32 minutes.

Regarding the feasibility of adding another attendant, it is necessary to compare the cost of one attendant and customer waiting time to the cost of two attendants and no waiting time (simulated analysis for the two attendants indicates no customer waiting time) to answer the fourth question. Using the cost of $6 for the attendant's wages plus fringe benefits and $6 for customer waiting time, the results are:

Two-Hour (Approx.) Period	One Attendant	Two Attendants
Customer waiting time (14 minutes × $6/hour)	$ 1.40	—
Attendant's cost (2 hours × $6/hour)	12.00	$24.00
Total cost of two-hour (approx.) period	$13.40	$24.00

Assuming this analysis is representative of the actual situation over many months rather than for approximately two hours, the cost for one attendant is lower than for two attendants.

In the problem, a value of $6 per hour was used for the customers' waiting time. If the firm values its customers highly, it will place a high value on its customers' waiting time, say double that of the attendant's cost per hour. In the problem, a low value was placed on the customers' waiting time. However, in theory, the value should be an average of all future profits on these customers discounted back to the present time. This is analogous to the price paid for a share of common stock, i.e., all future earnings discounted back to the present time.

This example illustrates the single-channel Monte Carlo method, which utilizes random numbers for originating data. The random numbers are used in creating hypothetical data for a problem whose behavior is known from past experience. If no past data is available, the individual must decide whether the variables in the phenomenon under study can be assumed to act at random. The use of the cumulative probability distribution for arrival and service time should closely parallel the real world.

Multichannel Monte Carlo Method Using Random Numbers

Before discussing a multichannel problem, it is helpful to discuss a system consisting of two or more stations where the arrivals cannot pass from one line to another. This type of waiting-line problem is really a single-channel one rather than a multichannel problem. Once an arrival has selected a particular line, he becomes a part of that single service facility. For example, on a toll road, each pay station is placed next to a specific route which has different destinations from the other routes. Obviously, an automobile waiting for one station will not switch to a pay station for a different route.

Multichannel queuing theory treats the condition where several service stations are in parallel and each element in the waiting line can be served by more than one station. Each service facility is prepared to deliver the same type of service and is equipped essentially with the same type of facilities. The arrival selects one station without any external pressure. When a waiting line is formed, a single line usually breaks down into shorter lines in front of each of the service stations.

In multichannel problems using random numbers for simulated arrivals and service times, the prior method could have been utilized. However, an approach slightly different from the preceding one is set forth. Consider a manufacturing plant which has a tool crib located in the center of the plant. Currently, two attendants (hourly wage rate plus fringe benefits is $5) are assigned to issue tools and parts to plant personnel. The plant superintendent notices that a waiting line of production workers (average hourly rate is $10 including fringe benefits) forms several times a day. The superintendent is questioning whether two attendants assigned to the tool room are adequate to keep overall factory costs at a minimum.

Empirical data has been gathered on the problem. It indicates the average time between requests for tools and parts is five minutes while the length of service time has the following distribution:

6 minutes	.10
7 minutes	.20
8 minutes	.30
9 minutes	.30
10 minutes	.10
	1.00

With this information and a random number table (Appendix D), the arrival and service times can be simulated.

The first task is to simulate the arrivals of the production workers at the tool crib. Since we are dealing with 10 digits (0 through 9) in a table of random numbers, we can select one of these to represent an arrival. Since the number 5 (or any other number) appears on the average once in each group of 10 digits, it represents the chance of an arrival. Using the table of random numbers (start in upper left-hand corner of Appendix D), the number of 5s in each 10-digit random number represents the arrival during that period. In the first 10 digits, the number 5 appears once. Similarly, in the second 10 digits, the number 5 appears once. The remaining arrivals are determined in like manner. Shown in Table 10–3 are arrivals for a two-hour period or 24 five-minute periods.

After simulating the arrivals at the tool crib, it is necessary to simulate the service time that is required by each of the arrivals. Service times can be distributed as follows:

1. Let 0 represent the probability of a service time of six minutes since we have a .1 probability of this amount of service time.
2. Let 1 and 2 represent the probability of a service time of seven minutes since we have a .2 probability of this amount of service time.
3. Let 3, 4, and 5 represent the probability of a service time of eight minutes since we have a .3 probability of this amount of service time.
4. Let 6, 7, and 8 represent the probability of a service time of nine minutes since we have a .3 probability of this amount of service time.
5. Let 9 represent the probability of a service time of ten minutes since we have a .1 probability of this amount of service time.

The simulated service times are shown in Table 10–3. This time the random numbers are found in the last row of Appendix D, that is, the random number 4 is associated with a service time of 8 minutes; the random number 0 is associated with a service time of 6 minutes; and so forth.

Table 10–3
Simulated Arrival and
Service Times

Period Number	Number of Arrivals	Service Time (Minutes)						
1	1	8	①					
2	1	6	②					
3	—		—					
4	1	9	③					
5	1	9	④					
6	2	8	⑤	9	⑥			
7	2	9	⑦	9	⑧			
8	2	8	⑨	8	⑩			
9	3	9	⑪	10	⑫	8	⑬	
10	—		—					
11	2	6	⑭	9	⑮			
12	—		—					
13	—		—					
14	—		—					
15	—		—					
16	1	7	⑯					
17	2	9	⑰	8	⑱			
18	1	7	⑲					
19	1	9	⑳					
20	1	8	㉑					
21	2	10	㉒	8	㉓			
22	—		—					
23	1	8	㉔					
24	2	8	㉕	9	㉖			

Now that arrivals and service times have been simulated, we want to determine the optimum number of attendants in the tool crib. The first-in, first-out rule will be observed. Notice that the number of simulated arrivals exceeds the number of time periods by 2. The sample is too small, causing the inequality between the arrivals and time periods.

In order to establish a method for arrivals within each five-minute period, the following rule will be observed. If there is one arrival, we will assume that the production worker arrives at the beginning of the five-minute period. If two arrivals occur within a five-minute period, one will be assumed to arrive at the beginning of the period, and the other to arrive at the end of the third minute during the period. If three arrive, one will be assumed to arrive at the beginning of the period, the second one to arrive at the end of the third minute, and the third one to arrive at the end of the fifth minute. Ideally, the distribution of arrivals should be based upon observed patterns. For a conservative point of view, all workers can be assumed to arrive at the beginning of the period.

The simulated problem in Figure 10–5 represents a two-hour period. Time is represented on the left-hand margin. To make it easier for referencing arrivals in Table 10–3, the same circled numbers are assigned in Figure 10–5. The following symbols are used:

Arrival   ○
Being served |———————|
Waiting |- - - - -|

Figure 10–5

Tool crib operation with two servicemen. (N.A. = no arrivals during five-minute period.)

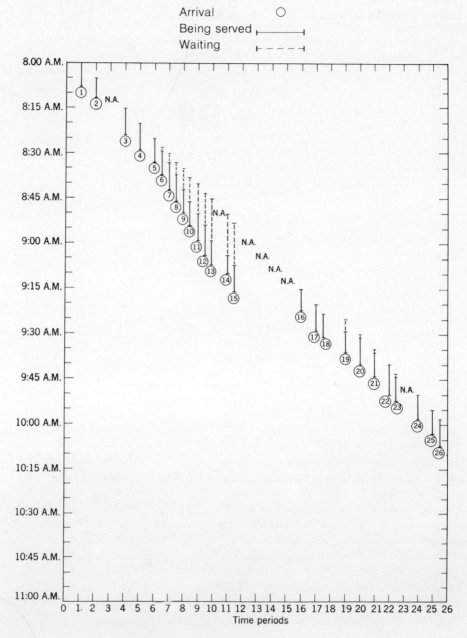

Based upon Figure 10–5, the total waiting time is 93 minutes, or an average waiting time per arrival of 3.6 minutes (93 minutes divided by 26 arrivals). If the average time between arrivals is five minutes, the number of arrivals for an eight-hour day is 96 (8 hours per day times 12 arrivals per hour). Also, if the average waiting time is 3.6 minutes, total waiting time is 345.6 minutes (96 arrivals times 3.6 minutes) or 5.8 hours of lost time per day for production workers.

Before computing the total cost for two attendants in the problem, it is necessary to simulate the problem with three attendants. This is shown in Figure 10–6, except three solid lines exist simultaneously because three production men can be serviced at one time. The total waiting time is calculated to be 12 minutes or 0.5 minute (12 minutes divided by 26 arrivals) lost per production worker. With 96 arrivals in an eight-hour day, the total time lost is 0.8 hour of lost time per day (96 arrivals times 0.5 minute).

A cost comparison for two, three, and four attendants per Table 10–4 is used to determine the optimum number of servicemen that minimizes the total cost of the plant operation. The cost for three attendants results in lower total costs. Again, a larger sample is recommended to finalize the results.

Chapter Summary

The treatment of queuing theory in this chapter is a cross section of various waiting line models and methods. They allow for the application of queuing theory to many business areas: the factory, the office, the sales floor, and public places. By using imagination and experience, the reader can readily identify other areas where queuing discipline can be utilized. In many cases, a firm can realize considerable cost savings without making a substantial investment in the queuing study itself. Operations research groups should give considerable thought to the use of this technique for high-return projects.

	Two Attendants	Three Attendants	Four Attendants
Customer waiting time	5.8 hours	0.8 hour	—
Cost per hour	$10	$10	$10
Waiting time cost (waiting time × cost per hour)	$ 58	$ 8	—
Attendant's cost (8-hour basis × $5 per hour)	80	120	$160
Total daily cost	$138	$128	$160

Table 10–4
Cost Comparison of Two, Three, and Four Attendants

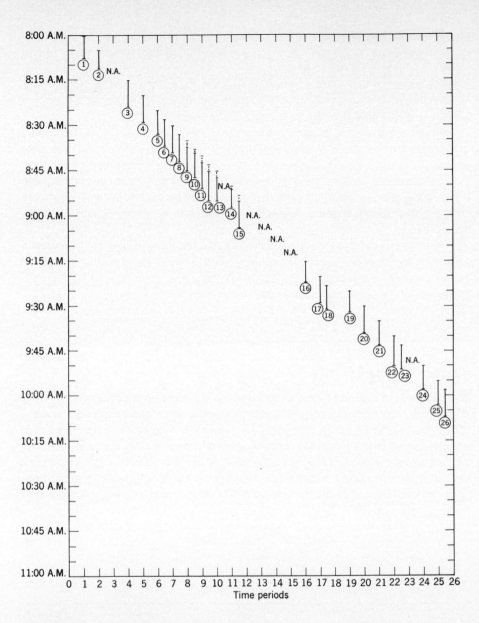

Figure 10–6
Tool crib operation with three servicemen. (N.A. = no arrivals during five minute period.)

Questions

1. What is queuing theory?
2. What are the fundamental differences between uniform and random arrival rates?
3. What are the advantages of the Monte Carlo method for single-channel and multichannel queuing problems over earlier models?
4. Give other applications for queuing theory not found in the chapter.

Model Formulation Exercises

1. In the formulation of a uniform arrival and service rate queuing problem, what type of mathematical series is used to solve for the average waiting times of the arrivals who have to wait? Hint: the first one who waits plus the last one who waits, both values divided by two, is the formula for the average waiting time.

2. When A. K. Erlang formulated his single-channel (as well as multichannel) queuing models with Poisson arrivals and exponential service, why did he make the assumption that the service rate must be greater than the arrival rate? In other words, why in the mathematical derivation of single-channel queuing models is the mathematical notation ($\mu > \lambda$) used?

3. Although in the example for the single-channel minimum cost service rate a plus cost service rate is selected over a minus cost service rate, what happens when both values are plus (see Mathematical Exercise 4e)? To state it another way, what criteria is used to determine the correct minimum cost service rate?

4. The procedures set forth in the chapter for the single-channel Monte Carlo approach to queuing are also applicable to multichannel problems. In a similar manner, the procedures for multichannel are applicable to single-channel problems. When formulating a Monte Carlo approach to a specific queuing problem, what determines which approach should be used?

5. For the various models and approaches to queuing given in the chapter, the assumption was that the first one in line would be the first one served. Give three situations where it is necessary to change the first-come, first-served basis.

Mathematical Exercises

1. The Midland Manufacturing Company operates several tool rooms within one of its major manufacturing plants. The arrival of its production men is observed to be at a uniform rate of 30 men per hour while the tool room service attendant is observed to handle these requests at the uniform rate of 24 per hour.
    (a) What is the waiting line likely to be at the end of four hours?
    (b) Would it be profitable for the company to add another attendant assuming the time of the production men to be worth $4.50 per hour (wage rate plus fringe benefits) and the attendant's time costs $2.50 per hour (wage rate plus fringe benefits) based on an eight-hour day?
    (c) Suppose the uniform service rate increases to 40 per hour for one attendant. Would it pay to add another person?

2. The Newcomb Corporation must make a decision regarding its policy of hiring a repairman to fix machines which break down at an average rate of four per hour according to a Poisson distribution. Nonproductive time on any of the

machines is costing the firm $10 per hour. The firm can hire two different types of repairmen, one slow but inexpensive ($2.50 per hour), the other fast but expensive ($4.50 per hour). The slow repairman can repair machines exponentially at an average rate of six per hour while the fast repairman can repair machines exponentially at the rate of eight per hour. Based upon the foregoing data, which repairman should be hired?

3. A stenographer performs stenographic services for five persons. Arrival rate is Poisson and service times are exponential. Average arrival rate is four per hour with an average service time of ten minutes. Cost of waiting is $8 per hour while the cost of servicing is $2.50 each.
   (a) Calculate the average waiting time of an arrival.
   (b) Calculate the average length of the waiting line.
   (c) Calculate the average time which an arrival spends in the system.
   (d) Calculate the minimum cost service rate.

4. Trucks are known to arrive at a dock in a Poisson manner at the rate of eight per hour. Service time distribution is approximated exponentially with an average rate of five minutes. The cost of waiting is $10 per hour while the cost of servicing is $4 per unit.
   (a) Calculate the average number of trucks in the system.
   (b) Calculate the average time a truck spends in the system.
   (c) Calculate the average queue length for the trucks.
   (d) Calculate the average time a truck waits before being served.
   (e) Calculate the minimum cost service rate.

5. Arrivals at a telephone booth average ten minutes between calls. The length of time an individual is on the phone is assumed to be distributed exponentially with a mean of three minutes.
   (a) What is the average length of the queues that form from time to time?
   (b) Should the telephone company install a second booth if half of the arrivals have to wait over three minutes for the telephone?

6. Incoming materials arrive at a receiving dock at an average rate of five per hour (Poisson distribution). The material is handled by a lift truck whose service time is exponential with an average service rate of seven loads per hour. Production management desires to know (a) the average number of loads waiting on the docks to be moved, (b) the average length of time that an arriving load will spend waiting for service, and (c) the lift truck average service rate in order to have an expected waiting time of 20 minutes for a load. [Hint for first part: average length of nonempty waiting line $= \mu/(\mu - \lambda)$.]

7. The Askcraft Machine Company operates a warehouse which services its foremen. The foremen arrive at a random rate of six per hour. The warehouse attendant is able to service these arrivals at a uniform rate of four per hour. If the attendant's cost is $3.50 per hour and the foremen's cost per hour is $5, use

the Monte Carlo simulation method to determine the optimum number of attendants to assign to the warehouse in order to minimize cost. Use a two-hour period for your decision. Assume any foreman in line will be serviced.

8. A sample of 300 arrivals (customers) at a checkout counter of a store indicates that an average time between arrivals is five minutes. A study of the time required to service the customer, that is, adding up the bill, receiving payment, cashing checks, giving stamps, and the like, yields the following distribution:

Service Time (Minutes)	Frequency
1.5	10%
2.0	20%
2.5	30%
3.0	20%
3.5	10%
4.0	10%

Using a simulated sample of 20 periods, calculate (a) the average customer waiting time, (b) the idle time of the checkout clerk, and (c) the average time a person spends in the system. Assume all arrivals come at the beginning of each five-minute period.

9. A single-service gasoline station has determined the following arrival and service times:

Between Time Arrivals (Minutes)	Percent of Cases	Service Time (Minutes)	Percent of Cases
0	3	1	6
1	4	2	12
2	8	3	17
3	11	4	19
4	16	5	17
5	14	6	12
6	10	7	8
7	9	8	5
8	8	9	3
9	5	10	1
10	4		
11	3		
12	2		
13	1		
14	1		
15	1		

Simulate the operation of this service station from 8:00 A.M. to 10:04 A.M. (time for last arrival). Assume that any customer(s) in the line at 10:00 A.M. will be serviced. Determine (a) the average length of the waiting line, (b) the average time a customer waits before being serviced, and (c) the average time a customer spends in the system. (d) Also determine whether or not it would pay to add another attendant if the attendant's cost is $2.50 per hour and the customer's time is valued at three times that amount. (Note: treat random number 00 as 100.)

10. The General Service Company has made a study of the average time for requests of its two office copiers. Requests were found to total 12 times an hour for both machines. The time it takes to run off the desired copies has the following distribution:

Service Time (Minutes)	Frequency
6	10%
7	20%
8	30%
9	30%
10	10%

The office manager is wondering if another machine might help alleviate the apparent traffic jam at the two machines. He has assigned the problem to you and suggested that a two-hour period be used for a preliminary analysis of the situation. (If the third machine appears warranted, the problem will be simulated on the firm's IBM 370/138 for a conclusive answer.) Assume that the waiting time of the average office employee is $3 per hour and the hourly cost of the machine with materials to be $2.50 per hour. Are the present two office copiers adequate?

Bibliography

R. L. Ackoff and M. W. Sasieni, *Fundamentals of Operations Research,* New York: John Wiley & Sons, 1968.

H. Bierman, C. P. Bonini, and W. H. Hausman, *Quantitative Analysis for Business Decisions,* Homewood, Ill.: Richard D. Irwin, 1973.

R. B. Cooper, *Introduction to Queuing Theory,* New York: The Macmillan Company, 1972.

W. J. Fabrycky, P. M. Ghare, and P. E. Torgersen, *Operations Economy, Industrial Applications of Operations Research,* Englewood Cliffs, N.J.: Prentice-Hall, 1966.

D. Gross and C. M. Harris, *Fundamentals of Queuing Theory,* New York: Wiley-Interscience, 1974.

F. S. Hillier and G. J. Lieberman, *Operations Research,* San Francisco: Holden-Day, 1974.

G. F. Newell, *Applications of Queuing Theory,* London: Chapman & Hall, Ltd., 1971.

C. M. Paik, *Quantitative Methods for Managerial Decisions,* New York: McGraw-Hill Book Company, 1973.

J. A. Panico, *Queuing Theory,* Englewood Cliffs, N.J.: Prentice-Hall, 1969.

N. U. Prabhu, *Queues and Inventories,* New York: John Wiley & Sons, 1965.

J. A. White, J. W. Schmidt, and G. K. Bennett, *Analysis of Queuing Systems,* New York: Academic Press, 1975.

Chapter 11

Simulation

The technique of simulation has long been an important tool of the designer. Scale models of machines have been used for many years to simulate plant layouts. Simulation, as used initially by operations research, had its origin in the work of John von Neumann and Stanislaw Ulam in the late 1940s. Using Monte Carlo analysis in conjunction with a mathematical technique, they solved nuclear shielding problems that were either too expensive for experimentation or too complex for analysis. With the advent of computers in the early 1950s, simulation has made substantial progress. Countless business problems are being solved since computer simulation is an economical and fast method of performing the vast amount of calculations required.

Requirements for Formulating Simulation Problems

Before specifying the most important aspects when formulating simulation problems, it would be helpful to define simulation. It has been defined as the use of a system model that has the desired characteristic of reality in order to reproduce the essence of the actual operations. It has also been defined as a representation of reality through the use of a model or other device which will react in the same manner as reality under a given set of conditions. None of these definitions include all of its fundamental requirements, namely, the use of mathematical models, computers, statistics or stochastic processes, facts, assumptions, and alternative courses of action. A more general and all-inclusive definition of simulation is: a quantitative technique that utilizes a computerized mathematical model in order to represent actual decision making under conditions of uncertainty for evaluating alternative courses of action based upon facts and assumptions.

Simulation is useful in solving a business problem where many values of the variables are not known or are partly known in advance and there is no easy way to find these values. The problem is likened to the sequence for which no ready-made formula is known for the nth (last) term. The only known fact is a rule (recursion relation) which allows us to find the next term from the previous terms. Basically, the only way to discover the nth term is to apply the same rule over and over again until the nth term is reached. Simulation utilizes a method of finding these successive states in a problem by repeatedly applying the rules under which the system operates. This successive linking of one particular state to a previous state is an important feature of simulation.

For the most part, simulation involves the construction of some type of computer mathematical model that describes the system's operation in terms of individual events and components. Further, the system is divided into the elements and the interrelationships of those elements with predictable behavior, at least in terms of a probability distribution, for each of the various possible states of the system and its inputs. Simulation is a means of dividing the model-building process into smaller component parts and combining them in their natural, logical order. This then allows computer analysis of the effects of their interactions on one another. Due to statistical error, it is impossible to guarantee that the optimal answer will be found, but the answer should be at least near optimal if the problem is simulated correctly. In essence, the simulation model performs experiments on the sample input data rather than on the entire universe (statistically speaking), since the latter would be too time consuming, inconvenient, and expensive.

Because the variants of simulation—the operational gaming method, the Monte Carlo method (treated in the previous chapter), and the system simulation method—differ somewhat from another, they are discussed below. In addition, applications of the Monte Carlo method are illustrated in the chapter.

Operational Gaming Method

Operational gaming (the first method of simulation) refers to those situations involving conflict of interest among players or decision makers within the framework of a simulated environment. The two most widely used forms of operational gaming are military games and business management games. Military gaming is essentially a training device for military leaders, enabling them to test alternative strategies under simulated war conditions. On the other hand, participants in business games must make decisions based upon historical information. These decisions then influence and create the environment under which subsequent decisions must be made. Its characteristics are sequential decisions, rapid feedback, and new responses.

Military Games *Military games* for amusement, and for the physical and mental preparation of war, are as old as civilization. Andrew Wilson, in his book, *The Bomb and the Computer,* traces war games back to the Chinese game *weich'i,* which appeared about 3000 B.C. The name translates literally as "envelopment." It was played with colored stones on a map.

Historically, European war gaming goes back to the game of chess—the first so-called modern version of which was invented by a Prussian in the seventeenth century. The game was played with 30 different pieces and 14 various moves on an enlarged board. In 1824 another Prussian, von Reisswitz, put the game on a plaster relief model of a countryside and substituted color-coded blocks, representing troop units, in place of chess pieces. Called *Kriegsspiel* (literally war game in German), it was quickly picked up by the military in other countries and used in testing operational plans.

By World War I, virtually every major world power was employing war games to determine its strategies. The subsequent history of war gaming is a story in itself and is marked by a number of outstanding successes. Today the military services conduct extensive war gaming to evaluate equipment, to test strategy and plans, and to train commanders and combat staffs. The individual services operate their own independent gaming establishments. One example is the United States Army's Fort Leavenworth War Games Facility, for which Booz, Allen Applied Research, Inc., gaming teams assist in evaluating problems.

Business Management Games *Business management games* have gained wide acceptance in business and education. The first such business game, which Booz, Allen & Hamilton helped develop, was known as "Top Management Decision Simulation." It was introduced by the American Management Association in 1957. Since then, management games of various kinds and levels of sophistication have been developed all over the world. Growth in the number of games and participants has been tremendous because computer capabilities have increased.

The primary use of management games is to help the participants, be they executives in industry or students in business schools, develop their ability to make difficult interdependent business decisions in real life, evaluate new ideas, and introduce new techniques of decision making—all in a simulated environment. These games offer the participants a high degree of personal involvement and competitive spirit. The results gained are in direct proportion to the skills of the participants.

The use of management games in the business world is in some sense equivalent to the use of laboratory experiments in the physical sciences. The outcome of good or bad decisions can be examined quickly and without fear of real loss. Simulations of business environments provide valuable experience in conceptualizing ideas and in logical thinking. Furthermore, games can be used to introduce operations research techniques and give participants training in model building and analysis. A sophisticated, but not necessarily complex, management game can also serve as a stepping-stone for development of information processing systems and corporate behavior models.

With the advent of interactive computing, the use of management games as a teaching, training, or research device is even more feasible. The decision-making process is enhanced by operations research because it affords the user an opportunity to utilize the techniques interactively on various sample data via remote terminals. Data retrieval and manipulation are simplified to a great extent. Thus, advancements in computers and utilization of OR techniques have led to the development of interactive management games.

Modeling the Business Game   The essence of a business simulation model is one that accepts input, analyzes or processes it according to a set of rules or formulas, and generates an outcome per the analysis. Figure 11–1 illustrates a typical business game consisting of three modules: marketing, manufacturing, and financing.

The *marketing module* simulates the behavior of customers in response to price and product availabilities, their preferences being modified by the firm's personal selling, advertising, sales promotion, and research and development activities. Basically, the market consists of two types of customers: the "loyal" customers, who do not switch brands unless price varies and the "switchers," who can be lured

Figure 11–1
Major modules— marketing, manufacturing, and financing—for firms operating in a simulated business game environment.

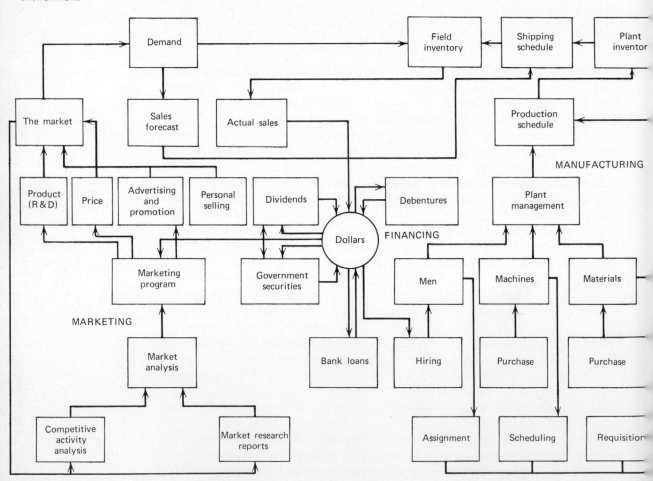

Applications—Simulation of a Firm's Functional Areas

- **Integration of marketing efforts**—defines the proper level, mix, allocation, and timing of diverse marketing efforts for products by employing a market simulator.
- **Optimum allocation of warehouses**—analyzes where warehouses should be placed for a low-cost physical distribution system.
- **Evaluation of alternative investments**—allows an evaluation of the more promising investment opportunities when large sums of money are involved.
- **Effective production scheduling**—employs decision rules to simulate factory operations that lead to effective production scheduling and control.
- **Improvement of the budgetary process**—analyzes various budgeting plans for the coming year for the purpose of selecting the best one.
- **Evaluation of financial structure**—permits an evaluation of the relationship among the elements of a firm's financial structure to help control the firm's cost of capital.
- **Test changes in company practices**—allows a firm the opportunity to test changes in its policies and practices for practicality before implementation.
- **Evaluation of investment portfolios**—analyzes the performance of a firm's investment portfolio under various market conditions.
- **Analysis of assembly lines**—determines the optimum number of personnel at each work station on the company's assembly line.

---

away by personal selling, advertising, sales promotion, and research and development activities of the firm.

A firm may not be able to supply all the demand in a market region if it is "out of stock." A percentage of the excess demand (the really loyal customers) may be back ordered, and the rest is redistributed among the other firms to the extent that they can supply the excess beyond their original market share. The rest of the unsupplied demand, if any, is assumed to be lost.

The effects of personal selling, advertising, sales promotion, and research and development activities are cumulative and lag over time. These activities have both competitive and cooperative aspects. For convenience, they are referred to as "effective advertising and research." Product promotion and product development are necessary to stimulate the demand. Hence, the marketing module determines:

Market share for each product in each region

Actual sales versus demand

Back orders, if any

Within the *manufacturing module,* each firm has a plant, a work force, and raw materials which form the three basic factors of production. The products that a firm manufactures require different combinations of these factors. The scarcity of the three factors limits production. Production changes are proportional to the quantities ordered. Finished goods can be stored at the plant or shipped to the market region warehouses. Thus, the manufacturing module:

Determines actual production schedules subject to the constraints of machines, work force, and raw materials

Modifies shipping schedules, if necessary

Updates factory and warehouse inventories

Costs are incurred in manufacturing, shipping to warehouses, and storing inventory. Inventory costs are charged on average inventory during the period. All costs are linear and each firm has the same internal cost structure.

The *financing module* summarizes the results of all activities and actions undertaken during a given period. Each period, the firms must make financial decisions relative to investment in government securities, payment of dividends, issuing of debentures, and purchase of new equipment. Other financial revenues and obligations arise as the result of activities in the production and marketing of a firm's products. Bank loans that partially cover the cash obligations for a firm are automatically drawn as required and are paid back when possible. Inability to meet the financial obligations beyond the outstanding line of bank credit can result in the firm's bankruptcy.

The cash transactions simulate the continuous flow of receipts and payments so that the income from operations offsets the expenses. The financing module uses standard cost accounting for manufacturing operations and computer cost variances. It calculates the working relationship among income, expenses, and cash flows of each firm.

The business game reports to the teams the outcome of their decisions and actual activities that took place during the simulation. These reports are the basis for making decisions in the following period(s). They can be grouped in various ways depending on the information required and ease of interpretation. The usual standard reports are:

Market reports

Competitive performance reports

Finished goods and production report

Factory and warehouse status report

Profit-and-loss statement

Balance sheet

Cash-flow statement

To aid effective decision making during the simulation exercise, the decision-assisting tools of operations research are available to the teams. These tools demonstrate to the participants the role of operations research techniques in decision making and expose them to model building and analysis. For example, linear programming can evaluate and allocate production resources effectively during the simulation exercise. The linear programming model optimizes the production decisions subject to the constraints and criterion of optimization. Markov analysis can explain the movement and retention of customers among firms. Also, statistical techniques can establish relationships between different variables in the market place. Statistical analysis of the latest market data can help forecast demands of products and assist in pricing and product promoting decisions.

Monte Carlo Method

For a complete understanding of the Monte Carlo method (the second method of simulation), it is necessary to refer to the work of von Neumann and Ulam mentioned earlier in this chapter. During World War II, physicists at the Los Alamos Scientific Laboratory were puzzled by the behavior of neutrons. The two mathematicians suggested a solution which amounted to submitting the problem to a roulette wheel. Step by step, the probabilities of the separate events were merged into a total picture which gave an approximate but workable answer to a problem. Von Neumann gave it the code name "Monte Carlo" for the secret work of Los Alamos. The Monte Carlo method, which is actually the study of the laws of chance, was so successful on neutron diffusion problems that its popularity spread and it is now an important operational research technique.

Even though the Monte Carlo approach suggests the use of roulette wheels or dice, random numbers are used (refer to Appendix D). This method can solve probability-dependent problems where physical experimentation is impracticable and the creation of an exact formula is impossible. Basically, we are studying problems with a long sequence of probability-determined steps or events. Although we can write mathematical formulas for the probability of a given step or event, we are often unable to write a useful equation for the probabilities of all steps or events.

With this brief background of the Monte Carlo method, a definition will help clarify its meaning. *The Monte Carlo method* is simulation by sampling techniques, that is, instead of drawing samples from a real population, they are obtained from a theoretical counterpart of it. Monte Carlo involves determining the probability distribution of the variables under consideration and then sampling from this distribution by means of random numbers to obtain data. In effect, a set of random numbers generates a set of values that have the same distributional characteristics as the real population.

System Simulation Method

System simulation (the third method of simulation) is a process in which real-world data—useful in the analysis of a complex problem—is processed through a model which reproduces the operating environment. The simulation model allows an analysis of the system reponse to alternative management actions, providing a sound basis for decision.

System simulation differs from the Monte Carlo approach in several respects. This method generally draws samples from a real population instead of drawing samples from a table of random numbers (or some special model). No theoretical counterpart of the actual population is used in system simulation. Another distinction is that the simulation method makes use of a mathematical and/or logical model which can be analytically solved to assist an individual in reaching a decision. However, when situations are complex and do not lend themselves to analysis by a mathematical model (which can be analytically solved), the Monte Carlo technique is employed. An example of this is the condition of an uncontrollable input to a system whose probability distribution is known and can be handled analytically, but whose sequential pattern cannot be adequately expressed for an analytical solution.

The distinction between these two basic techniques (Monte Carlo and system simulation) is actually not great. A system simulation example might help highlight the basic difference in the two approaches. This problem seeks the prediction of consumer reaction to new products, without extensive and costly surveys. The model exposes some 500 hypothetical individuals with certain characteristics to a set of communication channels, each of which carries a particular message. During each simulated week, an individual is subjected with varying probabilities of exposure to several communication channels and to particular corrections made in these channels. Predetermined rules decide if an assertion is accepted, depending on the individual's attitudes toward the communication source, previous acquaintance, acceptance of the assertion, and previous position on similar messages. As one might guess, a model of this kind is complex since it incorporates reasonable hypotheses regarding human behavior. This system simulation problem points out at least two basic differences—need for data not found in random tables and the use of a mathematical model.

Systematic Computer Approach to Simulation

The planned approach, an integral part of undertaking an OR project, is equally applicable to simulation. However, constructing the computer model, using a random number generator, and analyzing the data should be explained for a better understanding of simulation.

After the *first* step, or the *observation phase,* which leads to a *formulation* of the real problem under study (the *second* step), collection and processing of data follows. Because a certain amount of data must have been collected and processed before the real problem is defined, the medium on which data are recorded in the initial step of the planned approach may not be the most efficient medium for use in the later stages of computer processing. The conversion of the data from one medium to another may play an important role in determining data processing efficiency. Information that is handwritten, acceptable in the observation phase, must be converted to punched card, to magnetic tape, disk, or some other computer input medium.

The *third* step of the planned approach, when applied to simulation, is *formulation of the computer model* by determining how many variables to include in the model. Very little difficulty is encountered with the output variables since these are determined at the outset. The real difficulty arises in the choice of the input variables. Too few input variables may lead to invalid or incomplete models, whereas too many may result in no computer simulation because of insufficient computer memory capacity. Moreover, too many input variables will cause unnecessarily complicated computational methods.

Computer programming time is an important consideration in formulating mathematical models for computer simulation. The time required for writing a computer program depends upon the number of variables used in the model and the model's complexity. When variables of the model are stochastic in nature, both programming time and computation time are likely to increase. Reductions in the amount of programming time must be balanced against model validity and the computer's computational speed. The programmer should give serious thought to simulation languages, such as GPSS (General Purpose System Simulator) and SIMSCRIPT. The gain in time savings from use of these languages might mean the difference between success and failure from a timing aspect. Other considerations in the formulation of mathematical models for simulation are computational efficiency and compatibility with the data that has been collected.

An examination of the basic designs used in formulating mathematical models for computer simulation reveals that they are either generalized or modular (building block). The first type attempts to predict the operation of an entire system. The simulation of some segment of our economic system is an example of this generalized approach. The vast number of interrelationships and related complexities make the task almost impossible. Even though these models might be useful in formulating initial hypotheses in the third step of the planned approach, they seldom hold up when subjected to rigorous statistical testing procedures. For this reason, the modular approach to computer models is largely used for OR problems. The advantage of working with models which are block recursive is that computers are able to perform their operations in a sequential fashion. The use of a block recursive model in a simulation study reduces the computational time required to generate the time paths of the output variables. It should be remembered for the planned approach that more than one mathematical model can be and usually is formulated in this third step.

Once a set of mathematical models has been formulated describing the behavior of the system under study and their parameters have been set for operating characteristics, an initial judgment concerning the adequacy of the models can be made. This *testing phase* is the *fourth* step of the planned approach. Prior to actual computer runs, the inputs and assumptions of the simulation models are tested to determine how well a given hypothetical probability distribution fits the system under study. These tests are basically taken from statistics. At this point, one or more of the models will fail to meet the test requirements, leaving at least one promising model to formulate into a computer program.

Preparing flow charts and/or decision tables is the initial step in outlining the logical sequence of events for the selected computer model. This serves as the basis for writing the actual computer program. Programming can take any one of three directions: (1) use computer machine language; (2) write in a general-purpose language (FORTRAN, ALGOL, COBOL, or PL/1) or (3) utilize one of the special-purpose simulation languages. Once the model has been programmed and errors deleted from the program, initial values must be assigned to the model's variables and parameters before simulation of the system can begin. This initializing of the model often requires trial and error methods.

An important part of the computer program is the development of techniques for generating data. Data can be read in from punched cards, but computer storage devices are preferable because they are faster; or it can be generated internally by special subroutines, such as a random number generator, in which random numbers are developed as needed by a computer program. The last consideration in the computer programming steps is to determine the type of output reports needed. Programming languages impose no restriction on the format of the output records. However, the special simulation languages require adherence to the output requirements of that particular language.

The optimum model computer program, having been formulated, programmed, and debugged as part of the fourth step of the planned approach, must now be validated. This is the most difficult task because it involves a large number of practical, theoretical, statistical, mathematical, and philosophical complexities. In general, two tests can validate a simulation model. How well do the simulated values of the output variables compare with available historical data? Secondly, how reliable are the simulation model's predictions of the behavior of the real system in the future?

Once the validation of the computer model is complete, the *fifth* step of the planned approach seeks a complete *verification* of the model. To conduct these actual simulation experiments, we must focus our attention on questions of experimental design. We must select factor levels and combinations of levels as well as the order of experimentation. Within our factors and combinations, we must ensure that the results are reasonably free from error. The computer output generated for the system being simulated requires analysis prior to a final managerial decision. This analysis is considerably more difficult to interpret than analysis of real-world data. The problems of randomness, the assumptions set forth, the dynamic nature of business today and in the future, the large number of variables and parameters, to name the more important ones, cause this difficulty. For these reasons, the *sixth* (final) step of the planned approach requires establishing proper *controls* to detect how changes may affect the current simulation model. What might be the best simulation model today may not be best tomorrow. This is why one cannot say a simulation model is either true or false; rather, one can only say it is relevant to the current state of the system.

To gain some insight into the formulation of simulation models, using the Monte Carlo method, several examples are presented below. Since this is a cross section of current applications, it should not be construed as an all-inclusive grouping of OR simulation studies. New applications are being discovered periodically, adding new dimensions to our understanding of this dynamic OR tool.

Improving Assembly Operations

An interesting simulation example involves designing an assembly line. The need for assembly line design occurs when a new product is to be assembled, increased production requirements exceed the capacity of the existing line, assembly methods must be changed because of product design changes, or costs can be reduced by improving the existing line. Thus, the extent of the design effort is dependent on the problem.

There are several steps in the design process. The first is to establish a clear definition of the objectives or requirements. To design an assembly line, the engineer must know the assembly line's job, the production requirements, and the flexibility required. In addition to establishing the objectives, a clear definition of any factors which will constrain or limit alternatives must be established. In defining constraints, the designer should keep an open mind, avoiding limitations of historic operational modes.

The second step is to describe one or more alternative assembly line designs. The third step is to evaluate each proposed design and determine whether it meets the requirements. After the proposed assembly line is described, it can be simulated. The engineer will then know whether the proposed line will meet the production requirements and whether any facilities will be underutilized. The engineer can iterate steps two and three, and by examining the results of step three, may modify the proposed designs. The results may suggest other alternatives which were not apparent at the outset.

The assembly line simulation model is based on a collection of many assumptions; each assumption relates to only a small part of the assembly line. Examples are: the probability that a unit will fail at a certain station, and the probability that a station will not complete a unit in the given cycle time. The accuracy of the model is dependent upon the accuracy of the assumptions. Where changes in an existing line are being simulated, the assumptions can be quite accurate. The operation times can be observed and for each station, the distribution of those times can be determined from a time study. Where a new product line is simulated, the distributions may be assumed to be the same as those found on lines with similar operations. Where a new type of operation is being evaluated, the engineer can assume the best and the worst conditions, and thereby bracket the expected performance. The confidence which is placed in the simulation results can be no greater than the confidence which is placed in the individual assumptions.

Finally, the fourth step of the process compares the alternatives and makes a selection. The engineer must consider not only the production capability, but also the costs of installing and operating the line. Simulation results give the assembly, repair, and utility labor requirements, but do not specify equipment, space, or installation costs (including the cost of interrupting or disrupting the existing operations).

Determining Size of the Maintenance Force

One area of manufacturing that has received considerable attention in simulation studies is determining the size of a maintenance force. The Monte Carlo approach to simulation for this problem is certainly a lot less costly than experimenting in the plant. With actual experimentation, there is no assurance that an improvement will be realized; in addition, lost production and poor labor relations can result. The following section presents a problem for determining the size of a maintenance crew, with the lowest cost maintenance policy as the goal.

The manufacturing management of the Ace Tool and Manufacturing Company, after considerable bargaining with its union, must now employ maintenance personnel to service its machinery. The previous method of having the machine operators service the machines is no longer permissible. Hence, the company wants to determine the optimum employment of new maintenance personnel to minimize production losses caused by downtime on machinery. The number of personnel required is a primary consideration since their wages and fringe benefits must be balanced against the cost of the expected idle machines and operators.

The starting point in the study is to compile data on machines as they now operate. This can be done by recording the total number of incidents where equipment needs service each hour and the time required to perform the service. All service times greater than full minutes have been assigned the next full minute, resulting in a conservative approach to the problem. The data for this study are shown in Tables 11-1 and 11-2. Table 11-1 shows the delays per hour while Table 11-2 indicates the service time for machine downtime in the plant (based on present machine operators).

Data in Tables 11-1 and 11-2 are plotted in Figures 11-2 to 11-5. The first two figures are histograms, Figure 11-2 showing the distribution of all machine operation delays per hour and Figure 11-3 depicting the distribution of downtime in minutes for each time service is required (based on present machine operators). The cumulative distribution of machine delays from Figure 11-2 is graphed in Figure 11-4. Similarly, the graph of Figure 11-5 is taken from Figure 11-3, the distribution of service time per breakdown (based on present machine operators). For these last two graphs (Figures 11-4 and 11-5), the accumulated frequencies are constructed by starting with the lowest number of events, summing the frequencies, and plotting them. Thus, a percentage or probability scale is developed.

Events for this study can now be simulated through the use of a random number table (Appendix D). The random numbers will represent probabilities, shown as percentages in Figures 11-4 and 11-5. They are used to obtain machine delays and servicing time values in the problem. For example, random number 18 is selected to represent delays per hour in Figure 11-4. Starting at the right side of the chart, a horizontal line is drawn until it intersects the distribution curve. A vertical line is then dropped down to the x-axis (see dashed line on the graph). In this example, the delays per hour would be 19 for the first hour. Simulating in this manner from the cumulative distribution gives us the machine delays that are close to actual operating conditions. The same type of simulation is applicable in determining service times. A random number is selected for each delay and the service time is obtained from Figure 11–5. A conservation approach is used, that is, a random number of 20 is interpreted as eight minutes (see dashed line on the graph). For any hour of the study, the number of service calls is dependent upon the delays. In the first hour, 19 service times must be simulated since this number of delays was experienced through the use of random numbers. A simulated sample of three hours of machine servicing time is shown in Table 11–3.

Delays per Hour	Number of Occurrences	Relative Frequency (percent)	Cumulative Frequency (percent)
17 and under	19	5	5
18	35	9	14
19	40	10	24
20	74	19	43
21	95	24	67
22	70	18	85
23	45	10	95
Over 23	20	5	100

Minutes	Number of Occurrences	Relative Frequency (percent)	Cumulative Frequency (percent)
Under 7	18	5	5
7 to 8	82	25	30
8 to 9	136	40	70
9 to 10	82	25	95
Over 10	16	5	100

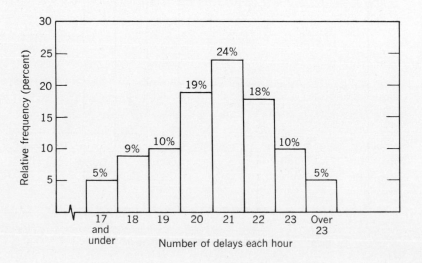

Figure 11–2
Distribution of machine delays per hour.

329

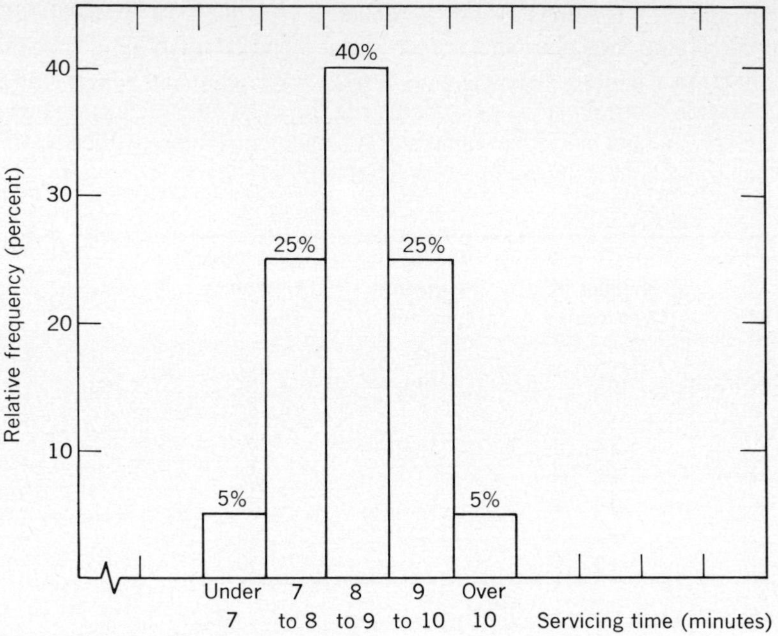

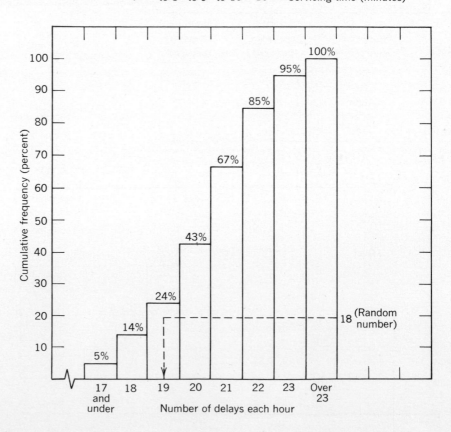

Figure 11–3
Distribution of downtime (minutes) for each time service is needed (based on present machine operators).

Figure 11–4
Cumulative percentage of machine delays per hour.

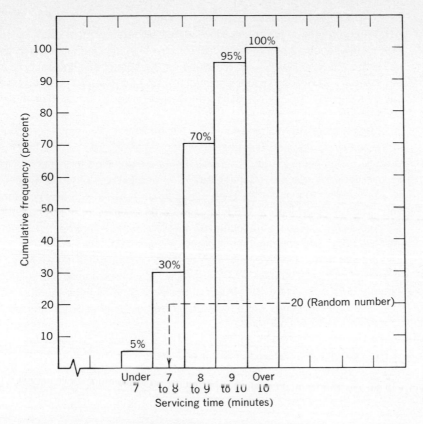

Figure 11–5
Cumulative percentage
of service time per
breakdown (based on
present machine
operators).

Simulation of Delays in One Hour		Simulation of Individual Servicing Time per Hour		Total Hourly Servicing Time Expressed in Minutes
Random Number	**Delays in Hour**	**Random Numbers**	**Individual Service Time in Minutes**	
18	19	20,68,57,79,84	8,9,9,10,10	
		72,95,08,85,79	10,10,8,10,10	
		34,40,67,24,86	9,9,9,8,10	
		54,35,81,07	9,9,10,8	175
09	18	88,30,90,90,88	10,8,10,10,10	
		72,22,75,69,86	10,8,10,9,10	
		45,48,32,63,00	9,9,9,9,7,	
		32,74,13	9,10,8	165
41	20	68,65,99,76,66	9,9,11,10,9	
		12,72,59,02,72	8,10,9,7,10	
		75,97,69,07,00	10,11,9,8,7	
		01,46,29,64,88	7,9,8,9,10	180

Table 11–3
Simulation Sample of
Three Hours of Machine
Servicing Time (Based on
Present Machine
Operators)

The simulated sample in Table 11–3 is based on the present machine operators performing the required repairs. However, consideration must be given to the fact that maintenance workers should have more skill and familiarity with machinery than machine operators. Thus, maintenance personnel should reduce the present service time (based on machine operators' service time) on each machine delay, say by two minutes. This fact is incorporated in Table 11–4, based on three and four servicemen.

The operators' waiting times in Table 11–4 for three servicemen were calculated in the following manner. The total servicing time required for the first hour of the study is 175 minutes (Table 11–3) which must be adjusted for faster service time of 38 minutes (2 minutes per service call × 19 delays) and personal time allowance of 30 minutes (10 minutes for each serviceman per hour × 3 men) during the first hour. The servicing time of 175 minutes less 38 minutes for greater efficiency plus 30 minutes for personal time totals 167 minutes for three servicemen. Thus, servicemen are not busy throughout the first hour, which means their busy time is 167 minutes with 13 minutes of idle time. Similarly, the operators are not waiting. The same type of calculations applies to all other rows. When moving to the columns representing four servicemen, 40 minutes of personal time must be considered.

Based upon an hourly wage including fringe benefits of $4 for maintenance personnel and $15 per hour for an idle automatic machine (rate includes profit lost in not producing parts and idle operator cost), the OR study indicates the employment of three service maintenance men is best, as shown in Table 11–5. This problem was worked manually, but it would have been better to utilize a computer for a larger sample, resulting in a more reliable answer. Nevertheless, the method used here gives a picture of what the computer program would be doing.

Table 11–4
Activity of Service
Maintenance Men*

		Three Servicemen				Four Servicemen			
Hour of Study	Total Servicing Minutes Required	Busy Time	Idle Time	Operators' Waiting Time	Cumulative Operators' Waiting Time	Busy Time	Idle Time	Operators' Waiting Time	Cumulative Operators' Waiting Time
		In Minutes				In Minutes			
1	137	167	13	—	—	177	63	—	—
2	129	159	21	—	—	169	71	—	—
3	140	170	10	—	—	180	60	—	—
4	167	180	—	17	17	207	33	—	—
5	119	149	31	—	—	159	81	—	—
6	179	180	—	29	29	219	21	—	—
7	105	135	45	—	—	145	95	—	—
8	130	160	20	—	—	170	70	—	—
9	150	180	—	—	—	190	50	—	—
10	166	180	—	16	16	206	34	—	—
11	141	171	9	—	7	181	59	—	—
12	155	180	—	5	12	195	45	—	—
					81 minutes				0 minutes

*(An allowance of ten minutes of each serviceman per hour for personal time is included in the activity before he is considered idle.)

Simulation is equally applicable to other maintenance problems. In particular its use can be helpful in determining an optimum policy for replacing machine parts, motors, tubes, transistors, light bulbs, and the like. Several maintenance procedures are available to the firm: (1) repair or replace the item when it fails, (2) repair or replace all items of the same kind when the first one fails, (3) repair or replace all items of the same kind and items that are comparable to the ones that failed, and (4) repair or replace the items after so many hours or weeks of use based on an estimated average service life. For these conditions, cumulative probability distributions are determined in order that random numbers, representing probability values, can be utilized to simulate experience. The simulation method set forth above can be used for these problems.

	Number of Maintenance Personnel	
	Three	Four
Total time lost by machines (operators) per Table 11–4	81 min.	— min.
Idle machine (operator) cost	$15/hour	$15/hour
Value of machines' (operators') lost time	$ 20.25	$ —
Total pay of maintenance personnel for 12 hours ($48 per man)	144.00	192.00
Total cost (idle machine and maintenance)	$164.25	$192.00

Determining Production-Inventory Levels

Simulation can not only be applied to certain phases of inventory, such as setting reorder points and determining usage during the reorder period, but also is rightfully applicable to integrating production scheduling models and inventory control models for a combined production-inventory system. The interaction of those two areas makes for a more involved simulation problem, requiring several steps.

The first step is a general decision model to forecast demand. After forecasting sales, the next step is to compute production rates according to some rule set forth by the OR group. The purpose of this decision rule is to specify an inventory position which the manufacturing manager considers ideal. This means that the production manager, at a point in time nearest to the present and still within control, would like to make a decision which will come as close as possible to a desired inventory position, subject to any technical constraints or changes in the production rate. This decision rule for calculating the desired inventory could be simple in form but, at the same time, must be flexible enough in its outcome. For example, inventory could be maintained at one-half month's forecasted sales. Once the desired inventory has been established, an initial value for the production rate is used. However, the rate is checked against the absolute limits (upper and lower) of manufacturing. It may have to be reset if it exceeds manufacturing limits. Also the production rate is checked against any relative upper and lower limits specified by the previous rate set. If exceeded, the production rate is reset. This rate is stored for use in the appropriate period during simulation.

The simulation model proceeds to generate demands for each day of the current manufacturing period. The generation of demand is under the control of the user, who has specified the seasonal and trend factors plus the actual forecasts. The user has the ability to vary the forecasts in order to determine the effect on the inventory decision rule. Daily production is added to inventory while demand is subtracted from inventory. Back orders are recorded when they occur and are filled from production, upon availability. Through simulation, average inventory and demand are tabulated. At the end of a period, say a week, two weeks, or a month, control is given to the decision model for a new rate to be set, based upon the current factors. Thus this simulation model allows the firm to relate the current factors of supply to demand.

The simulation model uses cost values for carrying costs of inventory, cost of being out of stock, and stockout costs to determine a near-optimal solution. The term "near" is used since the model is only as good as its forecasting ability, its inventory decision rule, and its cost factors, which may be only good estimates. However, the demand generator in a simulation model allows the user to control error in forecasting so that its effect on the model can be predicted. Only by testing with such models can one fit a decision rule to given conditions that will give the lowest cost basis to the firm and best service criterion to customers.

Minimizing Total Inventory Cost

To illustrate a straightforward inventory system using Monte Carlo simulation, attention must be focused initially on the objective of the inventory system. The aim of management is to operate the business so that total costs are at a minimum—the least total cost curve is the sum of the ordering costs, carrying costs, and lost revenue. Application of the Monte Carlo method requires that an event occur according to some probability density distribution for each variable that is to be sampled. First, the density function for demand (units) and delivery time (weeks) must be determined (illustrated in Tables 11–6 and 11–7 respectively) along with their cumulative probabilities. Likewise, corresponding random numbers are assigned that reflect the frequency of an event in the cumulative probability distribution. During the simulation process, random numbers are generated for demand and delivery time according to the Monte Carlo numbers assigned in Tables 11–6 and 11–7 respectively.

For this problem, a manual simulation is illustrated in Table 11–8. Fourteen weeks of operation were arbitrarily selected although several years of simulated data using a computer is recommended. For the simulation process, the reordering point level is set at 15 units and the ordering quantity variable is 20 units. Inventory carrying costs have been computed to be $10 per unit per week, and the cost of placing an order is $25. Also, the lost revenue (selling price less costs) per unit of stockout is $100 per day or $500 per week.

To illustrate the simulation process per Table 11–8, we will start with an inventory on hand of 20 units at the beginning of the first week. Based on a simulated demand of 4 units (random number 68 represents 4 units of demand per Table 11–6) in the first week, the balance at the end of the first week is 16 units (20 units less 4 units), which is still higher than the reordering point level of 15 units. For the second week, demand is simulated to be 3 units, resulting in an ending inventory of 13 units. Since the balance is below the reordering level, the delivery time of two weeks (random number 50 represents a delivery time of two weeks per Table 11–7) is generated. Hence, delivery is expected in two weeks. As indicated in the fourth week, 20 units are received into inventory. The rest of the table follows the foregoing simulation procedures.

Moving on to the inventory carrying costs, ordering costs, and lost revenue columns in Table 11–8, calculations are made in the following manner. In the first week, 16 units on hand are multiplied by the weekly carrying costs of $10 per unit, which totals $160 for the first week. Similarly, the calculated carrying costs for the second week are $130 plus the ordering costs of $25, totaling $155. All other weeks are calculated in this manner. However, demand during the eleventh week cannot be met, resulting in an out-of-stock condition. The result of not being able to meet the demand of one unit is $500 of lost revenue for the week. Based upon averaging the total cost column in Table 11–8, the problem has been solved in terms of an average weekly inventory cost of $198.21.

There are other important factors in this inventory problem. Utilizing a computer, management can reevaluate its total inventory costs by varying the carrying cost per unit, the ordering cost, and the lost revenue. Thus, management can ask, "What would the result be if . . ." and expect a reasonably accurate answer employing simulation procedures.

Demand (Units)	Frequency	Cumulative Probability Distribution	Distribution of Random Numbers
0	2	2	00–01
1	8	10	02–09
2	22	32	10–31
3	34	66	32–65
4	18	84	66–83
5	9	93	84–92
6	7	100	93–99

Table 11–6
Cumulative Probability Distribution and Distribution of Random Numbers for Customer Demand (units)

Delivery Time (Weeks)	Frequency	Cumulative Probability Distribution	Distribution of Random Numbers
1	23	23	00–22
2	45	68	23–67
3	17	85	68–84
4	9	94	85–93
5	6	100	94–99

Table 11–7
Cumulative Probability Distribution and Distribution of Random Numbers for Delivery Time (weeks)

Chapter Summary

A major stimulant to using simulation lies in its ability to deal with complex, dynamic, and interacting phenomena. If the process or phenomena permit quantitative description, they can be modeled and experiments can be simulated. Unlike analytical optimization solutions, simulation models tend to be better descriptions of reality. The availability of more powerful and less costly computer systems has and will continue to hasten the growth of simulation.

The method of conducting a simulation study revolves around the planned approach. The most critical step in the study is the construction of a model which is simple enough to permit experimentation and yet complete enough to capture the relevant aspects of the business situation being simulated. The test of a simulation model is its ability to capture the essence of reality with a minimum of details. A prerequisite for model construction is a clear definition of the objective for the study. An increasingly important phase of any simulation model is using random numbers (or a random number generator) to simulate the process of the real world. It should be remembered that new knowledge about the real world, caused by the dynamic nature of business, can be a basis for reevaluating the simulation study.

Table 11–8

Fourteen-Week Simulation
of Demand, Delivery,
Inventory, and Total Costs

	Demand		Delivery		Inventory		Inventory			
Week	Random Number	Demand (Units)	Random Number	Delivery (Weeks)	Units Rec'd	Bal. on Hand	Carrying Costs	Ordering Costs	Lost Revenue	Total Costs
0						20				
1	68	4				16	$160			$160
2	52	3				13	130			
			50	2				$25		155
3	90	5				8	80			80
4	59	3			20	25	250			250
5	08	1				24	240			240
6	72	4				20	200			200
7	44	3				17	170			170
8	95	6				11	110			
			85	4				25		135
9	81	4				7	70			70
10	93	6				1	10			10
11	28	2				0			$500	500
12	89	5			20	15	150			
			15	1				25		175
13	60	3			20	32	320			320
14	03	1				31	310			310
	Average weekly cost $198.21									

Questions

1. Distinguish between the Monte Carlo simulation method and the system simulation method.
2. How practical are large-scale simulation models of the firm? Explain.
3. It has been said that certain types of business problems can be solved more easily by using OR techniques other than simulation. What problem types may they be and why?
4. In addition to those areas mentioned in the chapter where simulation has been applied, where else can it be applied?

Model Formulation Exercises

1. Although simulation has been applied effectively in modeling and solving many business problems, what are some of the shortcomings of applying simulation to business games? In other words, why does simulation work well at solving management problems, but fail, to a large degree, at modeling executive decisions in a business game environment?

2. In the modeling of a business game, what other modules in addition to marketing, manufacturing, and financing could be included for a more representative model of the typical business firm?

3. In the formulation of simulation problems, why should the difficulty of finding good or near-optimal solutions increase as the number of variables are added?

4. In the problem presented in the chapter for determining the size of the maintenance force, the cumulative percentages of machine delays per hour (Figure 11–4) and the cumulative percentages of service time per breakdown (Figure 11–5) were illustrated in graphic form. What is another method of presenting this information for simulating the problem?

5. In the simulation of the problem in the chapter involving the minimization of total inventory cost, would there be much difference in the answer given for the small sample of 14 weeks and that of simulating several years on the computer? In other words, how sensitive is the final answer to various sample sizes?

Mathematical Exercises

1. The King Manufacturing Corporation is concerned about its solvency if a recession should hit the firm. The risk of cash insolvency can be defined as the probability that the firm's cash balance will fall below zero at the end of a recession. Using the assumption that the firm's outstanding debt can be success-

fully refunded at maturity, the firm's cash balance at the end of the recession (C_e) is given as follows:

$$C_e = C_b + \widetilde{R} - \widetilde{V} - F - I - \widetilde{T}$$

where C_b = cash balance at beginning of recession (initial cash balance of $350,000)

R = collections on accounts receivable during recession

V = total variable cash expense during recession, excludes federal income taxes ($0.60 on $1 of sales)

F = total fixed cash expenses during recession, excludes interest ($20,000 = daily fixed cash expenses and $2,000 = daily fixed noncash expenses)

I = total interest payment during recession (rate of 0.03 percent per day) on a debt of $2,500,000 in its capital structure

T = total federal income tax payments during recession (50 percent rate)

Since the sales volume is a random variable, the $\sim$ sign is used to distinguish random variables from constants. The probability distributions of recession sales and recession collection periods are given below:

Probability Distribution of Daily Sales During Recession	
Sales	Probability
$80,000	.1
70,000	.4
60,000	.4
50,000	.1

Probability Distribution of Increment in Collection Period During Recession (S = Daily Sales During Recession)				
Increment in Collection Period	Probability			
	$S = \$80,000$	$S = \$70,000$	$S = \$60,000$	$S = \$50,000$
10 days	.5	.4	.1	.1
20 days	.2	.3	.2	.2
30 days	.2	.2	.3	.2
40 days	.1	.1	.4	.5

Since we know the probability distributions of recession sales and recession collection periods, the equation to determine the firm's risk of cash insolvency (the probability that the firm's ending cash balance is negative) can be used.

Based upon a recession during the next 360 days (one year), what is the probability that the firm will become insolvent? Rather than simulating the problem, determine what steps would be involved in solving the problem.

2. Electron Manufacturing, Inc., is a manufacturer of specialized electrical measuring devices. The lead time of obtaining the needed materials for production is shown in Table 1. The probability of material shortages during the past year is given in Table 2. For the 20 devices just placed into production, what is the average delay that can be expected because of material shortages? Assume that the past will be representative of the future.

Table 1

Lead Time/Materials	Probability	Cumulative Probability
1 week	.10	.10
2 weeks	.15	.25
3 weeks	.20	.45
4 weeks	.25	.70
5 weeks	.25	.95
6 weeks	.05	1.00

Table 2

Material Shortages	Probability	Cumulative Probability
5 items	.10	.10
4 items	.20	.30
3 items	.20	.50
2 items	.30	.80
1 item	.10	.90
0 item	.10	1.00

3. The Public Service Commission is considering the employment of an additional filing clerk in its Motor Carrier Insurance Department. The filing clerk is responsible for processing insurance filings for truck owners so that they may legally transport commodities in this state. Each clerk works eight hours per day and is paid at the rate of $2.50 per hour. There are presently two clerks. Since the work being performed is a public service, the idle time of truck owners waiting to have their insurance filed is determined to be $5 per hour. Waiting time should be computed in excess of eight hours in order to complete the processing of the filings for that day.

Given below are the number of filings per day and the processing times along with their respective frequencies:

Number of Filings Per Day	Frequency	Processing Times— Minutes Per Filing	Frequency
60	30	6	10
70	10	8	25
80	15	10	35
90	10	21	20
100	35	14	10

Based on the foregoing data, should another clerk be hired?

4. The Automatic Machinery Company receives a different number of orders each day and the orders vary in the time required to process them. The firm is interested in determining how many machines it should have in the department to minimize the combined cost of machine idle time and order waiting time. In addition, the firm knows the average number of orders per day and the average number of hours per order. However, the number of machines that will result in minimum total variable costs cannot be analytically determined because analytical approaches do not take into account the sequential pattern of the number of orders or the sequential pattern of the number of hours to process an order. The firm has turned to you with the following data for a solution:

Probability Distribution— No. of Orders Per Day	
No. of Orders	Probability
0	.10
1	.15
2	.25
3	.30
4	.15
5	.05

Probability Distribution— No. of Hours Per Order	
Hours/Order	Probability
5	.05
10	.05
15	.10
20	.10
25	.20
30	.25
35	.15
40	.10

Cost/hour of idle machine time = $4/hour

Cost/hour for orders back-ordered per day = $6/hour

What is the best approach for solving the problem? Solve using this approach.

5. The Orlando Manufacturing Company has a large machine which contains three identical vacuum tubes that are the major cause of downtime. The current practice is to replace the tubes as they fail. A proposal has been made to replace all three tubes whenever any one of them fails in order to reduce the frequency with which the equipment must be shut down. The objective, then, is to compare these alternatives on a cost basis. Presently, the equipment must be shut down for one hour to replace one tube or for two and one quarter hours to replace all three tubes. The total cost associated with shutting down the equipment and replacing the tubes is $30 an hour in terms of lost production. The cost of each vacuum tube is $10. The probability distribution between breakdowns, based upon past experience for replacing one tube, is given as follows:

Hours Between Breakdowns Before Replacing Each Tube	Probability
20	.05
40	.10
55	.30
70	.30
85	.20
100	.05

The probability distribution between breakdowns, based upon limited experience for three tubes, is given as follows:

Hours Between Breakdowns Before Replacing Three Tubes	Probability
170	.10
175	.20
180	.40
185	.20
190	.10

Simulating this problem, what is the best policy for the firm—replace one or all three vacuum tubes at a time? Outline alternative approaches to the solution of the problem.

6. The Progressive Manufacturing Company has 20 machines which are basically alike and run eight hours per day. These machines break down from time to time despite the preventive maintenance practices of the firm. Four repairmen are on duty during the eight hours. The machines are such that only one repairman can work on them at a time. Sometimes more than four machines are down simultaneously while at other times all repairmen are idle. Even more frequently, two and three men are idle. Management is questioning the need for four repairmen. The data compiled by the operations research analyst indicates there is one chance in ten that a machine will break down in any given hour. A study of the necessary repairs discloses this probability distribution:

Time Required to Repair Each Machine	Probability
20 min.	.05
25 min.	.25
30 min.	.35
35 min.	.30
40 min.	.05

The cost of idle machine time to the firm is $8 an hour while the repairman hourly rate, including fringe benefits, is $4 an hour. Allow ten minutes per hour for each repairman's personal time. Based upon the foregoing data, what is the optimum number of repairmen for the firm?

Bibliography

D. C. Basil, P. R. Cone, and J. A. Fleming, *Executive Decision Making Through Simulation,* Columbus, O.: Charles E. Merrill, 1965.

D. N. Charafas, *Systems and Simulation,* New York: Academic Press, 1965.

J. R. Emshoff and R. L. Sisson, *Computer Simulation Models,* New York: The Macmillan Company, 1970.

G. W. Evans, G. F. Wallace, and G. L. Sutherland, *Simulation Using Digital Computers,* Englewood Cliffs, N.J.: Prentice-Hall, 1969.

G. S. Fishman, *Concepts and Methods in Discrete Event Digital Simulation,* New York: John Wiley & Sons, 1973.

G. Gordon, *System Simulation,* Englewood Cliffs, N.J.: Prentice-Hall, 1969.

F. S. Hillier and G. J. Lieberman, *Operations Research,* San Francisco: Holden-Day, 1974.

C. McMillan and R. F. Gonzalez, *Systems Analysis, A Computer Approach to Decision Models,* Homewood, Ill.: Richard D. Irwin, 1968.

R. Meier, W. T. Newell, and H. L. Pazer, *Simulation in Business and Economics,* Englewood Cliffs, N.J.; Prentice-Hall, 1969.

J. H. Mize and J. G. Cox, *Essentials of Simulation,* Englewood Cliffs, N.J.: Prentice-Hall, 1968.

T. H. Naylor, J. L. Balintfy, D. S. Burdick, and D. Chu, *Computer Simulation Techniques*, New York: John Wiley & Sons, 1966.

T. H. Naylor, *Computer Simulation Experiments with Models of Economic Systems*, New York: John Wiley & Sons, 1971.

A. Newell and H. A. Simon, *Human Problem Solving*, Englewood Cliffs, N.J.: Prentice-Hall, 1972.

J. W. Schmidt and R. E. Taylor, *Simulation and Analysis of Industrial Systems*, Homewood, Ill.: Richard D. Irwin, 1970.

C. H. Springer, R. E. Herlihy, and R. I. Beggs, *Advanced Methods and Models*, Homewood, Ill.: Richard D. Irwin, 1965.

K. D. Tocher, *The Art of Simulation*, London: The English Universities Press, 1963.

Part VI

Future of Operations Research

Chapter 12

Operations Research — Present And Future

Chapter Objectives
☐ To present operations research techniques not found in previous chapters that center on solving well-structured business problems.
☐ To demonstrate the use of combined OR methods, such as venture analysis, to solve complex business problems.
☐ To formulate procedures using heuristics or "rules of thumb" for solving poorly structured business problems.
☐ To set forth the current state of behavioral models that incorporate the human element as an essential part of the model-building process.
☐ To show the present and future directions of operations research within a business framework.

Chapter Outline
Integer Programming
Nonlinear Programming
Goal Programming
Venture Analysis
Heuristic Programming
Behavioral Models
Operations Research at Present
Operations Research in the Future
Conclusion
Questions
Bibliography

Operations research will take on new and exciting directions as newer techniques and variations of established techniques are added to the available quantitative tools. Additional current "tools of the trade" that have been developed and are expected to be expanded in the future to solve well-structured problems are *integer programming, nonlinear programming,* and *goal programming.*

In addition to these techniques, a most important trend is currently developing in operations research. It involves the combining of different OR methods to produce new quantitative techniques. Instead of being concerned with the maximization of profits or minimization of costs in one selected area, the trend is to include many or all functional relationships in a system. For example, operations research groups are building mathematical models to include the entire life cycle of a new product in order to maximize profits in the long run. One such approach, called *venture analysis,* will become more prevalent in the future and will undoubtedly provide a new thrust in solving operations research problems.

Although this book has concentrated on "well-structured" business problems (all of the constraints and variables are set forth with quantified values in a mathematical model) that have been successfully solved by OR groups, there is a growing trend to solve problems that are "poorly structured," sometimes called "ill-structured." Unfortunately, the most difficult and pressing problems facing managers tend to be poorly structured—ones that cannot be stated in a precise mathematical model with appropriate values for solution. The approach used in their solution involves programming them on a computer *heuristically.* This means employing "rules of thumb" to explore the most likely paths in arriving at a conclusion rather than examining all of the possible alternatives to find the optimum one.

Behavioral models, an emerging and dynamic direction for operations researchers, represent an attempt to merge the behavioral and quantitative schools of management thought. They are presented here as they can be developed within the framework of the planned approch. The present and future directions of operations research are treated, with the focus on how management can best utilize OR to improve its planning, organizing, directing, and controlling functions. The book concludes with a discussion centering on the real function of operations research, i.e., assisting management in reaching optimal (or near-optimal) decisions.

Integer Programming

A class of programming problems which is obtained from the general linear programming model by imposing the additional requirements that the variables can take on only integral values is referred to as *integer linear programming*.[1] It is adaptable to problems that allow only whole numbers for the final solution. For example, assume that an optimum production plan requires buying several different types of machines. Obviously, only whole machines can be bought. Other applications include allocation of salesmen to sales districts, capital budgeting for research and development, and optimum location of warehouses.

Although it is tempting to round off noninteger solutions in problems involving indivisible resources (especially if the rounding is small relative to the values of the variables involved), such rounding can result in solutions far from the optimal integer solution, as shown in Figure 12–1 for two products. The best solution in the noninteger problem is at point *A* while point *B* represents the rounded solution (the closest integer point to point *A*). Nevertheless, point *C* produces the best contribution on an integer programming basis.

In Figure 12–2, the best convex region of a linear programming problem is shown. When the integer restriction is imposed, the feasible solution set contains only the critical points. By adding new restraining lines connecting the outside integer points, we can pretend the entire convex set of points, bounded by the axes and the new constraints, is a new problem. Its characteristics are such that the feasible region contains all integer points contained in the original feasible region and every extreme point of the new feasible region is an integer point. The linear programming chapter demonstrated that optimal solutions occur at extreme points.

A variation of integer programming is *mixed integer linear programming*. This technique applies to problems in which some of the variables are continuous while others have only integer values. For example, a container manufacturer must cut various sizes of blanks from sheet stock with minimum waste. One of the restrictions is that whole blanks must be cut from sheets. Thus, mixed integer linear programming is more applicable for this kind of problem than linear programming is. This OR technique has been applied to production planning, investment analysis, and similar problems.

[1]For more details, refer to: Robert J. Thierauf and Robert C. Klekamp, *Decision Making Through Operations Research*, 2d Ed., New York: John Wiley & Sons, 1975, pp. 383–409.

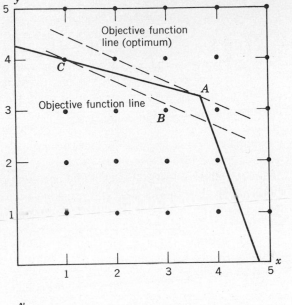

Figure 12–1
Linear programming problem with possible integer solutions.

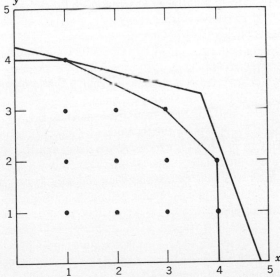

Figure 12–2
Linear programming problem with integer restrictions imposed.

Nonlinear Programming

Nonlinear programming problems which have been studied extensively are those in which the constraints are linear and the objective function is nonlinear.[2] Consider, for example, a durable consumer product whose production time remains the

[2]For more details, refer to Thierauf and Klekamp, loc. cit.

same as volume is increased. However, in order to sell more and more of the product, the price must be reduced, resulting in a nonlinear objective function. Other problems of this type include promotion expenditures, advertising campaign expenditures, and distribution analyses. For many of these problems, the objective function is written as the sum of a linear form plus a quadratic form, that is, the objective function contains squared terms. Computational procedures for finding optimal solutions have been developed when the objective function has certain properties. In some cases, calculus methods can be employed to solve the problem. In other cases, *quadratic programming* procedures are more effective in solving the problem. Fortunately, the simplex method can be modified for quadratic programming problems.

Other problems that are solvable by nonlinear programming methods include those whose objective function and constraints are nonlinear. In addition to a nonlinear objective function for a durable consumer product, the production constraints may exhibit nonlinear characteristics, caused by working the manufacturing departments overtime. As production line personnel work longer hours each day, their efficiency decreases, resulting in nonlinear constraints rather than linear constraints within the problem.

Specialized Nonlinear Programming Procedures For many nonlinear programming problems, the computational procedures may not always yield an optimal solution in a finite number of steps. One must settle for procedures that provide only an approximate optimal solution or may require an infinite number of steps for convergence. This is in contrast with the simplex algorithm of linear programming in which an optimal answer is obtained within a finite number of steps.

To ensure that an optimal solution for problems with nonlinear constraints can be obtained, stringent restrictions must be placed on both the constraints and the objective function. One technique for solving problems which have nonlinear constraints is the *classical optimization method*. This technique, based on calculus, is a theoretical tool. Classical optimization techniques can be generalized to handle cases in which the variables are required to be nonnegative and the constraints may be inequalities. These generalizations are primarily of theoretical value and do not usually constitute computational procedures. Another technique to solve this class of problems is searching for a *tangency case* and employing calculus methods for a final solution. Not only are the simplex algorithm and calculus methods used for solving nonlinear programming problems, but also other computational procedures are employed, such as dynamic programming (see Chapter 8).

The *gradient method* or the steepest ascent (descent) method, like the simplex method, is an iterative process which moves from one feasible solution to another in order to improve the value of the objective function. If the objective function is envisioned as a surface in space, this method takes steps in the locally steeped direction that lead either up or down the curved surface until a peak, valley, or some upper or lower constraint is reached. As with ordinary maxima-minima, this process is not limited to the three-dimensional slopes that can be visualized. Calculus techniques, computing what is called the gradient vector, can lead through iterative steps to reach a solution. The gradient method differs from the simplex method since it does not guarantee that each successive solution will be nearer the optimum and may require an infinite number of iterations for convergence. This method, which is designed for use on computers, can be used when both the objective function and the constraints contain nonlinearities.

One of the easiest ways for solving nonlinear programming (like integer programming) problems is to transform them into a form that permits application of linear programming. The nature of the transformation required to change a nonlinear (or integer) programming problem into an acceptable form for the simplex method varies with the type of problem being studied. While some problems require no approximation, others do. In any event, these should be as accurate as possible. The simplex algorithm, then, proves to be one of the most powerful devices for solving nonlinear or integer programming problems.

Goal Programming

Goal programming is a special application of linear programming, capable of handling a single goal with multiple subgoals, or multiple goals with multiple subgoals.[3] In this sense, conventional linear programming is a special case of goal programming which consists of a single goal with single or multiple subgoals. In conventional linear programming methods, the objective function must be unidirectional — either to maximize profits (or effectiveness) or to minimize costs. It is this unidirectional quality of the objective function that limits the application of the simplex method to aggregate production planning.

Since goal programming is capable of handling multiple goals in multiple dimensions, conversion of various factors to costs or profits may no longer be necessary. In other words, two hours of idle time in work group *A* or two hours of overtime in work group *B* do not have to be expressed in terms of estimated costs. Since the multiple goals are often achieved only to the detriment of one another, a hierarchy of importance among these goals is required. This allows consideration of low-order goals only after higher-order goals are fulfilled. Therefore, various kinds of problems can be solved if management provides a ranking of goals in terms of their contribution or importance to the organization.

Management, for instance, might consider the costs of shortages to be higher than costs of changing the employment level, and the latter costs to be higher than inventory costs, thus establishing three separate goals (the levels of production, employment, and inventories). The hierarchy among these incompatible multiple goals may be set in such a way that those with lower priorities are considered only after higher-priority goals are satisfied or have reached points beyond which they cannot be improved under the given conditions. This implies that there could be deviations from some or all goals, although the aim is to get as close to these goals as possible within the given constraints.

[3]Sang Lee and Veekko Jaaskelainen, "Goal Programming: Management's Math Model," *Industrial Engineering*, February 1971, pp. 30–35.

If shortages of one product are considered more critical than shortages of some other product, the largest weight should be assigned to the *deviational variables* for that product. In other words, we can assign differential weights to each variable within the same hierarchial order group, provided that they are in the same dimension.

The same reasoning can be applied to all variables. If it is more important to avoid underemployment in some groups than in others, different weights could be assigned to variables in the various groups. Similarly, different weights could be assigned to deviations from goals in the lowest-order group, representing excess inventories. In order to minimize the capital employed in production, goal programming minimizes the sum of each of the deviational variables in the objective function multiplied by the weights assigned to these variables.

In the simplex method, deviations from goals are designated as slack variables and are used only as dummy variables. In goal programming, these deviations, either positive or negative, are real variables and the objective function is expressed only by these variables. Once the goal programming model is developed, the computational algorithm is almost identical to the procedure followed in the simplex method.

Production Planning through Goal Programming   To illustrate goal programming, consider a manufacturing plant which has a current operational capacity of 500 hours a day. With this capacity, the company produces two products: *A* and *B*. Production of either product requires one hour in the plant. Because of the limited sales demand, only 300 units of product *A* and 400 units of product *B* can be sold. The profit from the sale of product *A* is $10, whereas the profit from product *B* is $5.

The president of the company has listed the following goals in order of importance:

1. Avoid underutilization or production capacity.
2. Sell as many units as possible; however, since the profit from the sale of product *A* is twice that of product *B*, he is doubly anxious to achieve the sales goal for product *A* relative to product *B*.
3. Reduce overtime.

He must choose a strategy which will achieve all of his goals as nearly as possible.

Since overtime is allowed, production may take more than 500 hours of operating time. The operational capacity may be expressed as follows:

$$x_1 + x_2 + d_1^- - d_1^+ = 500$$

where $x_1 =$ the number of product *A* to be manufactured

$x_2 =$ the number of product *B* to be manufactured

$d_1^- =$ idle time when production of products *A* and *B* does not exhaust production capacity

$d_1^+ =$ overtime operation

The number of products that can be sold for A and B is expressed as follows:

$x_1 + d_2^- = 300$

$x_2 + d_3^- = 400$

where d_2^- = underachievement of sales goals for product A

d_3^- = underachievement of sales goals for product B

In addition to these variables and constraints, priority factors must be assigned to the deviations from the goals as follows:

P_1—the highest priority assigned by management to the underutilization of production capacity: d_1^-.

P_2—the priority factor assigned to the underutilization of sales capacity: d_2^- and d_3^-. Also, management wishes to assign twice the importance to d_2^- as that assigned to d_3^-.

P_3—the priority factor assigned to the overtime in the production operation: d_1^+.

Based on the foregoing constraints, the goal programming model can be formulated per Figure 12–3. The objective is the minimization of deviations from goals. Hence, the objective function is expressed only in terms of the deviational variables. The deviational variable associated with the highest preemptive priority must first be minimized to the fullest possible extent. When no further improvement is possible in the highest priority order group, the deviations associated with the next highest priority are minimized. The optimal solution to the above problem can be obtained by applying the simplex method of linear programming.

$$\text{Minimize:} \quad Z = P_1 d_1^- + 2P_2 d_2^- + P_2 d_3^- + P_3 d_1^+$$

$$\text{Subject to:} \quad x_1 + x_2 + d_1 \qquad\qquad - d_1^+ = 500$$

$$x_1 \qquad\quad + d_2^- \qquad\qquad = 300$$

$$x_2 \qquad\qquad + d_3^- \quad = 400$$

$$x_1, \quad x_2, \quad d_1^-, \quad d_2^-, \quad d_3^-, d_1^+ \geq 0$$

Figure 12–3
Goal programming model for the production of products A and B.

Venture Analysis

One of the most extensive and sophisticated mathematical models that utilizes various OR methods for assessing uncertainty and risk is called *venture analysis*.[4] Its purpose is to analyze logically and quickly, any investment opportunity that may be offered to a company. For example, a company might consider introducing a

[4]Franz Edelman and Joel S. Greenberg, "Venture Analysis: The Assessment of Uncertainty and Risk," *Financial Executive*, August 1969, pp. 56–62.

new product (Figure 12–4), acquiring another company, building a new plant, or modernizing its distribution system. Whatever the objective, the computer evaluates the interactions of all the factors that might influence the project and the company's cash flow. With answers that the computer provides, a company is better able to maximize its profit at minimal risk.

When the introduction of a new product is being considered, several problem areas are troublesome to the manager engendering a desire to delay decisions until a more sound basis can be developed for choosing among the many alternatives. The major problems are (1) the complexity of the market plus investment and cost factors influencing profitability of the venture, (2) the multitude of alternatives to be evaluated quantitatively before selecting a course of action, (3) the risks introduced by forecast uncertainties, and (4) the possible counteractions by customers and competitors.

Venture analysis considers these problems and evaluates alternate strategies, thereby permitting more explicit consideration of the risks introduced by the forecast uncertainties and the potential counteractions of customers and competitors (who must adjust their tactics in the face of a new factor in the market). Thus, for the commercialization of a new product, venture analysis is extremely helpful for developing decisions in the early stages of planning. As might be expected, this type of analysis relies heavily on computer programming and processing.

Figure 12–4
Venture analysis—basic steps in marketing a new product.

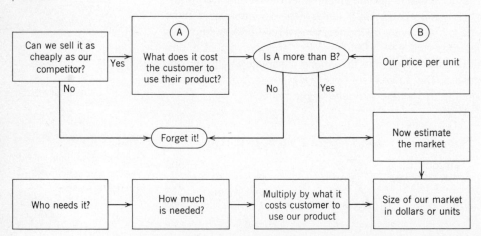

Simulation of Venture Analysis Model A typical venture analysis model is a simulation model. All inputs are communicated to the model through a dialogue between management-user and the computer time-sharing system. The dialogue consists of answering a series of questions posed by the model. The answers form the data base for a particular analysis. A teletype keyboard or video display terminal may be used for purposes of the dialogue.

The basic inputs to the model are of two types: probabilistic (i.e., uncertain) and deterministic (i.e., assumed known). Sales, cost of sales, capital purchases, engineering expenses, and general and administrative expenses are treated as probabilistic quantities, that is, uncertainty is considered. Interest rate, corporate assessment rate, number of years to be considered, depreciation life, depreciation type, and the like are considered to be deterministic, or known precisely. The probabilistic data conveys to the model management's assessment of the uncertainty associated with each of the key variables. It consists of management's subjective estimates of the likelihood that the variables will attain specified values.

A set of standard financial computations are performed, thereby determining values of profit, cash flow, return on assets, and similar items. These computations are repeated a large number of times employing different combinations of values for the key variables, as described by management's uncertainty assessments. Each repetition of the computation produces new values (profit, cash flow, etc.). This information establishes the risk profiles of the performance measures. The risk profiles—the model outputs—are printed on the same teletype keyboard or video display used to supply the input data. The outputs are available within a few minutes of entering the data. Upon management review and evaluation, necessary input changes can be made and the computations repeated.

The values of key input variables and their uncertainty profiles are functions of many factors. For example, revenue is a function of selling price, total market, and market share. Thus, these factors may be interrelated; market share is a function of relative selling price, total market is a function of selling price, selling price may be related to manufacturing cost, and manufacturing cost may be a function of quantity manufactured, which is related to market size. No attempt has been made here to define these complex interrelationships within the model. Instead, it is assumed that meaningful estimates, based on a detailed analysis performed outside of the venture analysis model, can be made for all pertinent data.

The venture analysis model, in essence, is a management laboratory in which managers can experiment before the fact with a variety of investment alternatives. One experiment may consist of choosing a set of specific values for the key input variables, then utilizing these values to compute after-tax profit, cash flow, indebtedness, payback period, return on assets, and present worth (discounted cash flow). In each experiment, the choice of values for key variables is based upon random sampling of the variables' probability distribution—the uncertainty profiles. The experiment is then repeated a large number of times, each time choosing from the specified uncertainty profiles a new set of values for the key variables and computing an after-tax profit. In this manner, frequency distributions—the number of times the computed results fall within specific intervals—are created for each of the computed quantities. The risk profiles are obtained directly from the frequency distributions and represent the chance that the committed quantity will exceed various specified values.

Heuristic Programming

Heuristic programming, as it is known in OR literature, has its roots in the artificial intelligence research of Herbert Simon of Carnegie Institute of Technology, together with Allen Newell of Carnegie and J. C. Shaw of the Rand Corporation.[5] Their goal in artificial intelligence research is to write programs instructing the computer how to behave in a way that, in human beings, would be called intelligent. Given enough observations, experiments, analysis, and modeling, they can instruct a digital computer to process information as humans do.

A simplified definition of *heuristic programming* that utilizes the computer as a major tool of analysis is given as follows:

> Heuristic programming utilizes rules of thumb or intuitive rules and guidelines and is generally under computer control to explore the most likely paths and to make educated guesses in arriving at a problem's solution rather than going through all of the possible alternatives to obtain an optimum one.

Because of the reliance on computers, most heuristic programming problems take the form of a set of instructions to solve a problem—the way the user might do it with enough time. To cover all contingencies likely to occur in a problem, generally a group of heuristics are needed. Since these heuristics are much too difficult to follow at the user's pace of problem solving, the computer identifies and evaluates the more feasible alternatives quickly and accurately.

Inasmuch as a computer heuristic program, like a computer algorithm, terminates in a finite number of steps, a heuristic program produces a *good* answer while an algorithm gives an *optimal* one. Although an algorithm appears better on the surface than a heuristic approach, many so-called algorithms end up in actual practice as heuristic programs because judgments have to be made by the user in their application which negate their optimality. Their principal difference is that a heuristic program can be constructed rather freely in a common-sense, intuitive manner. On the other hand, an algorithm must be constructed based on a mathematical model so that its optimality proofs can be substantiated. Thus, a computerized heuristic program actually appears preferable to an algorithm for many of the poorly structured and well-structured problems facing the firm.

Project Scheduling through Heuristic Programming A heuristic program for project scheduling,[6] shown in Figure 12–5, is based on three heuristics:

1. Allocate resources (workers) serially in time. This means to start on the first day and schedule all jobs possible, then do the same for the second day, and so forth.
2. Give preference to jobs with the least slack when several jobs compete for the same resources.
3. Reschedule noncritical jobs, if possible, in order to free resources for critical jobs having no slack.

---

[5] For more details, refer to Thierauf and Klekamp, op. cit., pp. 521–39.

[6] The source for material in this section is: Jerome D. Wiest, "Heuristic Programs for Decision Making," *Harvard Business Review,* 1966, pp. 140–43.

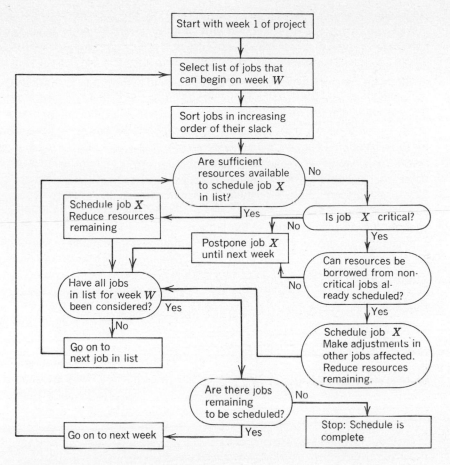

Figure 12–5
Heuristic program for scheduling a project. (Week *W* is week under consideration; job *X* is job under consideration.)

To demonstrate how these three heuristic rules operate within the computer program, they will be applied to one part of the main project. This subsection of the project consists of jobs, each of which requires a certain amount of time and a given number of workers (Table 12–1). The assumptions for this group of jobs are: all eight workers are interchangeable; jobs are undertaken only if sufficient personnel are available for the entire week; and certain jobs must be completed before others can begin. For example, job 8 in Table 12–1 cannot begin until jobs 5 and 6 have been completed.

The subsection under study can be illustrated as a network diagram in which each job appears as an arrow and each connection (small circles) indicates the predecessor relationship. This is depicted in Figure 12–6, where a horizontal time scale indicates the period during which the job is active. It should be noted that all jobs are started as early as their predecessors will allow. Dashed lines indicate slack time in the network. The number above each arrow indicates the job number; the number in brackets shows the number of workers required. The personnel requirements in Figure 12–6 were calculated by summing vertically the crew size of all jobs active during a specific week. For example, personnel requirements for the fourth week are 5 workers for job 5 plus 4 workers for job 6 plus 5 workers for job 7, or 14 workers.

Since we have only 8 workers available to assign to the project in any one week, we will have a problem from the beginning of the second scheduled week through the end of the fifth scheduled week. The problem is how to allocate the workers in order to complete the project as soon as possible. One way to find the shortest feasible schedule would be to enumerate all possible schedules. For the first week, there is only one possible choice of jobs (job 1), whereas for the second week, with three jobs available, there are several possible combinations. Each of these combinations represents a branch on a tree diagram and multiple choices fan out from each of these on succeeding weeks. A tree of all possible schedules is very large even for this small subsection of the project. The heuristic program trims this tree significantly since it selects just one branch at each decision point. Occasionally, the heuristic program will retrace its steps to see if a better branch can be found.

Starting with the first week and using the first heuristic (allocate workers serially in time), only job 1 is available to start in this period. There are sufficient workers to schedule it, that is, the 8 workers required for job 1 during the first week of the project equals the 8 workers available. Slack is zero since it is a job on the critical path.

Table 12–1

Subsection of a Larger Project—Time and Men Required

Job Number	Preceding Jobs	Time (Weeks)	Number of Men Required
1	—	1	8
2	1	2	4
3	1	2	2
4	1	1	4
5	4	3	5
6	3	2	4
7	2	2	5
8	5 and 6	1	8
9	8	2	8

Figure 12–6

Network diagrams for subsection of a larger project—time and men required.

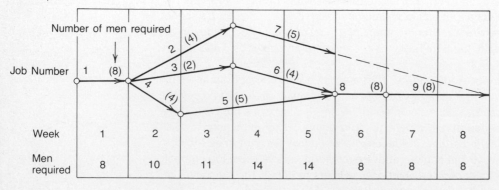

For the second week, three jobs, jobs 2 through 4, can be started. However, not enough workers are available to schedule these three jobs since they require 10 workers. The second heuristic calls for scheduling jobs with the least slack first, or jobs 3 and 4 in the second week. Since job 2 has three weeks slack, jobs 3 and 4 will take first preference, followed by job 2. The calculations for the second week are:

Schedule job 4 (slack = 0): $8 - 4 = 4$ workers remain

Schedule job 3 (slack = 0): $4 - 2 = 2$ workers remain

Postpone job 2 (slack = 3): Job 2 must be postponed since 2 workers cannot start on a job that requires the use of 4 workers at a time

In the problem, we assume that jobs cannot be interrupted once started. In the third week, 11 workers are required (Figure 12–6), although only 8 workers are available. The scheduling for the third week is as follows:

Continue job 3 (slack = 0): $8 - 2 = 6$ workers remain

The third heuristic is now brought into play—noncritical jobs, still active, can be postponed if they do not delay the project. Job 2 satisfies this rule. This allows us to start job 5 in the third week, which has no slack, making it critical.

Schedule job 5 (slack = 0): $6 - 5 = 1$ worker remains

Postpone job 2 (slack = 2): Job 2 again must be postponed since 4 workers are needed at one time

Figure 12–7 shows the updated network diagram at the end of the third week. In this figure, the number of workers required for the remaining weeks is recomputed.

Figure 12–7
Network diagram after three weeks—subsection of a larger project.

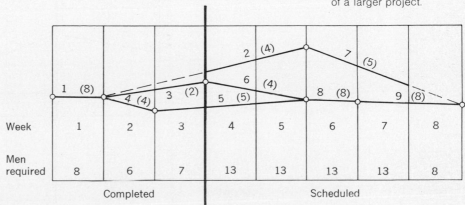

359

The scheduling for the fourth week is given as follows:

Continue job 5 (slack = 0): 8 − 5 = 3 workers remain

Postpone job 6 (slack = 0): Need 4 workers

Postpone job 2 (slack = 1): Need 4 workers

At the beginning of the fifth week, all jobs are critical, except job 2. Notice that at this point, the project has been delayed by one week due to the fact that job 6 was not started. The scheduling for the fifth week is as follows:

Continue job 5 (slack = 0): 8 − 5 = 3 workers remain

Postpone job 6 (slack = 0): Need 4 workers

Postpone job 2 (slack = 1): Need 4 workers

The scheduling for the sixth and seventh weeks is the same:

Schedule job 6 (slack = 0): 8 − 4 = 4 workers remain

Schedule job 2 (slack = 1): 4 − 4 = 0 workers remain

The network diagram for seven weeks is found in Figure 12–8. At this point, the project is two weeks behind schedule, the result of not starting job 6 on time.
The program decisions for the remaining weeks of the project are:

Eighth week— Schedule job 8 (slack = 0): 8 − 8 = 0 workers remain

Ninth week— Schedule job 9 (slack = 0): 8 − 8 = 0 workers remain

Tenth week— Continue job 9 (slack = 0): 8 − 8 = 0 workers remain

Eleventh week— Schedule job 7 (slack = 1): 8 − 5 = 3 workers remain

Twelfth week— Continue job 7 (slack = 0): 8 − 5 = 3 workers remain

Figure 12–8
Network diagram after seven weeks—subsection of a larger project.

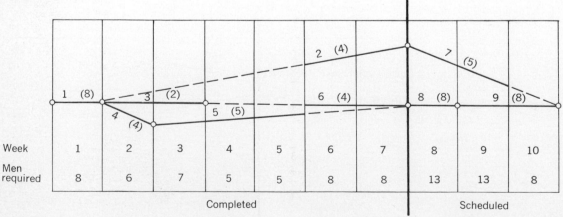

Week	1	2	3	4	5	6	7	8	9	10
Men required	8	6	7	5	5	8	8	13	13	8

Completed   Scheduled

The final scheduling of all jobs appears in Figure 12–9. The personnel limit of 8 workers has resulted in a four-week increase in the project's length. The heuristic program has found an acceptable schedule even though other feasible schedules exist. Due to the project's size, none are shorter than the one found.

Figure 12–9
Completed network diagram after 12 weeks — subsection of a larger project.

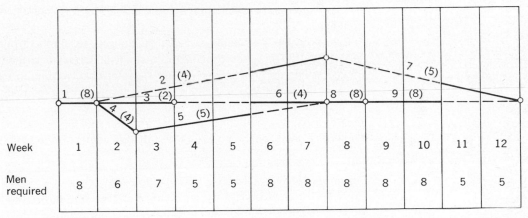

	Week	1	2	3	4	5	6	7	8	9	10	11	12
	Men required	8	6	7	5	5	8	8	8	8	8	5	5

Behavioral Models

The term *behavioral science* came into popular usage during the 1950s, although it had been applied to business firms much earlier, starting with the Hawthorne experiments of Elton Mayo and F. J. Roethlisberger at Western Electric from 1927 to 1932. The science of behavioral research from the 1950s to the present day has been and continues to be concerned with three levels of analysis. First is the behavior of the individual; that it, research is directed toward such topics as personality, motivation, attitudes, learning, coping with change, and leadership style. Second is the behavior of the group, such as interaction patterns, group conflict, problem solving, emergent leadership, and group norms. The third level of behavioral research deals with the organization as a whole. The effects on human behavior related to the design of the firm's total system and comparison of organizations are examples of this last level of analysis.

A contrast of the important differences between behavioral research and operations research might be helpful. Although both study the operation of organizations, the behavioral scientists are primarily interested in how decisions are made, while operations researchers are concerned with how they ought to be made. However, both research methodologies are problem oriented. Behavioral research is generally inductive since it tends to draw from statistics, psychology, and sociology while operations research is largely deductive, drawing largely from nonstatistical OR techniques. In essence, behavioral scientists are concerned with describing the nature of operations while operations researchers are interested in prescribing their nature.

Despite these differences and the fact that the behavioral sciences have had little or no impact on operations research, there is a great need to integrate behavioral research into the discipline of OR. The motivation and satisfaction of the employee have a profound effect on the way functions are performed as well as the way in which decisions are made. The usefulness of a custom-made mathematical model which optimizes the firm's goals and objectives is severely limited if it ignores the human problems that directly affect the model. A firm's success depends on its functioning as a coordinated unit, one that melds the human element with its environment.

Based on the integration of these disciplines, researchers need to construct *behavioral models* which explain and quantify the behavior of the human element. These models can be defined as the study of observable and verifiable human behavior that employs scientific procedures, such as the experimental method and the planned approach. They are largely inductive with special focus on why customers or employees behave as they do whether as an individual, a member of a small or large group, or a member of a market segment or firm.[7]

Designing Behavioral Models   Designing behavioral models is similar to developing any OR mathematical model. Using the six steps of the planned approach, model designers begin by studying the underlying behavioral facts, opinions, and symptoms concerning the problem (first step). A thorough understanding of the behavioral process leads to a definition of the real problem (second step). It could be customer dissatisfaction with specific products or poor morale within certain departments, or the real behavioral problem might be focused on the power structure of the physical distribution system or on the firm's relationship with its creditors. Whatever the source of the real problem, it must be defined clearly and objectively.

Before attempting to formulate tentative hypotheses or alternative solutions to the behavioral problem (third step), some fundamental law or established theory should be employed to provide an underlying structure or logical framework for developing hypotheses or solutions. For example, in certain marketing problems, "carryover effects," which can be defined as the effects that current marketing expenditures have on sales beyond the current period, should be an integral part of the marketing behavioral model. Similarly, certain employee behavioral models that relate to need levels and corresponding satisfactions thereof should include man's hierarchy of needs. Thus, the third step of the planned approach links the problem to be solved with some underlying law or theory when developing tentative behavioral models or hypotheses.

Next, the model designers study the behavioral process in some detail. Based on an ample number of observations, the observed data are summarized and tested according to the hypotheses. The modelers list the variables that appear to play an important role in the behavioral environment being studied. Thus, they begin with some behavioral notion of what affects these variables and run statistical tests of

[7]For more details, refer to Thierauf and Klekamp, op. cit., pp. 544–65.

how in actual practice each has correlated with the elements for which they are trying to find valid relationships.

Having arrived at a list of important variables, they structure the variables in a logical, mathematical way. As the model builders develop different behavioral models based on selected hypotheses, they drop and downgrade the variables that have lesser importance. Similarly, they eliminate those models (built on the selected hypotheses) that appear least promising by testing them against the observed data. Finally, they select the most promising behavioral model that conforms as closely as possible to the observed data (fourth step). Although the final mathematical model need not have the extreme complexities of the real world, its structure most follow reality so that the results parallel the real world.

Using the concept that the model is only an approximation of the real behavioral environment, the decision makers want an accurate and workable solution. In effect, they employ the computer to focus on what is the most likely to occur, then select a safe range around it. Desiring that range to be as narrow as possible, they will try to make good decisions within its boundaries. Throughout the implementation phase (fifth step), the computer is assisting the decision makers—not replacing them—in verifying the optimum behavioral solution.

Because a behavioral model is dynamic and depicts a situation over time, the model builders must be alert to shifts that take place in an ever-changing world. Thus, there must be provision for periodic evaluation which ensures that the model is still representative of the real world (sixth step).

Operations Research at Present

Most of the current operations research techniques have been treated in this book. The reader should have noticed the similarity of problems being solved by different OR techniques. For example, inventory problems have utilized EOQ models, dynamic programming, simulation, or some combination. One firm might be able to solve a specific problem by one method, whereas another firm might need an entirely different approach to solve its problem. No matter what approach is undertaken by the OR group, there is one basic direction—enabling management at all levels to make better, and hopefully, optimal decisions.

The increasing use of quantitative methods of operations research is currently having a dramatic effect on lower and middle management. Many of the present decision-making activities of these managerial levels are capable of being programmed. Computers can perform the necessary operations and, in turn, feed to these levels the optimum answer or courses of action. Examples were shown throughout the book, some of which are control of inventories—raw materials, work in process, and finished goods; optimum scheduling; and best routing of shipments. Once problems have been programmed, it is no longer necessary for managers to give as much time and thought in reaching decisions on the firm's problems. Instead of being bogged down with the routine decisions of their departments, they can now relegate these to a management information computer system. Thus lower and middle management can now spend time planning for their respective areas, training their personnel, and, perhaps for the first time, getting their respective jobs "under control."

levels effected by OR

The impact of quantitative methods on top management has likewise been dramatic. While the primary functions of lower and middle management are organizing, directing, and controlling the firm's activities, the primary concern of those at the highest level is planning the objectives, policies, and procedures that provide a framework for guiding the firm in a changing environment. Computer feedback from a management information system that utilizes the "management by exception" concept allows top management to review and evaluate all significant deviations (favorable and unfavorable) from the present profit plan. This information is instrumental in formulating the future plans of the firm. The use of computer models, then, has freed management from routine work in order to concentrate on the overall direction of the firm. However, there are a growing number of problems that are too complex for present quantitative methods or too time consuming for solution. The freeing of top management from some routine tasks will allow them to concentrate on these more difficult problems.

Operations Research in the Future

what OR help manage here about

The dynamics of the business world today, but more so in the future, are forcing companies to concentrate on the planning process, in particular planning for change and planning necessitated by change. The dynamics of products (the shortened life of products), markets (technically superior products displace established products in the marketplace here and abroad), industrial processes (the shortened and changing state of manufacturing processes), and government and society (legal and social constraints imposed on the firm which are continually changing) will be causing firms to plan carefully for the short, medium, and long range. In addition, the entry of more sophisticated computers, with their ability to handle unbelievable amounts of data, the continuing trend toward growth by merger and acquisition, and growing problems with labor unions will highlight the need for effective planning. It will be only through the use of optimum plans which consider all the relevant changing factors that the firm can benefit, rather than its competition. The planning function, then, is and will continue to be a logical candidate for quantitative study since operations research actually uses a planned approach in problem solving. Several OR methods are available for planning, some of which were indicated throughout this book.

Tomorrow's managers will be affected by organization structure changes. This will be particularly noticeable in the middle management area. It is becoming more and more important for firms to innovate with the market as the focus. This means that the marketing department takes preference over other areas of the firm. To state it another way, firms must bring their products to the right market at the right time in order to satisfy a particular market segment. This may necessitate a change in market structure. For example, direct shipments may eliminate the need for a middle manager since such transactions can be handled by a computer.

The dynamics of business will cause changes at the top management level. There will be the employment of numerous staff specialists to advise top management on special aspects of their jobs. Most of these specialists will have direct access to the computer through input/output terminal devices that allow them to use some mathematical model in order to solve a pressing management problem. The president may have a planning staff—an operations research specialist, an economist, a marketing research specialist, and a scientific adviser. Similarly, the marketing, manufacturing, finance (and accounting), engineering, R & D and personnel executives will be served by staff specialists so that knowledge from many disciplines will be used to solve complex business problems. By no means will computer mathematical models be limited to the OR group in the future. Many disciplines will have taken up the planned approach in solving complex well-structured or poorly structured problems as well as behavioral problems.

The methods of operations research that will be developed in the future will arise out of the necessity to solve particular problems. Among these will be the construction of a mathematical model for the entire firm. This model will demonstrate inter-relationships of all its parts more clearly than they have ever been understood before. It might, for example, permit management to make far more accurate judgments about the potential value of a possible acquisition and its resultant effect on the firm in the long run. This model might also enable management to gauge in advance the probable impact on the firm of various external conditions, such as development of new technology, and to take action accordingly. Newer on-line, real-time computers with massive storage facilities should be capable of handling such mathematical models for most firms. It is hoped that future computers will have the hardware to simulate a supplier-manufacturer-distributor-retailer relationship model in a routine manner. Thus, large-scale OR models will not be restricted to the firm but will be available to many areas of business activity.

Conclusion

The increasing managerial use of quantitative methods, backed up by the use of computers, is now considered a major turning point in the traditional way of viewing managerial functions. This revolution has given management at all levels improved information for decision making. The very structure of the firm has been changed to allow the optimum use of these OR computer techniques. The resulting answers from OR methods, models, and techniques have helped to liberate management so it can spend its energy on arriving at key decisions and laying plans for the growth of the business. It has made possible more effective centralized control of large, complex corporations. Information resulting from quantitative methods of operations research has helped and will continue to assist management in making sense out of the bewildering number of changes taking place in the real world. Management is now and will continue to do a much better job of sorting out the innumerable courses of action, testing its relative profit potentials, and reducing the resulting risks.

As mentioned often throughout the book, management should utilize the output from OR studies as an additional insight for solving its problems. If there are other important factors bearing on the problem that were not or could not have been included in the OR study or certain basic assumptions were made, the manager must weigh these factors in light of the OR results. To blindly concur with the output from an OR project when other concomitant factors apply is sheer folly on the manager's part. While the function of an operations research group is to advise the manager with their recommendations based on an objective approach to a problem, the manager still must temper these recommendations if certain critical conditions apply. Thus, the fact that managers have the authority and responsibility as well as eventual accountability for important decisions is reason enough for seeking the objective assistance of operations research. Similarly, managers have so many demands placed on them that they need all of the assistance available, including quantitative methods, to cope with the complexity of their positions.

Questions

1. Of what importance is the simplex method in solving integer and nonlinear programming problems?
2. Distinguish between linear programming and goal programming.
3. What are the problems associated with large, complex OR models, such as venture analysis?
4. How does heuristic programming differ from other mathematical programming techniques?
5. (a) How do behavioral problems differ from well-structured problems? Explain.
   (b) How do behavioral problems differ from poorly structured problems? Explain.
6. What is the most difficult part of a behavioral model? Explain.
7. What are the emerging directions of operations research now and in the future?
8. What effect will computerized OR models have on the various levels of management?
9. How can management best utilize operations research in decision making?

Bibliography

F. S. Hillier and G. J. Lieberman, *Operations Research*, San Francisco: Holden-Day, 1974.

R. I. Levin and C. A. Kirkpatrick, *Quantitative Approaches to Management*, New York: McGraw-Hill Book Company, 1975.

C. McMillan and R. F. Gonzalez, *Systems Analysis*, Homewood, Ill.: Richard D. Irwin, 1968.

D. W. Miller and M. K. Starr, *Executive Decisions and Operations Research*, Englewood Cliffs, N.J.: Prentice-Hall, 1969.

H. M. Wagner, *Principles of Management Science, With Applications to Executive Decisions*, Englewood Cliffs, N.J.: Prentice-Hall, 1975.

Appendixes

Appendix A

Vectors, Matrices, and Determinants

The mathematical methods in this appendix have applications not only in linear programming and transportation methods, but also in Markov analysis, queuing theory, and other quantitative techniques. Vectors, matrices, and determinants will be presented with a minimum of mathematical notation. This approach does not reduce the potential value of these methods.

Vectors

A *vector* is defined as a line with direction and length. All vectors are assumed to start at point zero. Consider vector V_1 consisting of a single number, say 4. This is represented in Figure A–1. Similarly, vector V_2 with a -3 value is represented by a single dimension per Figure A–1. Thus a vector can be seen to have direction (+ and −) and length (4 units and 3 units).

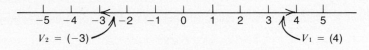

$$V_2 = (-3) \qquad V_1 = (4)$$

Figure A–1

Vectors, having two elements, can be graphed. They can be expressed either as row vectors $(a_1, a_2, a_3, \ldots)$ or column vectors $\begin{pmatrix} a_1 \\ a_2 \\ \ldots \end{pmatrix}$. Consider, for example, vector $V_3 \begin{pmatrix} 3 \\ 3 \end{pmatrix}$, which is graphed in Figure A–2. Whereas one component vector can be graphed in a single dimension, it takes two-dimensional space to graph a two-component vector. Similarly, a three-component vector $V_4 \begin{pmatrix} 1 \\ 2 \\ 3 \end{pmatrix}$ can be represented in three-dimensional space, as in Figure A–3. In general, it takes n-dimensional space to represent an *n*-component vector. Any vector larger than a three-component vector cannot be graphed.

Figure A–2

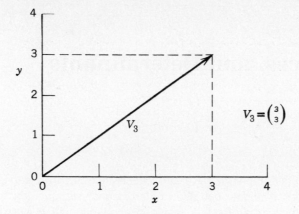

$V_3 = \begin{pmatrix} 3 \\ 3 \end{pmatrix}$

Figure A–3

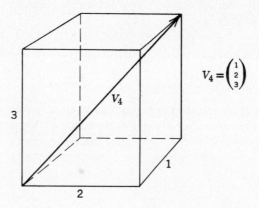

$V_4 = \begin{pmatrix} 1 \\ 2 \\ 3 \end{pmatrix}$

A vector may have one or more negative coordinates, as shown in Figure A–4. The vector $V_5 \begin{pmatrix} 3 \\ -3 \end{pmatrix}$ indicates the end of the vector is located by moving 3 units in a positive direction on the *x* axis and 3 units in a negative direction on the *y* axis. The rules for positive and negative signs are taken from geometry.

The length of any vector that does not lie exactly on one of the axes is not known from looking at its vector representation. Referring to geometry, it can be computed in the same manner as the hypotenuse of a right triangle. In Figure A–4, the length of the vector $V_5 \begin{pmatrix} 3 \\ -3 \end{pmatrix}$ is computed as follows:

$$(V_5)^2 = (3^2) + (-3^2)$$
$$= 18$$
$$V_5 = \sqrt{18}$$
$$= 4.3$$

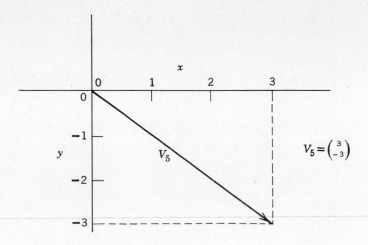

$$V_5 = \begin{pmatrix} 3 \\ -3 \end{pmatrix}$$

Vectors can be added and subtracted if the two given vectors have the same dimensions, that is, they are the same type of vectors and have the same number of elements. The vector $V_6 \begin{pmatrix} 2 \\ 1 \end{pmatrix}$ can be added to vector $V_7 \begin{pmatrix} 1 \\ 3 \end{pmatrix}$, the sum being $V_8 \begin{pmatrix} 3 \\ 4 \end{pmatrix}$. Both vectors need a two-dimensional space to be represented graphically. The resulting vector V_8 is a diagonal, passing through the origin of the parallelogram formed by the vectors V_6 and V_7. This is shown in Figure A–5.

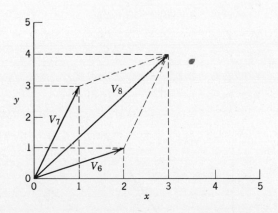

Just as vectors can be added and subtracted, a vector can be multiplied by any number to form a multiple of the original vector. The multiplier is called a *scalar*. The process of multiplicaton is accomplished by multiplying each coordinate of the vector by the scalar. Consider the example in Figure A–6. The vector $V_9 \begin{pmatrix} 2 \\ 3 \end{pmatrix}$ has been multiplied by a scalar, the number 2, with a resulting vector $V_{10} \begin{pmatrix} 4 \\ 6 \end{pmatrix}$. The resultant vector V_{10} is called a scalar multiple of vector V_9.

Figure A–6

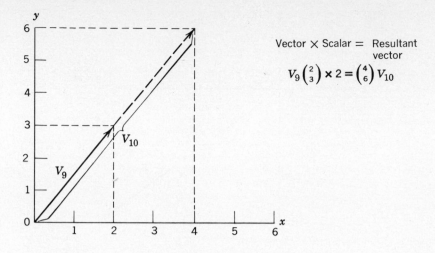

Vector × Scalar = Resultant vector

$$V_9 \binom{2}{3} \times 2 = \binom{4}{6} V_{10}$$

Figure A–7
All vectors are scalar multiples of each other.

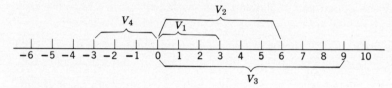

Vector	Scalar			
$V_2 = V_1 \times$	$2 = (3) \times$	$2 = (6)$		
$V_3 = V_1 \times$	$3 = (3) \times$	$3 = (9)$		
$V_1 = V_3 \times$	$\frac{1}{3} = (9) \times$	$\frac{1}{3} = (3)$		
$V_2 = V_3 \times$	$\frac{2}{3} = (9) \times$	$\frac{2}{3} = (6)$		
$V_4 = V_2 \times$	$-\frac{1}{2} = (6) \times$	$-\frac{1}{2} = (-3)$		
$V_4 = V_3 \times$	$-\frac{1}{3} = (9) \times$	$-\frac{1}{3} = (-3)$		

Figure A–8
V_5 and V_6 are reference or basis vectors while V_7 is a scalar multiple of V_5 and V_6.

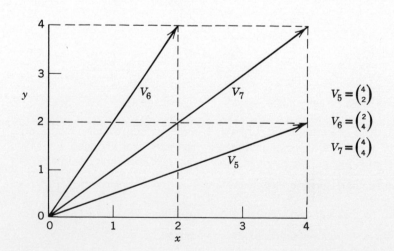

$$V_5 = \binom{4}{2}$$

$$V_6 = \binom{2}{4}$$

$$V_7 = \binom{4}{4}$$

By using one dimension for a moment, all vectors found are scalar multiples of each other. This concept, shown in Figure A–7 for the x axis, is also applicable to the y axis. This concept can also be applied to two dimensions. In Figure A–8, vectors V_5 and V_6 are reference vectors while vector V_7 is a vector in space that can be described as a scalar multiple of the two reference or basis vectors, V_5 and V_6. In three dimensions, three reference vectors would be required, one for each dimension.

Vector V_7 in Figure A–8 can be formed with the basis vectors V_5 and V_6 by finding the appropriate scalars with which to multiply the reference or basis vectors:

Vector V_7 = (some scalar)(V_5) + (some scalar)(V_6)

Letting A equal the appropriate scalar for vector V_5 and B equal the appropriate scalar for vector V_6, the resulting equation is:

$$V_7 = A\binom{4}{2} + B\binom{2}{4}$$

Since we know that the resultant vector $V_7 = \binom{4}{4}$, the preceding equation can be written as:

$$\binom{4}{4} = \binom{4A}{2A} + \binom{2B}{4B}$$

$$4 = 4A + 2B$$

$$4 = 2A + 4B$$

Using simultaneous equations, multiply the top equation by 2, subtract, and divide the result by 6:

$$8 = 8A + 4B$$
$$-(4 = 2A + 4B)$$
$$\frac{4}{6} = \frac{6A}{6}$$

$$A = \frac{2}{3}$$

Substituting A into the first equation yields:

$$4 = 4\left(\frac{2}{3}\right) + 2B$$

$$4 = 2\frac{2}{3} + 2B$$

$$4 - 2\frac{2}{3} = 2B$$

$$\frac{1\frac{1}{3}}{2} = \frac{2B}{2}$$

$$B = \frac{2}{3}$$

This may be checked by substituting the scalars (A and B) back into the original equation as follows:

$$
\begin{aligned}
V_7 &= A\binom{4}{2} + B\binom{2}{4} \\
&= \frac{2}{3}\binom{4}{2} + \frac{2}{3}\binom{2}{4} \\
&= \binom{2\frac{2}{3}}{1\frac{1}{3}} + \binom{1\frac{1}{3}}{2\frac{2}{3}} \\
&= \binom{4}{4}
\end{aligned}
$$

The two-dimensional space in Figure A–9 contains two vectors, V_8 and V_9, and a third vector, V_{10}. It is not possible to find the direction of a third vector using vectors V_8 and V_9 since both have y coordinates of 0. Being scalar multiples of each other, V_8 and V_9 are called *dependent vectors*. In mathematics, dependent vectors cannot be *basis vectors,* which is the name given to a pair of vectors that can be used to derive a third vector, such as V_{10}.

Figure A–9
Vectors V_8 and V_9 are dependent since they are not basis vectors, but they are scalar multiples of each other.

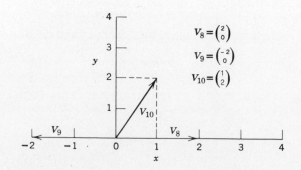

Previously, we stated that an n-dimensional vector can be represented as a linear combination of n linearly independent vectors. The problem is to determine the specific combination of given linearly independent vectors with which to form a given vector. Consider the two linearly independent vectors, $V_1 \begin{pmatrix} 2 \\ 3 \end{pmatrix}$ and $V_2 \begin{pmatrix} 1 \\ 2 \end{pmatrix}$. The problem is to determine what linear combination of V_1 and V_2 will form the resultant vector $V_3 \begin{pmatrix} 40 \\ 50 \end{pmatrix}$. In other words, find the scalars (A and B) for the following equation:

$$\begin{pmatrix} 40 \\ 50 \end{pmatrix} = A \begin{pmatrix} 2 \\ 3 \end{pmatrix} + B \begin{pmatrix} 1 \\ 2 \end{pmatrix}$$

$40 = 2A + B$ (multiply by 2) $80 = 4A + 2B$

$50 = 3A + 2B$ $\dfrac{50 = 3A + 2B}{A = 30}$

$40 = 2(30) + B$

$40 = 60 + B$

$B = -20$

The scalars ($A = 30$ and $B = -20$) can be checked by substituting them back into the original equation as follows:

$$\begin{pmatrix} 40 \\ 50 \end{pmatrix} = (30) \begin{pmatrix} 2 \\ 3 \end{pmatrix} + (-20) \begin{pmatrix} 1 \\ 2 \end{pmatrix}$$

$$= \begin{pmatrix} 60 \\ 90 \end{pmatrix} - \begin{pmatrix} 20 \\ 40 \end{pmatrix}$$

$$= \begin{pmatrix} 40 \\ 50 \end{pmatrix}$$

Note that the specific linear combination above was obtained by transforming vectors into linear equations. Likewise, linear equations can be transformed into vectors. Linear programming, which involves a set of linear equations, can be solved by the vector method. It should be pointed out that most linear programming problems are not this simple. However, the foregoing material should provide a general understanding of vectors.

Matrices

Matrix algebra is extremely useful in solving a set of linear equations. Any linear programming problem can be solved with the help of matrix algebra; in particular, the algorithm (a systematic procedure) of the simplex method is based on the concepts of matrices and inversion of matrices. Therefore it is essential that the individual become familiar with matrices.

A *matrix* is a rectangular array of ordered numbers, arranged into rows and columns. The purpose of a matrix is to convey information in a concise manner and in an acceptable form for mathematical manipulation. Taken as a whole, a matrix has no numeric value. Any matrix in which the number of rows equals the number of columns is called a *square matrix*. A vector is a special case of a matrix with only one row or one column. Given below are several examples of matrices:

$$
\begin{array}{ccc}
(a) & (b) & (c) \\
\begin{pmatrix} 2 & 4 \\ 1 & 5 \end{pmatrix} & \begin{pmatrix} 2 & 1 & 3 \\ 4 & 0 & 1 \end{pmatrix} & \begin{pmatrix} 4 & 4 & 4 \\ 1 & 8 & 6 \\ 7 & 1 & 2 \end{pmatrix} \\
2 \times 2 \text{ matrix} & 2 \times 3 \text{ matrix} & 3 \times 3 \text{ matrix}
\end{array}
$$

The number of rows and columns in a given matrix determines the dimension or order of the matrix. Matrix (a) is a 2×2 matrix, matrix (b) is a 2×3 matrix, and matrix (c) is a 3×3 matrix. When specifying the order or dimension of a matrix, the first number relates to the row and the second number refers to the column of the matrix. Thus the dimension of a matrix with m rows and n columns is $m \times n$. Rows in the matrix are numbered from top to bottom while columns are numbered from left to right. The values within a matrix are referred to as the *elements* of the matrix.

Referring to the matrix (b) above, we can observe that this matrix consists of two row vectors placed together or three column vectors placed together. This is shown as follows:

$$
\begin{pmatrix} 2 & 1 & 3 \\ 4 & 0 & 1 \end{pmatrix} \quad \begin{pmatrix} 2 \\ 4 \end{pmatrix} \quad \begin{pmatrix} 1 \\ 0 \end{pmatrix} \quad \begin{pmatrix} 3 \\ 1 \end{pmatrix}
$$

Thus it can be shown that vectors and matrices are interrelated.

Two given matrices can be added only if they have the same dimensions. Once it is established that the number of rows and columns of the two matrices are identical, their respective elements can be added together. Matrix addition is known as *elementwise* addition. The rules for matrix subtraction are the same as those for matrix addition. The subtraction process is an elementwise subtraction. The following are examples of matrix addition and subtraction:

Addition

$$\text{Matrix } A + \text{Matrix } B = \text{Matrix } C$$

$$
\begin{pmatrix} 2 & 4 & 2 \\ 6 & 2 & 6 \end{pmatrix} + \begin{pmatrix} 1 & 1 & 2 \\ 4 & 4 & 6 \end{pmatrix} = \begin{pmatrix} 3 & 5 & 4 \\ 10 & 6 & 12 \end{pmatrix}
$$

$$
\begin{pmatrix} 2 & 4 & -2 \\ -6 & 2 & 6 \end{pmatrix} + \begin{pmatrix} 1 & -1 & 2 \\ 4 & -4 & 6 \end{pmatrix} = \begin{pmatrix} 3 & 3 & 0 \\ -2 & -2 & 12 \end{pmatrix}
$$

Subtraction

$$\text{Matrix } A - \text{Matrix } B = \text{Matrix } C$$

$$
\begin{pmatrix} 1 & 3 & 4 \\ 8 & 1 & 2 \end{pmatrix} - \begin{pmatrix} 1 & 9 & 2 \\ 4 & 1 & 1 \end{pmatrix} = \begin{pmatrix} 0 & -6 & 2 \\ 4 & 0 & 1 \end{pmatrix}
$$

$$
\begin{pmatrix} 1 & -3 & 4 \\ 8 & 1 & -2 \end{pmatrix} - \begin{pmatrix} 1 & -9 & 2 \\ 4 & 1 & -1 \end{pmatrix} = \begin{pmatrix} 0 & 6 & 2 \\ 4 & 0 & -1 \end{pmatrix}
$$

The definition for multiplication of a row vector by a column vector can be easily extended to cover matrix multiplication. Two matrices can be multiplied together if the number of columns in the first matrix equals the number of rows in the second matrix. Unless this condition is met, the multiplication is impossible. However, if two matrices placed side by side do not meet the test, swapping positions may qualify them for multiplication but may fail to give the correct solution since matrix multiplication is not commutative. The following are some examples of matrices that can or cannot be multiplied:

First Matrix (A)   Second Matrix (B)

First Example:

$$\binom{4}{5} \times (3 \quad 8) \qquad \text{can be multiplied}$$

$$2 \times \textcircled{1} \leftarrow = \rightarrow \textcircled{1} \times 2$$

Second Example:

$$\begin{pmatrix} 4 \\ 1 \\ 6 \end{pmatrix} \times \begin{pmatrix} 1 & 4 & 8 \\ 4 & 2 & 6 \end{pmatrix} \quad \begin{array}{l} \text{cannot be multiplied} \\ \text{(consider swapping positions)} \end{array}$$

$$3 \times \textcircled{1} \leftarrow \neq \rightarrow \textcircled{2} \times 3$$

$$\begin{pmatrix} 1 & 4 & 8 \\ 4 & 2 & 6 \end{pmatrix} \quad \begin{pmatrix} 4 \\ 1 \\ 6 \end{pmatrix} \quad \begin{array}{l} \text{can be multiplied} \\ \text{after swapping positions} \end{array}$$

$$2 \times \textcircled{3} \leftarrow = \rightarrow \textcircled{3} \times 1$$

Third Example:

$$\begin{pmatrix} 4 & 1 & 4 \\ 8 & 7 & 3 \\ 2 & 4 & 2 \end{pmatrix} \quad \begin{pmatrix} 1 \\ 9 \\ 6 \\ 2 \end{pmatrix} \quad \begin{array}{l} \text{cannot be multiplied} \\ \text{(consider swapping positions)} \end{array}$$

$$3 \times \textcircled{3} \leftarrow \neq \rightarrow \textcircled{4} \times 1$$

$$\begin{pmatrix} 1 \\ 9 \\ 6 \\ 2 \end{pmatrix} \quad \begin{pmatrix} 4 & 1 & 4 \\ 8 & 7 & 3 \\ 2 & 4 & 2 \end{pmatrix} \quad \text{still cannot be multiplied}$$

$$4 \times \textcircled{1} \leftarrow \neq \rightarrow \textcircled{3} \times 3$$

Using the first example above, we know the two matrices can be multiplied. If we look at the outer numbers (2 for Matrix A and 2 for Matrix B), this indicates the size of the matrix for the answer. If we know the final answer is a 2 × 2 matrix, four elements must be contained in the matrix. To obtain any element in the final answer, it is necessary first to determine the row and column location of that element in the solution. Using the first example below, we want to know how the element 32 was computed. This element is in the first row and the second column. To compute it, we multiply the first row of matrix A by the second column of matrix B, or $4 \times 8 = 32$.

$$\text{Matrix } A \times \text{Matrix } B = \text{Matrix } C$$

$$\begin{pmatrix} 4 \\ 5 \end{pmatrix} \times (3 \quad 8) = \begin{pmatrix} 12 & 32 \\ 15 & 40 \end{pmatrix}$$

1st row (4) × 1st col. (3) = 1st row, 1st col. (12)

1st row (4) × 2nd col. (8) = 1st row, 2nd col. (32)

2nd row (5) × 1st col. (3) = 2nd row, 1st col. (15)

2nd row (5) × 2nd col. (8) = 2nd row, 2nd col. (40)

A more involved matrix multiplication (3×3 matrix) is shown below.

$$\text{Matrix } A \quad \times \quad \text{Matrix } B \quad = \quad \text{Matrix } C$$

$$\begin{pmatrix} 4 & -4 & 0 \\ 1 & -2 & 6 \\ 7 & -1 & 2 \end{pmatrix} \times \begin{pmatrix} -2 & 6 & -3 \\ 0 & 7 & 0 \\ -4 & 8 & 1 \end{pmatrix} = \begin{pmatrix} -8 & -4 & -12 \\ -26 & 40 & 3 \\ -22 & 51 & -19 \end{pmatrix}$$

	Matrix A	Matrix B			Where figure is located in answer
1st row	$(4 \quad -4 \quad 0) \times$ 1st col.	$\begin{pmatrix} -2 \\ 0 \\ -4 \end{pmatrix}$	$= -8 + 0 + 0$	$= -8$	1st row, 1st col.
1st row	$(4 \quad -4 \quad 0) \times$ 2nd col.	$\begin{pmatrix} 6 \\ 7 \\ 8 \end{pmatrix}$	$= 24 + (-28) + 0 =$	-4	1st row, 2nd col.
1st row	$(4 \quad -4 \quad 0) \times$ 3rd col.	$\begin{pmatrix} -3 \\ 0 \\ 1 \end{pmatrix}$	$= -12 + 0 + 0$	$= -12$	1st row, 3rd col.
2nd row	$(1 \quad -2 \quad 6) \times$ 1st col.	$\begin{pmatrix} -2 \\ 0 \\ -4 \end{pmatrix}$	$= -2 + 0 + (-24) =$	-26	2nd row, 1st col.
2nd row	$(1 \quad -2 \quad 6) \times$ 2nd col.	$\begin{pmatrix} 6 \\ 7 \\ 8 \end{pmatrix}$	$= 6 + (-14) + 48 =$	40	2nd row, 2nd col.
2nd row	$(1 \quad -2 \quad 6) \times$ 3rd col.	$\begin{pmatrix} -3 \\ 0 \\ 1 \end{pmatrix}$	$= -3 + 0 + 6$	$= 3$	2nd row, 3rd col.
3rd row	$(7 \quad -1 \quad 2) \times$ 1st col.	$\begin{pmatrix} -2 \\ 0 \\ -4 \end{pmatrix}$	$= -14 + 0 + (-8) =$	-22	3rd row, 1st col.

3rd row $(7 \quad -1 \quad 2) \times$ 2nd col. $\begin{pmatrix} 6 \\ 7 \\ 8 \end{pmatrix} = 42 + (-7) + 16 \ = \ 51$ 3rd row, 2nd col.

3rd row $(7 \quad -1 \quad 2) \times$ 3rd col. $\begin{pmatrix} -3 \\ 0 \\ 1 \end{pmatrix} = -21 + 0 + 2 \quad = -19$ 3rd row, 3rd col.

Finally, note that the multiplication of a matrix by a vector follows the rules of regular matrix multiplication as set forth above. The multiplication of a matrix by a scalar is accomplished by multiplying each term in the matrix by the scalar value.

Associated with every $m \times n$ matrix is another matrix whose rows are the columns of the given matrix, in exactly the same order. To state it another way, the first row of the original matrix becomes the first column in the derived matrix, the second row becomes the second column, and so forth. This derived matrix is called the *transpose* of a matrix. The transpose is a method often used to show data in a different form. The transpose of a matrix is shown as follows:

Original Matrix   **Transpose of a Matrix**

$$\begin{pmatrix} 4 & 4 & 2 \\ 2 & 1 & 7 \\ -8 & 6 & 8 \end{pmatrix} \qquad \begin{pmatrix} 4 & 2 & -8 \\ 4 & 1 & 6 \\ 2 & 7 & 8 \end{pmatrix}$$

Each element of a squared matrix that is 2×2 and larger has associated with it a *cofactor*. A cofactor can be defined as that element or group of elements that remains when a row and a column have been removed from the matrix with the appropriate sign. In the matrix below, the cofactor of the circled element 4 has been formed:

Original Matrix − Row and Column Removed = Cofactor

$$\begin{pmatrix} 4 & 1 \\ 3 & 5 \end{pmatrix} \qquad\qquad \begin{pmatrix} 4 & 1 \\ 3 & \end{pmatrix} \qquad\qquad \begin{pmatrix} & \\ & 5 \end{pmatrix}$$

The same type of procedure is performed for the other three cofactors as follows:

Original Matrix − Row and Column Removed...   Cofactor

$$\begin{pmatrix} 4 & 1 \\ 3 & 5 \end{pmatrix} \qquad \begin{pmatrix} 4 & 1 \\ & 5 \end{pmatrix} \qquad \begin{pmatrix} -3 & \end{pmatrix}$$

$$\begin{pmatrix} 4 & 1 \\ 3 & 5 \end{pmatrix} \qquad \begin{pmatrix} 4 & \\ 3 & 5 \end{pmatrix} \qquad \begin{pmatrix} & -1 \end{pmatrix}$$

$$\begin{pmatrix} 4 & 1 \\ 3 & 5 \end{pmatrix} \qquad \begin{pmatrix} & 1 \\ 3 & 5 \end{pmatrix} \qquad \begin{pmatrix} 4 & \end{pmatrix}$$

The original matrix has been transformed into its cofactors. Notice that the sign of two cofactors has been changed. In order to determine the sign of the cofactor, it is necessary to add together the location of the row and column which have been re-moved. If the total is an even number, the sign of the cofactor is unchanged. In the example above, the second cofactor (-3) was formed by deleting the first row and second column ($1 + 2 =$ odd). The odd number means the sign is changed (from $+3$ to -3).

After finding the cofactors, the matrix of cofactors must be computed in order to form the adjoint of a matrix. If each of the numbers in the original matrix were re-placed by its cofactor, we would form the matrix of cofactors. Using the same ex-ample, this is shown as follows:

Original
Matrix
$$\begin{pmatrix} 4 & 1 \\ 3 & 5 \end{pmatrix} \qquad \begin{pmatrix} a & b \\ c & d \end{pmatrix}$$

$$\qquad\qquad\quad a \qquad\qquad\quad b \qquad\qquad c \qquad\qquad d$$

Cofactors
$$\begin{pmatrix} \\ & 5 \end{pmatrix} \quad \begin{pmatrix} \\ -3 & \end{pmatrix} \quad \begin{pmatrix} & -1 \\ & \end{pmatrix} \quad \begin{pmatrix} 4 & \\ & \end{pmatrix}$$

Matrix of
Cofactors
$$\begin{pmatrix} 5 & -3 \\ -1 & 4 \end{pmatrix}$$
Original numbers (a, b, c, and d) have been replaced by their cofactors.

In 3×3 matrices and larger, the deletion of a row and a column which intersect each other forms a cofactor of a 2×2 size or larger. Consider the following example:

Original Matrix

**Cofactor formed by deleting
1st row and 1st column
(even: sign unchanged)**

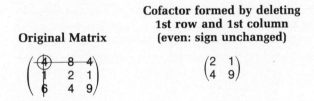

Since determinants can be used in solving for the value of a cofactor, they will be explained in the next section. It is sufficient to say that the numerical value of a 2×2 determinant can be found by multiplying together the elements lying on the primary diagonal (p) and subtracting the product of the elements lying on the secondary diagonal (s). In our example,

p $\qquad$ s
$$2 \qquad 1$$
$$4 \qquad 9$$

the numerical value of the determinant (cofactor) is 14 (18–4). Again, the sign of the cofactor will reflect the location of the row and column removed. Since we have de-leted the first row and the first column in the example, the sign remains unchanged.

The *adjoint* of a matrix is the transpose of the matrix of cofactors; it is useful in the study of games and optimum strategies. The adjoint of a matrix can also be very useful in finding the inverse of a given matrix. Returning to the earlier example, the adjoint of the matrix is as follows:

Original Matrix   **Matrix of Cofactors**   **Adjoint of Matrix**

$$\begin{pmatrix} 4 & 1 \\ 3 & 5 \end{pmatrix} \qquad \begin{pmatrix} 5 & -3 \\ -1 & 4 \end{pmatrix} \qquad \begin{pmatrix} 5 & -1 \\ -3 & 4 \end{pmatrix}$$

An *identity* (unit) *matrix* is a square matrix whose primary diagonal (p) is formed entirely of ones and the remainder of the terms are zeros. Several examples are:

2 × 2 matrix   **3 × 3 matrix**   **4 × 4 matrix**

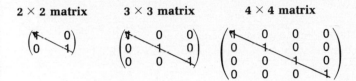

The initial tableau for the simplex method of linear programming with a squared matrix is a good example. Notice that the identity matrix is a combination of vectors (each of one unit in length) which forms a basis for space. For example, the 3 × 3 matrix used in three dimensions is graphed in Figure A–10. Because each axis of the space is one unit in length, finding scalar multiples of these bases is relatively easy.

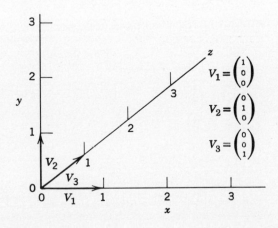

Figure A–10
Three-dimension graph.

The last area of the matrix algebra covered is the inversion of a matrix. This is used in the simplex method of linear programming. The following example is used:

Original Vector		**Original Matrix**		**New Vector**
(2 1)	$\times$	$\begin{pmatrix} 4 & 6 \\ 8 & 10 \end{pmatrix}$	$=$	(16 22)
$1 \times ②$	$=$	$② \times 2$		can be multiplied

The multiplication of vector (2   1) by the original matrix $\begin{pmatrix} 4 & 6 \\ 8 & 10 \end{pmatrix}$ will change the vector (2   1) to a new vector in two dimensions since the matrix acts as a combination of scalars. Remember that vectors are a special case of a matrix. Multiplying the inverse of a matrix by the new vector (16   22) will return a vector from some point in space to its original location, (2   1) in the problem.

An inverse can be formed for this problem. There are eight procedures, four involving rows and four involving columns, that can be used on the original matrix to form an inverse. The method must be limited to rows or columns but not both. The row and column procedures are:

1. One row may be interchanged with another row.
2. A row can be multiplied by a constant.
3. One row can be added to or subtracted from another row.
4. A multiple of a row can be added to or subtracted from another row.
5. One column can be interchanged with another column.
6. A column can be multiplied by a constant.
7. One column can be added to or subtracted from another column.
8. A multiple of a column can be added to or subtracted from another column.

These procedures (rows and columns) have as their objective the conversion of the original matrix into an identity matrix. Row procedures are used in the example.

Original Matrix	**Identity Matrix**	**Steps Performed**
$\begin{pmatrix} 4 & 6 \\ 8 & 10 \end{pmatrix}$	$\begin{pmatrix} 1 & 0 \\ 0 & 1 \end{pmatrix}$	1. Set up the original matrix and the identity matrix
$\begin{pmatrix} 1 & 1\frac{1}{2} \\ 8 & 10 \end{pmatrix}$	$\begin{pmatrix} \frac{1}{4} & 0 \\ 0 & 1 \end{pmatrix}$	2. First row multiplied by $\frac{1}{4}$ (rule 2)
$\begin{pmatrix} 1 & 1\frac{1}{2} \\ 0 & -2 \end{pmatrix}$	$\begin{pmatrix} \frac{1}{4} & 0 \\ -2 & 1 \end{pmatrix}$	3. Multiply first row by 8 and subtract it from 2nd row (rule 4)
$\begin{pmatrix} 1 & 1\frac{1}{2} \\ 0 & 1 \end{pmatrix}$	$\begin{pmatrix} \frac{1}{4} & 0 \\ 1 & -\frac{1}{2} \end{pmatrix}$	4. Second row multiplied by $-\frac{1}{2}$ (rule 2)
$\begin{pmatrix} 1 & 0 \\ 0 & 1 \end{pmatrix}$	$\begin{pmatrix} -\frac{5}{4} & \frac{3}{4} \\ 1 & -\frac{1}{2} \end{pmatrix}$	5. Subtract $1\frac{1}{2}$ times row 2 from row 1 (rule 4)

The calculations can be checked by multiplying the inverse times the new vector (16   22) to determine if the multiplication will return the vector back to its original point (2   1). This is calculated as follows:

	New Vector		**Inverse of Original Matrix**	**Original Vector**
	(16 22)	$\times$	$\begin{pmatrix} -\dfrac{5}{4} & \dfrac{3}{4} \\ 1 & -\dfrac{1}{2} \end{pmatrix}$	= (2 1)

Another way of stating what has occurred is to say that the inverse represents the group of scalars which returns the new vector back to its original point. The inverse of a matrix can be thought of as the reciprocal of a matrix.

An inspection of the example used in Chapter 6 for the simplex method of linear programming might help clarify the use of matrix inversion. The original and identity matrices are shown below:

	Original Matrix	**Identity Matrix**
First Tableau	$\begin{pmatrix} 2 & 3 \\ 3 & 2 \\ 1 & 1 \end{pmatrix}$	$\begin{pmatrix} 1 & 0 & 0 \\ 0 & 1 & 0 \\ 0 & 0 & 1 \end{pmatrix}$
Third and Final Tableau	$\begin{pmatrix} 0 & 1 \\ 0 & 0 \\ 1 & 0 \end{pmatrix}$	$\begin{pmatrix} 1 & 0 & -2 \\ 1 & 1 & -5 \\ -1 & 0 & 3 \end{pmatrix}$

The original matrix must be square for a complete inversion to occur. Many linear programming problems will reach an optimum solution before a complete inversion takes place. Those square matrices in linear programming problems that fail to reach a complete inversion are tending in that direction. Moreover, the procedural steps in the simplex method of linear programming are somewhat different from the row and column procedures when forming an inverse.

Determinants

The last subject to be discussed as a mathematical background for Chapter 6 and following chapters is *determinants*. Whereas the matrix does not imply any mathematical operation, a determinant does imply certain operations. When a determinant appears in its regular form, it is said to be *unexpanded*. To evaluate a determinant, we expand it according to certain rules in order to obtain a single numerical value. Thus a determinant is a square array of numbers arranged into rows and columns and has a numerical value. The number of rows always precedes the number of columns when specifying the size of the determinant. They are extremely useful in solving simultaneous equations. Several examples of determinants are found below.

A 2×2 determinant has one primary diagonal and one secondary diagonal. Determinants larger than 2×2 have multiple primary diagonals and multiple secondary diagonals. As stated in the previous section, the numerical value of a 2×2

$$\begin{vmatrix} 1 & 4 \\ 6 & 2 \end{vmatrix}$$ 2×2 determinant

$$\begin{vmatrix} 4 & 6 & 5 \\ 1 & -1 & 6 \\ 8 & 9 & 7 \end{vmatrix}$$ 3×3 determinant

$$\begin{vmatrix} 15 & -4 & 8 & 9 \\ 11 & -6 & 7 & 2 \\ 8 & -1 & 6 & 5 \\ 4 & 0 & 4 & 2 \end{vmatrix}$$ 4×4 determinant

determinant is found by multiplying together the elements lying on the primary or main diagonal (p) and subtracting the product of the elements lying on the secondary diagonal (s). The value of the 2×2 determinant above is -22, determined as follows:

$$\begin{vmatrix} 1 & 4 \\ 6 & 2 \end{vmatrix}$$ Value $= (2)(1) - (6)(4)$
$= 2 - 24$
$= -22$

The mathematical process for finding the value of a 3×3 determinant is determined with a slight modificaton of the procedure used on a 2×2 determinant. For the 3×3 determinant above, it is obvious that neither the second and third primary diagonals nor the second and third secondary diagonals pass through all three elements. This can be remedied by repeating the first two columns of the determinant, which appear as follows:

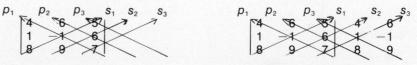

The value of the determinant equals $(p_1 + p_2 + p_3) - (s_1 + s_2 + s_3)$:

$$[\,(7)(-1)(4) + (8)(6)(6) + (9)(1)(5)\,] - [\,(8)(-1)(5) + (9)(6)(4) + (7)(1)(6)\,]$$

$$\underbrace{}_{p_1}\quad\underbrace{}_{p_2}\quad\underbrace{}_{p_3}\quad\underbrace{}_{s_1}\quad\underbrace{}_{s_2}\quad\underbrace{}_{s_3}$$

$$(-28 + 288 + 45) - (-40 + 216 + 42) = 305 - 218 = 87$$

The preceding two examples have made use of diagonals to find the numerical value of a determinant. However, the diagonal method is rather restrictive from the standpoint of the size of the determinant. There is another procedure for finding the numerical value of any size determinant, called *expanding* a determinant. Any square determinant can be solved for its numerical value by expanding any one of its rows or any one of its columns. If a determinant is expanded by a row, this means selecting a particular row and then eliminating, in turn, each column which intersects that row. Expanding a determinant by a column means choosing a specific column and eliminating each row which intersects that column. Recall that the sign must be changed if the sum of the row and column which are eliminated is an odd number. Otherwise, if the sum of the number of the row and column that are eliminated is an even number, the sign is not changed.

Using the 2×2 determinant set forth previously, we shall expand this determinant by its first row. A line has been drawn through the first row to indicate this.

Step 1

$$\begin{vmatrix} 1 & 4 \\ 6 & 2 \end{vmatrix}$$

Since the first row is being expanded, the first column that intersects the first row needs to have a line drawn through it.

Step 2 $2 \times \textcircled{1} = 2$

Multiply the one element which is not lined out by the circled element 1. The sign is unchanged because we are adding together the number of the row and the column which were eliminated. The value in the first part of the expansion is 2.

Step 3

$$\begin{vmatrix} 1 & 4 \\ 6 & 2 \end{vmatrix}$$

Expanding on the first row, the second column that intersects the first row is column 2.

Step 4 $6 \times \textcircled{4} = -24$

Multiply the one element which is not lined out by the circled element 4. The sign is changed because we are adding together the number of the row and the column which were eliminated. The value of the second part of the expansion is -24.

Step 5 $2 - 24 = -22$

Add together the value of the two parts of the expansion for a value of the determinant, or -22. (Same answer as obtained with diagonal method.)

Returning to the previous illustration for a 3×3 determinant, we will expand this determinant by its first column. When a row and a column are eliminated, a 2×2 determinant remains. The value of this 2×2 determinant, in turn, is multiplied by the circled element. The method for changing the sign remains. The original 3×3 determinant is:

3 × 3 determinant
$$\begin{vmatrix} 4 & 6 & 5 \\ 1 & -1 & 6 \\ 8 & 9 & 7 \end{vmatrix}$$

First part of expansion
$$\begin{vmatrix} 4 & 6 & 5 \\ 1 & -1 & 6 \\ 8 & 9 & 7 \end{vmatrix} = \begin{vmatrix} -1 & 6 \\ 9 & 7 \end{vmatrix} \times 4 = -61 \times 4$$

$\times 4 = -61 \times 4 = -244$
Row 1 + col. 1 = even,
sign is unchanged

Second part of expansion
$$\begin{vmatrix} 4 & 6 & 5 \\ 1 & -1 & 6 \\ 8 & 9 & 7 \end{vmatrix} = \begin{vmatrix} 6 & 5 \\ 9 & 7 \end{vmatrix} \times 1 = -3 \times 1 = 3$$

Row 2 + col. 1 = odd,
sign is changed

Third part of expansion
$$\begin{vmatrix} 4 & 6 & 5 \\ 1 & -1 & 6 \\ 8 & 9 & 7 \end{vmatrix} = \begin{vmatrix} 6 & 5 \\ -1 & 6 \end{vmatrix} \times 8 = 41 \times 8 = 328$$

Row 3 + col. 1 = even,
sign is unchanged

The sum for three parts of the expansion
$= -244 + 3 + 328 = 87$ value of determinant
(same value as for diagonal method).

The procedure for expanding a 4 × 4 determinant is the same as for a 3 × 3 determinant, except that the deletion of a row and a column would leave a 3 × 3 determinant to be multiplied by the circled element in each step. As one might suspect, the calculation for the value of a larger determinant becomes quite complex, usually requiring the use of a computer.

Determinants, as noted previously, are quite useful in solving simultaneous equations. The following set of simultaneous equations will be used to illustrate this point:

$4X + 6Y + 3Z = 18$

$3X + 5Y + 6Z = 24$

$2X + 8Y + 4Z = 12$

The value for each of the unknown variables (X, Y, and Z) is determined by solving a particular set of two determinants which form a fraction. The determinant which forms the numerator of each fraction changes with each variable (X, Y, or Z). The determinant which forms the basis for the denominator of each fraction remains the same. The determinants used to solve for X are shown as follows:

$$X = \frac{\begin{vmatrix} 18 & 6 & 3 \\ 24 & 5 & 6 \\ 12 & 8 & 4 \end{vmatrix}}{\begin{vmatrix} 4 & 6 & 3 \\ 3 & 5 & 6 \\ 2 & 8 & 4 \end{vmatrix}} \quad \text{numerator} \\ \quad \text{denominator}$$

Inspection of the determinant for the denominator reveals that this is nothing more than coefficients of the three unknowns arranged in the same form as they appear in the above equations. The same cannot be said for the numerator. The column of coefficients for the unknown variable X has been replaced by the value to the right of the equality sign in the original equations. However, the second and third columns are identical to those found in the denominator. In like manner, the determinant for the numerator of the unknown variable Y is formed by eliminating the coefficients for Y and replacing it with the values to the right of the equality sign in the original equations. The determinant for the last unknown variable Z is formed in a similar fashion. The determinants for X, Y, and Z are shown below with their respective values:

$$X = \frac{\begin{vmatrix} 18 & 6 & 3 \\ 24 & 5 & 6 \\ 12 & 8 & 4 \end{vmatrix}}{\begin{vmatrix} 4 & 6 & 3 \\ 3 & 5 & 6 \\ 2 & 8 & 4 \end{vmatrix}} = \frac{-252}{-70} = 3.6$$

$$Y = \frac{\begin{vmatrix} 4 & 18 & 3 \\ 3 & 24 & 6 \\ 2 & 12 & 4 \end{vmatrix}}{\begin{vmatrix} 4 & 6 & 3 \\ 3 & 5 & 6 \\ 2 & 8 & 4 \end{vmatrix}} = \frac{60}{-70} = 0.8571$$

$$Z = \frac{\begin{vmatrix} 4 & 6 & 18 \\ 3 & 5 & 24 \\ 2 & 8 & 12 \end{vmatrix}}{\begin{vmatrix} 4 & 6 & 3 \\ 3 & 5 & 6 \\ 2 & 8 & 4 \end{vmatrix}} = \frac{-204}{-70} = 2.9143$$

Now we have solved for the unknown variables X, Y, and Z, the values can be verified by substituting them into the original equations. The values (X, Y, and Z) satisfy the equations:

$$4X + 6Y + 3Z = 18$$
$$4(3.6) + 6(-0.8571) + 3(2.9143) = 18$$
$$14.4 - 5.14 + 8.74 = 18$$
$$18 = 18$$

$$3X + 5Y + 6Z = 24$$
$$3(3.6) + 5(-0.8571) + 6(2.9143) = 24$$
$$10.8 - 4.286 + 17.486 = 24$$
$$24 = 24$$

$$2X + 8Y + 4Z = 12$$
$$2(3.6) + 8(-0.8571) + 4(2.9143) = 12$$
$$7.2 - 6.857 + 11.657 = 12$$
$$12 = 12$$

In Chapter 9 on Markov analysis, a 4×4 determinant will be solved. The problem has actually five equations with four unknowns. Due to the structure of Markov analysis, one equation can be dropped, which permits us to utilize a 4×4 determinant.

This concludes a brief discussion of vectors, matrices, and determinants. The simplex method of linear programming is based on the concept of matrices, vectors, and inversion of matrices. Some of the material presented in this appendix will be useful in other chapters. It is important that the reader become familiar with these three areas of mathematics and their basic properties.

Appendix B

Calculus Approach to Selected OR Models

Basic EOQ Model (page 64)

The preferred approach for solving the economic ordering quantity utilizes differentiation (calculus). In the typical graph of EOQ (refer to Figure 2-2), the slope of the total cost curve is the sum of the slopes of the two lines—inventory carrying costs and ordering costs. Starting with the left-hand portion of the graph, the inventory carrying cost has a positive slope while the ordering cost has a negative slope. As the quantity Q increases on the x axis, a point is reached where the negative slope of the ordering cost line has decreased to the same value as that of the inventory carrying cost line (slopes numerically equal but opposite) so that their total, the slope of the total cost line, is zero. In the EOQ model, the rate of change for the total cost with respect to Q, the economic ordering quantity, is zero when the total cost curve has a zero slope.

To review, the equation developed under the algebraic method is:

$$\frac{Q}{2}CI = \frac{R}{Q}S$$

Restating the equation in terms of total costs (TC), the equation is:

$$TC = \frac{Q}{2}CI + \frac{R}{Q}S$$

Differentiating the preceding equation, the resulting expression is the slope of the total cost curve:

$$\frac{d(TC)}{d(Q)} = \frac{CI}{2} - \frac{RS}{Q^2}$$

In calculus, the first derivative is set equal to zero in order to determine where the rate of change of the total cost curve relative to Q is zero:

$$\frac{CI}{2} - \frac{RS}{Q^2} = 0$$

$$Q^2CI = 2RS \qquad \text{(Equation 2–1)}$$

$$Q^2 = \frac{2RS}{CI}$$

$$Q = \sqrt{\frac{2RS}{CI}}$$

The above solution yields the same formula (Equation 2–1) as the algebraic method. However, this does not say whether total costs are at a minimum or maximum with respect to the economic ordering quantity. In calculus, the use of the second derivative test will resolve this problem:

$$\frac{d^2(TC)}{d(Q)^2} = + \frac{2RS}{Q^3}$$

A minimum total cost point rather than a maximum total cost point with respect to the EOQ is indicated by a plus sign in the second derivative test. The plus sign indicates that the total cost curve is increasing upward.

Optimum Number of Orders Per Year (page 68)

The equation for the optimum number of orders per year under the algebraic method where the total inventory carrying costs are equated to the total ordering costs is:

$$\frac{AI}{2N} = NS$$

Restating the equation in terms of total costs (TC), the equation becomes:

$$TC = \frac{AI}{2N} + NS$$

Using the appropriate rules for differentiation, the resulting equation is:

$$\frac{d(TC)}{dN} = -\frac{AI}{2N^2} + S$$

Setting the first derivative equal to zero and solving for N, the final formula is:

OPTIMUM DAYS' SUPPLY
PER ORDER (PAGE 69)

$$\frac{-AI}{2N^2} + S = 0$$

$$S = \frac{AI}{2N^2}$$

(Equation 2–2)

$$2N^2S = AI$$

$$N^2 = \frac{AI}{2S}$$

$$N = \sqrt{\frac{AI}{2S}}$$

The second derivative test indicates that a minimum cost point has been reached since the plus sign indicates a total cost curve that is tending upward.

$$\frac{d^2(TC)}{d(N)^2} = + \frac{AI}{N^3}$$

Optimum Days' Supply Per Order (page 69)

The equation for the optimum days' supply per order under the algebraic method where the total inventory carrying costs are equated to the total inventory ordering costs is:

$$\frac{RCI}{730/D} = \frac{365S}{D}$$

When stated in terms of total costs, the equation becomes:

$$TC = \frac{RCI}{730/D} + \frac{365S}{D}$$

Employing differentiation, the equation becomes:

$$\frac{d(TC)}{dD} = \frac{RCI}{730} - \frac{365S}{D^2}$$

391

Setting the first derivative equal to zero and solving for D, the final formula becomes:

$$\frac{RCI}{730} - \frac{365S}{D^2} = 0$$

$$\frac{RCI}{730} = \frac{365S}{D^2}$$

$$D^2 RCI = 266,450S \qquad\qquad \text{(Equation 2–4)}$$

$$D^2 = \frac{266,450S}{RCI}$$

$$D = \sqrt{\frac{266,450S}{RCI}}$$

As in the previous equation, a plus in the second derivative test indicates that a minimum cost point has been reached.

$$\frac{d^2\,(TC)}{d\,(D)^2} = + \frac{730S}{D^3}$$

Optimum Amount of Dollars Per Order (page 70)

The equation for calculating how many dollars of an inventory item to purchase at one time under the algebraic method where inventory carrying costs are equated to total ordering costs is:

$$\frac{OI}{2} = \frac{AS}{O}$$

When restated in terms of total costs (TC), the equation is:

$$TC = \frac{OI}{2} + \frac{AS}{O}$$

The resulting equation when applying the rules for differentiation becomes:

$$\frac{d\,(TC)}{d\,(O)} = \frac{I}{2} - \frac{AS}{O^2}$$

By setting the first derivative equal to zero for O, the final equation is:

$$\frac{I}{2} - \frac{AS}{O^2} = 0$$

$$\frac{I}{2} = \frac{AS}{O^2}$$

$$O^2 I = 2AS$$ (Equation 2–6)

$$O^2 = \frac{2AS}{I}$$

$$O = \sqrt{\frac{2AS}{I}}$$

A plus in the second derivative test indicates that a minimum cost point has been obtained.

$$\frac{d^2\,(TC)}{d\,(O)^2} = +\,\frac{2AS}{O^3}$$

EOQ Model for Simultaneous Sales and Production for One Item (page 80)

Just as calculus was used above in solving for optimum inventory formulas when buying from the outside, an inventory model for an optimum lot size where there is a simultaneous sales and production for one item can also be solved using calculus. After mathematical expressions have been determined for production setup costs and inventory carrying costs, it should be apparent from the above derivations of inventory models that total manufacturing costs are at a minimum when the total cost curve has a zero slope. Hence, the first derivative is again set equal to zero in order to determine the optimal EOQ. The mathematical derivation is as follows:

$$TC = \frac{RS}{Q} + \frac{Q}{2}\left(\frac{P-U}{P}\right)CI$$

$$\frac{d(TC)}{d(Q)} = -\frac{RS}{Q^2} + \frac{CI}{2}\left(\frac{P-U}{P}\right) = 0$$

$$\frac{RS}{Q^2} = \frac{CI}{2}\left(\frac{P-U}{P}\right)$$

$$Q^2\left[CI\left(\frac{P-U}{P}\right)\right] = 2RS$$

$$Q^2 = \frac{2RS}{CI\,(1 - U/P)}$$

$$Q = \sqrt{\frac{2RS}{CI\,(1 - U/P)}}$$ (Equation 2–10)

Applying the second derivative test to the statement of this model,

$$\frac{d^2(TC)}{d(Q)^2} = + \frac{2RS}{Q^3}$$

The plus sign indicates that a minimum total cost point has been reached with respect to the optimum number of units per production run.

Single-Channel Queuing Minimum Cost Model (page 301)

Calculus is the preferred approach to solving the single-channel minimum cost service rate formula. A minimum cost service rate can be found by differentiating total (TC_m) with respect to the service rate in units per period (μ), setting the results equal to zero. In calculus, the first derivative is set equal to zero to determine where the rate of change of the total cost curve related to μ is zero. The mathematical derivation is:

$$\frac{d\,(TC_m)}{d\mu} = -\,C_w\lambda\,(\mu - \lambda)^{-2} + C_f = 0$$

$$(\mu - \lambda)^2\,C_f = \lambda C_w$$

$$(\mu - \lambda)^2 = \frac{\lambda C_w}{C_f} \qquad\qquad \text{(Equation 10–6)}$$

$$\mu - \lambda = \pm\,\sqrt{\frac{\lambda C_w}{C_f}}$$

$$\mu = \lambda \pm \sqrt{\frac{\lambda C_w}{C_f}}$$

Applying the second derivative test to the statement of this model, a minimum cost service rate has been found.

$$\frac{d^2\,(TC_m)}{d\,(\mu)^2} = + \frac{2C_w\lambda}{(\mu - \lambda)^3}$$

Appendix C

Areas under the Curve

	.00	.01	.02	.03	.04	.05	.06	.07	.08	.09
0.0	.50000	.50399	.50798	.51197	.51595	.51994	.52392	.52790	.53188	.53586
0.1	.53983	.54380	.54776	.55172	.55567	.55692	.56356	.56749	.57142	.57535
0.2	.57926	.58317	.58706	.59095	.59483	.59871	.60257	.60642	.61026	.61409
0.3	.61791	.62172	.62552	.62930	.63307	.63683	.64058	.64431	.64803	.65173
0.4	.65542	.65910	.66276	.66640	.67003	.67364	.67724	.68082	.68439	.68793
0.5	.69146	.69497	.69847	.70194	.70540	.70884	.71226	.71566	.71904	.72240
0.6	.72575	.72907	.73237	.73536	.73891	.74215	.74537	.74857	.75175	.75490
0.7	.75804	.76115	.76424	.76730	.77035	.77337	.77637	.77935	.78230	.78524
0.8	.78814	.79103	.79389	.79673	.79955	.80234	.80511	.80785	.81057	.81327
0.9	.81594	.81859	.82121	.82381	.82639	.82894	.83147	.83398	.83646	.83891
1.0	.84134	.84375	.84614	.84849	.85083	.85314	.85543	.85769	.85993	.86214
1.1	.86433	.86650	.86864	.87076	.87286	.87493	.87698	.87900	.88100	.88298
1.2	.88493	.88686	.88877	.89065	.89251	.89435	.89617	.89796	.89973	.90147
1.3	.90320	.90490	.90658	.90824	.90988	.91149	.91309	.91466	.91621	.91774
1.4	.91924	.92073	.92220	.92364	.92507	.92647	.92785	.92922	.93056	.93189
1.5	.93319	.93448	.93574	.93699	.93822	.93943	.94062	.94179	.94295	.94408
1.6	.94520	.94630	.94738	.94845	.94950	.95053	.95154	.95254	.95352	.95449
1.7	.95543	.95637	.95728	.95818	.95907	.95994	.96080	.96164	.96246	.96327
1.8	.96407	.96485	.96562	.96638	.96712	.96784	.96856	.96926	.96995	.97062
1.9	.97128	.97193	.97257	.97320	.97381	.97441	.97500	.97558	.97615	.97670
2.0	.97725	.97784	.97831	.97882	.97932	.97982	.98030	.98077	.98124	.98169
2.1	.98214	.98257	.98300	.98341	.98382	.98422	.98461	.98500	.98537	.98574
2.2	.98610	.98645	.98679	.98713	.98745	.98778	.98809	.98840	.98870	.98899
2.3	.98928	.98956	.98983	.99010	.99036	.99061	.99086	.99111	.99134	.99158
2.4	.99180	.99202	.99224	.99245	.99266	.99286	.99305	.99324	.99343	.99361
2.5	.99379	.99396	.99413	.99430	.99446	.99461	.99477	.99492	.99506	.99520
2.6	.99534	.99547	.99560	.99573	.99585	.99598	.99609	.99621	.99632	.99643
2.7	.99653	.99664	.99674	.99683	.99693	.99702	.99711	.99720	.99728	.99736
2.8	.99744	.99752	.99760	.99767	.99774	.99781	.99788	.99795	.99801	.99807
2.9	.99813	.99819	.99825	.99831	.99836	.99841	.99846	.99851	.99856	.99861
3.0	.99865	.99869	.99874	.99878	.99882	.99886	.99899	.99893	.99896	.99900
3.1	.99903	.99906	.99910	.99913	.99916	.99918	.99921	.99924	.99926	.99929
3.2	.99931	.99934	.99936	.99938	.99940	.99942	.99944	.99946	.99948	.99950
3.3	.99952	.99953	.99955	.99957	.99958	.99960	.99961	.99962	.99964	.99965
3.4	.99966	.99968	.99969	.99970	.99971	.99972	.99973	.99974	.99975	.99976
3.5	.99977	.99978	.99978	.99979	.99980	.99981	.99981	.99982	.99983	.99983
3.6	.99984	.99985	.99985	.99986	.99986	.99987	.99987	.99988	.99988	.99989
3.7	.99989	.99990	.99990	.99990	.99991	.99991	.99992	.99992	.99992	.99992
3.8	.99993	.99993	.99993	.99994	.99994	.99994	.99994	.99995	.99995	.99995
3.9	.99995	.99995	.99996	.99996	.99996	.99996	.99996	.99996	.99997	.99997

Directions: To find the area under the curve between the left-hand end and any point, determine how many standard deviations that point is to the right of the average, then read the area directly from the body of the table. *Example*: The area under the curve from the left-hand end and a point 1.86 standard deviations to the right of the average is .96856 of the total area under the curve.

Appendix D

Random Numbers Table

1581922396	2068577984	8262130892	8374856049	4637567488
0928105582	7295088579	9586111652	7055508767	6472382934
4112077556	3440672486	1882412963	0684012006	0933147914
7457477468	5435810788	9670852913	1291265730	4890031305
0099520858	3090908872	2039593181	5973470495	9776135501
7245174840	2275698645	8416549348	4676463101	2229367983
6749420382	4832630032	5670984959	5432114610	2966095680
5503161011	7413686599	1198757695	0414294470	0140121598
7164238934	7666127259	5263097712	5133648980	4011966963
3593969525	0272759769	0385998136	9999089966	7544056852
4192054466	0700014629	5169439659	8408705169	1074373131
9697426117	6488888550	4031652526	8123543276	0927534537
2007950579	9564268448	3457416988	1531027886	7016633739
4584768758	2389278610	3859431781	3643768456	4141314518
3840145867	9120831830	7228567652	1267173884	4020651657
0190453442	4800088084	1165628559	5407921254	3768932478
6766554338	5585265145	5089052204	9780623691	2195448096
6315116284	9172824179	5544814339	0016943666	3828538786
3908771938	4035554324	0840126299	4942059208	1475623997
5570024586	9324732596	1186563397	4425143189	3216653251
2999997185	0135968938	7678931194	1351031403	6002561840
7864375912	8383232768	1892857070	2323673751	3188881718
7065492027	6349104233	3382569662	4579426926	1513082455
0654683246	4765104877	8149224168	5468631609	6474393896
7830555058	5255147182	3519287786	2481675649	8907598697
7626984369	4725370390	9641916289	5049082870	7463807244
4785048453	3646121751	8436077768	2928794356	9956043516
4627791048	5765558107	8762592043	6185670830	6363845920
9376470693	0441608934	8749472723	2202271078	5897002653
1227991661	7936797054	9527542791	4711871173	8300978148
5582095589	5535798279	4764439855	6279247618	4446895088
4959397698	1056981450	8416606706	8234013222	6426813469
1824779358	1333750468	9434074212	5273692238	5902177065
7041092295	5726289716	3420847871	1820481234	0318831723
3555104281	0903099163	6827824899	6383872737	5901682626
3007929946	4031562749	5570757297	6273785046	1455349704
6085440624	2875556938	5496629750	4841817356	1443167141
7005051056	3496332071	5054070890	7303867953	6255181190
9846413446	8306646692	0661684251	8875127201	6251533454
0625457703	4229164694	7321363715	7051128285	1108468072
5457593922	9751489574	1799906380	1989141062	5595364247
4076486653	8950826528	4934582003	4071187742	1456207629

Dudley J. Cowden and Mercedes S. Cowden, *Practical Problems in Business Statistics*, 2d ed., © 1960, by permission of Prentice-Hall, Inc., Englewood Cliffs, N.J.

Appendix E

Answers to Mathematical Exercises

Chapter 1

1. (a) Graph the data.
    (b) Capacity—25,001 to 30,000; 28,000 units; and $210,000
        Capacity—30,001 to 35,000; 32,000 units; and $240,000
        Capacity—35,001 to 40,000; 36,000 units; and $270,000
        Capacity—40,001 to 45,000; 40,000 units; and $300,000
    (c) Percent capacity—62.2%, 71.1%, 80.0%, and 88.8%
    (d) $1.25 fixed cost per unit at 80% capacity
    (e) 40,000 units

2. 11,076 units at breakeven
    13,219 units must be sold to make a profit of $15,000.

3. (a) Breakeven—$143,369 (present) and $134,907 (proposed)
    (b) Total variable costs—$63,369 (present) and $54,907 (proposed)
    (c) Take on new line.

4. (a) Graph the data.
    (b) 127 units and 7,873 units
    (c) Profit = $15,000
    (d) Selling price — $20

5. Selling price = $7.95

6. (a) Plant B
    (b) Plant A = 47.6% capacity and plant B = 50.0% capacity

7. (a) Use company salesmen.
    (b) Breakeven = $20,000,000

8. Make the part; above 66.67% capacity, it pays to manufacture the part.

9. Indifference point = 2,500 units
    Total cost: Machine 1 = $51,000; Machine 2 = $40,600; and Machine 3 = $38,000 at 5,100 units; lowest machine cost—Machine 3

10. (a) Graph the data.
    (b) Use 1 up to 3,500 units; use 2 over 3,500 units to 13,000 units; and use 3 over 13,000 units

Chapter 2

1. (a) EOQ = 231 units (approx.)
   (b) 8.7 orders per year (approx.)
   (c) 42 days' supply (approx.)
   (d) $4,157 (approx.)

2. (a) EOQ = 1,330 units (approx.)
   (b) 48 days' supply (approx.)
   (c) 7.5 orders per year (approx.)

3. Offer should not be accepted. Counteroffer 1.4% or better.

4. Accept Grabbers, Inc., proposal—lowest cost.

5. Quantity of 500 should be purchased.

6. (a) EOQ = 343 parts (approx.)
   (b) 80 orders per year
   (c) No—additional cost with air freight—$57,337.50

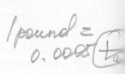 1/pound = 0.0005 (t)

7. Best price, $9.15; range: purchase 1,001 pallets

8. Reorder point = 1,375 units

9. Reorder point = 525 bags

10. (a) EOQ = 121,543 units
    (b) Reorder point = 4,000 + safety stock

11. (a) EOQ = 68,700 units (approx.)
    (b) Reorder point = 12,000 + safety stock
    (c) As usage goes up, the reorder quantity does likewise.

12. (a) 4.7 cycles (approx.) per year
    (b) $B-2,000$, 16 days; $F-1,000$, 33 days

13. 8.4 cycles (approx.) per year

Chapter 3

1. Accept A and B $6,500 (original problem)
   Marginal (or joint) probability under statistical independence
   Accept A and B $5,000 (revised problem)
   Joint probability under statistical dependence

2. (a) Accept *A* and *B* $7,500 (original problem)
   (b) Joint probability under statistical dependence
   (a) Accept *A* and *B* $10,000 (revised problem)
   (b) Marginal (or joint) probability under statistical independence

3. Assign .833 probability to recession.

4. (a) .99 versus .8; continue manufacturing.
   (b) .007 versus .8; do not continue manufacturing.

5. (a) *P*(correct setup|4 GP) = .999
      P(correct setup|3 GP, 1BP) = .983
      P(correct setup|2 GP, 2BP) = .112
      P(correct setup|1 GP, 3BP) = .0104
      P(correct setup|4 BP) = .0001
      Compare all values to .9
   (b) Marginal, joint, and conditional probabilities

6. Product *X*—yields highest expected profits

7. Vendor *B*—lowest expected future cost

8. (a) Total expected sales = $2,602,370
   (b) Joint probability under statistical dependence

9. (a) Highest profit per unit—$0.25 at 200,000 units
   (b) Highest profit at 400,000 units, $60,000

10. Quote $2.30, use Method *A*.
   Marginal probability under statistical independence

11. Choose *DCA* for lowest development cost of $2,267,250.

Chapter 4

1. (a) See Tables 4–1 and 4–4 for approach.
   (b) Expected profits:
      stock 50—$250.00
      stock 51— 253.50
      stock 52— 251.75
      stock 53— 244.00
      Expected losses:
      stock 50—($ 8.00)
      stock 51—(4.50)
      stock 52—(6.25)
      stock 53—(14.00)
   (c) EVPI = $4.50

2. (a) 1,120 units
   (b) $65.80 with variable demand
   (c) $68.23 under certainty

3. (a) 26 dozens
   (b) $23.30 with variable demand

4. (a) $MP = $1.33, $ML = $8.00
   (b) No, carry 81 units.

5. (a) Manufacture 70,000 pairs.
   (b) Total expected profits—$126,000

6. (a) Investment appears sound, expected profits of $15,412.50 per year for five years
   (b) Time value of money, rate of return, comparison with other projects, reliability of data, etc.

7. Carry 31 units

8. Carry 18 units

Chapter 5

1. Rank according to "expected value" estimates—2, 4, 3, 1, and 5.

2. (a) Draw PERT network.
   (b) Critical path: 0–1–3–6–8–9–10

3. Critical path: 0–1–2–11–12–13–14
   See text for recommendations.

4. (a) Draw PERT network.
   (b) Slack time: 3 days, none, 7 days
   (c) Critical path: 1–2–4–6–8
   (d) End completion date remains unchanged.
   (e) Slack time: 7 days—event 7

5. Sales prices $90,000
   Costs—var. and fixed   83,000
   Profit $ 7,000

6. Critical path initially 1–4–6–7; modified crash plan—$19\frac{1}{3}$ weeks and cost—$235,500; and total crash cost $268,500

7. (a) Recommend 13 weeks, profit of $21,000.
   (b) 79 percent chance of completing the contract one week after the normal delivery time

Chapter 6

1. S$-$1,000 Model $= 355\frac{1}{2}$ units
   S$-$2,000 Model $= 0$ units
   Contribution, $14,220
   Slack time:
     M. F. Dept., 178 hours
     E. W. Dept., $311\frac{1}{4}$ hours
     A. Dept., 0 hours

2. (a) Model Z$-$1,200 $= 150$ units
       Model Z$-$1,500 $= 70$ units
   (b) Increase contribution by $4,000.
   (c) Range for Model Z$-$1,200, 100 to 150 units
       Range for Model Z$-$1,500, 70 to 120 units
       Any combination of the above that totals 220 units
   (d) Model Z$-$1,200 $= 55$ units
       Model Z$-$1,500 $= 0$ units
       Model Z$-$1,800 $= 150$ units
       Contribution, $11,000
   (e) Solution is not unique.

3. Range for Magazine 1, 20 to 35 runs
   Range for Magazine 2, 10 to 16 runs
   Any combination of the above that totals $120,000

4. Product $A = 20,000$ units
   Product $B = 0$ units
   Product $C = 7,500$ units
   Contribution, $9,750

5. (a) $X_1 = 3,000$ pounds
       $X_2 = 5,000$ pounds
       $X_3 = 2,000$ pounds
   (b) Lowest cost $= 96,000
   (c) Slack pounds, $X_6 = 3,500$

6. (a) Resin $= 40\%$
       Fiber $= 40\%$
       Glass cloth $= 20\%$
   (b) Lowest cost composition, $48 per pound

7. (a) Lean cow meat $= 50$ pounds
       Blade beef $= 20$ pounds
       Pork trimmings $= 30$ pounds
   (b) Lowest cost $= 43 per 100 pounds

8. (a) Product C = 300 units
Product D = 600 units
Product E = 500 units
Product F = 1,100 units

(b) Contribution, $17,900

(c) Slack time:
Planner, 0 hours
Milling, 0 hours
Drilling, 950 hours
Assembly, 200 hours

Chapter 7

1. Total cost = $28,900

2. Factory 1 to Jacksonville, 600
Factory 2 to Newark, 1,000
Factory 3 to Newark, 200
Factory 3 to Jacksonville, 200
Factory 3 to San Diego, 1,000
Total cost = $16,400

3. (a) Total cost = $7,800

(b) Drop out column C, slack column now totals 550.

(c) Insert a row for an artificial factory, but using a very high cost (M) so this factory will not enter the final solution.

4. Total cost = $11,000

5. Dalton to Plant C, 800 units
Dalton to Plant D, 1,200 units
Doran to Plant A, 800 units
Doran to Plant C, 100 units
Doran to Plant E, 500 units
Riggs to Plant B, 1,000 units
Riggs to Plant E, 1,000 units
Total cost = $30,300

6. $J_1 = 5W_3$
$J_2 = 15W_2$
$J_2 = 5W_3$
$J_3 = 10W_1$
Lowest cost/hour, $137.25

7. From $A \begin{pmatrix} 2 \\ 5 \\ 1 \end{pmatrix}$ to $\begin{pmatrix} R \\ T \\ U \end{pmatrix}$

   From $B \begin{pmatrix} 6 \\ 2 \end{pmatrix}$ to $\begin{pmatrix} S \\ U \end{pmatrix}$

   From C (6) to (S)

   From D (3) to (U)

8. To press 1:
   Order 3,   6,000
   Order 6,   44,000
   To press 2:
   Order 1,   28,000
   Order 3,   2,000
   Order 4,   20,000
   To press 3:
   Order 2,   15,000
   Order 3,   7,000
   Order 5,   <u>38,000</u>
            160,000

9. Machine 1:
   Product D 1,240
   Machine 2:
   Product B 1,240
   Product C 1,800
   Product D 510
   Machine 3:
   Product A 1,620
   Product B <u>760</u>
         7,170

Chapter 8

1. Production schedule:
   1st month $= 650$
   2nd month $= 820$
   3rd month $= 950$
   4th month $= 920$
   5th month $= 800$
   6th month $= 500$
   Total inventory cost $= \$27,409$

2. Sales Area 1 = 2 salesmen
   Sales Area 2 = no salesmen
   Sales Area 3 = 7 salesmen
   Total profits = $218,000
   Note: it is recommended that at least one salesman be in each sales area.
   Thus, one salesman from sales area 3 should be shifted to sales area 2.

3. (a) Sales Area 1 = 3 salesmen and Sales Area 2 = 4 salesmen
   (b) Maximum profits = $173,000
   (c) Sales Area 1 = 3 salesmen, Sales Area 2 = 3 salesmen, and Sales Area 3
       = 1 salesman
       Maximum profits = $244,000
   (d) Sales Area 1 = 3 salesmen, Sales Area 2 = 3 salesmen, and Sales Area 3
       = 0 salesman. Note: It is recommended that at least one salesman be in
       each sales area. Thus, one salesman from sales areas 1 or 2 should be
       shifted to sales area 3.

4. Districts 1 and 2—1 truck in District 1 and 4 trucks in District 2 or 2 trucks in
   District 1 and 3 trucks in District 2
   Districts 3 and 4—1 truck each

5. Part 23, 4 units
   Part 56, 2 units
   Part 42, 1 unit
   Total cost = $380 ($390)

6. 1st or 2nd interview, hire outstanding engineer; 3rd interview, hire engineer

7. If return in months 1 or 2 is $800,000, make the $2 million investment, otherwise
   wait. If return in months 3 or 4 is either $600,000 or $800,000, make the $2 mil-
   lion investment, otherwise wait. If no investment made by month 5, make the
   investment at the return prevailing in month 5.

Chapter 9

1. Best-Cut = .330, Jones = .435, and Henry's = .235

2. $K = .40$, $A = .374$, $B = .226$
   $K = .43$, $A = .279$, $B = .291$

3. (a) Yes
       Test areas 1 and 2 = 27.8%
   (b) Test area 1 = 25%
       Test area 2 = 43.8%
       Select campaign for test area 2

4. (a) $H = .244$, $A = .268$, $B = .283$, $C = .205$
   (b) $H = .25$, $A = .25$, $B = .25$, $C = .25$

5. (a) $A = .59$, $B = .16$, $C = .25$

    (b) $A = .5820$, $B = .1587$, $C = .2593$

6. Neither advertising program is profitable for the firm.

Chapter 10

1. (a) 24 men in line after 4 hours

    (b) Add another attendant.

    (c) One attendant for 40/hour service rate

2. Hire fast repairman, total cost of $116 per day.

3. (a) $\frac{1}{3}$ hour

    (b) $1\frac{1}{3}$ persons

    (c) $\frac{1}{2}$ hour

    (d) 7.58 persons per hour

4. (a) 2 trucks

    (b) $\frac{1}{4}$ hour

    (c) $1\frac{1}{3}$ trucks

    (d) $\frac{1}{6}$ hour

    (e) 12.47 trucks per hour

5. (a) .13 person

    (b) No need for a second booth

6. (a) $3\frac{1}{2}$ loads

    (b) 0.36 hour

    (c) 7.1 loads per hour

7. Use 2 attendants for lowest cost.

8. (a) 1.03 minutes

    (b) 48.5 minutes (about half of the time)

    (c) 3.74 minutes (From Appendix D, random number for arrivals: upper right-hand corner, starting with 4637567488, and go downward, let 5 = an arrival; random number for service time: last row starting with 4076486653, go across and use each number)

9. (a) .95 customer

    (b) 3.04 minutes

    (c) 7.59 minutes

    (d) Hire 2 attendants (From Appendix D, random numbers for arrival and service times: first 2 columns downward, starting in left-hand corner—15, 09, 41, 74, etc.).

10. Use 3 machines for lowest cost.

Chapter 11

1. See text for approach.

2. Average delay expected $= 3.5$ weeks (for random numbers used)

3. Do not add an additional clerk.

4. Monte Carlo simulation: cost comparison for various number of machines — 11 machines with a lowest total cost

5. Replace three vacuum tubes at a time; consider preventive maintenance, new equipment, etc.

6. Lowest cost with 2 repairmen

Index

107D
9